LUDVIG IRGENS-JENSEN
The Life and Music of a Norwegian Composer

LUDVIG IRGENS-JENSEN
The Life and Music of a Norwegian Composer

Arvid O. Vollsnes

Translated by Beryl Foster

TOCCATA
PRESS

English edition first published in 2014 by Toccata Press; an earlier version of this book appeared as *Komponisten Ludvig Irgens-Jensen*, Aschehoug, Oslo, 2000

British Library Cataloguing in Publication Data
A catalogue record for this book is available from the British Library.

ISBN 978-0-907689-73-7 (hd)

Set in 11 on 13 point Minion Pro
by Kerrypress, Luton

Printed and bound by CPI Group (UK) Ltd, Croydon, CR0 4YY

FSC www.fsc.org MIX Paper from responsible sources FSC® C013604

Contents

List of Illustrations

Introduction

On 2 December 1930 large headlines in the Oslo daily newspaper *Tidens Tegn* announced

A remarkable day in Norwegian music history
Irgens Jensen's St Olav Cantata was performed for the first time yesterday
The most significant and deepest work in our modern music

The success that the 'St Olav Cantata', or the dramatic symphony *Heimferd* ('Homeward Journey'), had at that time in Oslo has scarcely been surpassed by any Norwegian choral work. Not only was it performed to a full house; the Philharmonic Society had to put on no fewer than nine extra concerts in the first two months after the first performance.[1]

Irgens-Jensen again enjoyed banner headlines on 19 September 1934, when the front page of *Dagbladet*, one of the main Norwegian dailies, read:

Irgens Jensen proclaimed as world genius
Three world publishers fight over Passacaglia

His Passacaglia is probably the only large-scale Norwegian orchestral work since Grieg and Svendsen to achieve frequent performance: it enjoyed wide international circulation in the composer's lifetime and has been recorded four times.[2] In her study of Norwegian contemporary music in 1948, the composer-critic Pauline Hall, whose strictures were much feared, called it 'a shining feather in the cap of Norwegian music'.[3] Few other Norwegian composers have received such an enthusiastic reception from their contemporaries or enjoyed the successes Irgens-Jensen knew.

Little has been written – in Norwegian, let alone other languages – about Norwegian music-history between the two World Wars in general or about Ludvig Irgens-Jensen in particular. There is one broad survey, in Nils Grinde's *Norsk musikkhistorie* ('History of Norwegian Music'), first

[1] The significance of *Heimferd* as a musical work and symbol is discussed below: *cf.* especially pp. 159–69.

[2] Most recently (2011) on a Naxos CD (8.572112), with the Bournemouth Symphony Orchestra conducted by Bjarte Engeset – the first commercial recording by an orchestra outside Norway.

[3] 'Musikk', in Haakon Shetelig, Fritiof Brandt and Alf Nyman (eds.), *Vår tids kunst og diktning i Skandinavia I*, J. G. Tanum, Oslo, 1948, p. 213.

published in 1971 and since revised in several later editions;[4] and a five-volume history of Norwegian music, recently published in Norwegian, contains an even broader discussion.[5] A handful of specialist studies have emerged, and some themes have been examined in intermittent theses and articles.[6] Published archival material is scarce, as is the secondary literature. This lacuna is striking because the period is Norway's 'second golden age' after the heyday of Grieg and Svendsen, and Irgens-Jensen was one of the most highly prized composers of these years.

His compositions were met with early acknowledgement even though he was initially perceived as a 'modernist', whose music featured elements perceived as new in the Norway of the period after the First World War. But he was not amongst those who called: 'Clear the way – something new is coming!'[7] And yet, his modest appearance notwithstanding, he succeeded in creating an individual style, one which gains in significance when examined in the context of the development of Norwegian music-history. Nonetheless, the change in which he took part was a quiet one, not a vociferous revolution.

Although Irgens-Jensen's compositions were undertaken within the wider, European perspectives of his own outlook, throughout his life he was often described in terms of national music and attitudes, even by musicians and critics who should have known better. In his later years he was also perceived as a conservative, not least by younger colleagues and writers, but that was at the time of the high modernism of the 1950s and '60s which, as it did elsewhere, brought the sharpest stylistic rupture in the history of Norwegian music – a break for which, paradoxically, Irgens-Jensen himself had prepared the ground in the 1920s.

The reception and interpretation of his music seems sometimes to have occurred on false premises: it seems plain that some commentators did not know, or understand, it. To help with the interpretation of the many reviews cited in this book, I have tried to foster an awareness of who is writing and what motives may lie behind some of the statements in question: musical life in a small country like Norway is relatively restricted and 'intimate', and people often have to occupy a number of roles; it was thus inevitable that the people prominent in musical life knew one another and often met socially. I therefore discuss Irgens-Jensen's music not only through stylistic examination but also from a biographical, historical and socio-cultural

[4] The most recent edition was published by Musikkhuset Forlag, Oslo, 1993; an English translation (as *A History of Norwegian Music*) was published by the University of Nebraska Press, Lincoln, 1991.

[5] Arvid O. Vollsnes (ed.), *Norges musikkhistorie*, Vols. 1–5, Aschehoug, Oslo, 1999–2001.

[6] For full details, *cf.* the Bibliography, pp. 335–40, below.

[7] This statement was used by Hans Jørgen Hurum in his eulogy in 1969: *cf.* p. 260, below.

position. That requires the assessment of some musical and intellectual traditions, together with the clear influences to which the composer and the reception of his works were exposed – all to give a broader and more complete interpretation of the music. That part of Norwegian music history which forms the background to the composer's works is explained briefly, and the various sides of the debate which took place in the 1920s and '30s about 'modernism' and 'national music' are likewise examined.

Those of Irgens-Jensen's large-scale works I have chosen for closer discussion are central to his production and, as a collection of historical pictures, should give an impression of the whole. Two of them – the Passacaglia and *Heimferd* – are dealt with extensively, as are the circumstances around their creation and reception, since this approach generates useful historical perspectives.

Music-history is often regarded as dependent on a chronology, to be flushed out by description and analysis. To be first seems to be important: a pioneer, a new theory or new aesthetic outlook will attract critics and researchers as much as other musicians and composers. The struggle of some artists for recognition – sometimes provoking a headlong attempt at originality – has indeed brought them their footnote in history, but real artistic significance comes only if the works they create have solidity and substance, which is certainly the case with Irgens-Jensen.

His surname is found in both hyphenated and unhyphenated forms. In early reference works and dictionaries it is generally entered without a hyphen. Since the composer is sometimes found listed under 'Jensen', the family arranged in 1956 for the surname to be changed by deed-poll to 'Irgens-Jensen' to avoid such misunderstandings.[8] Rather than constantly oscillate between usages, and at the cost of perpetuating the occasional anachronism, that is the form I have used throughout this book, except in quotations from or references to sources which cite the name as 'Irgens Jensen' or 'Jensen' – although some of the early sources jump the gun and already hyphenate the name.

[8] It is not always obvious in a Norwegian name which part is the surname.

Acknowledgements

Writing the biography of a person one has seen only a few times in the concert-hall but with whom one has never exchanged a word is a challenging task. Distance may bring the advantage of a degree of objectivity, although one misses the more direct understanding of the subject's ways of thought, emotional life, environment and other external conditions.

My interest in the music of Ludvig Irgens-Jensen came particularly through his orchestral works. With the enthusiasm of youth I was constantly looking for him at concerts and saw a well-dressed, slightly delicate figure who, unlike some of his fellow-composers, appeared retiring and modest. Perhaps that is why, in spite of his outstanding success, there are so few good interviews with him in newspapers and musical journals, although the Norwegian Broadcasting Company (NRK) did interview him shortly before his death in 1969. A number of important manuscripts and sketches were given to the Norwegian Music Collection in the University Library (today part of the National Library) in Oslo but, apart from the sketch-books, drafts of poems and his own letters, together with letters from others, which were found in the attic at the Irgens-Jensen home, not many personal papers have been preserved.

Much of my account is based, therefore, on interviews and conversations with those who were close to Irgens-Jensen or came to know him on professional grounds. Two contacts were especially valuable: the composer's sister, Dagny Irgens Jensen (1905–94),[1] and his son, Olav Irgens-Jensen (born in 1927). They kept themselves well informed both about Norwegian musical life and the composer's works. In addition to their memories, I set much store by their considered and wise evaluations, and they readily allowed me to use all the material they had: music, manuscripts, letters, pictures, recordings, cuttings and so on. I received valuable information also from the tape-recordings that the late Øystein Gaukstad, the principal librarian in the Norwegian Music Collection in Oslo, was far-sighted enough to have made with the composer David Monrad Johansen and the conductor Odd Grüner-Hegge; the information from Grüner-Hegge, a friend of Irgens-Jensen's from boyhood, was particularly valuable.

[1] Dagny chose not to hyphenate her surname.

The orthography in the quotations of Norwegian text does not follow any norm: the spelling of the original is used (except where obvious typographical errors could be corrected), including titles of works, names and such like, which can differ somewhat from the titles and names that have become normal today.

During my work over all these years I have had help and inspiration in many different ways from my colleagues, many now retired or deceased, in the Department of Musicology at the University of Oslo, especially Finn Benestad, Nils Grinde, Dag Schjelderup-Ebbe and Kjell Skyllstad, and also, in the initial phases, from the late Øivind Eckhoff. Other colleagues in the University's institutes and collections (particularly Lexicography) have also been of considerable help.

The personnel at the Norwegian Music Collection deserve huge thanks for their excellent archive of collections and cuttings, and for much help and patience.

Many people have had to show patience during the many years this account has been underway, and so my thanks go first to my dear wife Brit and my family for their help, support and encouragement. The work has had to be done in fits and starts, usually losing any contest with daily business at the University. But in 1993–94 I had a sabbatical and more peace to work, so that large sections could be completed and put together.

Thanks, too, to all the colleagues, friends and acquaintances who have given me challenges and thereby given the book another angle and direction from those originally foreseen – to its benefit, I hope.

Particular thanks are due to Simax/Grappa and the other copyright-holders and the musicians for granting me this opportunity to use samples from various recordings on the CD included with this book.

At Aschehoug Publishers, the publishers of the original, Norwegian edition of this book,[2] I was in the excellent hands of Birger Huse, their Senior Editor, and he has followed this English version conscientiously, too. My friend Beryl Foster gracefully clarified my thoughts through her English translation, and Martin Anderson of Toccata Press helped revise the text for an international audience. Seth Blacklock and Guy Richards provided help with the proof-reading.

A grant from the Research Council of Norway towards the production costs of this book is gratefully acknowledged, as is support from NORLA for the translation.

[2] *Komponisten Ludvig Irgens-Jensen, Europeer og nordmann*, Aschehoug, Oslo, 2000.

I
Musical Life in Kristiania around 1910

Ludvig Irgens-Jensen was born and grew up in Kristiania,[1] a fact which calls for some knowledge of musical life in the city in the years from around 1910, the time when he was reaching musical maturity. In 1910 Norway had about 2.4 million inhabitants, some 30 per cent of them living in towns and cities. Kristiania was home to about 10 per cent of the population and had recently experienced a rapid increase in size: between around 1875 and 1900 the number of inhabitants more than tripled, from 77,000 to 227,000, and the city became a melting-pot for urban and rural culture.

All cultural activity in Kristiania was private in origin, apart from the large museums and collections such as the National Gallery and the Norwegian Folk Museum, for which the state and city, wholly or in part, were responsible. Even the National Theatre, opened in 1899, was a limited company; the state had contributed only the site for the building.

The single most determinant element in Norwegian culture in the years leading up to the First World War was the fact that Norway had obtained its independence from Sweden in 1905. That brought a constant emphasis on national culture, which culminated in the Anniversary Exhibition in Kristiania in 1914, the centenary of the Constitution.[2] It was both an industrial exhibition and a genuine cultural event, with exhibitions, choral festivals and other concerts, and a number of compositions were written for the occasion.[3]

In the period up to 1920 Norwegian cultural attitudes were influenced also by events outside the national boundaries: first and foremost, obviously, was the First World War, which had an unsettling influence, economically, socially and ideologically; the Russian Revolution also had an ideological impact in Norway. Two national economic surges, both before and after the War, helped create unrest because they gradually led to a boom, where

[1] The Norwegian capital did not revert to its ancient name, Oslo, until 1925.

[2] Signed at Eidsvoll on 17 May 1814. Later that year Norway, formerly united with Denmark, became 'a kingdom united with the kingdom of Sweden'.

[3] The most prominent was Christian Sinding's *Cantata for 1914*, Op. 117 (with a text by Nils Collett Vogt). A number of larger works were premiered, too, among them Eyvind Alnæs' Piano Concerto, Op. 27, and Hjalmar Borgstrøm's Violin Concerto in G major, Op. 25.

people made or lost fortunes almost overnight and banks and other enterprises fell into bankruptcy.

Simultaneously, technological development was making dramatic advances. Water supplies and drainage networks were built in several parts of the city, transport systems were developed, the telegraph and telephone became more widespread. Electric lighting began to penetrate many more homes and illuminated the streets. Irgens-Jensen himself remembered the strong impression made, at the end of the 1890s, by the first evening that electric light lit up the family home.[4]

In spite of the limited size of the city, and its comparative poverty, cultural life in Kristiania in 1910–20 was relatively rich, and music enjoyed a high social standing, as is documented by the broad coverage given to all sorts of topical musical material in the daily papers and weekly journals. But much was missing from musical life, the biggest lacuna being the absence of a national institution of music education. There was a Music Conservatory in Kristiania, but it was principally a school for organists, offering a professional training that musicians would require to take up the permanent positions that were available in churches.

There were a few composition teachers to choose from in Kristiania in the early years of the twentieth century. Two particularly important figures were based at the Music Conservatory. Catharinus Elling (1858–1942) was a popular and respected teacher, especially in counterpoint and harmony.[5] He was affiliated to the Music Conservatory until 1909; later he took a few private pupils. Among his students were Fartein Valen (1887–1952), David Monrad Johansen (1888–1974), Arne Eggen (1881–1955) and Pauline Hall (1890–1969), all leaders of the next generation in various ways, Valen as an international atonalist, Monrad Johansen as an outspoken representative for the national movement, Eggen as a traditionalist but important president of the Society of Composers for years, Hall a champion for modern European trends (first Impressionism and later Neoclassicism).

The other important composition teacher was Gustav Fredrik Lange (1861–1939), whose main interest was the violin; most of his pupils were violinists.[6] But he also had some students in theory, particularly harmony

[4] Recounted by his family.

[5] Elling's status as a composer has yet to be adequately acknowledged. His output includes an opera, *Kossakkerne* ('The Cossacks'), two symphonies, a violin concerto, a piano quartet and two string quartets. In his own time he was recognised principally as an organist, choral conductor and ethnomusicologist – he notated some 1,400 folk melodies from the southern part of Norway.

[6] Most of his compositions involved the violin as well, among them the *Ballade*, Op. 9, *Two Norwegian Rhapsodies*, Op. 12, *Drei Stücke in norwegischer Weise*, Op. 15, *Romance*, Op. 21, and *Norwegian Dance*, Op. 22 – all for violin and piano.

and counterpoint, and his *Praktisk harmonilære* ('Practical Harmony')[7] and *Musiklære* ('Music Theory')[8] had a wide circulation and were repeatedly reprinted. Amongst his best-known composition pupils were Bjarne Brustad (1895–1978) and the short-lived Arvid Kleven (1899–1929), both later advocates for contemporary European music. Brustad, who succeeded Lange as teacher of theory at the Conservatory in 1937, described his teacher thus:

> Although Lange was an all-round musician with extensive knowledge, he was congenial and pleasant, cheerful and direct, with a distinguished appearance; he inspired respect, for he was a fine and sure giver of advice both in musical and personal questions; one could rely on him, and one could be fond of him.[9]

Another student of Lange at the Conservatory was Odd Grüner-Hegge (1899–1973), a close friend of Irgens-Jensen from childhood and later renowned as a conductor; he also had some instruction from Otto Winter-Hjelm (1837–1931) who, despite advanced age, was happy to take such a gifted young pupil.

But many Norwegian music students also went abroad – usually to Berlin, Leipzig or Paris – as they had done since early in the nineteenth century, often bringing back new ideas that did much to enliven the musical culture they had left.

In the capital the National Theatre had its own permanent orchestra, with a strength of 43 musicians under the direction of the composer Johan Halvorsen; it generally functioned as a standard theatre orchestra, playing overtures, entr'actes and similar music for the productions in the Theatre; but it also played for performances of opera there and regularly gave concerts of its own, some twenty purely orchestral events annually in the period 1910–19 (as well as a number of outdoor concerts).

Another institution, *Musikforeningen* (The Music Society), was a looser organisation which had existed since 1871, when Grieg had been one of the founders. It was a closed society with its own choir (of 120) and orchestra (60 men), which had some support from the municipality after 1889. The conductor from 1886 until 1911 was the composer Iver Holter, who was followed by Karl Nissen (1879–1920 – he, too, short-lived) until 1918. The Music Society gave six to eight concerts a year. In 1919, almost all of the 27 professional – though part-time – musicians went over to the newly founded *Filharmonisk Selskap* (Philharmonic Society), which came to play

[7] Norsk Musikforlag, Kristiania, 1897.

[8] Cappelen, Kristiania, 1904

[9] *Liv og yrke: ord og tone*, Tanum, Oslo, 1971, p. 17.

an important role in musical life.[10] In most years there were also visits from orchestras from abroad, particularly from Germany, Sweden and Finland.

Opera functioned under difficult conditions, too. Until 1915 the National Theatre gave fairly regular operatic performances, for the most part of well-known operas – and sure successes – by Mozart, Rossini, Bizet, Gounod, Verdi and Puccini. They also managed two performances of Wagner (*The Flying Dutchman* and *Lohengrin*). Otherwise the biggest success at the Theatre was Lehár's *The Merry Widow*, which had its Norwegian premiere in 1906. Gradually, performances of opera at the Theatre became more sporadic and operetta was given more space. In all, in the first twenty years of the National Theatre, 26 different operas were performed, of which seven were purely Norwegian, by composers such as Ole Olsen, Johannes Haarklou, Sigwardt Aspestrand and Gerhard Schjelderup.[11]

Opera was also performed in the Central Theatre, where the repertoire was very similar to that presented at the National Theatre. The dream of a permanent opera theatre was held intensely in a number of circles and in 1917 the idea was given a boost with the promise of a large sum for the building of an opera house from the Norwegian-American ship-owner and -builder Christoffer Hannevig. Unfortunately, Hannevig's most important assets were sequestered by the American state after the entry of the United States into the First World War and he later went bankrupt.[12]

In 1918–21 a private company calling itself the Opéra Comique put on productions in Kristiania and smaller towns of Norway. In Kristiania there were almost daily performances during the season, with well-known singers and conductors, both Norwegian and foreign – Kirsten Flagstad, for example, gained practical experience during these years by singing a range of varied roles with the Opéra Comique.[13]

Various other musical organisations with specific interests were also to be found in Kristiania, among them *Holters Korforening* (Holter's Choral Society) and *Cæciliaforeningen* (The Cecilia Society), which aimed to tackle the major choral challenges (oratorios and masses), often in co-operation with the Music Society. *Kvartettforeningen* (The Quartet Society) was another active institution, giving several chamber-music concerts each year.

But most concerts given by professional musicians were solo recitals, and singers, pianists and violinists, Norwegian and foreign, appeared in

[10] The founding of the Philharmonic was also dependent on the transfer of some of the musicians of the National Theatre orchestra to the Philharmonic, which caused a good deal of controversy. It ended with the Theatre retaining fifteen (later increased to nineteen) musicians together with the conductor, Johan Halvorsen, but its orchestra was then no longer able to give symphony concerts.

[11] *Cf.* Ingeborg Kindem, *Den norske operas historie*, Mortensen, Oslo, 1942, p. 97.

[12] *Ibid.*, pp. 105–9.

[13] *Ibid.*, pp. 123–25.

an almost endless line. An important group behind the scenes were the agents, concert-arrangers and impresarios, who had an important role both nationally and internationally, not only as intermediaries, but also as cultural-political participants and people of influence.

Amateur music-making blossomed, too, organised in churches, societies and other groups and unorganised in private homes. Choirs continued to be very popular, but with time the number of amateur orchestras grew and bands proliferated, especially in schools. *Arbeiderbevegelsen* (The Workers' Movement) had its permanent choirs and ensembles, which both performed traditional repertoire and encouraged their members to create their own songs. There was also a direct parallel to this sub-culture in the many temperance lodges.

In schools, music was taught from primary up to grammar school, with a focus on general education, patriotism and the Christian legacy, and so hymns and educational songs were included in classes outside singing lessons. The treasury of songs from this period was presented both in ordinary schools and in the many 'folk high schools'.[14] The ideal of the healthy, honest and heroic Norwegian man (personified in the character of Fridtjof Nansen[15]) is clearly presented in this repertoire; the role of women was less clearly defined.

This emphasis on cultural values had consequences for teacher-training colleges, where the teaching of music was compulsory, and there were indirect implications for other aspects of musical life: up and down the country more and more churches obtained organs, resulting in a growing demand for organists with a solid musical training – and they played not only for services but also spread music around the community when they appeared as conductors of choirs and bands.

In the well-to-do home, the piano continued to be the most widely used instrument, although sales of accordions, both simple and sophisticated, now began to grow. It was also a prime time for music-publishers and music-shops, since sheet music was now bought instead of being borrowed from the lending libraries. More and more popular music was published, not only folk-dances – much of what today one would call round-dances or *gammaldans*[16] – but also music from revue and cabaret, from operetta and theatrical productions. Hit tunes from abroad (particularly from Sweden

[14] People's colleges, which run courses that do not lead to a degree.

[15] Nansen showed his intellectual side as a scholar, and his courage, strength and endurance in his Arctic expeditions; his moral side was displayed through his humanitarian work for the oppressed and refugees, and he played a political role in the formation of the sovereign Norwegian state in 1905 and as an ambassador.

[16] That is, the popular dances from around the turn of the century: waltzes, polkas, reinlenders, galops and so on.

and Germany) were also included. The *skillingsviser* (street songs that sold for a *skilling*, a small-value coin) continued to enjoy an audience among many sections of the population.

With the influence of gramophone records, cinema music and café music, taste gradually changed from German popular music to British and American. The waltz remained popular but, particularly from the 1920s, jazz came to take precedence, especially in the towns. Indeed, it was often used as a collective term for modern dance music: the cake-walk, one-step, two-step, Boston, shimmy and so on – all were labelled 'jazz'. This change in tastes also brought in new sounds, with the predominance of instruments like the trumpet, clarinet and saxophone, and new forms of percussion.

Even though the external conditions for the performance of concert music changed during these years, it was far more difficult to effect corresponding changes in the repertoire. The dominant personalities amongst the critics and the leading composers, like Otto Winter-Hjelm, Hjalmar Borgstrøm and Johannes Haarklou, were very conservative and keen on preserving the status quo: for them Grieg still offered the very best of Norwegian music. Wagner began to gain a foothold of sorts, but as late as the First World War there were still critics who considered Brahms to be a radical. The real radical music of Stravinsky and Schoenberg was not contemplated in Norway until well into the 1920s; as late as 1920–22 Debussy and Ravel were still spoken of as modernists. Ravel's *La valse* (from 1920) was characterised by one critic as 'ugly and revealing bad taste' when it was performed by the Philharmonic in December 1922.[17] Reger's music, too, was almost unilaterally condemned in the press. Mahler and Richard Strauss enjoyed a warmer reception, and Bruckner's symphonies finally came into the repertoire during the First World War, earning overwhelmingly positive reviews. Carl Nielsen's Third Symphony, the *Sinfonia Espansiva*, avoided the worst insults when it was given its Norwegian premiere by Johan Halvorsen and the Philharmonic at the end of 1919 – but he had paved the way by performing the Second and Fourth Symphonies the year before with his National Theatre Orchestra.

As might be expected, the more modern and forward-looking of the younger composers – not least Alf Hurum, Fartein Valen and Pauline Hall – had problems obtaining a fair hearing for their works in Norway: the dominant older critics and colleagues found it difficult to tolerate anything new that might have had its origins abroad. In any event, European musical modernism was partly halted, or at least hindered, by the First World War: in Norway modernism was almost turned away at the border.

[17] Arne Erpekum Sem, writing in *Tidens Tegn* on 12 December 1922.

As a rule, Norwegian composers could not survive by their music alone (not a problem only for Norwegian composers, and not only then, of course): they had to take other work, as critics, performers (as organists in particular) or teachers. There were few grants, and a commission was a rare thing indeed – Christian Sinding, for example, was one of Norway's most prominent composers, but he was given a commission only on the centenary of the Constitution in 1914.

Even though Kristiania by now had become a large city in Norwegian terms, it was nevertheless small and poor in comparison with the major conurbations of Europe, a peripheral outpost for culture. Critics from other Nordic countries nonetheless praised the standard of orchestral playing in the city, which was recognised as being superior to that found elsewhere in the north.

This was the musical environment in which Ludvig Irgens-Jensen chose to become a composer and which provided the background for his development as an artist.

II
First Years

Ludvig Irgens-Jensen was born into comfortable material circumstances. The family on his father's side ran the store Jensen & Co. in Torvgata in Kristiania, a well-known and successful enterprise established in 1866 by the composer's paternal grandfather, Ludvig Christian Jensen (1834–1910), with his second wife, Martine, *née* Bjerregaard (1834–1917), as partner, to sell 'delicacies and delicatessen'.

Ludvig Christian Jensen belonged to the Jerndahl family, who for several generations had been mill-owners and master-millers in Moss, some 50 kilometres south of Kristiania. His father was the master-miller Christian Jensen Jerndahl (1789–1839) and his mother Petrea Schou (1810–78), both from Moss. The name Jerndahl came from the farmstead Jerndal (Jerndahl, Jønndal) in Råde near Moss, which is recorded as far back as 1648. When L. C. Jensen began his business career, he took his father's middle name as his family name.

The composer's father, Peter Marinius Jensen, was born in Moss in 1860 but grew up in Kristiania. After matriculation in 1882, he began to study law but had to break off his studies to join his father's firm. In 1890, P. M. Jensen married Elisabeth Frederikke Gløersen, born in Kristiania on 11 June 1865.[1] She was the daughter of clerk of the supreme court Paul Irgens Gløersen (1830–1901) and Birgitte Irgens (1835–1912). The Gløersen family can trace their ancestors back to the aristocratic Sparre family in Denmark in the thirteenth century, and through the Mylting family (from Asdal on Jutland) in the female line back to the Norwegian royal house in Viking times. The Irgens family also stems from Denmark – from Holstein. Johannes Irgens, an ancestor of the Norwegian branch, came to Norway in 1651 to take over the running of the Røros copper works, in which the family was the largest shareholder.

Elisabeth and Peter Marinius Jensen had three children: Brynjulf Bjerregaard (b. 1891), Ludvig Paul Irgens (b. 1894) and Dagny Birgitte Irgens (b. 1905). Peter M. Jensen died in 1939 and Elisabeth in 1945.

Jensen & Co. expanded rapidly after 1866, becoming widely known at home and abroad for its specialities in fine groceries, both retail and

[1] She was thus exactly two days younger than Carl Nielsen.

The reindeer trade mark of Jensen & Co.

wholesale. It grew so swiftly, in fact, that parts of the operation had soon to be divided into separate companies. First, in 1893, the game and salmon business was separated from the main enterprise under the name of, and run by, P. M. Jensen's younger brother, Karl A. Jensen. Three years later P. M. Jensen then set up a separate meat and delicatessen business under his own name, which he managed in addition to Jensen & Co. Another brother, Adelsten Jensen, founded the clothing firm Adelsten Jensen, which was to become a well-known chain of shops. The trademark of Jensen & Co., a reindeer, was familiar from packages, marmalade containers and advertisements in the press, and for several decades a standard advertisement was to be found in Norwegian music journals and concert programmes. P. M. Jensen worked hard all his life to expand the two firms he ran; he passed the management over to his son Brynjulf only in 1939. The business is still run by his family today, although it now concentrates on import and wholesale.

P. M. Jensen was a well-known and respected figure in Kristiania, with a personality which made a strong impression on the people he met. He was generous and helpful, and at the same time an efficient manager – though his son Ludvig thought that he was occasionally too trusting. He lived an active life, working early and late in the business, and he was an unusually enthusiastic outdoors man, to the point of going ice-bathing (even in old age he still took a daily swim in a public swimming pool); he also often went to lectures at the University. Coming and going in Norwegian winters is usually complicated by the requirement of lodging one's overcoat in a cloakroom before going into a restaurant, theatre or concert hall. P. M. Jensen rarely wore a coat so that he didn't waste time having it hung up somewhere; for the same reason he used a cloth cap instead of a hat, since he could easily tuck it into his pocket. Once at a fashionable party where the men wore their tails, someone noticed that he had not bothered to find the correct breast buttons for his starched dress shirt but had simply used a pair of ordinary wooden matches. On one occasion he said to Ludvig: 'The art is to have small needs'.[2]

Ludvig grew up, then, in a solid merchant family and, as was often the case in such environments in Kristiania, he developed a deep interest in art and culture. Some old accounts from Cammermeyer's bookshop (found in Irgens-Jensen's woodshed) show that in the course of three weeks in January–February 1919 the family bought a series of art books, amongst them a large work on the *Ursprung und Entwicklung der chinesischen Kunst*, Burckhardt's *Geschichte der Renaissance*, Josephson's *Teckningar* ('Drawings') and *Seltene Radierungen* by Goya – as well as *Le spleen de Paris* by Baudelaire, *Chansons* by Verlaine, *Science et méthode* by Poincaré, *A Tale of Two Cities* by Dickens, *Poor Folk* by Dostoyevsky and the latest novels by the Norwegian authors Hamsun, Falkberget, Johan Bojer and Gabriel Scott. In addition, there was a collection of Danish folk-songs, a series of composer biographies, and the *Grosse Kompositionslehre I–III* by Hugo Riemann.

Both Irgens-Jensen's parents came from families where music was enthusiastically cultivated and they were themselves musical. At the age of 72 his father wrote in the student annals of the class of 1882:

> I have the same interests as before – enjoying music, reading and being out in the countryside. When I look back on my life, I have to be happy that I have had these interests, but I seem more and more to have to complain that the business and the necessary newspaper and professional reading have taken so much time at the cost of the other interests. [...]
>
> When one is just about at the end of the road, one inevitably asks oneself if after all it would not have been better to have a little more time to spare for one's family, brothers and friends, because all the work in the business and the many interests have meant that I have done too little for them.[3]

Like the rest of his family, Peter Jensen was a regular theatre- and concert-goer. The children had music-lessons. And there was regular music-making at home. Elisabeth sang songs by Kjerulf and Grieg, an interest she had in common with her sister, Mathilde, a trained singer who died only 25 years old. P. M. Jensen played the piano excellently and maintained this accomplishment despite the many duties of his business life. Both of Ludvig's siblings were musical and played the piano.

Ludvig Paul Irgens Jensen was born in Kristiania on 13 April 1894. Not much is known about his childhood beyond what his sister Dagny was able to recall.[4] The family lived in Niels Juels-gate before moving to

[2] Recounted by Olav Irgens-Jensen (the composer's son).

[3] *Studentene fra 1882*, Malling, Oslo, 1932, p. 80.

[4] 'Erindringer om min bror', manuscript in the possession of Olav Irgens-Jensen, *c.* 1984.

Irgens-Jensen at the age of two-and-a-half

Fastingsgate 1, a large brick house in a pseudo-Gothic style designed by the town architect, Holm Munthe. At one time they also had a summer house by the fjord, 'Bråten', in Bygdøy near the city, and a large cottage at Lillevann near Voksenkollen in the hills just north of the city, and there, and in town, family life evolved in the usual manner.

Ludvig was born with reduced sight in one eye, a handicap he learned to overcome so that he could carry out every task as did children with normal sight. Indeed, his early drawings demonstrate that he was a keen observer: a drawing from his first day at school shows all the pupils at their desks in the classroom and in the correct perspective.

An active and reckless child, he developed fast and made many friends. He was left-handed, but he wrote equally well with both hands and could also write with both hands at the same time, both in parallel and in mirror image. At one time he was pre-occupied with making sailing boats that could genuinely sail – hard work, because the entire wooden shape had to be hewn out with a chisel and the sides of the hull had to be thin, and trimmed exactly. On one occasion, occupied with this work, he generated considerable uproar when he cut through the artery in a wrist, the blood spurting up to the ceiling.

In an interview shortly before his death[5] Irgens-Jensen emphasised that there was one person in particular who meant more to him – personally and musically, in his youth and afterwards – than anyone else: Odd Grüner-Hegge (1899–1973). The young Irgens-Jensen frequently visited the Grüner-Hegge family, where he found an intellectually rich and fashionable environment: Mrs Grüner-Hegge painted and sketched, and there was much music-making. There were four boys in the family. The eldest, Thorleif, became professor of psychology at the University of Michigan, Ann Arbor; the second, Rolf, became a businessman; the third, Finn, took up the violin professionally; and the youngest, Odd, became first a composer and then a highly regarded conductor, both abroad and in Norway, where he was for several years chief conductor of the Philharmonic Society orchestra, later (1960–69) becoming head of the Norwegian Opera, after Kirsten Flagstad.

Odd and Ludvig went to the same school, where they were both in the school choir, directed by Johannes Berg-Hansen, a well-known conductor and singer. Odd, Ludvig's junior by five years, had an unusually beautiful treble voice and was regarded as a musical prodigy: he also composed and could play demanding piano works. His first printed composition was written when he was six, and so he was taken along to Edvard Grieg, on whose lap he sat to play his own little pieces.

Odd was thus included in the games and music-making of the bigger boys, and it was he who gradually became closest to Ludvig. They often played piano-duet editions of the standard orchestral works and had endless discussions about music, aesthetics and music theory. In time Grüner-Hegge, always a loyal friend, would become a useful critic of Irgens-Jensen's music.

Another life-long friend was Leif Bruun (1897–1981), who was very musical and from childhood had viola and violin lessons with the best local teachers. He became an engineer in Sweden and spent some years in Denmark around 1930 before returning home to Norway when he bought

[5] With Torstein Gunnarson on NRK (Norwegian national radio), April 1969, in connection with his imminent 75th birthday. This interview is preserved as UBO/NMS lyd/b194–195 at the National Music Collection of the National Library. Page numbers refer to my transcription of this material, enclosed in these boxes. The transcription is direct: subsequent extracts from it contain verbal and spontaneous comments which do not reflect Irgens-Jensen's painstaking use of written language.

The Irgens Jensen family in 1907: from the left, Ludvig's mother Elisabeth, his brother Brynjulf, sister Dagny, father Peter and Ludvig himself

a small foodstuffs factory. Bruun was much engaged in the musical life of Oslo and after the Second World War he became for many years a member of the board of the Oslo Philharmonic Society.

In 1913 Irgens-Jensen passed his secondary-school examination at the Vestheim school; indeed, he was one of only nineteen students in all of Norway who passed *summa cum laude* – out of 860 candidates. That summer, as a present from his father, he was given a trip abroad, and so, with his elder brother Brynjulf, he went on a month-long tour of Germany, drawing musical inspiration from what he discovered in Berlin, Dresden and Bayreuth, including Wagner's *Tristan* and the whole of *The Ring*. His admiration for Wagner's orchestration was unreserved and later, in 1915, he studied *Tristan* in detail with Grüner-Hegge, even though the overwhelming scale of Wagner's conception was at odds with his more sober outlook.

In that autumn of 1913 he enrolled at the University of Oslo and in 1914 became *cand. philos.*, that is, he took the 'second examination' and completed the preliminary tests in philosophy with the highest possible mark, 1.0. He began to attend lectures in English literature and in philosophy and for a short time considered going in for these subjects. In a later interview in the newspaper *Dagbladet*[6] the interviewer described that period:

[6] Published on 29 November 1930; the interviewer was 'Mais', a well-known journalist whose real name was Marie Fearnley.

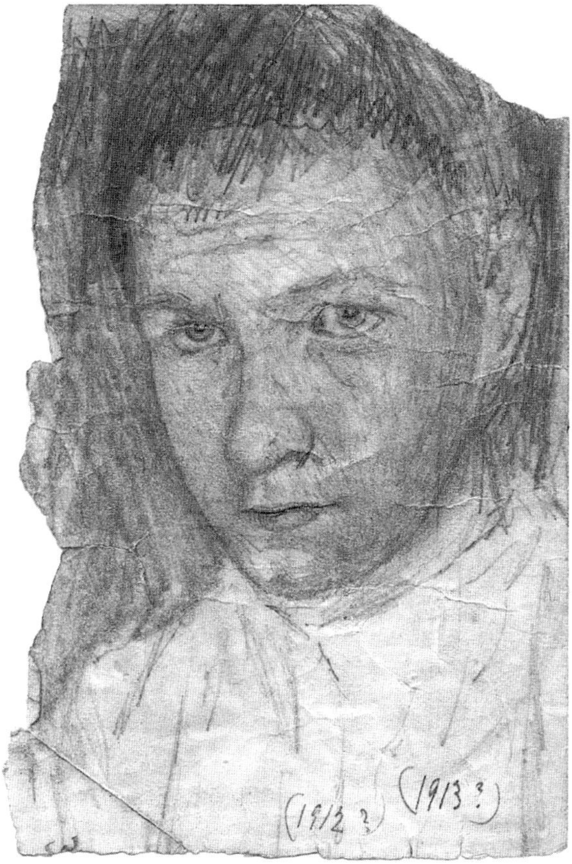

Pencil sketch for a self-portrait, from 1912 or 1913

> Originally he had thought of becoming a philologist. He went to the university lectures every day with his briefcase under his arm. But the briefcase was full of scores. While a professor was lecturing on Old English, he was enjoying the favourite composers he had brought with him, and if it happened that a professor on occasion pounced on this diligently reading pupil, he got confused nonsense as an answer. Philology was just a cover, which he soon threw overboard.

In truth, this description does not fit with what is known about Irgens-Jensen's character: if he applied himself to a particular pursuit, he did so thoroughly and systematically. He thought long and hard about the path he should choose as a career. One of the choices was between language/ literature and philosophy – a subject which then also embraced many elements of psychology, with which he was much taken. He was especially interested in the phenomena of the imagination as it was so close to the artistic mind.

Irgens-Jensen's sketch-books detail his plans and reveal how thoroughly he worked. One entry documents how he would organise an ideal day:

> Timetable
> Play c. 4 hours per day
> 1 hour's practice (Naturally, as it comes. I just mean
> 1 " Bach that none of these must be completely ignored)
> 1 " things for Finn[7]
> 1 " composition
>
> Read c. 2 hours about music
> 1 hour acoustics
> 1 hour music-theory
> (harmony, counterpoint,
> study of scores etc.)
>
> 1 hour? cultural history, history of religions (Buddha, Zarathustra)
> music history (mediaeval music, folk music) etc.
>
> read 1 hour psychology
> or philosophy (Bergson, Kant)
> 1 [hour] literature and literary history
> (by and about Goethe)
> 1 hour Homer or Dante
> 1 hour French
> 1 hour English (Shakespeare, Milton)
> 2 hours Greek
>
> On average now c. 3 lectures a day adding c. 4 hours
>
> In addition a quick methodical reading of physics and mathematics
> (Besides acoustics and optics,
> light – in relation to psychology and physiology)
>
> altogether 17 or 18 hours
> (one hour food and dressing)
> 5 or 6 hours sleep.

Although he later crossed out these pages with thick pencil strokes, the unrealistic nature of his expectations does point to a degree of ambition

[7] Presumably, music to practise before playing it with Finn Grüner-Hegge.

Irgens-Jensen in 1913 as a newly fledged student with his family on the doorstep of Fastingsgate 1

and perfectionism. And he was 'miserly with his time', as he later put it:[8] for example, while he ran through the Palace Park on his way to the University, he would use the occasion for relaxation exercises for his wrists, which grew stiff with constant piano practice.

Literature absorbed much of his time and energy, and he constantly bought books by Norwegian and foreign authors. In the 1969 NRK interview with Torstein Gunnarson,[9] he touched on this interest briefly:

> TG: You have a huge amount of reading behind you. I have the impression that reading is a part of Irgens-Jensen. You have read a great deal of Norwegian and foreign literature?
>
> LIJ: Yes, I suppose I have. But I have had to be careful of my eyes, or my eye. There has not been very much reading from that. In my youth I tried to get by. I certainly did.
>
> TG: What did you chiefly read, when you talk of your youth?
>
> LIJ: I began to be fond of literature quite early, I have to say.
>
> TG: What did you throw yourself into then? Norwegian first?
>
> LIJ: Certainly that, yes.

[8] Related to his son.

[9] *Cf.* note 5, p. 26.

TG: But I know that Ibsen and Kinck[10] held a unique position?

LIJ: Did I write that somewhere? Yes, now I remember. I mentioned them, because I had to mention some that I …. But I did have others ….

TG: Literary gods?

LIJ: Yes. I was very enthusiastic about Kinck, I remember, in my youth.

TG: And Aukrust?[11]

LIJ: Yes, I read him when he appeared and also some of it later.

[...]

LIJ: Yes, you asked me about the literature, I read quite a bit from countries outside Norway, too. I was a good deal taken with Baudelaire and the Belgians [Verhaeren, Maeterlinck], but especially Baudelaire. And at that time around the First World War a lot of strange things appeared, right from the days of symbolism in France and further afield. It was very strange, and there is much which is recurring now, and which has caught on now. […] It was regarded almost as gibberish at the time.

Irgens-Jensen also wrote poetry and verse himself. A few drafts are to be found in his sketchbooks from his time at grammar school. Although Appendix 2[12] presents some drafts of shorter poems from these sketchbooks, one example is worth including here because it seems to reveal something of the very young Irgens-Jensen's thinking about the function of form:

Høststemning	*Autumn Mood*
Jeg vandrer alene blandt kjendte trær	I wander alone among well-known trees
og husker de gamle steder	remembering the old places
Vissent løv rasler stilt hvor jeg gaar.	Faded leaves rustle silently where I pass.
Jeg tænker paa vaarens vuggende trær,	I think of the spring's trees swaying,
paa alle de drømte glæder	of all the dreamt-of pleasures
Men vissent løv kranser hvert et minde.	But faded leaves wreathe each memory.

These drafts for the most part are free in form, but there are also many poems – not only autumnal elegies – with strict meter and end-rhymes. One of them asserts that formal binding in art can bring more artistic freedom – something that can be recognised also from his music:

[10] Hans E. Kinck (1865–1926) was later to play a pivotal role in Irgens-Jensen's music – *cf.* pp. 69 and 183–96, below.

[11] Olav Aukrust (1883–1929) was a well known Norwegian poet.

[12] Appendix 2, pp. 323–34, below, examines Irgens-Jensen's poetry in more detail.

Digter	*Poet*
Den som er lenket i rytmer og rim	He who is fettered in rhythm and rhyme
– er friest av alle	– is the freest of all
Han kun si hvad han vil	He can *say* what he *will*
– og faa sagt *hva han* maa	– and *get to say* what he *has to*
Rytmer og rim!	Rhythm and rhyme!
Lyttende glemmes éns strenge kritik	Listening, one's strict critique is forgotten
Én hører kun – en sagte	one hears only – a gently
strømmende selsom musik	streaming strange music

It is also clear that he was taken with the idea of an artistic career from a very early age. On a slip of paper from this time he scribbled down some points on the subject:

> Describe an artist's development, from the youthful time of awakening, the time of eternal possibilities, when one knows everything and wants everything, when the desire is honest, but the technique poor, to a time when one has one's own firm sure form, one's inevitable limitations, no new possibilities, the grey ordinary time.
>
> Does one's development go from being idealistic, dedicated to the service of art, to becoming an egotist who allows himself to be served by art at the table of life? Is it not a more natural shifting of motive: from art as a medium to art as an aim?
>
> Naturally, if these two are carefully set against one another... It is sad for the one suddenly to be reminded of the dreams of his youth. It is hard for the other to see that the way he must go is not the one the world now values.

Irgens-Jensen had other talents he wanted to develop, too, not least his gift for drawing and painting. He had a sharp eye for colour and form: his papers contain sketches from his first years at school as well as drawings, pastels and paintings from his secondary-school years, which he obviously thought were worth retaining. Right up to the last years of his life he captured the atmosphere of his mountain walks and the view from his home with pastel chalks and with watercolours. When a Ukrainian artist, Daniel Vladimir (Baranoff-) Rossiné,[13] came to his home during the First World War to paint two portraits of his sister, Ludvig paid close attention to what the visitor was doing. Irgens-Jensen approached art systematically; he always had a drawing pad with him, making quick, small sketches on his

[13] Rossiné (1888–1944) later became an internationally known artist. His wide interest in the arts included music, and he invented an 'optophonic piano', intended to generate light and sound at the same time.

A brief moment of relaxation during his demanding, self-imposed programme of study

walks and noting colours in a sort of shorthand, a colour circle with light/dark in a double cone, so that he could remember them if he later wanted to transfer them into watercolours.

He may even have had plans to become a painter. In the winter of 1918, at the age of 23, he went to Copenhagen to study art in the galleries and museums there with a class-mate from high school, William Lunden (1895–1979), who was then working in the city for the porcelain firm Bing & Grøndahl. In Copenhagen Irgens-Jensen moved in with Lunden and his wife Vera Burgund (1895–1994), also a class-mate from his senior-school days, for six months.

Music, though, was becoming ever more important for him. In the sole letter preserved from his time in Copenhagen, written to his father, he talks only about music, which was, of course, a shared passion – though the filial naivety of the style does not correspond with his other writings of the time:

> (Tuesday after Easter) [postmark: Copenhagen, 2 April 1918]
> Dear Papa!
> I have heard a wonderful performance of the St John Passion in Our Lady's church, which is a splendid basilica – you have certainly been there many times yourself.
> I met Ole Sandvik[14] there. He is studying old church music on a grant.
> On Sunday I heard Rossini's Mass [*Solennelle*] at the same place, in a still more perfect performance. I was very pleasantly surprised. I could never have believed that he could have written such serious and uplifting music. Many

[14] Ole Mørch Sandvik (1875–1976), Norwegian musicologist.

of the arias really resemble love arias more than church music. But there were passages so heartfelt and beautiful that one has seldom heard the like.

Yesterday I heard Mahler's longest symphony (No. 3). It lasted 1 1/2 hours and must be the longest symphonic work by far. For the occasion I bought myself a large work on M. for 9 marks. He has written 10 tremendous, world-famous symphs. and not one of them has been performed at home! No doubt we will not get to hear them for several years, because they demand more than we are able to manage for a creditable performance.[15] And they need a creditable performance; there is a rich and fine sound which is their strength. His handling of the orchestra must be without parallel. But themes and melodies were occasionally unimportant, even banal. But no doubt that is often intentional. He looks for the ordinary, folk-song simplicity. Besides there is irony in his music. – [In the margin:] A most interesting personality – surely one of the greatest in new music!

Ludvig, then, was a creature of many talents. But he was no fragile indoor plant: he was an outstanding skier and won cups for sailing and tennis. He had inherited his father's interest in the outdoors and, from the age of twelve, he took up mountain-climbing, practising free climbing on the slopes at the top of Kolsås – a wooded mountain-ridge west of Oslo, and a well-known training area for the Oslo climbers. Here he showed such daring that the veteran climber Ferdinand Schjelderup[16] rang Ludvig's parents to warn them about his recklessness. In 1914, when he was twenty, an invitation to apply for membership of the only Norwegian mountaineering club triggered a reflection in his sketchbook on what climbing brought him:

[27 September 1914]

Ought I to do it? I don't have that much interest in the sport any longer. It contrasts unsuitably with my art (if I dare use that expression), although difficult – and – challenging piano-playing could call for precisely this nerve-stimulating, strengthening sport as a contrast! – When I touch the mountain, I feel a quite healthy satisfaction; it is fun to overcome these difficulties – and yet this is much less the case for me now than before – perhaps one day it will completely disappear.

Once I would say: I am never as safe as when I have the inevitable precipice beneath me. Then it's a matter of having the right amount of distrust and to rely on oneself. And live only for that moment. Everything else goes away, all thoughts and anxieties and dreams. –

15 He was right: the first Mahler symphony to be performed in Norway was No. 1 in 1919.

16 Schjelderup's son, Thorleif (1920–2006), achieved fame in his own right as an author and ski-jumper, winning the bronze medal in the 1948 Winter Olympics; his second wife, the American (later Norwegian) soprano Anne Wiggins Brown (1912–2009), created the role of Bess in Gershwin's *Porgy and Bess* in 1935.

Irgens-Jensen was active – and reckless – as a child and began climbing from the age of twelve. Here he and a classmate (Ludvig is the one with the rope) celebrate a successful climb on Kolsås, a wooded mountainous ridge west of Oslo popular with climbers.

But now at least I have abandoned this excitement of seeking harmony in mortal danger. But for how long? If sorrows come – will I then be an enthusiastic mountain climber or even less keen? But in any case:

I do not at all want to be like a sheep in a flock, as a member of a club. Climbing, scrambling – cannot interest a man excessively for long. I cannot always only play children's games. If I dare use the demanding word aesthetic about myself (in a Kierkegaard-like way), I would say that, as an aest. [aesthete?] I have an aim: to enjoy the beauty of colour, lines, the gigantic and superhuman in the nature of the mountain, the autumnal and desolate – but I prefer to enjoy such things alone. Then I can talk to myself, be inspired; but it doesn't liberate an artist's powers to amble around with 'comrades' and club members and say that here it is very beautiful, does it? I can also (I believe to a high degree) enjoy solitude. Yes, that is my real life.

On one occasion 'touching the mountain' nearly cost him his life. Skiing in the Jotunheim at Easter 1918, he came close to freezing to death when he and his cousin Emil Jensen were caught in a snowstorm. They had climbed

The nineteen-year-old Ludvig on Store Skagastølstind (2,405 metres) in the western part of Jotunheimen – the most famous mountain in Norway, first climbed by the British climber William C. Slingsby in 1876

to the summit of Nautgardstind (2,258 metres) and were on their way towards the tourist lodge at Glitterheim to spend the night there. Suddenly, bad weather struck; they could not see where they were and had to spend the entire night out in the cold. They finally sought shelter behind a large rock and, so as to keep warm and not to go to sleep, they walked round and round their rucksacks, into which from time to time they put their feet to warm them up. The next morning the weather relented a little and they discovered the cabin only a few hundred metres away. By then they were exhausted and were transported by sleigh down to Randsverk. Irgens-Jensen had a frost blister on the sole of one of his feet, which made walking difficult for a while, but there was no permanent damage – unlike his cousin who, having dozed off, had suffered frostbitten feet and had to have some of his toes amputated.

The next winter he again came close to losing his life when he and a friend were caught by an avalanche, once more in the Jotunheim. Ludvig managed to 'swim' on top of the slide because his ski-bindings came loose, but his friend was buried. Ludvig and the others in the party who were not taken by the avalanche managed to dig the friend out – who was alive but, having nearly suffocated, seems to have suffered a degree of brain damage from lack of oxygen.

At high school Irgens-Jensen was keen both on sport and play and on intellectual activities. 'He was decidedly the cleverest in the class,' said his class-mate Vera Lunden.[17] He was also a witty and amusing prankster, but never spiteful: his wit could be striking, but it was never wounding.

The young Irgens-Jensen could appear a shade eccentric. In connection with a performance of some of his songs, Gunnar Larsen (writing as 'Kollskegg' ('Black-beard'), then a new journalist on *Dagbladet* and later its editor) remembered an earlier meeting with him:

> It was in a large garden on the splendid island of Tjømø that I met Ludvig Irgens Jensen for the first time. It was actually a Sunday with a sea breeze and sailing boats, kind elderly ladies sat together on the lawn in wicker chairs in the shade of the huge trees chattering, small children in diminutive bright dresses and white trousers ran around outside in the sunshine, butterflies fluttered and the bees hummed, as the books have it.
>
> In a secluded corner a young man, dressed for town, was eating birch leaves. He had raised these pieces of the plant to a delicacy of highest rank in his eccentric imagination and I surprised him during his consumption of a juicy twig with small red lice. He told me, as we strolled up towards the house, about the life and purpose of plants, about flowers and millipedes and their symbolism in France; he seemed to express an enthusiastic and inexplicable sympathy for Ejlert Bjerke's works.[18]
>
> A single chord sounded from the open window. Bach, said Irgens Jensen.
>
> The artistic scion of the old Torvgaten food dynasty has, in the years which have passed, combined his extensive knowledge about and feeling for fine and distinctive poetry with his deep and sensitive musicality and created a series of small pearls of vocal music, which have attracted unusual attention amongst people who understand such things. [19]

This article may have contributed to the wariness he came to show towards all journalists. He later generally refused requests for interviews and, in the few to which he consented, he usually expressed himself with extreme caution. This fear that the private might become public is partly responsible for the picture of the composer as a shy, taciturn and reserved figure, someone who, when he had become well known, also protected himself with an unlisted telephone number. Yet that image does not gel with the portrait his friends paint, of a warm and generous person with a droll sense of humour and keen self-irony, clear and well-balanced attitudes and a rare wealth of knowledge.

[17] In conversation with the author, c. 1971.

[18] Ejlert Bjerke (1887–1963) was a Norwegian writer with a couple of psychological novels among his publications.

[19] *Dagbladet*, 31 March 1924.

Larsen's article nonetheless presents an important side of his character. His 'inexplicable sympathy' for the research of Ejlert Bjerke surely comes from his interest in psychology and, in particular, in the effects of colour and after-images, extensively discussed by Bjerke. Psychology had only begun to uncover the explanatory patterns in the labyrinths of the mind, and the discipline had started to gain a foothold in Norway.

Irgens-Jensen's intellectual acuity was not matched by a concern for such practical matters as clothes. He didn't much care how he looked, even having to write himself a reminder on a scrap of paper that has been preserved from this period:

> Correct morning attire: top hat, black jacket, striped trousers, grey-patterned tie, grey spats and grey gloves, black shoes.

In the period up to the First World War many of the better-off families in the capital were liberal in their views on education and gave their children ample room for self-development. Thus it was with the Irgens-Jensen family, who were nonetheless unsettled, his mother in particular, by the fact that their richly gifted son did not seem to want to complete a normal education and, despite his obvious abilities, was unclear about what he wanted to do. Irgens-Jensen's notebooks reveal that he, too, was tormented by this vacillation. The decision, taken in 1920, at the age of 26, to go in for music fully and completely – and publicly, with the appearance of a collection of 38 songs[20] – brought considerable relief.

Irgens-Jensen never wanted a formal music education. He did have piano lessons early in life, although it is unclear in which year he began. While he was at school, he was a pupil of Christian Johnson (1861–1915), a well-known and much-sought-after teacher. Later in high school he played with Karl Nissen, son of the famous pianist Erika Nissen and himself also an outstanding concert pianist and teacher.

In 1915 Irgens-Jensen began to study with Nils Larsen (1888–1937), who after his return from a career as pianist abroad, had set up a piano institute. Larsen was also a composer, but posterity remembers him best as one of Norway's foremost piano-teachers, responsible for a long line of the leading Norwegian pianists who made their debuts from the 1920s onwards, among them Odd Grüner-Hegge, Kari Aarvold Glaser, Elisabeth Reiss, Ivar Johnsen, Robert Riefling, Robert Levin, Eline Nygaard and Amalie Christie. For how long Irgens-Jensen studied with Larsen is not known (they remained friends for years). It was during this time that he developed most rapidly as a pianist. The repertoire he tackled was demanding and included Bach's *Well-Tempered Clavier*, Beethoven's last sonatas, Chopin's

[20] *Cf.* pp. 51–59, below.

waltzes and studies and Schumann's collected piano works, all of which he came to master.

His relentless practising led to the muscular stiffness he would attempt to cure as he ran through the Palace Park. For advice in overcoming the problem he went to Dagmar Walle-Hansen (1871–1954), a concert pianist and teacher who in 1914 had returned to Norway after fifteen years' concertising abroad; she had also been an assistant teacher to Leschetizky in Vienna. Walle-Hansen, who had a reputation for being able to help with tension and occupational myalgia, insisted that Irgens-Jensen begin all over again, a finger at a time, so that he understood how the musculature worked as he played. Systematic and deliberate as ever, he noted the exercises down in one of his sketch-books, indicating how many times they should be played each day, some up to 200 times. He also diagnosed the faults in his own playing:

> Show her how uneven my *runs* are (e,g., the Ballade, the ascending passage on page 4, in D flat (E flat, E, F).
>
> Stiffness in turning under [the thumb]. Is my hand naturally not very flexible?
>
> How quickly I tire from the *tremolo* (Kreutzer, dev. in reprise cf. 1st movement) (Moonlight Sonata)
>
> How tense my *octaves* become (C min. Nocturne (p .2))

Irgens-Jensen never appeared in public as a solo pianist, although he did step forward on several occasions as an accompanist, particularly in performances of his own songs. After a concert on 4 April 1923, one critic wrote:

> He proved himself in this performance, which was perhaps his first, to be a real pianist, a consummate master of the keyboard. It takes real accomplishment to accompany a song like 'Besværgelse' ['Conjuration'] with its sometimes fiendish piano part.[21]

Another writer considered that he was an 'authoritative and authentic interpreter of the often really difficult piano parts'.[22] Jens Arbo, who was to become one of the critics who best understood the composer and later wrote the first authoritative biographical article on him,[23] reported that he accompanied 'with devotion and authentic authority'.[24]

Hjalmar Borgstrøm, himself a (relatively conservative) composer and a critic for *Aftenposten* allowed on several occasions that Irgens-Jensen

[21] 'R. M.' (Reidar Mjøen), in *Dagbladet*, 6 April 1923. On 'Besværgelse', *cf.* pp. 55–57, below.

[22] Valentin Siewers (who generally signed his reviews as '+') in *Morgenbladet*, 6 April 1923.

[23] 'Ludvig Irgens-Jensen', in *Norsk biografisk leksikon*, Aschehoug, Oslo, 1936, Vol. 7, pp. 3–6.

[24] *Musikbladet og Sangerposten*, No. 10, 1923, p. 87.

played 'satisfactorily' and, writing in 1924, compared him with his erstwhile teacher:

> Nils Larsen accompanied the first two sections of the programme, while Irgens-Jensen occupied the place at the grand piano for two of his own compositions. Nils Larsen is certainly the more brilliant of the two; but Irgens Jensen also played proficiently.[25]

In an interview given shortly beforehand, Irgens-Jensen spoke about his playing:

> 'Who is accompanying?'
> 'I am, unfortunately.'
> 'You are also a pianist?'
> 'No. My technique is all to pieces. But anyway I want to try to give a reasonable impression of the songs. Some think I do it well; others don't. No matter how it is, I shall unfortunately be accompanying on Wednesday.' [26]

Some amateur recordings from the 1960s nonetheless reveal that, even at an advanced age, he had a considerable technique, a lively delivery which was full of nuance, and a natural sense of phrasing, dynamics and the dramatic.

As a composer Irgens-Jensen is most often described as an autodidact. In the 1969 interview with Torstein Gunnarson he was asked about this aspect of his development:

> TG: Our music history makes it clear that you are an autodidact, self-taught.
> LIJ: Well, yes. I certainly had the opportunity to hear music all the time and the opportunity to read music and scores, etc. When one 'has absorbed' a great deal, then perhaps one cannot be called an autodidact.
> TG: That's why I want to ask the question, what does it mean when it is maintained that you are an autodidact?
> LIJ: It was I myself who mentioned it at one time. I have not had any teachers of composition or in any other subject, except just piano for many years. Also I have had friends who have given me brilliant advice through the years and one could very well call them teachers, first and foremost Grüner-Hegge, but also several others.[27]

Why, then, if he deliberately chose the best Norwegian piano-teachers, did he not go to the Music Conservatory or to a private teacher for lessons in the traditional subjects for the study of composition: music theory, harmony, counterpoint, analysis, orchestration, as well as for correction and guidance with his own works? Nor did he travel to study at an institution abroad, even though his parents could easily have afforded it. There are

[25] *Aftenposten*, 11 April 1924.
[26] *Aftenposten*, 1 April 1924.
[27] *Loc. cit*, p. 3.

Irgens-Jensen was a keen drawer and painter. These drawings are of his sister Dagny, from c. *1916*

several potential explanations. One might be that, although paying for piano lessons was entirely normal, taking lessons in composition signalled ambition of an altogether higher order – and Irgens-Jensen's modesty may have ruled that out. Another possible explanation can be found in an interview he gave in 1930:

> In my earliest youth I felt a sovereign contempt for the conservatories with their binding rules and bans, says Irgens Jensen. I thought all such restrictions put an unnatural hamper on the imagination. I went ahead on my own account and laughed at my contemporaries who swore by fugues and the small forms. But the experience has been dearly bought. I eventually realised that I had got stuck, understood that music followed its own unbreakable laws and so started on little songs and smaller orchestral works. I worked hard.[28]

The 'sovereign contempt' for the conservatory was a general expression of how he thought a conservatory education would turn out. Nor did the Music Conservatory in Kristiania have any structured course in composition, even though a number of well-known composers eventually had their grounding there.[29] And the fear that his imagination and artistic energy

[28] *Dagbladet*, 29 November 1930.
[29] *Cf.* pp. 16–17, above.

A self-portrait from 1917. 'Snillen' ('the kind one') was added by his sister.

might be hindered would have been reinforced by his distaste for showing others what he was working on.

Accordingly, he chose to remain outside traditional teaching. He began to compose at an early age, although the first sketches to have survived date from only 1913. At that time, of course, he considered his composing to be a private affair; there was hardly any conscious thought of becoming a composer. His younger sister was the only witness to these early attempts: when, at night, he sat at the piano to compose, she could hear him through the air-ducts of the house.

Though his material existence was comfortable, his working conditions were far from ideal. Living at home, he had a grand piano and a harmonium at his disposal. But the piano was in his parents' drawing room and, without his own work-space, he was constantly disturbed both by family and friends and repeatedly had to clear all his sketches and music away from the piano. He therefore preferred to work at night to have peace, even though it meant a disordered daily rhythm in relation to the rest of the family.

Odd Grüner-Hegge nurtured a suspicion that his friend had begun to compose in secret, but even a direct question was met with an evasive answer:

> Of course it happened that we discussed composition and he was very interested in what I was doing, naturally. But I discovered fairly soon, at any rate after a couple of years, I think it was in 1918 for the first time, that I had taken him by surprise by saying: 'Do you compose, too?' 'Who said so?' 'Your sister.' It was, of course, a lie. 'Oh, did she say that,' he said and went like that... [made a face]' 'So you are composing, then,' I said.[30]

Irgens-Jensen systematically took in books on harmony, counterpoint and other aspects of music-theory, as well as on orchestration and music-history. He endlessly discussed all aspects of music with Grüner-Hegge, and they competed in discovering new music. His music library grew; he bought everything he came across and ordered scores from abroad, playing through them on the harmonium. And, often with Grüner-Hegge, he attended the rehearsals and concerts of the Music Society and National Theatre orchestras, listening and learning.

He was always well informed about developments in musical life at home and abroad, not least through foreign music-journals: his library contains copies of the first year of *Melos* (1920), which was a leading mouthpiece for new music. He also read new musicological publications and sought inspiration in older ones. He studied old music, both the music itself and through the literature – in the years 1927–30, for example, he subscribed to the *Handbuch der Musikwissenschaft*. In Grüner-Hegge's opinion, he had not only a wider knowledge of contemporary musical life in Europe than most critics but also a thorough understanding of the history of music.

All reminiscences of Irgens-Jensen praise his knowledge and wide orientation. As early as 1924 the critic Elling Holst Bang[31] warned against the presumption of a 'lack of training', by which he meant formal education:

> As a reassurance to those whose first question to an artist is always, 'Whom did you study with?', it ought perhaps to be added that it probably will not work for Irgens Jensen as it did for the old masters of music history – if he, the autodidact, were placed under scrutiny by erudite judges and theoreticians, it would soon be shown that the parties could just as easily change places.[32]

Common to all the major Norwegian composition teachers at that time was a grounding in a continental conservatory tradition anchored in harmony and counterpoint. To judge from their own music and from other documentation, such as the writings of Catharinus Elling and Gustav Fr. Lange, their musical ideals were the 'old', moderate Romanticism. In these

[30] Grüner-Hegge in a tape-recording made by Øystein Gaukstad and preserved in 1972 at the National Music Collection as UBO/NMS lyd b/287–289.

[31] Holst Bang (1887–1969) was also a composer known for sentimental songs published under the pseudonym Sven Prås

[32] 'Baadnlaat – Siciliano av Ludvig Irgens-Jensen', *Musik*, December 1924, p. 7.

early years Irgens-Jensen's goals were rather different – and without any systematic teaching in composition, he had to come to his judgements independently, without the authoritative weight of a teacher's opinions, for good or ill. But he showed a particular interest in the classics, Beethoven especially but also Schubert and Mendelssohn. He mentions several other favourites in an interview in 1930:

> 'Do you fear the Romantics?'
> 'It is not a question of fear. I have my heroes Bach and Palestrina, Chopin and Brahms, all of whom have made important music.' [33]

In the 1969 radio interview with Torstein Gunnarson, he touched on his relationship to contemporary developments:

> TG: Has it been difficult or easy for you to avoid the trends and directions of current interest?
>
> LIJ: I don't believe I thought much about it. It was certainly difficult at that time for those who wanted to find themselves, true. I ... toiled and struggled to get something together and shape it, I remember, in my youth. So gradually there were some songs and things and ... and they satisfied me. Actually, I kept up with what music I could get hold of and bought it. I can mention, for example, that I knew Schoenberg's atonal things as early as 1913, when I got hold of them and played them with a certain interest. But there wasn't anything in that for me.
>
> The whole time I was very taken with Max Reger and it was really only when I got away from him that I began to write for myself, in something like '17–18 only, I think it was. And all this of course I have... I don't really want to go into this very much.

Gunnarson then asked about his relationship to Grieg:

> LIJ: I am very fond of Grieg's music. That was some of the first music I admitted into my life, and I can certainly say that I am still just as fond of most of it. [...] One thinks of how his music has delighted us through the years. We hear the same works innumerable times. Let us say the best songs, for example, so it is something of a miracle.[34]

His interest in Schoenberg might appear surprising. Yet, as he intimated in the interview, he was playing Schoenberg's *Sechs kleine Klavierstücke*, Op. 19, in 1913, only two years after they were composed; he studied them, analysed them in every detail, learned them by heart (according to Grüner-Hegge), evaluating them meticulously – before rejecting Schoenberg's musical language as a possible direction for his own compositions. The same thing happened with Richard Strauss' music which, as Grüner-Hegge again

[33] *Dagbladet*, 29 January 1930.
[34] *Loc. cit.*, p. 7.

reported,[35] they studied closely in 1914–15, especially *Tod und Verklärung* and *Till Eulenspiegel*.

Two of the composers for whom he expressed enthusiasm were still held to be 'radicals' by some of the more conservative Norwegian critics of the day: Brahms and Reger, both of whom show supreme mastery of polyphony and form, something he admired also in Bruckner. He collected cuttings about Bruckner performances – the only ones on a foreign composer to be found in his posthumous papers.

In addition, his sister mentioned[36] that in his youth he had a predilection for Robert Schumann's songs and piano-cycles, which he played constantly. It was his intense practising of Schumann's *Études symphoniques*, indeed, that brought about the muscular strain that required treatment.[37] He was also much taken with Schumann's personality and his tragic fate.

The common denominator for these composers is that they were all regarded as 'Romantic', even though most of them belonged to the 'Classical' line where the 'universal' expression of emotion was most important, not the personal and private sphere of the individual artist. It is typical that Irgens-Jensen never mentioned Wagner and Richard Strauss, nor did Tchaikovsky receive any comment – Irgens-Jensen may well have shared Fartein Valen's views on the 'exhibitionism' of his music.[38]

The first piece of Irgens-Jensen's own music Grüner-Hegge was allowed to see was a quintet with voice in five sections based on Baudelaire's vast poem 'Le Voyage' from *Les Fleurs du mal*. Each section took no less than an hour, so that the entire work would have lasted five hours had it ever reached performance. Grüner-Hegge described it thus:

> There was certainly an enormous richness, but it was also rather disordered in form, but also a wealth of ideas which completely bowled me over. I remember how astounded I was by it.[39]

During his time at high school Irgens-Jensen had taught himself shorthand to be able to note down important points in lectures and any thoughts of his own – just as he had developed a colour-shorthand for his painting. He then carried the experience over to music, writing most of the ideas and sketches of his compositions in a sort of musical shorthand of his own invention which others could not read. He wrote at lightning-speed to

[35] *Loc. cit.*

[36] *Loc. cit.*

[37] *Cf.* pp. 30 and 39, above.

[38] Recounted by several of Valen's friends, among them Steinar Ihle at a Valen seminar at the Bergen Festival in 1981.

[39] *Loc. cit.*

get the inspiration down, and sketches, mostly of songs, streamed out, as Grüner-Hegge observed in wonderment:

> I believe he had some 500 songs at that time. He produced incessantly – wrote at night, and came to me the next day: 'Listen to this!' It really was a flourishing time. [...] Then he came every day and wanted to hear my opinion of the various things, and thus a collaboration came about, so that I gave my pedantic comments on everything he had done and in fact made him shape it in a more – what shall I say? – orderly way, both in the part-writing and odds and ends. And he really was a master of this. He knew his Bach well and knew everything that comes under the name of part-writing very well, it was in his blood. But I got him to write smaller things – for example, songs – and finish them, really finish them. It was just sketches he made, he couldn't be bothered to write music, as he said. He couldn't be bothered to finish a thing, he wanted the pleasure of composing it, he didn't take pleasure in writing it out. It didn't interest him, as he said very grandly. Later his attitudes changed.
>
> [...] Quite obviously I quickly gave up composition when I found such a talent beside me. Take, for instance, the ease with which he could change things. I could just say one thing, and the next moment he could come up with ten suggestions, separate suggestions. There was an abundance. He could say that he was not sure, but one does not need to reproach someone who has such a profusion that he can easily find ten ways out of a difficulty. That really was abundance. I must say that I believed in him, that he was a genius.
>
> [...] I weeded out and used my critical sense, my sense, certainly not very developed, that I was right, but I did it. However, I think that at any rate I had good judgement. And I believe Ludvig benefited from it. And, as I have certainly said before, he came up with so many alternatives for how one could solve the different things, that I could say 'Take number three'. Then just correct this and that, do this and that and so on and so on.
>
> [...] But his self-criticism, as time went on, that became severe.[40]

Grüner-Hegge also commented on their common interest in a number of leading composers of the time. Irgens-Jensen's early songs contained

> absolutely beautiful details. And all the harmony in these things, that is indeed a tasty morsel, if we look at it thoroughly. Naturally we were both very taken by Max Reger's art of modulation.[41]

They played and analysed some of Reger's violin sonatas

> which all ended with a fugue. A great fugue.[42] And it is clear that such a thing impressed young men, and especially its refinement of sound, Reger's

[40] *Ibid.* Grüner-Hegge's '500 songs' might be an exaggeration.

[41] *Ibid.*

[42] Grüner-Hegge's memory plays him false here: among Reger's nine violin sonatas, there is none that really 'ends with a great fugue'.

Odd Grüner-Hegge (left) and his brother Finn, who also studied music. Both were friends of Irgens-Jensen from his youth.

modulatory sophistication. [...] We suffered the childhood illness called Max Reger, which was of course prevalent at that time. And the childhood illness, Mahler, which for me became an adult illness. Just look at his simple things, which at the time were called 'banal', something as sophisticated as those songs of his, for example. It is so beautiful, especially in this simplicity! There is not one thing where one cannot say: there is only one person who could have written that and that is Mahler. His distinctive quality strikes one so much in these things. Even this 'Viennese style', when I think about the folk-song style down there, which pervades these things – one is moved by it. It is fabulous.

Precisely because of the sophisticated sound of these composers, it took me longer; that is to say, I didn't take Brahms so quickly to my heart as I took a Mahler, for example, and maybe also Reger.[43]

[43] *Ibid.* One young Norwegian composer who shared their enthusiasm for Reger was Fartein Valen, who had studied at the Hochschule für Musik in Berlin in 1909–11. Back in Norway, he persuaded the pianist Dagny Knutsen to ask to play the Reger Piano Concerto for the Concert Society, which she did in a concert in Kristiania on 19 November 1916. Though the critics tore the work apart, the performance was seen by many young Norwegian musicians as a turning point in their fight for new music. Nor did the critical reactions put off the conductors Johan Halvorsen and Karl Nissen, who presented Reger's *Variations and Fugue on a Theme of Mozart* at concerts in the same season (1916–17) with, respectively, the National Theatre Orchestra and the Music Society.

Besides going through the piano repertoire, old and new, Irgens-Jensen played chamber music with Finn Grüner-Hegge and Leif Bruun, and piano duets with Odd Grüner-Hegge and Nils Larsen, both original pieces and transcriptions of symphonies and other large-scale works. With almost no gramophone records at the time and relatively few new orchestral works being performed in Oslo, they had to make do with scores and piano-duet transcriptions of the orchestral repertoire. Odd Grüner-Hegge told me[44] that around 1920, when they could not obtain the piano editions of Mahler's symphonies, Irgens-Jensen had sat down and written them out himself, a practice which, in Grüner-Hegge's opinion, had brought some considerable benefits:

> One had to learn all one's scores, and it took a long time to learn a score by rote. One didn't take it in through the ears, one took it in through the eyes. In this way one learned to read a little. Thus one could imagine the sound and the orchestration; there are many colours which go in and sound silently in one's ear.[45]

Clearly, music took more and more of Irgens-Jensen's time during the time of the First World War, and he was in these years first and foremost concerned with songs. But songs were not his only concern: Marie Fearnley suggested in a profile-interview[46] that he might also have been working with gigantic symphonic works, which later had to be discarded:

> And it was not trifles that came to light. The most tremendous projects were revealed, symphonic works that would have taken two hours to perform. A richly concentrated music, which just needed clarifying. One of his friends described these, his first works, as a thick jungle with enormously high trees.

This statement appears to accord with what Grüner-Hegge suggests of the dimensions of *Le voyage* – although, of course, there may have been many other large-scale works in incubation.

In spite of Irgens-Jensen's excess of energy, he could occasionally be driven dry, leading to short-lived depressions, particularly if the musical ideas would not come or develop as he wanted. In such periods he would occasionally stay in bed or resort to drawing and painting as well as his insatiable reading, his sister commenting[47] that in these years he pursued an extensive rotation between art forms.

When he was eighteen, he wrote in one of his note-books:

[44] In conversation in 1970.

[45] Radio interview, 1972, *loc. cit.*

[46] *Dagbladet*, 29 January 1930.

[47] In an interview with the author.

This wonderful feeling for beautiful things. The silence of the forest and the snow-white shadows, which makes one so weak – so sick. It is best just to sink down, fade away, in a beautiful impression – before the beautiful impression disappears. Is there here a fear of life's mad rush and transitoriness?

Also this, that beautiful things can put one into such a sad mood. What one wants becomes so small, so desolate and loses its glow. Here is the beauty, this moment is the best – now all the forests sigh and the leaves fall.

Similarly, Nietzsche's conception of art, and the laws for its creation: All art has the deepest pessimism as its basis.

[Added in the margin] I must try to investigate this feeling, so that I can also come to determine the morbid effects of art.

III
Early Songs, Early Success

Interest in the art-song – the *Lied* – has been strong in Norwegian music since the time of Halfdan Kjerulf and Edvard Grieg, whose careers jointly spanned the second half of the nineteenth century. But in the years between the two World Wars that interest waned: there were fewer song-recitals – the so-called 'time of a thousand singers'[1] had passed – and the commitment of composers to the genre diminished correspondingly. Irgens-Jensen's deep interest in literature and his lyrical sense nonetheless led him naturally into the writing of art-song.

In his compositions he tried to be himself from the first. In his younger years he was considered by several critics both a modernist and someone who wanted to preserve tradition and use the standard forms, and the song offered a vehicle that suited modernity of expression and at the same time could remain loyal to tradition: in the years up to his debut in print in 1919 by far the largest part of all his compositions, drafts, sketches and notes are focussed on song. There were, as Grüner-Hegge put it, 'heaps of songs':[2] over 300 are preserved in manuscript, many in different versions. Also dating from this time are sketches for a violin sonata, some fragmentary violin pieces (probably written for performance by Finn Grüner-Hegge and Leif Bruun) and the sketches of some large-scale piano-works.

He would sketch musical ideas directly into poems published in anthologies and concert programmes, noting the ideas, melodic and harmonic, that the texts had inspired in him. His style, initially a question of trial and error, soon displayed rapid development both in his treatment of melodic lines and in a growth of a radical style, tonally and harmonically. It would be almost impossible to place the early works in chronological order: only a very few are dated, and stylistically they constitute a confused and unsystematic picture. Different versions of the same song, moreover, appear to stem from different times and deciding which is the more recent is difficult. Irgens-Jensen put most of these songs to one side; they were no longer

[1] Originally female singers: *cf.* Arvid O. Vollsnes, *Norges musikkhistorie*, Vol. 4, Aschehoug, Oslo, 2000, p. 175.

[2] In the interview with Gaukstad, *loc. cit. Cf.* also note 40, p. 46, above.

interesting after his prentice years. But he did not throw them away or destroy them. It may be that he considered doing something further with them but never found the time or the will to work on them again, but their mix of original ideas and a more traditional manner may yet justify a hearing for them. As noted, this early output contains cycles as well as individual songs; Odd Grüner-Hegge calls attention to *Le voyage* as the most important.[3]

One of the first songs among the composer's posthumous papers that can be dated exactly is *Ein Fichtenbaum* (Ex. 1), to a text by Heinrich Heine (1797–1856), which is inscribed '1 September 1913'; Irgens-Jensen was nineteen at the time and was working on several other Heine texts as well as on some by Nikolaus Lenau (1802–58).

The poem itself had a strong appeal for a romantic young man with a fascination for nature, symbolism and psychology (and the older Norwegian composers to have been inspired by it include Grieg, Agathe Backer-Grøndahl and Iver Holter), but the song it inspired is a rather uneven attempt from a young student; it would have sounded rather strange if it had been performed at the time. *Ein Fichtenbaum* is tonal. But it was around now that Irgens-Jensen had begun to study Reger's music and there are features in the fast and unusual changes in tonal focus that remind one of some of Reger's phrasing.[4] There is little motivic unity, melodic or rhythmic, and the form is unconventional. There are both four-part chords and triads with various added dissonances. Many of the 'classical' rules of part-writing and chord-progression are broken, and there are intentional false relations. The lines are at times dominated by wide leaps, often in the same direction, and the declamation of the text occasionally seems strained. Neither concrete textual reasons nor a consistent feeling of style appear to justify these 'transgressions'; instead, this is merely an inquisitive beginner trying to express himself. It is instructive that there are few direct parallels to be found with the Heine songs Irgens-Jensen included in *Gedichte von Heine*, his Op. 3, from 1920.

In 1919 he finally decided to 'go public' as a composer, with the publication of a number of songs. That was the year in which a certain Birger H. Olsen started Skandia Musikforlag, a new music-publishing business in Kristiania, and on 26 November publisher and composer signed a five-year contract. But the association brought Irgens-Jensen little success, and on 4 May 1920, less than seven months on, since nothing had been done to print the songs, he tried to withdraw from the contract.

[3] *Cf.* p. 45, above.

[4] *Cf.* pp. 44 and 46–47, above.

Ex. 1

pp
Ein
Fich-ten-baum steht ein-sam Im Nor-den auf kah - ler HšhÕ.
Ihn schlŠ-fert, mit wei-§er De-cke, um - hŸl-len in Eis und Schnee.
Er trŠumt von ei-ner Pal-me, die fern im Mor-gen-land,
ein-sam und schwei-gend hauert auf brenn-en-der Fel-sen-wand.

It seems that Olsen must initially have refused, but only a week later, the lawyer Georg Myhre wrote to the composer that Olsen had been to his office for a discussion and that the contract had now been torn up.[5]

Irgens-Jensen then decided to publish his first songs himself: 38 in all, which appeared in print before Christmas that same year – although choosing between the 300 and more which were to hand cannot have been easy. The choice of texts in these first published songs shows something of his broad literary interests. From his friend Arnulf Øverland (1889–1968) he singled out seven poems for his Op. 1, *I Mørket* ('In the Dark'), and four for Op. 5, *Digte av Øverland* ('Poems by Øverland'). Five poems by Heine provided Op. 3, *Gedichte von Heine*, and five translations from Slavic folk-poems by the Dane Thor Lange (1851–1915) are the basis for Op. 6, *Slaviske Digte* ('Slavonic Poems'). The German translations of oriental lyrics by Hans Bethge (1876–1946) were very popular at the time[6] and Irgens-Jensen selected nine poems for his Op. 2, *Japanischer Frühling*, and three for Op. 4, *Gedanken – Schwermut – Blüten* ('Thoughts – Melancholia – Blossoms'). The final five are separate songs, including *Vaarregnen* ('Spring Rain') of the Chinese Thu-fu (Du Fu, 712–70), in a Danish transcription by Aage Matthison-Hansen[7] and *Der blinker ei Stjerner* ('No stars shine') by Sigbjørn Obstfelder (1866–1900). Paul Verlaine (1844–96) is represented by the song *Qu'as-tu fait?* and Maurice Maeterlinck (1862–49) by *Den hellige Birgittas Salme* ('St Birgitta's Hymn').[8] The final song sets a poem, *Seifenschaum* ('Soap Bubbles'), by the unknown Richard Gerschow.

Four languages are represented in this choice of songs and a total of eight nationalities. Gerschow apart, the poets (or translators) are relatively familiar. The choice of both French and German writers suggests, moreover, that Irgens-Jensen took no side in a cultural debate which occupied minds in Kristiania after the end of the First World War – whether French culture should now occupy the prominent place that German culture had traditionally held in Norway.

One characteristic of these songs is that their collective titles underline their use of poetry, possibly because of modesty on the composer's part, but it may also be an attempt to draw attention to the high literary value of

[5] Letter dated 12 May 1920, in the possession of Olav Irgens-Jensen, who has safeguarded his father's correspondence.

[6] The best known Bethge settings, of course, are those from *Die chinesische Flöte* in Mahler's *Das Lied von der Erde*. *Cf.* also pp. 247–53, below.

[7] Aage Matthison-Hansen (1864–1938) was the son of the Danish composer Gottfred Matthison-Hansen (1832–1909), best known for his organ music; Gottfred's father Hans (1807–90) and his nephew Frederik (1869–1933), Aage's cousin, were also organist-composers.

[8] The translation of this poem may be by Irgens-Jensen himself.

the majority of the poems he set. Some of the Japanese and Slavonic verses, by contrast, may have been chosen because of their exotic imagery. The growing interest in late-nineteenth-century western-European literature, art and music, philosophy and religion in exotica – in many ways a natural outcome of the Romantic movement – led to a blossoming of translations of such material. Hans Bethge's enjoyed particular popularity, inspiring many composers to set them to music: in the course of a few years Richard Strauss, Arnold Schoenberg, Anton Webern and Egon Wellesz amongst others had joined Mahler in composing song-cycles or choral works based on Bethge's translations; in Norway, Bethge texts were also used by the composers Fartein Valen and David Monrad Johansen.

Translations of oriental poetry were not only popular; they were also regarded as modern. Many of Øverland's poems, too, were also considered to be modern on the grounds of both form and content; his writing was a worthy successor to the pioneering verse of the Norwegian radical poet Sigbjørn Obstfelder. Maeterlinck and Verlaine continued to represent modern French-language poetry in Norway. Heine, of course, was now considered a classic.

Irgens-Jensen's formal treatment of a poem is often strophic, but that is frequently because he has only a single strophe to work with; where there are several strophes, he generally uses a through-composed form, with each strophe having its own distinctive musical form. Most of these early opera are collections of separate songs, rather than cycles; the exception is *Japanischer Frühling*, where the songs are closely inter-related, with a fine correlation between the songs in sound and colour and in contrasts of expression over the cycle as a whole. The five songs printed individually display sensitivity to atmosphere and elegant musical solutions, and 'Guldskyen' ('Golden Cloud', the second of the *Slaviske Digte*, Op. 6), 'Ballade' (the third of the four *Digte av Øverland*, Op. 5) and 'Vuggevise' ('Lullaby', No. 2 of *I Mørket*, Op. 1) deserve a place amongst the most distinguished songs of their time.

But these early songs are not faultless. There are often many lines, frequently in a low register, and complicated rhythmic polyphony. Nor is Irgens-Jensen always true to the rhythm of the poems in his shaping of the melodic lines, and he seems insufficiently aware that top notes should not be set on the thinnest vowels. The frequent modulations and transitions, moreover, can make the songs appear unsettled and angular, at times evoking a different atmosphere from that which the poem clearly invites. But those polyphonic lines and shifting tonalities are a function of the modern style he wanted to use. Tonally, he goes further than the mediant progressions of the Romantic period. The tonality is sometimes blurred and can shift often and unexpectedly; it is also free, with one or more tonal centres, not always closely related. In the polyphonic texture different tonal centres arise in different lines, the resulting conflicts generating a feeling of bitonality. The harmony, in fact, is polyphonically derived, which occasionally contributes an impression of pan-tonality – even, in the most modern songs, the suggestion of atonality.

In fact, these songs, with their atonal character, were published before the first atonal works of Fartein Valen, who is generally regarded as the earliest atonal modernist in Norwegian music. When these Irgens-Jensen songs appeared in 1920, Valen had been working hard for years to find his own form of polyphony and atonality through the Violin Sonata, Op. 3, the *Ave Maria* for soprano and orchestra, Op. 4, and the Piano Trio, Op. 5. But none of these works was first performed or published before 1922 (the Sonata and *Ave Maria*), and the Trio was finished only in 1924. Both composers were inspired to explore this line through their interest in Reger, but while Valen, through his interest in Schoenberg, developed an expressionist line of thought, Irgens-Jensen was to continue a Classically inclined late Romanticism.

'Besværgelse' ('Conjuration'), Op. 5, No. 1, shows Irgens-Jensen's most radical style amongst these songs. The poem is taken from Øverland's collection *Advent*:

Brist ut inat,
min smertes røde lilje!
  Du har besat
mit væsen og min vilje.
	Break forth tonight
	red lily of my pain!
	  You have possessed
	my being and my will.

Du drakk min drøm *Din tørst blev aldrig slukket.* *Din mund er øm* *av blod, som du har drukket.*	You drank my dream. Your thirst was never slaked. Your mouth is soft with the blood you have drunk.
Duft i mit krat! *Jeg er en tom cisterne,* *tom og forladt.*	A fragrance in my undergrowth! I am an empty well, empty and deserted.
. . . . . .	. . . . . .
Brist ut i nat, *lilje og storm og stjerne!*	Break forth tonight, lily and storm and star!

In its time, this poem was certainly considered modern. But rhyme and rhythm are still traditional; it is its symbolism which was regarded as modern, although without becoming the kind of word-music cultivated by the French symbolists.

The lay-out of the song is complicated, with a host of small motifs. It begins relatively compactly with a clear tonality and rhythmic reiterations almost like imitation (Ex. 2). But later it becomes extremely complex, with ever more sophisticated rhythms set against one another; the piano part becomes almost impenetrably thick. The extended use of complex chords with unprepared and unresolved 'dissonances' helps give the song an atonal character.

Ex. 2

In addition, Irgens-Jensen employs a very fast rhythm over the modulations and transitions and at times this 'blurred' tonality becomes so thoroughly disrupted by the independent lines that in several sections it can be felt as atonal, as can be easily observed if the vocal line is isolated (Ex. 3): there are many 'unmelodic' large intervals and an angular outline that tends to chromaticism. The rhythm is at times quite subtle and precisely judged to match the declamation of the text, but recurrent periodicity is of no interest to the composer here.

'Besværgelse' observes no traditional form, is compact and is melodically unconventional. But Irgens-Jensen's purpose was not simply experimental, or to demonstrate 'modernist' tendencies: the form comes from his understanding of this particular poem and the symbols he found there. Their diversity demanded a multi-layered texture and a strong expressive style.

Ex. 3

A performance of some of these songs three years later earned an ambivalent review from one critic:

> There is in his music a bubbling and boiling of youth and the desire to create, and although it has still not fermented into completely mature wine, it bears witness of a distinct talent, which hopefully also has the sweetness of the purely lyrical atmosphere which is a necessary condition for good musical wine. His means of expression is at times rather harsher than necessary. And in a little ballad such as Heine's 'Es war ein alter König', the folk-tune is perhaps modernised too much. It is also a little difficult to find musically congruent notes for a verse like this: 'Duft i mit krat, jeg er en tom cisterne, tom og forlatt. Brist ut inat, lilje og storm og stjerne'.[9] The songs met with strong approval and occasioned several curtain calls for the composer.[10]

[9] 'A fragrance in my undergrowth!
I am an empty well, empty and deserted.
Break forth tonight,
lily and storm and star!'

[10] Valentin Siewers ('+') in *Morgenbladet*, 4 April 1923.

The tonality of some of the other songs ('Nimm mich auf, uralte Nacht', the first of the Heine settings in Op. 3, for example), is blurred, too; others (including several to Øverland texts) are much more simply planned. 'Ballade', Op. 5, No. 3, has a far clearer form, with the ring almost of a mediaeval ballad: it is stricter, not least in the rhythm, and has a lighter texture, but then neither is it as exciting and as ambitious as some of the more radical songs.

Obstfelder's poem *Der blinker ei stjerner*, one of the five independent songs, is arranged simply: there is a clear multi-layered texture in the piano part, as the opening shows (Ex. 4), but it is far simpler than that of 'Besværgelse' and the polyphony is clearer. There are also the pedal notes and certain melodic and harmonic features of modality and false relations that would become characteristic of Irgens-Jensen's later style.

Ex. 4

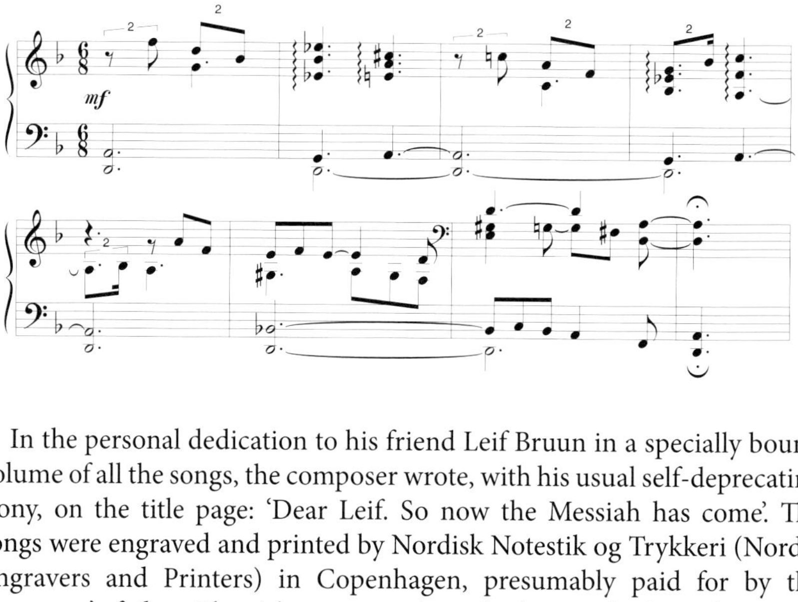

In the personal dedication to his friend Leif Bruun in a specially bound volume of all the songs, the composer wrote, with his usual self-deprecating irony, on the title page: 'Dear Leif. So now the Messiah has come'. The songs were engraved and printed by Nordisk Notestik og Trykkeri (Nordic Engravers and Printers) in Copenhagen, presumably paid for by the composer's father. The title page carries a by-line with the information that the music is 'Distributed by Oluf By, Music Publisher, Kristiania/ Composer's Copyright'.[11]

Almost half a century later[12] Irgens-Jensen said about this first period:

[11] In 1900 Oluf By started a concert-bureau, music-shop and publishing business, which he ran with his son Einar up to 1925, when it was absorbed by Norsk Musikforlag. By had several such distribution agreements, which were not usual at the time: to pay for engraving and the other production costs was too expensive for most composers who, with such an agreement, could at least count on some distribution of their music.

[12] In the NRK interview of 1969; *cf.* note 5 on p. 26, above.

> [I] toiled and struggled to get something together and to give it shape, I remember, in my youth. So gradually there were some songs and things and … and they satisfied me.[13]

In fact, his first appearance in print followed his first public appearance as a composer. That had taken place at two concerts, the first on 9 June 1920, at a pupils' concert arranged by the prominent soprano and teacher Elisabeth Munthe-Kaas (1883–1959) when Margit Aarberg Rom (Nergaard) (1888–1962) sang eight of his songs: 'Vuggevise' ('Lullaby') and 'Sne' ('Snow'), from the Øverland settings in Op. 1, *Vaarregnen* ('Spring Rain'), together with five songs from *Japanischer Frühling*: 'Heute', 'Betrachtung', 'Die Liebeslaut', 'An einen Freund' and 'Leichtes Spiel'.[14] For a 'public' concert, though, this recital was something of a private affair, with only limited advertising and no critics in attendance. But Aarberg Rom sang Irgens-Jensen songs also on several later occasions[15] and he was obviously very enthusiastic about her interpretations, writing to her many years later:[16]

> It was a great help to me that you sang my songs – before anyone else – and did it so excellently! It convinced me that it was possible to sing them just as I had intended – something which was rather vital for my future.

The first occasion on which any of the songs were performed before a wider public was on 4 October 1920. For her concert debut, the singer Hildur Øverland (*née* Arntzen) had rehearsed a number of them, encouraged by her husband, the poet Arnulf, and other close friends of the young composer. Accompanied by Pauline Hall at the piano, she sang 'I Mørket' ('In the dark'), 'Et Barn' ('A child'), both Øverland settings from Op. 1, 'Das Meer erstrahlt' from the Op. 3 Heine settings, and 'Hvorfor vil de røde flammer spille' ('Why will the red flames play') and 'Tre søstre' ('Three Sisters') from the Op. 6 translations of Slavonic folk-poems.[17] This time there were critics in attendance. The moderate Hjalmar Borgstrøm was sympathetic, at least about Irgens-Jensen's ability, if not his music:

> The five songs by Ludvig Irgens Jensen were not flattering to the voice either, even more so as the heavy jarring accompaniment did not set off the beauties

[13] Quoted more fully on p. 44, above, and in Irgens-Jensen's original Norwegian on p. 368, below.

[14] 'Leichtes Spiel' (the title of the poem) is more normally referred to by the first words of the text, 'Nichts leichter'.

[15] *Cf.* pp. 73 and 75, below.

[16] Letter bearing an illegible date, written at some point in 1961.

[17] Whether Hildur Øverland was the right person to perform these songs is a moot point. To judge from the reviews of later concerts and various comments from people who heard her, she seems to have had a marked dramatic talent and expression and thus to have been the sort of 'Wagnerian soprano' who could easily have overwhelmed the lyricism and delicate sensitivity of Irgens-Jensen's vocal lines.

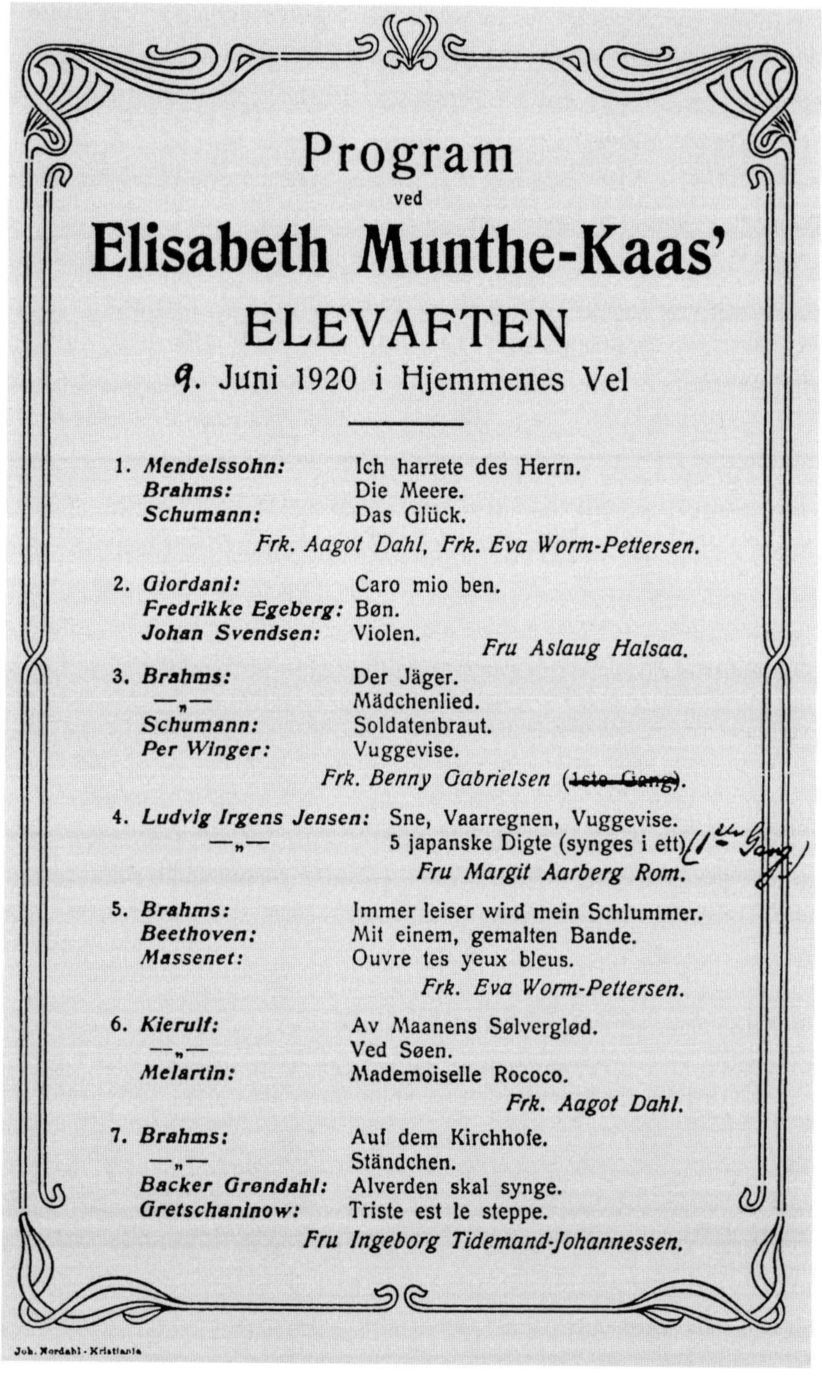

Program

ved

Elisabeth Munthe-Kaas'

ELEVAFTEN

9. Juni 1920 i Hjemmenes Vel

1. *Mendelssohn:* Ich harrete des Herrn.
   Brahms: Die Meere.
   Schumann: Das Glück.
   Frk. Aagot Dahl, Frk. Eva Worm-Pettersen.

2. *Giordani:* Caro mio ben.
   Fredrikke Egeberg: Bøn.
   Johan Svendsen: Violen.
   Fru Aslaug Halsaa.

3. *Brahms:* Der Jäger.
   —„— Mädchenlied.
   Schumann: Soldatenbraut.
   Per Winger: Vuggevise.
   Frk. Benny Gabrielsen (~~1ste Gang~~).

4. *Ludvig Irgens Jensen:* Sne, Vaarregnen, Vuggevise.
   —„— 5 japanske Digte (synges i ett) (1ste Gang)
   Fru Margit Aarberg Rom.

5. *Brahms:* Immer leiser wird mein Schlummer.
   Beethoven: Mit einem, gemalten Bande.
   Massenet: Ouvre tes yeux bleus.
   Frk. Eva Worm-Pettersen.

6. *Kierulf:* Av Maanens Sølverglød.
   —„— Ved Søen.
   Melartin: Mademoiselle Rococo.
   Frk. Aagot Dahl.

7. *Brahms:* Auf dem Kirchhofe.
   —„— Ständchen.
   Backer Grøndahl: Alverden skal synge.
   Gretschaninow: Triste est le steppe.
   Fru Ingeborg Tidemand-Johannessen.

Joh. Nordahl - Kristiania

The programme from Irgens-Jensen's debut concert as composer

> of the melody. That is not to say that the composer lacks talent – it is highly probable that he has it; but he lacks experience.[18]

The more conservative critics were not particularly gracious. Ulrik Mørk, on this first encounter, was dismissive:

> it is [...] remarkable that someone making a debut should present five songs by a composer making his own debut. Perhaps it would have been wiser of the two not to enter into a debut alliance. It is possible the young composer Ludvig Irgens Jensen has special gifts for writing music; I am not so sure of that after this first attempt. At any rate he cannot compose for the human voice; an oppressive monotony pervades both melody and piano accompaniment.[19]

Arne van Erpekum Sem likewise expressed reservations about the music but offered the young composer some words of encouragement:

> The singer gave a good account of herself in five songs, which were anything but easy and grateful, by Ludvig Irgens Jensen. The young debut composer is undoubtedly a musical talent who tries to go his own way, but it was impossible to gain a clear impression of his physiognomy from the songs we heard yesterday. In these the composer had only one colour on his palette and that was grey. These songs were rhythmically monotonous and, as far as both the voice and the accompaniment were concerned, colourless. And yet there were individual phrases, a characteristic harmony and a distinctive atmosphere, which made one listen and which gave a hint of a remarkable talent. But the new composer must learn more, and above all learn to mix his colours better.[20]

This was also the first occasion on which Jens Arbo wrote about Irgens-Jensen's music:

> The remarkable, fine songs by Hr. *Ludvig Irgens Jensen* were too uniform in the selection but bore witness to a distinct lyrical talent, from which one may be able to expect a rich development.[21]

Irgens-Jensen took these reviews with him when he went to Paris in October 1920, directly after Hildur Øverland's concert, and he was still there at the beginning of December when, back home, the songs were published and went into the shops. They were sent to the critics in the usual manner, beginning with those from the newspapers and music-journals in Kristiania. The reviews were mixed. The more conservative of them turned up their noses at this radical who strayed from convention;

[18] *Aftenposten*, 5 October 1920.
[19] *Ørebladet*, 5 October 1920.
[20] *Tidens Tegn*, 5 October 1920.
[21] *Nationen*, 9 October 1920.

others were more understanding, mostly of the composer's talent, if not the expression and apparent experimentation in the music. In a survey of recently published music, Borgstrøm – whose own music was linked with Wagner's and with Romantic programme music – called the modernism of the time to account. But he also emphasised Irgens-Jensen's ability and the expectations one might infer from his, Borgstrøm's, ideals:

> Nevertheless, there is a great deal that points a long way forward in these works, however much they have a tendency to the beginner's inclination for excess. Irgens Jensen is for me a seriously striving and truly inquisitive artist. He seems to have a real artistic nature, which does not compromise his conscience. And he has learnt a good deal. The composition technique is far advanced – in a neo-German form. [...] But this composer will clearly go further. One fine day he will surely present us with a substantial work of art.[22]

Ulrik Mørk, too, was now more encouraging:

> [Irgens-Jensen's songs] do not exactly lie very well for the voice; but when one goes into them more closely, they bear tidings of a talent which *will be* something, and whose further development one will follow with interest. In this comprehensive collection there is music to Norwegian, German, French, Slavonic and Japanese poetry. Several of them are very appealing. But when Jensen becomes a little older as a composer, he will be more miserly about displaying all his musical talents for all the world to see; he will understand that *multum* is better than *multa*.[23]

Trygve Torjussen, another conservative composer-critic, was similarly slighting about the music but recognised Irgens-Jensen's gift:

> The composer makes nothing easy for one. One has to fight one's way through a thicket of 'sharps and flats', rhythmically complex figures and an intricate and awkward piano part. Musically, the movement is also somewhat monotonous – and when it is finally concluded, one sits down with an industrial taste in one's mouth. 'So viel Wollen aber bis jetzt so wenig Können!'
>
> And yet Irgens-Jensen is not at all lacking in talent. He even has talent in abundance. For the time being this talent appears mostly on the intellectual path, that is to say, there is more theory in him as yet than living music.[24]

The critics' caveats notwithstanding, this was a promising debut. It helped his name become known, and the goodwill, even guarded, must have been heartening. In a letter to his father from Paris[25] he writes:

[22] 'Ny musik. 2. Vokalmusik', *Aftenposten*, 22 December 1920.

[23] *Ørebladet*, 22 December 1920.

[24] *Verdens Gang*, undated cutting.

[25] Probably from January 1921.

> You probably think that the reviews were not necessarily very good, but I had not expected them to be so kind. It is not an enjoyable exercise to have to review scores of songs, while the 'poor man's cake'[26] is frying in the pan.

It is odd, then, that Irgens-Jensen very soon withdrew all these published songs and had all the remaining copies returned to him. His sister believed that it was because he felt he was being cheated by the distributor. Perhaps an equally important reason was that he was developing quickly at this time and may already have grown away from many of the songs: he rejected several of them, and they were never performed; many of the others he now began to revise.[27] Still he was not satisfied. In a draft of a letter to the publisher Wilhelm Hansen preserved in his papers, he later wrote (perhaps in 1927–28):

> As you will maybe remember, you were so kind about 1 1/2 years ago to offer to publish some of my songs, which of course I greatly appreciated. However, I have constantly put off sending them with the thought in mind that time and distance would perhaps provide a sharper self-criticism. The longer one's things lie, naturally the more easily one sees the weaknesses and can remedy them, and that they are present in these things, I am more and more convinced of.
>
> I just wanted to say this as an explanation and excuse for my silence. […] At the same time I want to thank you very much for the great kindness and hospitality from which I benefitted.
>
> But for these thanks one ought not to have taken 1 1/2 years' contemplation!

Some years later, in 1934, he wrote in a note to the singer Signe Amundsen, who wanted to sing some of his songs:

> With regard to my songs, they are all old (10–15 years), and I have changed my opinion about a great deal since then. I do not think there are any of them which I am happy with now. I have made up my mind to go through them thoroughly and clarify what I now think is usable.

Irgens-Jensen remained in Paris (where he stayed with his friends Vera and William Lunden, who had moved to Paris a while before) at least until Easter 1921. But he had no sooner arrived there before he went to Berlin for a short period to visit Odd Grüner-Hegge, returning to Paris in the middle of November. In the middle of December he paid another flying visit to Berlin, again to visit Grüner-Hegge and this time also Arnulf Øverland. During the few weeks of this visit he heard Hindemith performing his First String Quartet with the Amar Quartet (in which Hindemith played viola)

[26] A traditional Norwegian Christmas fried cake.

[27] Several of these reworkings, which were sung by Hildur Øverland and Elisabeth Munthe-Kaas, among others, are preserved at the Norwegian Music Collection at the National Library in Oslo.

and was introduced to the composer through a mutual acquaintance. In his six months in Paris, he studied also art and French literature as well as music. He knew French well enough to be able to take part in conversations, but in a letter to his mother[28] he writes that he is too busy to take French lessons.

With its 2.5 million inhabitants,[29] the Paris of the 1920s was a leading music metropolis.[30] The season began early in October and during the period Irgens-Jensen lived there – from October 1920 to March 1921 – there were at least five or six concerts every day, and often more, with church concerts and professional and amateur recitals across the city, as well as the rich musical life in private *salons*. The 'official' concerts, mostly of chamber and orchestral music, generally featured two main categories: 'classical' French (and Belgian) music, particularly from Berlioz to Debussy and Ravel, and Austro-German music from Beethoven to Schumann and Wagner. But the newer French music also had its place, together with music by many young French (and Belgian) composers now long forgotten. The 150th anniversary of Beethoven's birth fell in December 1920, and so his music was much performed. Irgens-Jensen will have heard far more Schubert than he did in Norway. Brahms, though, was a rarity, and in the listings of *Le Guide du Concert* during Irgens-Jensen's sojourn there is not a single work by Bruckner,[31] Bruch, Mahler, Reger or Hindemith. Russian music, though, was very fashionable, as might be expected in a city with a large colony of Russian exiles. A few works by Stravinsky were performed, though fewer than one might have supposed, given that he lived in the city: the Suite from *The Firebird* was performed twice, but otherwise only three small pieces are to be found in the listings.[32] It is apparent also that Grieg held a special position in Parisian affections, quite on a par with the Russians.[33]

Paris offered an opera-hungry young man an enormous amount. In October 1920 the Opéra and the Opéra-Comique presented nine different

[28] Dated 15 February 1921.

[29] By way of comparison, the entire population of Norway at this time was 2.6 million.

[30] For additional information on Paris at that time, *cf.* Danièle Pistone, 'Musique et société dans les années vingt', in Stanislav Tuksar (ed.), *Music, Ideas and Society. Essays in Honour of Ivan Supicic*, Croatian Musicological Society, Zagreb, 1993, pp. 237–47.

[31] The French premiere of Bruckner's Fifth Symphony, for example, came only in 1969, when Eugen Jochum conducted it with his own visiting orchestra.

[32] Diaghilev's Ballets Russes, based in Paris, had premiered *The Firebird* in 1910, *Petrushka* in 1911 and *The Rite of Spring* in 1913; *Le chant du rossignol* and *Pulcinella* were to follow in 1920, *Renard* in 1922, *Les noces* in 1923 and *Apollon musagète* in 1928.

[33] *Cf.* Harald Herresthal and Danièle Pistone (eds.), *Grieg et Paris*, Presses Universitaires de Caen, Caen, 1996, for a discussion of the links between Grieg and Paris, and between French and Norwegian musicians more generally. The links between French music and Nordic composers will be explored also in Martin Anderson and Anders Edling (eds.), *The Elk on the Roof: Nordic Composers and Paris, 1900–39*, Toccata Press, London, forthcoming.

operas within two weeks, and this proliferation of repertoire lasted all season. Some of the French operas on their programmes are rarities today, such as Lalo's *Le Roi d'Ys*. There was an essential element of Italian opera (the 'Parisian' operas, *La bohème* and *La traviata* were given regularly), but German opera was not performed during the autumn season at either theatre.

In a letter to his father[34] Irgens-Jensen wrote:

> I don't think it is correct to say that musical interest here is inferior. The orchestral concerts on Saturday and Sunday are usually sold out, and that in spite of there being up to 4 at the same time (Sunday midday Colonne, Pasdeloup, Lamoureux and Conservatoire). It is almost impossible to obtain tickets for the opera, even many days in advance. Several times I have had to come up with 25 fr. and still only get a poor strapontin seat, that is a little ledge to pull down at the end of the benches themselves. When you consider that all the posh French snobs come late, you can imagine how much enjoyment one has in the first act.

It was not only the music he enjoyed. In the same letter he writes about the day-to-day diet at the Lundens':

> Well into autumn we lived almost exclusively as vegetarians, a practice I really introduced and which suits me extremely well: artichokes, beans, chestnuts, Jerusalem artichokes, crosnes [an edible tuber], salsifrage, you know them all very well, one better than the other, petits-pois in mayonnaise, which Mrs Lunden is a master of (generally in restaurants one usually gets rancid oil). The most delicious mushroom omelettes when we want to be extravagant. Afterwards Brie, Camembert, Roquefort, with bread that is better than the finest rolls at home. And then red country wine, too, preferably 'château Lunden', which means that it had been abundantly diluted with our domestic stimulant, water. Sometimes oysters, which are themselves a revelation. They come at ten Norwegian øre each. I have also tried snails and offal, less enjoyable.

From his sister's accounts we know something of what Irgens-Jensen took from his stay in Paris. He heard Schoenberg's atonal piano works again in recital, where they were met with laughter. There was also an opportunity to hear some of Stravinsky's works in concert, and on New Year's Eve he was present at a performance of Debussy's opera *Pelléas et Mélisande*.[35] He wrote in another letter[36] to his father:

> Musical life here far exceeds my expectations. Several perfect orchestras and quartets, which give a great deal of new French music the best

[34] Dated 21 January 1921.
[35] Postcard to Dagny Irgens Jensen, dated 2 January 1921.
[36] Postmarked 20 November [1920].

> performances. – The new composers, Ravel and Dukas, are extraordinarily talented. Furthermore there is a whole host of lesser known names. They are distinguished by depth and clarity and moderation. Their style appears far more sound and attractive than that of the German moderns.

In some of the music Irgens-Jensen composed at this time, especially in his setting of texts by French symbolists, there is clearly a 'French', Impressionist, character, and it is not unnatural to assume that this stay in Paris and another, two years later, were important influences in the development of his own musical style.

In the absence of documentary evidence, what was going around Irgens-Jensen's mind while he was in Paris – what he thought the stay might achieve for him – is obviously impossible to know. Having declared himself as a composer in Kristiania, he must have felt, at least to some degree, obliged to live up to the expectations he had generated. Again, he may still have harboured some doubts about whether a career as a composer was the right one for him, and the time spent in Paris – free from obligations, and surrounded by art, literature and music – must have given him the space he required to come to a final decision.

He went to Paris again in March 1922, with his sister, Dagny, this time to visit their brother Brynjulf, who was studying business-management in Paris with the food company Félix Potin. Dagny stayed for a month, with Ludvig remaining a little longer. Her memoirs[37] recalled a chance meeting on the journey:

> On the train through Sweden we sat on our own in a carriage with a rather peculiar looking man. He was rather thin with a large wide-brimmed hat, sat reading diligently, not a book, but a score, eating a large bar of chocolate at the same time. When he went out for a moment, I was bold enough to stand up on the seat and look at the luggage label on his suitcase, despite Ludvig's protests. It said Fartein Valen. And so it was not long before they were talking about music and kept going until we went to our berths on the ferry. Next morning as we were walking on deck, we met him again and Ludvig invited him to breakfast. Valen was so shy and reserved that he almost wrung his hands before he finally managed to say thank you. Then there was music talk again – until Valen had to take a different train, as he was going to Berlin.

The two composers' conversation embraced their common interest in Max Reger and his musical ancestors, and Schoenberg's String Quartet No. 1 in D minor, Op. 7, which had made such a decisive impression on Valen in

[37] *Loc. cit.*

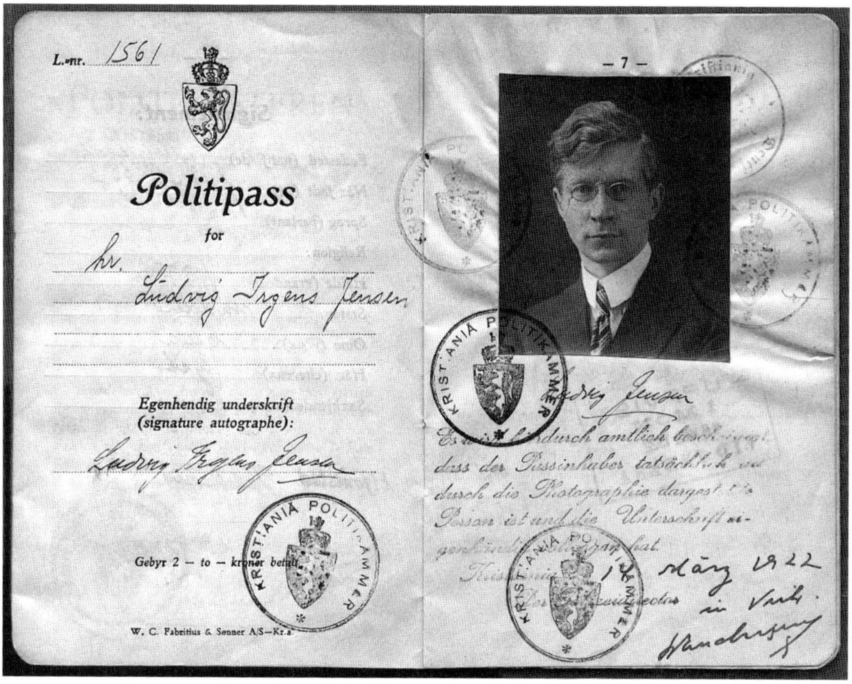

Irgens-Jensen's passport, issued in 1922

Berlin in 1913: he told Irgens-Jensen that he had been so moved that he had only been able to shake Schoenberg's hand and could not get a word out.[38]

Valen had recently heard the premiere of his own Violin Sonata, Op. 3, in Kristiania and now was on his way to Berlin and to Rome, where he spent the spring with the painter Hugo Lous Mohr and his wife. He wrote about his impromptu meeting in a card to his mother, Dorothea:[39] 'Yesterday evening I arrived here after a really lovely journey. Had pleasant travelling company with a Norwegian composer, Ludvig Jensen, as far as Sassnitz'.

In Paris the three siblings enjoyed the company of Leif Bruun and, for a while, that of Finn and Odd Grüner-Hegge and Sigurd Leversen, who was a good friend of the family and later became a merchant in Stavanger. They all had a voracious appetite for concerts and often went to two or three concerts in a day: church concerts, opera, chamber music and orchestral soirées. They were impressed by the large Parisian orchestras, which sometimes played with over a hundred musicians – far more than

[38] Gunnarson interview, *loc. cit.*, p. 3. Valen himself also described this experience in a letter to his sister Magnhild, postmarked 19 November 1913; *cf.* Arvid O. Vollsnes (ed.), *Fartein Valens brever*, Vol. 1 (1904–24), Lyche, Drammen, 1987, p. 145.

[39] Postmarked Berlin, 17 March 1922, *cf. ibid.*, p. 220.

the Norwegian orchestras they were used to. They heard works by Debussy, Ravel and Poulenc, and Schoenberg's *Pierrot Lunaire*. And at the opera they saw Feodor Chaliapin in Mussorgsky's *Boris Godunov* and Delibes' *Lakmé* – a rarity for Scandinavians. They visited galleries and exhibitions, of which Dagny eventually felt she had a surfeit; the others never seemed to tire of them. Ludvig still had much of the boy in him and constantly thought up little jokes. Dagny recalled[40] an excursion to Chartres:

> We inspected the cathedral from top to bottom, before Ludvig bribed the doorman, so we got the key and wandered around the three galleries, came right up to the roof and up into the tower. There he almost frightened the life out of Leif and me by pulling the rope of the huge bell, which gave a thundering clap, so that we nearly missed our footing. When we went out of the gallery, he suddenly hopped up onto the parapet of one of the side towers with a dizzying depth below him and balanced his way across it. He was certainly used to climbing, but there was nothing to hold on to. He was frightfully reckless and impulsive.

Irgens-Jensen was extremely productive as a composer in the years up to 1925. In spite of the difficulty of dating his manuscripts, the fact that most of the compositions are songs means that the type of lyric or author sometimes offers a clue; so, too, can the type of music-paper, although it can also introduce confusions, since new versions or corrections of several of the older songs are often on the same paper. The development of his musical handwriting is a rather safer guide: it evolves from a childlike, over-refined clear script with ordinary school ink to a fast and functional – but still easily understandable – rough script, leading to a beautifully written exemplary clean copy in black ink from a broad-nibbed music pen.

On a couple of sheets of music paper he once made an intriguing overview of opus numbers with dates. But whether these are plans for works or later dating after the works were finished, or a combination of both, is difficult to judge. On the cover of his *Kinesiske digte* ('Chinese Poems'), Op. 15, he wrote:

> Gott und Bajadere' / op. 10 / Lieder op. 11 /
> *Kinesiske digte* / op. 15 [the title applying to all the poems]/(*som.* [summer] *1922*)

Other sources reveal that *Der Gott und die Bajadere* (to a text by Goethe) was begun in 1921 (and completed in 1923), but nothing is known about Opp. 7–10, which should logically be from the period 1920–21. Which songs comprised Op. 11 is likewise unknown, nor is any further information to hand on what Opp. 13 and 14 might have been. The list continues, more

40 In her written memoirs, *loc. cit.*

comprehensively, on the cover of Op. 16, *Syv Sange* (Seven Songs) to texts by Einar Solstad:[41]

later principal exercises:

begun	Verhaeren Trilogy (unfinished) op 17
autumn 1921	Eros og Afrodite op 18 (unsuccessful)
	Kinck fragments op 19…
	Sonata in B min (unfinished) op 20
spring 1924	Barnerim og fabler [Nursery Rhymes and Fables] op 21…
sum 1924	Sonata in B flat major (violin and p.) op 22
spring and autumn 1924	Rosenstaden [The City of Roses] op 23
spring 1925	Mandskor [Male-voice chorus] Norge [Norway] op 24
[spring 1925]	4 male-voice songs … op 25
sum 1925	Variations and fugue op 26
March 1926	Prologue…

The surviving manuscripts contain no *Verhaeren Trilogy* – although late in his life in the middle of 1960s, he did work on an orchestral score with the working title *Fransk suite* ('French Suite'), which built on earlier songs to three texts by Verlaine: *Gaspard Hauser*, *Colombine* and *Femme et chatte*, together with one Verhaeren text, *Les deux enfants de roi*.[42] These Verlaine songs in their first form were written early in the 1920s (*Femme et chatte* was first performed on 2 April 1924) and so it may well be that *Les deux enfants de roi* dates from about the same time and was included in the *Verhaeren Trilogy*. Of *Eros og Afrodite*, Op. 18, and the Sonata in B minor nothing is known.

Like Finn Grüner-Hegge, Irgens-Jensen was very enthusiastic about the writings of Hans E. Kinck (1865–1926) and for a long time worked on music to the play *Bryllupet i Genua* ('The Wedding in Genoa') with the idea of using it as the basis of an opera; that is probably the music he referred to as *Kinck-fragmentene* ('the Kinck fragments'), Op. 19. Indeed, in the summer of 1923 Finn Grüner-Hegge dragged the reluctant Irgens-Jensen with him to Kinck to play some of this music for him. It was a successful meeting, but unfortunately the only one between the two of them, even though Kinck was very taken with both the young man and his music, writing afterwards[43] to 'express the hope that you will not forget me or my things. You are the man!' – to do something musical with my texts, one assumes. But many

[41] A Norwegian poet who died in Copenhagen in 1918, only 25 years old, from pneumonia following Spanish influenza.

[42] *Cf.* p. 254, below.

[43] Letter dated 3 August 1923.

years were to pass before Kinck's wish came to fruition, with the incidental music to his play *Driftekaren* ('The Drover') at the National Theatre in 1938.[44]

In the summer of 1922 he worked, among other things, on the *Kinesiske digte*, Op. 15, which set old Chinese poems, again in German reworkings by Hans Bethge. One of these songs, *Das Mädchen auf der Brücke*, was performed by the singer Dagny Constanze Knutsen with the pianist Waldemar Alme at the chamber-music concert of the Society of Composers in December 1922, which seems to have been the only public performance of any of his music in the entire year. But his public profile was about to expand considerably. In April 1923 he accompanied the soprano Berta Wang Halvorsen in a number of his earlier songs. In the same month he also had two orchestral songs performed, *Skumring* ('Twilight'), to a text by Einar Solstad, and 'Das Mädchen auf der Brücke', at a students' concert. That same month, on 10 April, also in Kristiania, he had an instrumental work performed in public for the first time: a Scherzo for violin and piano, played by the violinist Per S. Bolstad (1899–1931) and Waldemar Alme; unfortunately, the piano part was later lost. The players and composer alike received glowing reports in the press. Ulrik Mørk called Irgens-Jensen a 'dancing faun'[45] and Hjalmar Borgstrøm mentioned the 'ultra-modern character' of the work[46] – although his idea of what constituted ultra-modernism invites a degree of scepticism. Later that year, on 7 December, Irgens-Jensen had two songs – *Le flambeau vivant*, to a text by Baudelaire, and *Chrysantemum*, a Solstad setting – performed with orchestra at the Society of Composers concert.

Even though he was very productive as a composer in the 1920s, he also had time to produce countless pastels and aquarelles, and he continued to write small, subtle verses for his own pleasure.[47] The text of 'Debatten' ('The 'Debate') forms the basis of one of the most popular of his collection of songs *Fabler og barnerim* ('Fables and Nursery Rhymes'):[48]

De små dyr klaget på de store.	The little animals complained about the large ones.
Løven stevnet dem til debatt.	The lion summoned them to a debate.
Løven brølte:	The lion roared:
'Møtet er satt!	'The meeting is convened!
Begjærer noen ordet?'	Does anyone want to speak?'

[44] *Cf.* pp. 183–87, below.
[45] *Nationen*, 11 April 1923.
[46] *Aftenposten*, 11 April 1923.
[47] A selection of them will be found, with translations, in Appendix Two, pp. 323–34.
[48] Discussed on pp. 73–76, below.

Hans E. Kinck c. 1920, in a lithograph by Erik Werenskiold.

Kongelig myndig mønstret han dem.	Regally masterful he reviewed them.
De redde små hjerter bevet –	The fearful little hearts trembled –
Ingen knydde.	No-one murmured.
'Møtet er hevet!'	'The meeting is adjourned!'
Lettet pilte de små dyr hjem.	Relieved, the little animals hurried home.

On 2 April 1924 a number of the songs from around 1920 together with some new ones – twenty in total – were sung by Elisabeth Munthe-Kaas at an all-Irgens-Jensen recital in the Gamle Loge ('Old Lodge') in Kristiania, with the composer at the piano. The first interview with him to appear in print had been published in *Aftenposten* the day before; in it he admitted that he had 'about 150' songs to hand. The critical reception of the concert the next evening was this time quite different. Some of the critics had noticed certain stylistic changes in the songs, among them the perceptive Hjalmar Borgstrøm, who had an eye for talent even if its output was too modern for his taste:

> Irgens Jensen's music is decidedly modern; but it is unaffected by the French Impressionists and rather reminds one of Max Reger. The young composer is, of course, still in a period of development, and it was interesting yesterday to

> note the progress from the older to the more recent songs. Irgens-Jensen now writes more singably for the voice, his means of expression has become more sensitive, his sense of beauty is growing and his independent train of thought has gained a foothold. […] The new 'Sang for mor' ['Song for Mother'] is very beautiful and the poetic atmosphere in 'Kulden' ['The Cold'] reaches even more depth. The excellent 'Tanz' ['Dance'] must be singled out; the few bizarre things in it are fully justified.
>
> That Irgens Jensen possesses a conspicuous talent for composition has previously been reported several times and is repeated on this occasion. […] The composer accompanied satisfactorily.[49]

Similar praise for 'progress' came from Arne van Erpekum Sem:

> Irgens Jensen feels and thinks in a completely modern way; but he does not rely on any fixed direction and any direct influence can only be perceived with difficulty. With a sophisticated taste and a finely cultivated feeling for music he keeps away from all cheap effects and banal phrases, and with an apparently natural ease he creates the strangest, newest harmonic relationships and the most unusual, most refined tonal effects. […] In the new songs a clear growth is to be detected towards richer, more contrasting colouring, towards purer, more broadly sweeping lines and a greater talent for melodic invention.[50]

The concert was obviously something of an event and became the subject for a long feature by Jens Arbo[51] where, as usual, he wrote positively about Irgens-Jensen's music, putting both concert and music in a wider perspective:

> At the composer's own concert on Wednesday, Madame Elisabeth Munthe-Kaas sang several of the earlier songs, a selection of the best and also a good many of the new, which have still not achieved more than an intimate existence in manuscript. I found most worthy things in these new songs, generally quite mature and clear manifestations of a genuine, fine and independent lyrical talent. The objections to the first songs do not apply to Ludvig Irgens Jensen's most recent things; they have their considerable specific worth, a charming freshness and originality and, in addition, more warmth and naturalness than we have previously encountered from his creative pen. The means are the most simple – often amazingly concise in giving a completely pertinent poetic expression – and no banality or cheap effects arise in the twenty *romancer*[52] which range over a wide area. […] 'Vuggevise', too, to Øverland's beautiful poem, melted many hearts, and the devil-may-care 'Zigeunervise' ['Gypsy Song'] finally released the enthusiasm

[49] *Aftenposten*, 3 April 1924.
[50] *Tidens Tegn*, 3 April 1924.
[51] *Morgenbladet*, 7 April 1924.
[52] The generic term for Scandinavian art-song, equivalent to *Lied* or *mélodie*.

> in endless applause. Madame Munthe-Kaas interpreted the songs splendidly, the difficulties were as nothing and the fine intentions of the music were clearly expressed in the always sympathetic performance. The composer was his own accompanist and naturally the most authentic. Many songs had to be given 'da capo' – there was no economising with encores. The concert gives grounds for continued great expectations that the composer will also attain new merits in musical areas which lie beyond the song.

Fabler og barnerim

Among the '150 or so' songs Irgens-Jensen mentioned in his interview were several *Fabler og barnerim* ('Fables and Nursery Rhymes'), to his own texts, three of which were presented for the first time at another concert in that same month, on 9 April, when the singer was Margit Aarberg Nergaard,[53] with Irgens-Jensen again at the piano for his own songs. The unity of poetry and music in the *Fabler og barnerim* is striking. Here he simplified his musical style considerably, perhaps to allow it to respond more subtly to the gentle ambiguity of his texts – which may, of course, have been written with the music in mind.[54]

The programme for this concert was the first place he allowed his poems to appear under his own name. Previous performances had used his own translations of the original texts, and he had composed other songs to his own poems, although only *Sang for mor* ('Song for Mother') reached performance. He looked over the fables again in the late 1940s, when the two collections – each with three fables – were finally published. He then had two further collections ready, but did not publish them.[55]

The music in the fables is frequently strophic, but several of the longer texts introduce a degree of irregularity and become almost through-composed. As in many others of his shorter songs, he is rather free with form and texture, using small alterations in the repetitions seemingly in response to nuances of the text. Of course, the texts do not invite the large and elaborate musical forms that were evident in his first published songs. But it does not follow that they are intended for children or childlike minds, even though they are simple and unpretentious. These subtle texts demand a simple melody with uncomplicated declamatory rhythm and a straightforward chordal accompaniment. Occasionally, though, there are lines in the accompaniment which spice up the chording, such as added

[53] It was she who, under her maiden name of Rom, had first sung Irgens-Jensen's songs before an audience, in the concert of 9 June 1920; *cf.* p. 59, above.

[54] Several of the texts and translations can be found in Appendix 2, pp. 324–37.

[55] Five of these songs are now available from Music Norway in Oslo under the title *Fabler* ('Fables'); for more information, *cf.* Appendix One, List of Works, pp. 305–6.

Elisabeth Munthe-Kaas in the 1920s, when she often performed songs by Irgens-Jensen – on one occasion twenty of them in a single recital.

notes to his prevalent clean triadic harmonies. And although the tonality in the early songs was often blurred by frequent transitory and restless modulations, here it is more stable. Modality, too, which he previously employed more for its colouristic effect, now has more distinction and seems organically connected to the whole.

The stylistic simplification the critics had already noted now came even more clearly into view, as Borgstrøm again perceived:[56]

> On this occasion, too, Irgens-Jensen had three new manuscripts to show us. These were three nursery rhymes: 'Haren og ræven' ['The Hare and the Fox'], 'Baanlaat' ['Lullaby'; Ex. 5] and 'Katten og musen' ['The Cat and the Mouse']. The last two seemed to me to be the best; they were also demanded 'da capo'. I found it a little surprising that all these children's songs to humorous texts were in minor keys. Otherwise the composer made a praiseworthy effort to come close to the national tone of voice; but the piano part is conceived with many subtle oddities, which admittedly can be a characteristic asset. Nevertheless, I believe a sustained naïvety would have brought an even better result.

This is the first time that a 'national tone' is mentioned in conjunction with Irgens-Jensen's music, probably because of the simplification and use of

[56] *Aftenposten*, 11 April 1924.

modality, although the images from Norwegian nature must have reinforced the perception.[57] Today, of course, it is easier to see these songs and the large-scale *Norge*, a choral song for male voices to a text by Arnulf Øverland ('Skaberen reiste et trossig fjeld' – 'The Creator raised a defiant mountain'), composed immediately after the *Fabler*, from a European perspective since, despite their texts, they go far beyond the 'national'. Irgens-Jensen ironically described *Norge* as 'this beast of a male-voice song',[58] probably because it belongs to an old tradition of writing homophonic tonal music for male-voice choirs.

Reidar Mjøen was one of the critics who perceived the poet in the modernist – and who understood that the *Fabler og barnerim* carried in them the germ of something new:

> Margit Aarberg Nergaard had two whole sections in her programme by this remarkable and highly gifted composer, our youngest musical *enfant terrible*. Leaving aside his odd, dissonance-laced, rather feeble songs, where melody and accompaniment seldom go together and often only have rhythms in common, once or twice, as in 'Leichtes Spiel', something truly very experimental can appear. No one can close his ears to the fact that there is a poet within the composer! [...] The three small 'Barnerim' which were sung this evening for the first time – from manuscript – were extremely enjoyable. They made a particularly amusing effect through the laconic and witty way the funny little texts were matched in the music, with light touches of folk-song, even if in minor keys.
>
> Irgens Jensen himself accompanied his songs and reaped demonstrative applause for them.[59]

The simplification observed in the *Fabler og barnerim* can be seen in other songs from the period among the manuscripts held in the Norwegian Music Collection. In spite of the difficulties of dating the songs, it is at least clear from the new texts he chose that the change in style occurs from 1922 onwards. That explains also his further attempts to simplify the published songs in a process that would last a couple of years yet: performing copies from 1924 offer the final, and best, versions.

The songs written between 1913 and 1924 reveal a stylistic frame of reference which runs from the naïve and romantic to a number of experimental and radical elements which foreshadow later characteristics, a kaleidoscopic variety of songs which range from the expressionist to

[57] Elling Bang, in his article 'Baadnlaat – Siciliano av Ludvig Irgens Jensen', *loc. cit.*, made a similar observation. The varying orthography of the title – 'Baadnlaat', 'Baanlaat', 'Bånlåt' – is explained by the rapid transformations the Norwegian language was undergoing at the time.

[58] In an undated draft of a letter to the choral conductor Karl Skallerud.

[59] *Dagbladet*, 11 April 1924.

Ex. 5

The Lullaby, 'Bånlåt', from Fabler og barnerim
('The bear he pads amongst the forest trees, wades in marsh and violent streams.
Then he finds himself a cloudberry and lies down in the moss and dreams.
"I am very fond of lamb, I am very fond of lamb", thinks the bear.')

the simple, from a Germanic post-Wolf Lied tradition to delicate French sonorities. Unsurprisingly, the dominant theme is nature – often a symbol of the human condition and a cipher for existential questions; indeed, a number of the poems he used are psychologically profound. But there are few which come close to the expressionist poems that Schoenberg and Berg used in their songs, nor did he chose anything in line with Fartein Valen's religious mysticism.

The urge to simplify attended Irgens-Jensen all his life. Some other songs came up for further scrutiny many years later: the orchestral edition of *Japanischer Frühling* was completely 'simplified' as late as 1956.[60] One might wonder whether he had not been thinking instrumentally in the texture of many songs from the outset. In several of the manuscripts small notes of instrumentation are to be found: 'flute' is written over one line, 'cello' under another, and so on.

[60] *Cf.* pp. 247–53, below.

Ex. 5 (cont.)

Rosenstaden

Irgens-Jensen's song-cycle, *Rosenstaden* ('The City of Roses', i.e., Isfahan), was written around 1923–24, and is ripe for rediscovery as some of the songs are now published.[61] The cycle was originally in five sections to poems by the Finnish-Swedish poet Bertel Gripenberg (1878–1947) and, through exotic images of nature and experiences from the Near East, illustrates existential aspects of life seen through the eyes of a young man, not at least with love and eroticism inspired by the young girl Lindagull.

The most frequently performed song from this cycle is 'Ökenridten' ('The Ride in the Desert') from the third section, although unfortunately it is not in the published collection – although it was also orchestrated, and was performed in 1923. The music is tonal, and the harmonies resulting from the profiled lines are colourful and support the voice as it paints the content of the poem. In the piano version the obvious riding motive is presented in the left hand, establishing an ostinato going through large parts of the song in an almost minimalist manner (Ex. 6 gives the opening

[61] A few of the songs were published by Norsk Musikforlag in an album in 2002, and the Norwegian singer Solveig Kringelborn recorded two of them in the same year: *cf.* the Discography, p. 342, below.

bars). Against it a dark movement of major thirds (bars 3–4) obscures the seemingly established tonality, even creating a feeling of bitonality, before introducing a small triplet motive, which later proves very important in the accompaniment. These two bars are also in a major-third relationship, contributing to the tonal ambiguity.

Ex. 6

When the text enters in bar 16 ('Tysta öknens stjärnor skrida / öfver vidden dunkel blå' – 'Silently the stars of the desert move in procession / above the dark blue expanse'), the melodic line starts off one beat before the voice (Ex. 7). The voice and piano at first move in parallel, the piano line with moving 6-4 chords (major, minor, diminished triads in second inversion). This mobile piano ribbon in a way obscures the melodic line, which moves in changing B minor modes.

Ex. 7

The bitonal feeling from the introduction returns throughout the song, an obvious connection back to Irgens-Jensen's earliest compositions, not to the more simple textures of *Fabler og barnerim.*

Irgens-Jensen's modesty may have meant that he was never the best judge of his own music. In 1947, on his admission into the Kungliga Musikaliska Akademien (the Royal Music Academy in Stockholm), he had to fill out a form for biographical notes. Here, right at the bottom of a long list of works, which includes the titles of a series of choral songs, he wrote simply: 'A number of songs'.

In March 1924 Irgens-Jensen received a request to become a member of De yngre tonekunstneres samfund ('The Young Musicians' Organisation'), which intended to join forces with the older Norsk Tonekunstnersamfund ('Norwegian Musicians' Organisation'), in order to obtain more performances of Norwegian music. Whether he did join is unknown.

That autumn saw the launch of a new music journal, *Musik*, which lasted for a little over a year but even in that short span produced a good deal of material about new Norwegian music. Irgens-Jensen's standing was evidently fairly high. In the issue of December 1924 he was profiled as a composer, and one of his 'Fables' and a little piano piece, *Siciliano*, were printed – the first composer-profile to appear in the journal, and the first composition it published – and an article on 'Our younger Norwegian composers' in May 1925 spoke of him enthusiastically. The *Siciliano* is important because it gives the clearest presentation yet of what would become regarded as his personal style: a clearly balanced 'old' form, well proportioned independent lines in a polyphonic texture, largely functional tonality, but with a number of modal features both in melody and harmony. The first of his large-scale orchestral compositions to have survived, the Variations and Fugue in G minor, numbered as Op. 26 in one of the composer's notebooks, was soon to make these stylistic features clearer yet.[62]

In the mid-1920s Irgens-Jensen's old acquaintance O. M. Sandvik was working actively to establish the Norsk Musiksamling (Norwegian Music Collection), then at the University of Oslo. The collection was opened in 1927, but as early as 1925 Sandvik had persuaded a number of people to give money to buy in rare music and manuscripts; Irgens-Jensen was one of these – sitting, too, on the board of the Friends of Norsk Musiksamling, which surprised those who knew him, since he generally refused to sit on committees or boards. He may simply have felt the obligations of friendship.

Arnulf Øverland was still among those friends in the 1920s. Dagny Irgens Jensen recalled[63] how at parties Øverland would ask her brother to play new music for them. One of the pieces he often asked to hear was from Schoenberg's *Six Little Piano Pieces*, Op. 19 – but not for the reasons one might expect: in spite of his reputation as a 'modernist' poet, Øverland

[62] *Cf.* the discussion of the *Tema con variazioni* on pp. 86–98, below.

[63] In her written recollections, *loc. cit.*

did not especially like Schoenberg's music and would improvise a parody of such pieces at the piano, with an improvised verbose and esoteric introduction about the background and the spiritual struggle revealed in the piece. Another frequent visitor to the Irgens Jensen home was the writer and critic Elling Holst Bang; and from 1920 onwards Irgens-Jensen was often in the company of the composer David Monrad Johansen, who several times accompanied singers performing Irgens-Jensen's works. Together with Monrad Johansen and Odd Grüner-Hegge he also visited the composer Christian Sinding, an erstwhile acquaintance of the Irgens Jensen family, who was then well over 60 years old but always had a keen eye for younger talent. The composer Fartein Valen writes[64] of a visit to Sinding with Monrad Johansen and his wife, Irgens-Jensen and the violinist Arve Arvesen (1869–1951), which was followed by a visit to Monrad Johansen:[65]

> On Sunday I was invited with Irgens-Jensen to Monrad [Johansen] at Hvalstad. It was such a wonderfully clear winter day. We ate dinner there and then rested for a while and afterwards talked music. Irgens-Jensen had just had an orchestral piece performed [the Variations and Fugue in G minor], which he went through for us, and then we continued to talk about music. They are both so sweet and cordial to me. Irgens-Jensen said, 'We should really get together more with this man, so we could learn a bit from him'. He really meant it, you know. And the strange thing is that Monrad Johansen wouldn't give in until I promised to teach him counterpoint. At first I just laughed, but he would not give in, so I had to surrender. And then they said that we three must definitely get together a little more, because there are so few to talk about music with in this town. I thought it was so nice.

Irgens-Jensen and Valen never became close friends or confidants, even though they had many common traits, both in their early stylistic development and in their ideals, as well as sharing an interest in language and literature: they were both too shy and too cautious. But they continued to be interested in each other's development and respected each other's artistic integrity.

Irgens-Jensen, Monrad Johansen and Valen had another mutual acquaintance in the poet Olav Aukrust, whose distinctive and gentle lyrical poetry they appreciated. Irgens-Jensen met Aukrust several times before the poet's death in 1929 and in 1935 Aukrust's poem 'Rosa' provided the text for one of his finest songs for mixed choir.

[64] Letter to his sister Sigrid, dated 29 November 1926, preserved in the National Library in Oslo.

[65] He lived then *chez* Hulda Garborg, wife of the famous dialect writer, Arne Garborg. The visit Valen describes took place on the same day that Irgens-Jensen's *Variasjoner og fuge* ('Variations and Fugue') had had a public dress rehearsal by the Philharmonic in the Aula of Oslo University.

Arnulf Øverland in the 1920s. His wife Hildur was the first to perform Irgens-Jensen songs in public.

Dagny Irgens Jensen's memoirs record the practical forms her brother's kindness could take. The composer Alf Mørstad, for example, was a shy and nervous person who lived a difficult and lonely life in Nittedal in the countryside north of Oslo. Irgens-Jensen would often go to Nittedal both to cheer him up and give him a little extra teaching in harmony and counterpoint.

Nor was Irgens-Jensen's own life free from concern, as Dagny recollected:

> It was not easy to be a composer in the 20s in Norway; without father's support it couldn't have worked. And then he had the difficult choice between painting and music – which should he choose?
>
> Moreover he was so kind and helpful to others that he could easily be exploited – as often happens with kind people. He would constantly entertain, play for the ladies mother had to tea, play at his friends' parties, etc. Nor can I say that I was not guilty of having exploited him a little. When I came home tired from school and was sick and tired of lessons and studying, I often asked him to play something for me, something we both liked, for example 'Vogel als Prophet' by Schumann, Ravel's 'Pavane', some Bach or Chopin. At other times I also had help with arithmetic I couldn't manage, but it was worked out in a rather too advanced way, so it was easily apparent that I had had help.
>
> And he encountered little understanding of his music; he was told that there was not enough melody in it etc. But his closest friends, Odd [Grüner-Hegge] and Leif [Bruun] especially, had an interest in and understanding of his work. But he didn't earn a farthing [ett øre] before he broke through with the Passacaglia. It was not exactly likely to give a man self-confidence.[66]

[66] Recounted by Dagny Irgens Jensen in her recollections.

Irgens-Jensen playing for his friends in the early 1920s.
On the left, Elling Bang; on the right, Odd Grüner-Hegge.

Violin Sonata in B flat major

Both the Scherzo for violin and piano first performed in 1923 and Irgens-Jensen's great Violin Sonata in B flat major were, to judge from the sketches, probably begun in his youth, perhaps as early as 1913. The Sonata is uncharacteristic of his other works from this period, probably because it was originally conceived so many years before. It was written for Finn Grüner-Hegge, whom the composer himself would accompany in private performances.

At the beginning of the first movement, marked *Allegretto* (the tempo moves to *Molto vivace* followed by an *Allegro moderato* before regaining *Tempo I*), the music is tonally unstable: the modal and chromatic colouring of the lines cast doubt on whether the key is major or minor (Ex. 8). This dualism – which is characteristic of Nordic folk-music in general – is later found in his major orchestral works. In the Violin Sonata Irgens-Jensen is more explicit in his use of contrapuntal devices than in the *Fables*, and some of the phrases contain Norwegian elements, both motivic and rhythmic.

Ex. 8

As he later observed,[67] Grieg was one of the subjects he studied in his youth, and the 'Grieg motif'[68] and a number of 7-13 chords are used. But the fluctuation of tempo in each movement and the tension between triplet and duple rhythms are closer to Brahms. The second movement, a ternary *Andante serioso*, includes elements from the first and 'makes you experience a funeral march'.[69] The third movement, *Vivace*, likewise brings back material from the first movement, thus demonstrating the cyclic thinking found in all of Irgens-Jensen's multi-movement works. The rhythms of a Norwegian folk-dance, the *springar*, recall the Grieg sonatas, as does the central section, an intermezzo marked 'Siciliano'.

The Violin Sonata originally featured a fourth movement, a rondo, later presented as a separate piece; as performed today, the work comprises only three movements. Irgens-Jensen was to practise this kind of autotomy on several occasions, excising the triple fugue that crowned the first version

67 *Cf.* the 1969 radio interview quoted on p. 26, above.

68 So called because it was one of Grieg's melodic fingerprints, the 'Grieg motif' is a folk-derived falling three-note figure, a minor second followed by a major third. It is found through Grieg's music, perhaps most prominently at the start of the tune that opens the Piano Concerto.

69 Elling Bang in *Dagbladet*, 9 October 1926.

of the *Tema con variazioni* and severing the finale of the Symphony in D minor; it, too, became a separate piece, the *Rondo marziale*.[70]

Irgens-Jensen's circle of friends included the violinist Arve Arvesen and pianist Elisabeth Reiss, whose first performance of the Violin Sonata on 6 October 1926 attracted favourable reactions in the press – although the composer had to wait to read them, since he was then in Copenhagen. Arvesen was interviewed by several newspapers, telling one of them:

> Certainly the sonata is splendid. Irgens Jensen has the most remarkable artistic profile I know. Everything is so introspective with him. I said to him: It is strange you have your pince-nez on the outside, you should have them on the inside. He is dreadfully fastidious. He knows everything. You might as well ask him about the new Russian gymnastics! Yes, one can expect the very best from him.[71]

In another newspaper an interview with Arvesen was given the heading 'The best sonata since Sinding's and Grieg's', thanks to his proud claim for the work:

> This evening we are playing just two things, a little Brahms sonata and Irgens Jensen's sonata, says Arve Arvesen. We are very pleased to play it; I think it is the best sonata which has been written since Grieg and Sinding. We are giving the concert for its sake and I hope the public will have the right impression of the importance of the presentation of a new Norwegian work.
>
> Do you believe so strongly in Irgens Jensen?
>
> Yes, I do. He has such a distinct artistic profile. The sonata, which is his first, will perhaps stir up controversy, but peace is not always the best thing.
>
> Is it very modern?
>
> No, it is not modern or anything like it. One cannot speak of it like that. It is simply Irgens Jensen.[72]

Elling Bang's review in *Dagbladet* was so enthusiastic that it was turned into the 'Profile of the Week':

> his music appears surprising and new, because he fills the form with thoughts which are wholly his own. And to a certain extent the depth can be measured in the time it takes for us others to follow.
>
> It is also true of the sonata, which Elisabeth Reiss and Arve Arvesen performed for the first time yesterday with great success, so that scarcely any one of those present was unmoved by its penetrating language. The straightforward, fresh and natural wealth of melody, at the same time so subtle and so simple, is developed with an unaffected ingenuity in the detail

[70] *Cf.* pp. 95, 220–221 and 223, below.

[71] *Aftenposten*, 7 October 1926.

[72] *Tidens Tegn*, 6 October 1926.

> and such an impressive imagination that one sits in one intense hearing from the first to the last note.
>
> It is also impossible to describe in words what music alone can give. The sonata is a poetic work of large dimensions and huge inner strength. It is very rare to find a composer who has the imagination of a poet and is able to place it at the obedient service of an idea. And it is this which justifies going so far into the subject in the present case.[73]

The reviewer in *Aftenposten* found a national note in the Sonata:

> An interesting work, really quite sensational, a new example of the strong and remarkable talent of this young, productive composer. One has a hint of his nationality right from the opening theme; he is a compatriot of Grieg. But before the sonata was played to the end one could recognise, beside this artistry, a wealth of musical impressions, which accumulate into a picture of a wholly distinctive and independent, sensitive musician. In this work more strongly than in any other of Irgens Jensen's earlier works. His marked sense of rich, polyphonic part-writing groups him most closely with neo-classicism – of the Norwegian variety.
>
> But all this masterly control of material and form, which we often have admired in Irgens Jensen, most recently in his choral work 'Norge', is the least decisive step in the sonata; it pales into the background before the impression of the great, musical beauties and subtleties and poetic things contained in the work. And here one must call attention to the second movement, andante serioso, with its character of quiet, brooding, lyrical melancholy. It is absolutely beautiful music, confiding of a distinctive deep intimacy.
>
> The most important thing is that the whole work is borne by a musical spirit as true and noble, as refined, as in few other Norwegian chamber-music works. It was an honour for Elisabeth Reiss and Arve Arvesen to be god-parents to this new, outstanding work. And the honour was mutual. These two excellent artists have obviously, with a strong sense of responsibility, identified themselves completely and intensely with the work. It received a brilliant performance. Irgens Jensen, who on account of the matter has run away to Copenhagen, can feel delighted with the evening.[74]

The performance was therefore an artistic if not an economic success: in the account prepared by Rudolf (a.k.a. Rulle) Rasmussen's concert management, the deficit, 246.22 kroner, was 'met by P. M. Jensen' – once again, Ludvig's father had come to the rescue.

Irgens-Jensen had indeed run away from the excitement surrounding the concert, but since Arvesen and Reiss had repeated requests for another performance, he was able to hear the Sonata himself – but, true to form, instead of taking a bow onstage, he preferred to hide at the back of the hall.

[73] *Dagbladet*, 9 October 1926

[74] Reidar Mjøen, *Aftenposten*, 12 October 1926.

A third performance of the Violin Sonata took place during the Scandinavian Music Days in Stockholm in 1927, chosen by the Norwegian Society of Composers. It stimulated a letter[75] to Irgens-Jensen from the Danish composer Knudåge Riisager:

> Your clear style had such a refreshing effect because its modernity was striking and exactly that objective, pure music, which one so rarely encounters in much of what is called 'modern' music.

The two composers later became good friends.

In the 1930s the Sonata was performed a number of times, including performances by the violinist Helga Løkke with Robert Riefling, in connection with one of which a recording was made, in the studios of the Norsk Grammofonkompani on 20 May 1935. Unfortunately, this type of 'one-off' recording could not be duplicated for commercial sale, although the shellac discs were preserved and later transferred onto tape, a unique recording that, in spite of the hiss and crackle, shows that these performers were distinguished interpreters of the Sonata. The cost of the recording, ten sides in all, was met by the composer. In a draft of a letter of thanks to Riefling, he wrote: 'My warm and enthusiastic thanks for the brilliant performance my sonata received. It went absolutely superbly and the balance between the instruments was ideal'. But then, in what was to become almost a reflex action, he withdrew the Sonata in order to rework it.

The two original manuscripts of the work met differing fates: the first disappeared in Germany before the Second World War; the other was destroyed by a fire at Norsk Musikforlag in 1987, roasted inside the safe. Fortunately, there were copies, drafts and transcripts, which have furnished the basis for later performances.

Tema con variazioni

Irgens-Jensen's first mention of the work that ultimately became the *Tema con variazioni* is in the list he put together sometime in the mid-1920s: 'summer 1925 Variations and fugue op. 26'.[76] It seems probable that he completed the first version of the score in the summer of 1925.

As far as is known, his previous experience of writing for the orchestra extended to some sketches and a handful of orchestral songs. These variations were the first purely orchestral work he heard performed and recognised as a work that would last. He reworked it, of course, for the first time before a performance on 3 December 1934 in Oslo with Grüner-Hegge conducting the Oslo Philharmonic, eight years after the premiere;

[75] Dated 12 May 1927.

[76] *Cf.* p. 69, above.

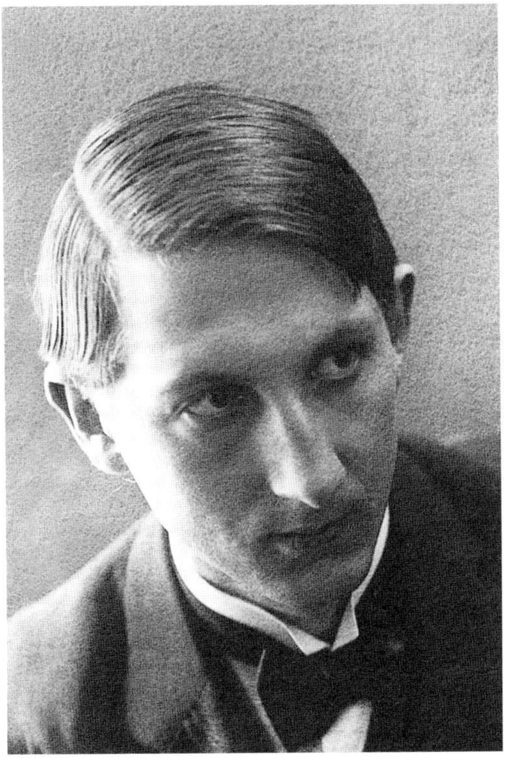

The Danish composer Knudåge Riisager was a good friend of Irgens-Jensen from the 1920s

the score was published in 1935. He later made a few more alterations and in 1949 Norsk Musikforlag published the final edition (which unfortunately contains a number of typesetting errors).

In his notebook, after writing out the theme (Ex. 9), Irgens-Jensen added: 'Nordic folktune'. In a preserved draft of a lengthy text intended to reply to a series of questions about this and other works, he explained its attractiveness:

> I seem to remember: that the theme (which I still love) proliferated. There were many v. of it, many more than I needed.[77]
>
> I think the theme is fine as material for v. – with its 1-2-1 construction and the simple modulations. (Perhaps one could have difficulty in recognising it *en route*, but a theme which one recognises too easily the whole time could become tiring.)[78]

[77] In one of Irgens-Jensen's sketch-books there is a draft of the theme (in G sharp minor) where the first note of the anacrusis is not the flattened seventh, but the tonic, which makes a duller effect.

[78] This was probably written around 1960, but it was never sent.

Ex. 9

But is there anything in the music which justifies its description as a folk-tune, let alone a specifically Norwegian or Scandinavian one?[79]

When the Variations are taken as a whole, it becomes clear that the theme in this instance has two essential aspects: the melodic and the harmonic, which are closely intertwined. The melody has a clear ABA′ form over eighteen bars (6 + 8 + 4). The A section is divided into three parallel parts, which form a sort of development through a rising sequence. The B section is in two parts, where the second part is a variation of the first, transposed up a perfect fourth. The A′ section is a variant, transposed by a fourth, of the A section, abridged. The theme is a predominantly diatonic and stepwise melody, and the triadic conflict that is found here becomes one of the elements in the contrasting B section. The tonality of the melody itself is deliberately meandering and, seen in isolation, is ambivalent: G (minor) is not confirmed until right at the end. Here a crotchet beat is chosen as a walking meter and the rhythm, too, glides peacefully along with simple subdivisions. The difference between feminine and masculine cadences is

[79] The Norwegian musicologist Bjarne Kortsen published a study of the modal aspects of the theme in 'Noen modale særtrekk i Ludvig Irgens Jensens musikk', *Norsk Musikktidsskrift*, Oslo, 1962, Vol. 2, pp. 62–65, but without reaching any convincing conclusion.

used deliberately, together with a veiled anacrusis effect. The triplets which come into the B section are underlined by being used as a 'refrain' the first time.

The theme is harmonised note for note, almost as a chorale. The chords in the a section are predominantly triads in root position, but the B section is purely two-part right up to the transition to the A′ section. There are many non-functional progressions and an avoidance of strict dominant progressions (apart from one to D minor in bar 7). There are several plagal cadences; even the transition to the concluding characteristic pedal note is a plagal cadence. In the B section open fifths (with a leap from a tritone) are encountered in a couple of cadences.

The melody is harmonised so that many of the chords in root position go to second inversion, the melody note being the fifth of the chord. The part-writing aspires to a degree of independence, even in the A section; false relations therefore occur in several places, also simultaneously (last quaver in bar 3). In bar 5 there are two seventh-chords, one after the other, as parallel accents.

A series of musical elements can justify the description of the theme as 'archaic'. The melody has something of the poise and balance of an old chorale, in spite of its asymmetric form. The reiteration of the different sections plays a part in creating this impression. The extensive use of root-position chords, the open fifths, the many non-functional progressions and the lack of a number of clear dominants also give the theme the archaic character it aims for. But it is very difficult to point to anything specific about the theme that could be characteristically only Norwegian or Nordic – that is, different from melodies of a similar character and tonality from a number of other countries.

The theme becomes the subject of a series of variations, with a pronounced climax towards the end. Here use is made of figure-variations, some *cantus firmus* variations and free variations, before a type of metamorphosis technique leads the original harmonic basis into some bass variations. These gradually become a four-bar chaconne which forms a contrapuntal variation within the variation, so that this section appears as a double variation in relation to the original melodic theme. But in one variation (starting on p. 93 of the published score) the chaconne is extended to five-bar phrases up to p. 98, and the Coda, where the bass theme (marked 'Bass 2' in Ex. 10) is augmented and wholly simplified against the augmented original melody. It could be that this section really formed part of the original fugue which was later abandoned.[80]

[80] On this point *cf.* pp. 95–96.

Ex. 10 shows the first bars of the coda, where the opening bass movement (marked 'Bass 1') is given for the sake of comparison. It is apparent here that the harmonic basis *and* the tonal centre through this bass movement become something quite different, and the coda and the whole work then also end in a 'crowning' B flat major.

Ex. 10

The work originally bore the title *Tema med variationer og fuge, g-moll* ('Theme with Variations and Fugue in G minor'). Irgens-Jensen's fondness for Brahms and Reger may have had some influence on his choice of form. Brahms' Handel and Haydn Variations, Opp. 24 and 56, and his Fourth Symphony with its passacaglia-finale were performed several times in Kristiania around the time of the First World War. Reger's two large orchestral variation-works, the *Variations and Fugue on a Theme of J. A. Hiller*, Op. 100, and *Variations and Fugue on a Theme of Mozart*, Op. 132, the latter first played in Kristiania by Johan Halvorsen and the National Theatre Orchestra in 1916,[81] and the Hiller Variations were also performed by the Philharmonic only two months before Irgens-Jensen's own Variations. David Monrad Johansen wrote of the Hiller Variations at the time: 'It is German classicism which has retired from life and proceeded into the study dressed in slippers, dressing gown and nightcap, amusing us with old man's talk'.[82] It is hardly surprising, then, that in the sketch for the score the second variation (pp. 8–11 in the printed score) is marked 'Reger': here is the tight, not to say thick, polyphonic texture with rapid

[81] *Cf.* note 4 on p. 47, above.

[82] Quoted in Hampus Huldt-Nystrøm, *Fra munkekor til symfoniorkester. Musikkliv i det gamle Christiania og Oslo*, Filharmonisk Selskap, Oslo, 1969, p. 216.

modulations and a *rubato* character which points towards Reger's variation technique.

Irgens-Jensen was particularly concerned with the formal sections and contrasts between the variations when he made his drafts and sketches of the structure. There is an especially interesting instance of structural 'part form' in variation 3 (pp. 12–17 of the printed score), where he makes an ABA form (19 + 20 + 19 bars) within the variation. The contrasting B section he himself called 'Trio' in his sketch. Variations 6 and 7 (pp. 45–57) are two 'free' variations. In the outline sketch Irgens-Jensen marked variation 6 'norsk' (Norwegian). In fact, he created a stylised *springdans*[83] in rhythm and structure, similar to the way in which Svendsen and Halvorsen deployed such dances in their *Norwegian Rhapsodies* (Ex. 11).

In one draft, for some unknown reason, he called the following variation '*jæsuittermarsj*' (Jesuit march). It is a ponderous *cantus firmus* variation

Ex. 11

(which also has an ABA form) and, in the a section, has perhaps an element of a 'March to the Scaffold' about it. The ninth variation (pp. 62–64) he suggested in a draft was a 'reflected image'. What it perhaps comes nearest to here is parts of Svendsen's tone poem *Zorahayda*, in particular in the use of the strings, although the use of the bass clarinet, alternating with the oboe to bring about a transformed theme, is reminiscent of Mahler. Between these phrases are striking Impressionist colours on strings and harp, and later on high woodwind, which have obvious parallels in Debussy's music.

In addition to the purely formal side, there are two essential effects which have a part in creating the large span of tension in the work as a whole and between the individual variations. One is the contrast between the 'homophonic' theme and the polyphonic treatment in the variations. The other is the tonal gravity, the moving and shifting of the tonal centres and the various forms of modality used. This modality is not always connected

[83] A traditional Norwegian dance in $\frac{3}{4}$ metre with a strongly accented second beat.

to the traditional church modes or the harmony associated with them; it also uses synthetic scales.[84]

The first performance was given on 29 November 1926, by the Oslo Philharmonic Orchestra conducted by José Eibenschütz. Monrad Johansen was enthusiastic:

> Ludvig Irgens Jensen, whose large orchestral work 'Theme with variations and fugue' began the evening, is a composer who in the last couple of years has attracted more and more notice. First through a series of bold and, in part, almost provocative songs. This spring, a monumental male-voice choral piece 'Norge' was performed and recently, just a month ago, came his great sonata for violin and piano. Through all his compositions one notices an uncontrollable need to show the many sides of his gift. A multitude of partly conflicting elements fight for mastery in his rich and full-toned compositions. This is perhaps because several of his songs are so difficult and have not won the sympathy with the public which their artistic quality deserves. But Irgens Jensen has developed a new and greater clarity. He has fought the tough and dispiriting fight that leads to simplification, to strength, to more intensity of expression, and in the variations he shows that the battle has been won victoriously. The work shows a stylistic mastery so superior that one quite forgets the complicated and immensely demanding style in which the composer has chosen to present his material. The whole feels simple and almost inevitable. Even such an individually stylistic device as a triple fugue, with which the composer in the most impressive way had to conclude and crown his work, makes no dent in this feeling. But what first and foremost makes the work so valuable is its deep and strong spiritual content. The theme has something of a mediaeval ballad about it and, through the long series of variations, the composer displays a strongly developed sense of beauty and a richness of feeling, which produce a wholly surprising effect. The charm, the grace, the grotesque, the pathetic, the strongly passionate, the gentle childlike mind – everything is expressed in a striking and distinctive way and finally unites in the tremendous fugue, where the theme of the variations also appears and maintains the atmosphere.
>
> The instrumentation is, in the best sense, euphonious, but the composer has renounced everything which could smack of external effect. The orchestral sound is palpable throughout and has many fine and characteristic features to display, which disclose a decided talent and sense of colour. Irgens Jensen has for the most part entered Parnassus as well armed as anyone and is fully ready to take up the fight with whomever it may be.[85]

[84] *Cf.* John Vincent, *The Diatonic Modes in Modern Music*, Mills Music, NewYork/San Francisco, 1951.

[85] *Aftenposten*, 30 November 1926.

Elling Bang again heard a national note:

> The theme is short, a pure and simple melody of religious character. Through the graceful gently humming first variation it sets out on its journey and undergoes a series of metamorphoses. The basic mood is lyrical, some of the variations rise to mighty pathos, others play on lighter strings, in part with a touch of humour. Common to all is the strictly concentrated form with its melodically true counterpoint, a fresh and imaginative ingenuity and not least the wholly Norwegian character throughout.[86]

Arne van Erpekum was similarly appreciative:

> This work, too, by the prolific composer bears witness to his strong and individual talent. Seen purely formally there is in this, his first orchestral work, possibly some lack of single-mindedness, and likewise a little more concentration would elevate the effect; but otherwise there is nothing that shows that Irgens Jensen here is dealing with the orchestra for the first time. On the contrary, the instrumentation is so sure and so euphonious, and the simple theme is used in the variations with such great imagination and contrapuntal proficiency, that the composer has at a stroke proved his rare aptitude for symphonic music. The work was a great success and the composer had to thank the public several times for the warm applause.[87]

Per Reidarson, though, was less responsive:

> Irgens Jensen's *Theme with variations and fugue* was something new. The theme is simple and gentle – akin to an old folk-tune, but it is so undistinguished that it does not stick in the mind so as to enable one to recognise it again in its transformations. The variations are, however, extremely well orchestrated and have many small fragments of tuneful contrapuntal effects. But as usual with Irgens Jensen the musical point is lacking. He *knows* a good deal of school technique and makes use of it with noble intentions, but it nevertheless sounded to me like just a long series of cleverly managed exercises in orchestration. – One must have something to say. The notes in themselves are nothing if they do not carry a message to us from a poet, one who understands how to use the notes, as a poet his words.[88]

Irgens-Jensen sent the reviews with a letter to Odd Grüner-Hegge in Berlin. The draft has survived:

> 1/12 26
>
> Dear Odd!
>
> Many thanks for your letter. I am late with this reply – wanted to wait until the Variations were well buried. They received kind sympathy, but I have the impression that most people did not find *the music* in them, did

[86] *Dagbladet*, 30 November 1926.

[87] *Tidens Tegn*, 30 November 1926.

[88] *Arbeiderbladet*, 30 November 1926.

not experience anything. There were not a few who were thoroughly bored, I think. In the reviews you'll see that the same things emerge. It is only David [Monrad Johansen] and Elling [Bang] who express true enthusiasm. Several (not just critics) find the work too protracted and monotonous.

Eibenschütz eventually found the right tempi – it is certainly not easy, but without it I believe the work would have become intolerably boring. He was very attentive, tried and finally succeeded in following my advice, helpful and industrious. However, it lacked detail and phrasing. The musicians played without authority and devotion, it was easy to be aware that they still didn't have the right feeling for the music.

There were a lot of rehearsals, and I have (or should have) gained rich experience: including that one cannot consider one's expression marks carefully enough, or more correctly that most musicians are unmusical and get it all wrong when they get a chance.

The instrumentation was as I had imagined it, that is to say I believe that in an ideal performance it will be as I have imagined. On the other hand, it appears that the line is still not as good as you and I had hoped. But it is not possible for me to detect any definite weak point. I think that for those who are drawn into the magic circle – who are moved by the atmosphere in the quiet section and delight in the details – for them the line is good enough. The others who keep cool and believe that one is writing exercises in composition technique quickly grow tired. (Thus it has always been and will always continue to be). In any case I think that it is not so easy now to regroup or shorten without the structure collapsing. Eibenschütz says it is a little too long and wants to make some cuts. It will be amusing to see what he will leave out.

How are you? Are you comfortable in your solitude and your work? I have much to think about now myself – and don't get anything done.

Well, this was not a letter worthy of you, you master of style. I am now also very tired and do not have a clear thought in my head.

Read in isolation, this letter and the reviews would suggest that the work had a good reception in the concert hall. In the event, there was another performance at the concert which stole the show – of Arthur Honegger's *Pacific 231*. This musical 'visual impression' of a 300-ton locomotive starting up and plunging into the night at 120 km per hour created a huge stir, with whistling and booing mixed in with the applause – it was too radical for the conservative members of the Oslo audience. Eibenschütz, moreover, played the Honegger 'da capo', thereby pushing Irgens-Jensen's variations to the back of people's minds. What should have been a triumphal orchestral debut for a young, promising composer – a large-scale work played by the Philharmonic – was overshadowed.

But some people had noticed the work and by 3 March 1927 the young conductor J. L. Mowinckel Jr.[89] had arranged a performance at one of his concerts with the Harmonien[90] in Bergen. Part of the advance publicity involved printing the theme in the main local newspaper, *Bergens Tidende*, on the day of the concert.

There had been some previous contact between Mowinckel and Irgens-Jensen. On Mowinckel's initiative a secret fund was set up for Odd Grüner-Hegge's musical education in Berlin, to which Mowinckel had contributed money, asking Irgens-Jensen[91] to make the payment so that he could remain anonymous.

Mowinckel now suggested[92] cutting the Variations from 28 to 25 minutes. An undated draft of a reply reveals that Irgens-Jensen was clearly conscious of 'a lack of singlemindedness' in the work and gave Mowinckel a free hand in making cuts, to the conductor's evident surprise.[93] Mowinckel explained the omissions he had made at the concert: 'Personally I am very pleased with many of the variations, but I can only reconcile myself to the form as a whole with difficulty'.

But these changes were only the beginning of a more drastic process of revision. There is a notebook amongst Irgens-Jensen's papers where he diagnoses what he feels are the shortcomings of the work:

> flaws: more major keys and rhythmic changes
> less cantus firmus, more figure variation
> larger layers of sound
> delay as much as possible the strict movement to the fugue.

But his severity was born of affection. In the draft of an unsent letter from around 1960, he writes: 'Besides Heimferd ['Homeward Journey'] and Driftekaren ['The Drover'] it is certainly the work I am most fond of (perhaps because it had a difficult birth)'.

His most sweeping change was made for the performance in December 1934, before which he removed a good deal of the work, slicing off the triple fugue almost in its entirety: only reminiscences now remain. He felt that that it 'appeared too long and not exciting enough. The rest of the material

[89] Son (1895–1940) of Johan Ludvig Mowinckel (1870–1943), who was three times prime minister of Norway (1924–26, 1928–31 and 1933–35), from a wealthy Bergen family which donated considerable sums to culture.

[90] Literally, 'The Harmonic Society', the name of the Bergen orchestra founded in 1765, the forerunner of the present-day Bergen Philharmonic.

[91] In a letter of 12 August 1926.

[92] In letters dated 15 February and 24 February 1927.

[93] Letter dated 5 March 1927.

in it is found in the last section of the work, and I am satisfied with it as it is now'.[94]

Even in the final printed edition of 1949 there were several more changes, largely technical details, but there was also another drastic structural change: a note in the score allowed the omission of twenty pages of music (pp. 24–44), and no surviving early recording of the Variations includes this part of the music. In a draft from c. 1950 Irgens-Jensen explained the impulse behind his optional surgery:

> When the work was performed in 193? [1934] without cuts, I clearly understand that the work as a whole gained by this shortening.
>
> The form revolves around contrasts, but there are so many of them, of peaks and troughs, that one can lose the perception of the whole (where one is in the work) and tire. – However, when the work was to be printed, I did not have the heart to delete these three variations, because they belonged with the original plan. The work is really a sort of '*éducation sentimentale*' where the different moods and – shall we say – approaches to life find expression. Childlike directness, nature-mysticism, gentleness, commotion, also the ironic and demonic. (Oh, well –)

This text also raises the intriguing possibility of a programmatic impulse in its inspiration:

> The work alternates betw. strict and more free v.
>
> If there is a programme behind it. That I will not answer, but it is interesting that you mention it. What do you read into this music?
>
> […]
>
> As I have touched on previously: I imagined something that the individual variations should try to express, or if one would have it given[?] an emotional philosophy of life, how we – perhaps most of all in youth – swing 'himmelhoch jauchzend, zum Tode betrübt'.[95]
>
> That is the explanation of the abrupt contrasts.

He drafted other notes on the work, too, including a summation of its character which was probably sparked by a performance in Budapest in 1935, when Odd Grüner-Hegge conducted the revised version:

> The T.c.v.[*Tema con variazione*] seeks through contrasting variations to symbolise the critical phase of a spiritual development, a development where an ethical philosophy of life issues forth ever more strongly.

And in another draft, written during the Second World War:

[94] Unpublished draft.

[95] 'Rejoicing unto Heaven, grieving unto death' – from Klärchen's Song in the Third Act of Goethe's *Egmont*.

> The work evolves through ever greater contrasts between strict and freer variations, between sacred and 'profane' (which moreover the human soul often does) [this last phrase crossed out]. 'Through dream, nocturne, vision and impressive imagination the composer progresses to clarification, and the work then ends in bright harmony.'[96]

The *Tema con variazioni* – as Irgens-Jensen called the work from 1934 onwards – enjoyed many performances abroad. Hermann Abendroth (1883–1956) was one of its champions, first conducting it in Lübeck on 26 and 29 June 1935, and later taking it to the Gewandhaus in Leipzig and to Bayreuth. It was chosen for the Scandinavian Music Festival in Copenhagen in 1938, drawing enthusiastic reviews from the Danish critics. One of them, Karl Bjarnhoff, contained an aside which disagreed with the early Norwegian reviewers:

> Sweden has its Gösta Nyström,
> Norway an Irgens Jensen.
> [...] But just as at the Swedish concert recently, so this evening, too, there was a work which rose far above the ordinary, and this work was Irgens Jensen's Theme with Variations. Irgens Jensen does not strive for originality. He does not want to be ultra-Norwegian at any price and, precisely because of this, he becomes in the deepest sense the most original; precisely because of this, his music acquires an element of something universal. His Theme with Variations was purely and simply pure gold, the value of which is equal across all frontiers. And there is this with Irgens Jensen, he does not appear sensational by virtue of an outright modernism or striking instrumentation. He drives his points home exclusively for the value of their content and for their classical form.[97]

Bjarnhoff's view that Irgens-Jensen did not attempt to be 'ultra-Norwegian' may seem to contrast with Elling Bang's discernment in 1926 of a 'wholly Norwegian character throughout'. Its archaic quality, not least because of its use of modality, may be to blame for the Norwegians' readiness to hear a nationalist element in the work, their expectations conditioned by a long-standing search for historical affiliation.

The *Tema con variazioni* can, of course, be both Norwegian and European. The work shows a Neoclassical attitude to clear form and lively polyphony, which was then, of course, a pre-occupation of Stravinsky, Hindemith and other composers then seeking formal clarity as part of their search for the new. In a few of the variations there is also a type of French 'classicism', with a *clarté* in the simple and elegant lines; elements of French Impressionism,

[96] Quoted in Jens Arbo, 'Filologen som overrasket verden med musikk', *Norsk Musikkliv*, No. 1, 1943, pp. 6–9.

[97] *Social-Demokraten*, 9 September 1938.

then considered exotic and modernistic in Norway, can also be found. Nonetheless, the work came to be regarded by younger composers as a firm and serviceable point of departure for the future of Norwegian music.

Whatever the influences on it, the *Tema con variazioni* is a genuinely personal work, with its musical durability proven by many performances down through the years. It is one of the finest pieces of music by any Norwegian composer to have been written between the two World Wars.

According to his sister, Irgens-Jensen was seriously in love several times. Usually these episodes did not last very long; while they did, they could be intense. Early in October 1926 he showed up on the boat to Denmark to bid farewell to Odd Grüner-Hegge and David Monrad Johansen, who were bound for Copenhagen. Grüner-Hegge was going on to Berlin to study; Monrad Johansen was to stay in Copenhagen for several days.

Grüner-Hegge relates[98] that as the ship was ready to leave, he and Monrad Johansen stood waving down to Irgens-Jensen on the quay.

> Then David says to him: 'Well, my friend, come with us to Horten then, and we'll have a dram on board!' At that time there was prohibition here. So just as they took away the gangway, Ludvig jumped aboard.

At that time the ship to Denmark stopped at Horten, a city on the fjord some 60 km south of Oslo, with service at the bar right from the departure from Oslo. Irgens-Jensen, though, stayed on board, not because of the availability of alcohol (he was a moderate drinker) but because he let himself be persuaded by the others to stay on until Copenhagen – this was immediately before the premiere of his Violin Sonata by Arvesen and Reiss. The lack of a ticket and money was one thing, but there was a worse problem: how would he be able to go ashore at Copenhagen? It was at that time compulsory to have a passport between the two countries and Irgens-Jensen did not have his with him. Fortunately, the then Norwegian minister in Copenhagen was on board and Grüner-Hegge knew him. The friends trooped up and explained the situation, and Irgens-Jensen was equipped with a letter of reference from the minister, which was enough to gain him admission to Danish territory.

Once in Copenhagen, he had to telegraph home for money and wrote briefly to his sister to send some music on to him. He had long had plans to approach Wilhelm Hansen Music Publishers in Copenhagen. He had no contract with any publisher and Wilhelm Hansen was (and still is) the largest

[98] Grüner-Hegge's and Dagny Irgens Jensen's recollections of this story differ in some details; this account is a synthesis of the two versions.

Three gentlemen in Copenhagen:
from the left, David Monrad Johansen,
Odd Grüner-Hegge and Ludvig Irgens-Jensen.

music-publisher in northern Europe and also had its own distribution in Germany.

The three enjoyed life in Copenhagen. The first day they had lunch in the restaurant at the Hôtel d'Angleterre. There they met a Norwegian-born operetta singer, Hjørdis Johnsen, whom Monrad Johansen knew from earlier appearances at the Opéra Comique in Oslo. Johnsen had with her a sweet, young Danish girl, in whom Irgens-Jensen became interested. She was Louise Ravn Christophersen, born on 16 October 1903 in Haraldsted, daughter of a land-owning farmer Johannes Ewald Christophersen and of Signe Ravn, of Brøndby Vester outside Copenhagen. It was arranged that the three would come for coffee at Mme Johnsen's in the afternoon and later in the evening go to a party. But since Irgens-Jensen had no luggage with him, he lacked suitable clothes. Grüner-Hegge related:

> Ludvig never had a proper suit. This relatively rich man really never had a proper suit. So that he could go to the party, I lent him my suit, one of mine, I had two. He had one of them to strut around in, and he had never looked so fine.[99]

After only a quarter of an hour at the party, Grüner-Hegge met Irgens-Jensen in an adjoining room and said: 'You are looking very serious'. 'I am engaged', he answered. When Grüner-Hegge told Monrad Johansen, he responded with:

> 'What stuff and nonsense!' and calmed me with: 'That is something *I* usually do'. But it was not that. 'I know Ludvig better,' I say. 'If he has once said that, he will stand by it. You will not change his mind.'[100]

While they were at the party, the whole of the western sky was lit up by flames, and a telephone call told Louise that her father's farm was on fire. She and Irgens-Jensen left immediately and, in all the chaos at the site of the fire, he was presented as her fiancé. He tried to help extinguish the conflagration as well as he could in his borrowed suit, which of course was ruined. The blaze had been started by a pyromaniac, and a strong wind whipped it up, to considerable destructive effect: the largest barn, containing the year's crop, too, was burnt down, and with it most of the animals; luckily, the dwelling houses were undamaged.

Some days later the family in Oslo received a card from Ludvig to announce that he was 'coming home with strange news'. They thought it concerned a publishing contract and were startled to discover that he was now engaged.

The engagement was short. Louise and her family very soon came to Oslo and the wedding was arranged. It took place in Brøndby Vester as early as 11 December 1926, straight after the success in the Philharmonic of the first performance of the *Variations and Fugue*, and barely two months after the couple had first met. Irgens-Jensen had not one best man but two: Grüner-Hegge, who returned from his studies in Berlin for the occasion, and Monrad Johansen. The wedding had consequences also for his friend Leif Bruun. During the celebration in Copenhagen he met Louise's cousin, Esther, and the following year they, too, were married.

During the wedding reception a telegram arrived from Christian and Augusta Sinding: 'The devil will have his birthday while the wedding bells

[99] Quoted from the taped interview, *loc. cit.*

[100] *Ibid.*

Louise Irgens-Jensen
(née Ravn Christophersen) in 1926

are ringing' – according to Norwegian tradition, 11 December was one of the two settlement days for paying interest on loans, and these days were called The Devil's Birthday.

Two days later the evening edition of *Aftenposten* reported that eminent guests had arrived with the morning train from abroad. One was Edvard Munch, fresh from the success of a brilliant new exhibition in Berlin.

> Also with the train from abroad this morning came the composer Ludvig Irgens Jensen, who has been in Copenhagen getting married. In the picture here he is seen with his wife. It is, however, a little difficult to see the radiant young lady's face behind her enormous bouquet.
>
> David Monrad Johansen also came from Copenhagen. He was in fact Mr. Irgens Jensen's best man.[101]

That first winter the young couple lived in the family's large cottage at Lillevann at Voksenkollen. The year after, they had a son, Leif Olav Jerndal Irgens-Jensen, born on 4 December 1927. The young family then moved

[101] *Aftenposten* (evening edn.), 1 December 1926.

to Theresegate. Not until just before Christmas 1930 did they move to Nordstrand, to the villa 'Fjell' ('Mountain'), beautifully situated with a view of the Oslofjord. Irgens-Jensen was to live there until his death in 1969. Louise survived him by 25 years: she died in the autumn of 1994.

Even if by 1926 Irgens-Jensen was famous enough for his marriage and homecoming to provide copy for the newspapers, his composing activities were hardly profitable economically. The music that had been printed or published was now withdrawn and he had no special income from material on hire or performances until long after TONO[102] was set up in 1927. He did not apply for stipends and so did not receive any, and so it was his family who had to come to the rescue to enable him to continue his work. His father gave him authority to draw money on the company, Jensen & Co. – an action with which his brother Brynjulf, who had come into the firm, was completely in agreement, saying: 'We should be able to afford to have one artist in the family'.[103]

Irgens-Jensen was not a member of the Norwegian Society of Composers (Norsk Komponistforening), but after a controversy over stipends in 1927,[104] the newly elected chairman, Arne Eggen,[105] invited many younger composers to become members, among them Irgens-Jensen:

> We wish to strengthen the society artistically much more, and the board has therefore decided to approach several of our best names, whose entry into the society will signify an increased artistic strength for our organisation.
>
> The subscription is now 5.00 kroner p.a. (as opposed to the former 10.00 kroner).[106]

He did indeed become a member, together with a number of other young composers.

Piano Quintet

After the success of the Violin Sonata and the *Variations and Fugue*, Irgens-Jensen was doubtless relieved to find public interest dying down again. And by 1927 he was working on his Piano Quintet. The date of its completion is unknown; it was not premiered until 2 February 1932, by the pianist Ivar Johnsen and the string quartet of the Oslo Philharmonic (Ernst Glaser,

[102] The international music agency of the Norwegian Society of Composers.

[103] Quoted in Dagny Irgens Jensen's memoirs, *loc. cit.*

[104] *Cf.* p. 110, below.

[105] Eggen (1881–1955) studied in Oslo and Leipzig before beginning his career as an organist. His works include a Symphony in G minor (1920), two operas (*Olav Liljekrans*, after Ibsen, 1931–40; *Cymbelin*, after Shakespeare, 1943–48), an oratorio, *Kong Olav* (1930; *cf.* p. 141, below), and some chamber music and songs. He remained chairman of the Society of Composers until 1945.

[106] Letter dated 12 January 1928.

Ludvig and Louise Irgens-Jensen with their son, Olav, in 1929

Oscar Holst, Bjarne Brustad and Guillaume Hesse). In the programme notes for that performance he gave a succinct description of the work:

> The style is polyphonic and has a serious character.
>
> The chorale [Ex. 12] which the material leads into, is the basic idea of the work, which all the thematic material is related to and derived from.
>
> The first movement is kept in sonata form. The main theme is strictly delineated and is frequently used as a *cantus firmus*, but the 2nd theme is syncopated and has a more lively character. The coda is formed as a rapidly moving fugato.
>
> The siciliano-like middle movement leads directly into the last section which is introduced by the chorale. This gives way to an impetuous motif which is developed in a restless hurry; later a ponderous march theme also turns up.
>
> The finale gradually brings in all the earlier material.

Ex. 12

In the company of Brustad's *Capricii* for violin and viola and Svendsen's Octet, the Quintet was so well received that the concert had to be repeated a week later. The same spring (in May) the Quintet and its musicians scored a success also at the Scandinavian Music Days in Helsinki.

The Piano Quintet was performed at a private concert during World War II,[107] but more than half a century passed before it was heard again, when the Risør Chamber Music Festival programmed it in 1999, in a performance by the pianist Gonzalo Moreno and an all-female quartet: Elise Båtnes and Katrine Buvarp, violins, Nora Taksdal, viola, and Ellen M. Flesjø, cello. The concert was broadcast on NRK and some minor stations in the USA. The performance was very well received by the public, and the critic Idar Karevold wrote:

> This is a vigorous work written in the best classical tradition and with a wide-ranging and demanding piano part [...]. It is lamentable that this work has not found its proper place in the standard repertory, at least for Norwegian ensembles. The genre of the piano quintet is a rarity in the worklists of Norwegian composers, and Irgens-Jensen's contribution is unique in its kind.[108]

[107] *Cf.* p. 206, below.

[108] *Aftenposten*, 25 June 1999. Although a number of the concerts in the 1999 Risør Festival were transplanted to the Wigmore Hall in London the following week, the Irgens-Jensen Piano Quintet was left behind – a fact of which the critic Martin Anderson complained in print ('Norway's Sounds and Visions', *The Independent*, 7 July 1999).

Now that the first performance of the Piano Quintet outside Norway has taken place,[109] and the first commercial recording is under discussion, it seems certain this work will live on and enjoy further performances.

[109] By Øyvind Aase and the Frosch String Quartet in the Concert Hall of the Pancho Vladigerov National Academy of Music, Sofia, Bulgaria on 3 October 2012.

IV
Modernism and Norwegian Musical Nationalism between the Wars

In the summer of 1928 Irgens-Jensen went on a round trip of Europe, first to Germany to visit Grüner-Hegge, then to Poland, taking in Katowice and Kraków, and on to Czechoslovakia. In Poland he visited his friend Erik Dahm, who was director of a factory in Katowice run by the Norwegian fish-hook manufacturers, Mustad. Elling Bang and Jens Arbo travelled with him, while his young wife stayed at home with their little son.

In May, shortly before his departure, a new orchestral work by Irgens-Jensen, his Passacaglia, had been declared one of the winners in a composition competition run by the Columbia Graphophone Company,[1] and for the next few years he was once again in the headlines, with a series of performances of the work, at home and abroad, first in Scandinavia and later in Europe and the USA, following its well-received premiere in January 1929 – there is no other twentieth-century Norwegian orchestral work which has been performed so often and have enjoyed such international circulation in its composer's lifetime as the Passacaglia.

That success took place against a domestic background of cultural controversy, a long-standing, and sometimes heated, debate on the place of modernism and nationalism in the Norwegian music of the 1920s. Nationalism had been a powerful force in Norwegian music since the time of Grieg – whose national symbolism was felt well beyond the confines of music. The background to this situation goes back to Norway's split from Denmark on 17 May 1814, when the country became independent and received its own constitution. But the freedom was short-lived: in October the young nation was forced by the countries victorious in the Napoleonic wars to accept the Treaty of Kiel and form a union with Sweden under the Swedish king Karl XIII, although with its own new, liberal constitution. So in the nineteenth century Norwegian society as a whole felt an urge to cast aside the culture that had characterised the former Danish hegemony and the present Swedish one – and to underline what were perceived to be historical national values and build a distinctive Norwegian cultural identity. This birth of the new Norwegian nation took the form of deliberate cultural

[1] For further details of this competition, *cf.* pp. 113–18, below.

conquest. Through (self-)conscious praise of Norway's glorious past, by collecting and publishing folk-tales, folk music and artefacts, a foundation for a national culture was laid. This material from the 'real' Norway, from mythical ideals of 'nature', from people living in the mountains and the remote valleys invigorated the young minds creating new literature, music and pictorial arts. Even more importantly, across in the new educational system, from the community schools to university, these national attitudes permeated both the teaching and the goals of the students themselves.

Romanticism was still very firmly rooted in Norwegian music around the time the First World War, perhaps because, unlike most other European countries, Norway's National Romantic movement was extended in time through the dominating influence of Grieg. Romantic attitudes were as much apparent in the choice of repertoire as in musical literature and journalism. A telling example is Ole Sandvik's and Gerhard Schjelderup's *Norges Musikhistorie* ('Norwegian Music History'),[2] published in 1921: it is permeated by Romantic attitudes in its description of music and emphasis on a strong connection with Norwegian 'soul', soil and landscape. Music critics joined these authors in preserving the ideals of Romanticism well into the twentieth century.

At this point it might be useful to list the more important composers active in the period under discussion, classified into three rather broad categories, according to age and attitude (Table 1, p. 108).

Impressionism came to Norway relatively early when, in 1906, Johan Halvorsen conducted a concert of music by Debussy with the National Theatre Orchestra.[3] Alf Hurum's *Tre akvareller* ('Three Aquarelles') for piano, composed in 1912, and his *Eksotisk suite*, premiered in Kristiania in 1918, were the first important Norwegian Impressionist works. In 1921 came Bjarne Brustad's *Orientalsk suite* and Arvid Kleven's *Lotusland*. Pauline Hall heard parts of her *Verlaine suite* performed in 1922. These orchestral works were not well received by the public and the press at first, although in 1929 Hall's suite was given a more favourable reception. But by then the mayfly life of Norwegian Impressionism was already over.

Neoclassicism evades precise definition since it embraces differing aesthetic attitudes. Many composers – chief among them Paul Hindemith – strove for a 'new objectivity', accompanied by a return to older forms and principles as sonata, concerto and fugue, to polyphony,

[2] Ole M. Sandvik and Gerhard Schjelderup, *Norges Musikhistorie*, two vols., Oppi, Kristiania, 1921. Schjelderup (1859–1933) was himself a composer, best known for his Wagnerian music-dramas, although he also wrote two symphonies and other orchestral pieces, chamber works and songs.

[3] Finn Benestad, 'Claude Debussy i norsk musikkliv frem til 1925', *Studia Musicologica Norvegica*, No. 2, Universitetsforlaget, Oslo, 1976.

Norwegian Composers Active between the World Wars		
The conservative, 'the old'	**'The younger old'**	**'The young'**
Otto Winter-Hjelm (1837–1931)		Alf Hurum (1882–1972)
Johannes Haarklou (1847–1925)		Fartein Valen (1887–1952)
Ole Olsen (1850–1927)		David Monrad Johansen (1888–1974)
Iver Holter (1850–1941)		Pauline Hall (1890–1969)
Christian Sinding (1856–1941)		Ludvig Irgens-Jensen (1894–1969)
Catharinus Elling (1858–1942)		Bjarne Brustad (1895–1978)
Per Winge (1858–1935)		Harald Sæverud (1897–1992)
Gerhard Schjelderup (1859–1933)		Arvid Kleven (1899–1929)
Hjalmar Borgstrøm (1864–1925)		Eivind Groven (1901–77)
Johan Halvorsen (1864–1935)	Per Reidarson (1879–1954)	Olav Kielland (1901–85)
Eyvind Alnæs (1872–1932)	Arne Eggen (1881–1955)	Harald Lie (1902–42)
Halfdan Cleve (1879–1951)	Trygve Torjussen (1885–1977)	Karl Andersen (1903–70)
	M. M. Ulfrstad (1890–1968)	C. G. Sparre Olsen (1903–84)
	Sverre Jordan (1889–1972)	Klaus Egge (1906–69)
		Geirr Tveitt (1908–81)
		Conrad Baden (1908–89)

to the perceived simplicity of earlier times. Others embraced new forms of tonality, including bi/polytonality, modes and synthetic scales, as can be heard in the music of many French and eastern European composers, most obviously Milhaud and Poulenc, Stravinsky and Prokofiev.

These subtleties were not widely discussed in Norway. Indeed, the conceptual framework for modern music was sorely under-developed. Terms such as 'atonal', 'modernism', 'radical', even 'new music', meant something different in Norway compared with, for example, Britain and Germany. 'Atonal' – which was generally used by conservative Norwegian commentators as an insult – included music using extended tonality, bi- and polytonality, twelve-note music and purely atonal music. Composers from Reger to Hindemith and Stravinsky to Schoenberg were all branded 'atonal' and unilaterally condemned by the conservatives, often even before their music had been heard. A variety of labels were then current, among them 'music of the future,' 'constructivism' and 'musical Communism' – this latter jibe, of course, reflecting the general bourgeois fear of Communism and 'Bolshevism' in the period after 1917. Composers who erred from familiar paths could find themselves called 'cerebral musicians'.[4]

Although the conservative groups in Norwegian musical life were well represented in the debate, the 'moderns' – in marked contrast with the plethora of such organisations which exist today – did not have any clique, group or organisation of their own that could offer a collective forum. They may well have had a common goal in their attitudes and in their desire

[4] *Cf.* Huldt-Nystrøm, *op. cit.*, p. 160, and in more depth in Arvid O. Vollnes, *Modernisme på norsk – Komponisten Ludvig Irgens-Jensen*, Garantiforlaget, Oslo, 1996, pp. 163–82.

for openness, but the stylistic gaps between them were too wide. In both Sweden and Denmark there were unifying leaders and cliques, but Norway did not have a truly modernist forum until 1938 with the formation of the society Ny Musikk ('New Music'), which became a section of the ISCM. Its prime instigator was Pauline Hall. She had a status and position similar to Nadia Boulanger in France, although she was not a teacher. On a number of occasions, though, Hall was close to giving up her work as a composer and critic, and in 1934 she even thought about emigrating.[5]

Music by the radically atonal Fartein Valen was the starting point for one of the most vigorous and long-lasting debates in Norwegian music between the Wars. Valen knew that his music was controversial and would receive harsh treatment from the Norwegian critics. The most unbridled attacks came after the premiere of his orchestral song *Ave Maria* in 1923. Some of the reviews of the first performance have passed into Norwegian musical folklore as a kind of joke, and an example of misplaced critical responsibility. The worst came from Per Reidarson – Valen's friend during their studies in Berlin – who characterised the music as

> an orchestral score, which, in a poor Max Reger-style, consisted of notes that aimlessly lay in wait and undulated up and down like a jellyfish in muddy water. A vocal line, the notes of which also never showed whether they should go up or down, and which therefore remained lying askew, howling, heaven knows what about. Haldis Halvorsen had the doubtful honour to appear as the priestess for this work. It was scarcely her fault that she sounded as if she was miaowing and crowing. Leif Halvorsen conducted with a certain skill, but the whole appeared painful, embarrassing, risible [...].[6]

Valen's three little songs, *Gedichte von Goethe*, Op. 6, written and published in 1930, unleashed a debate about atonality that would last for over three years. Most of the critics, though, were not out for Valen's blood in particular; their target was modernist music in general – music some of them wanted stopped at the border. In writing about Valen himself, the majority were polite and considerate, although the odd sarcastic remark did appear in their reviews. But even if the attitudes behind a number of the reviews were unashamedly hostile, it was rare to find unanimous condemnation.

The young composers won a qualified victory with some of the first performances of the music of Valen, Hall, Harald Sæverud and Irgens-Jensen, but they also made some small advances on a wider socio-political plane. One of the first, and most important, was an internal victory in the Society of Composers, the so-called 'Stipend Controversy' of 1927.

[5] Undated letter to Irgens-Jensen.

[6] *Arbeiderbladet*, 10 April 1923.

The Society had the right to recommend to the Department for Church and Education (as it was called then) candidates for a stipend, and an internal group in the society in 1927 proposed the young radical Harald Sæverud as first on the list. After some manipulation by the committee, the Society recommended instead the second composer on the list, the older and more conservative Per Reidarson, who – as his attack on Valen suggests – stood as a sort of leader of the reactionary 'clique'. In response, in a Saturday profile in *Dagbladet* on 3 September 1927, 'Pueblo' (the journalist Paul Gjesdahl) mercilessly attacked Reidarson and the attitudes he stood for, so angering him that he picked a fight with Gjesdahl in the interval of a concert in the Aula of the University. This 'Aula scuffle', as it became known, attracted much publicity and for several days there was speculation about a police report and a lawsuit. There were even threats of lawsuits against the voting committee members of the Society. The affair ended with the convening of an Extraordinary General Meeting of the Society which forced the members of the committee to stand for re-election. At the general meeting on 26 November an entirely new committee was elected, with Arne Eggen as chairman, a change which encouraged a long line of younger composers to join the Society, among them Irgens-Jensen.

Even if on this occasion Sæverud did not receive his stipend, it was still a victory for the radicals, exposing the conservatives and their machinations. The victory was reinforced when Reidarson had to justify his actions with a short, self-published paper in the autumn of 1928: *What is the Matter with Our Musical Life*, a grudging apology which again clearly illustrated his conservative attitudes and where, unconvincingly, he tried to lead all Norwegian music back to the style of Grieg's and Svendsen's time.

The debate raised the issue of the 'national' in music, and the extent to which it can reflect nationality – other, of course, than by incorporating elements of indigenous song and dance. Naturally, there are ideas behind and inside music that have a specifically musical character, and which can combine with extra-musical features – not least the ideology that can 'elevate' the music of, say, Grieg or Sibelius into something that sounds specifically 'Norwegian' or 'Finnish'.

Between the two World Wars, many Norwegian composers and cultural commentators began to speak of a new national music which was not built on Grieg's and Svendsen's examples and yet which could simultaneously both express something new and be connected with the past. The composer David Monrad Johansen used his post as a critic for *Aftenposten*, still the most widely read newspaper in Norway, to present the nationalist position. The broadest presentation of his musical vision was given in a lecture, 'National Values in Our Music', delivered to the Kristiania Music Teachers' Society on 22 May 1924.[7] In it he gave an historical overview of Norwegian music, seen from a nationalist viewpoint, and he emphasised the line of musical development in central Europe, which he regarded as being unbroken right up to Brahms; he felt that the occupants of the last branch of the family tree – Max Reger, together with his 'partner', Richard Strauss – heralded the autumn. The crux of his argument was a simple one: 'All art music has its source in folk music and if one wants to give a character-sketch of what, in the best sense, we mean by Norwegian music, then we must go to Norwegian folk music'. Among the characteristics he ascribed to it was an 'effervescent vivacity' which constantly brings forth something new, as with Grieg. It was, he continued, 'a consequence of certain peculiarities in our people. First and foremost, the unusual joy in colour which characterises everything that is called Norwegian art'. He then attempted to have his cake and eat it in a curious leap of logic:

> Just because it is the most emotional expression of a people's temperament, it is to a very high degree dependent on environment. And fortunately so. We would otherwise have been consumed long ago, we would also in a cultural regard have been enslaved by Communism. To want to deny that art is indigenous is to deny the individual, the personal in it, and no one seriously wants to do that.

Monrad Johansen and his fellow nationalists believed that Norwegian culture continued to live on 'unseen' even during the four hundred years of Danish rule from c. 1400 to 1814. Norwegians had to shake off the Danish yoke and colonial feelings of inferiority, rise up proudly and march onwards with the distinctive art of the people in their knapsack. This attitude meant that the hard-core nationalists rejected much Norwegian art-music – no matter what its quality – because it did not, as Pauline Hall sarcastically put it, have 'the authentic smell of the cow-shed'; they preferred, she wrote, that Norwegian music should 'march on the spot'.[8]

The term 'Norse' (*norrøn* in Norwegian) began to creep into discussion of music. Monrad Johansen's large-scale cantata-like work *Voluspå* ('The Prophecy of the Seeress', based on an Eddic poem about the gods and creation), composed in 1926, used a Norse text in an archaic translation and archaisms in the music to underline its extra-musical associations. Other composers were less aggressive: Alf Hurum's *Norrøn suite* ('Norse Suite') employed archaisms, modality and parallel chords to create a synthetic

[7] It was published, partly revised, in four parts in *Aftenposten* on 5–11 July that year.

[8] Pauline Hall, 'Musikk', in Shetelig, Brandt and Nyman, *op. cit.*, p. 209. A 'language debate' – to which this exchange was a clear parallel – was then raging in Norway; *cf.* pp. 140–41, below, for a fuller discussion.

'Norwegian Impressionism',[9] sometimes called 'Norse Impressionism'. This interest in the 'Norse' in music had begun in the 1800s, first among historians and folklore collectors, growing in importance with the composer and ethnomusicologist Catherinus Elling at the beginning of the 1900s. When the fashion took hold, Monrad Johansen's *Voluspå* was only one of a decades-long flood of such works, among them settings of *Draumkvedet* ('The Dream Lay'), a Norwegian mediaeval religious ballad, by Monrad Johansen (1924), Egge (1933) and Sparre Olsen (1937), Hurum's symphonic poem *Bendik og Årolilja* (1923), Arne Eggen's opera *Olav Liljekrans* (1940), Sæverud's orchestral *Galdreslåtten* ('The Magic Tune'; 1942), Tveitt's *Håvamål* for voice and orchestra ('Sayings of Odin' or 'Sayings from the High One' from the Poetic Edda; 1930), *Håkonarmål* for soprano, tenor, baritone, chorus and orchestra ('Sayings of Håkon'; date uncertain) and his ballet *Baldurs draumar* ('Baldur's Dreams', 1935), even Øistein Sommerfeldt's *Hafrsfjord*[10] for narrator and orchestra (as late as 1972) – an exhaustive list would fill many pages.

Irgens-Jensen never took part in any of these artistic ideological debates, although in a sketch-book from the beginning of the 1920s a scribbled draft of a verse offers an ironic view of the belief in a super-national heritage.[11]

The arguments in musical circles were symptomatic of the debate raging in Norway's cultural life as a whole. Some extremists were concerned exclusively with nationalist issues and worked for an isolationist line, believing Norwegian culture inherently superior to anything else the rest of the world could offer. Such provincialism was opposed, fortunately, by many of those who themselves took the national line. It is hardly surprising that, when the Second World War broke out, a section of the hardest isolationists and nationalists associated themselves with the occupying Germans and the Norwegian Nazi party, Nasjonal Samling (National Unification Party),[12] among them David Monrad Johansen. Another who became a Nazi was Per Reidarson, who seemed to have been motivated also by a lust for power. Most of the composers – among them Irgens-Jensen – as well as the overwhelming majority of the Norwegian population opposed the Nazi occupation, more or less actively. Nevertheless, the battle-lines were drawn for a clash of values, the echoes of which can still be felt in Norwegian musical life today.

[9] *Cf.* Grinde, *op. cit.*, p. 299, and Vollsnes, *Modernisme*, *op. cit.*, pp. 225–28.

[10] Hafrsfjord is a small fjord near Stavanger, scene of the final battle in the unification of Norway in around 872.

[11] It can be found in Appendix Two, pp. 330–31, below.

[12] The party which supported the Nazis as a puppet Norwegian government during the War. It was founded in 1933 by Vidkun Quisling – in direct imitation of the National Socialist Party in Germany – and led by him until his arrest, trial and execution after the end of the War.

V
The Passacaglia

While Irgens-Jensen was at work on his Piano Quintet[1] he also began a large-scale liturgical piece for soprano, choir and organ[2] which developed into a purely orchestral work with organ *ad lib*. It was completed the following year with the simple generic title of Passacaglia.

It is characteristic of the composer that he worked most swiftly – and, often, at his best – when he had a deadline hanging over him (as with *Heimferd*, the Symphony in D minor, the *Canto d'omaggio* and the music for his three theatre productions[3]). Even though the Passacaglia was composed relatively quickly, it didn't have quite as hurried a birth, as he revealed in an interview:[4]

> 'When did Passacaglia come into being?'
>
> 'A few years ago. But then it lay waiting for a chance to take part in this competition.'

'This competition' was one which originated with the Columbia Graphophone Company in the USA in 1927 to mark the centenary of Schubert's death the following year. On 28 June 1927 *The Times* published a report 'From Our Correspondent' in Vienna:

> it is proposed to hold a competition for the completion of Schubert's 'Unfinished' Symphony in B minor by the addition of a scherzo and finale.[5]
>
> This competition, for which the world will be divided into ten zones, comprising 26 countries, each with its own jury, will open next September and close in July, 1928. There will be one prize of $750 (£150) and another one of $250 (£50), besides an honourable mention, in each zone, and an international prize of $10,000 (£2,000) for the best of the international scores submitted to the international jury. The competition has met with approval in Austrian musical circles.

[1] *Cf.* pp. 103–5, above.

[2] Mentioned in two articles by Jens Arbo, one in *Aftenposten* on 7 May 1928, the other rather later: 'Filologen som overrasket verden med musikk' ('The Philologist who Surprised the World with Music'), *Norsk Musikkliv*, 1943, No. 1, pp. 6–9.

[3] *Cf.* respectively, pp. 181–87, 213 and 229.

[4] *Bergens Tidende*, 23 January 1929.

[5] At the time all that was known of the last two movements were the first sixteen bars of the scherzo and a little of the trio.

But it met with outrage in the rest of the musical world: the suggestion that anyone might have the audacity to consider tampering with such a masterpiece was considered well nigh sacrilegious, most opinions holding that the existing two-movement 'symphonic torso' was more valuable in itself than any 'synthetic' version completed by another hand. Moreover, it was then generally accepted that Schubert himself had finished working on the score and sent it to the composer and conductor Anselm Hüttenbrenner in Graz as complete.[6]

A month later, on 30 July, *The Times* published a letter from the American Frederick N. Sard, who had already organised that year's Beethoven centenary celebrations and now wrote, from Paris, as 'Director, Schubert Centenary', on behalf of the Columbia Graphophone Company (the British subsidiary of the Columbia Phonograph Company). Sard first explained the division of labour in the organisation of the competition:

> The Gesellschaft der Musikfreunde in Vienna [...] has accepted the artistic trusteeship of the contest for the Austrian zone [...]. For the German zone the Allgemeine Deutsche Musikverein (founded by Franz Liszt) has accepted the artistic supervision. For Italy, the venerable Academia [*sic*] di Santa Cecilia, founded by Palestrina, is the artistic trustee. And in France, it is the Conservatoire National de Musique which has accepted this *rôle*. This trusteeship is being extended in other countries.

He then went on to justify the terms of the competition:

> The plan for the competition was evolved from the study of beautiful precedents. To prevent the expansion of this letter, may I quote the most apposite examples, first from the Schubert works themselves? The piano sonatas of Schubert have been the subjects of various attempts at completion, the most successful of which is that by Krenek. The efforts of Gade and Ludwig to complete the Unfinished are well known;[7] and the latter was performed by the Berlin Philharmonic. Going farther afield we owe it to Sussmayer [*sic*] that the Mozart Requiem did not remain a torso; to Mahler

[6] Brian Newbould has since argued (in *Schubert and the Symphony*, Toccata Press, London, 1992, pp. 202–7) that, having sketched out the scherzo of the 'Unfinished', Schubert went on to sketch out the finale but then adapted it to form the 'Entr'acte' in B minor (and thus in the same key as the Symphony) in his incidental music to *Rosamunde*.

[7] According to Herbert F. Peyser (in 'The Epic of the Unfinished', *Musical Quarterly*, Vol. 14, No. 4, October 1928, pp. 639–60), the German composer Carl Reinecke claimed that the Dane Niels Gade (1817–90) wrote two movements to complete the 'Unfinished' but then made them part of a symphony of his own: No. 8 in B minor, Op. 47 (1969–71), premiered in Leipzig in 1872 – but none of the four movements of Gade's Eighth contains Schubertian material. August Ludwig conducted the Berlin Philharmonic in his own completion of the 'Unfinished' in Berlin on 8 December 1892; it was, Peyser reports, a failure.

> that the Weber sketches are now a unit;[8] to Rimsky that *Boris Godounov* was made an operatic whole, and, perhaps best of all examples, to Mozart and Wagner that the classical perfection of the Overture to *Iphigenia in Aulis*, of Gluck, received a capstone worthy of the structure.

Sard's protests cut no ice, and on 28 December *The Times* featured another report from its Vienna correspondent:

> the original international composers' contest launched by the Columbia Graphophone Company for the Franz Schubert Centenary Year, by which that composer's 'Unfinished' Symphony was to have been finished, has been abandoned. The scheme, it may be remembered, caused much adverse comment. The idea of an international composers' contest is maintained. Its object, however, is no longer the supplementing of the composition named by two movements designed to complete the work. Indeed, music composers are required to produce original symphonic compositions of one or more movements, subject to certain conditions.
>
> The compositions, apart from faultless formal structure, must be marked by the predominance of a vigorous melodic content, and the number of instruments employed must not substantially exceed the measure established by the classical orchestras of Schubert's time.

The ten zones into which the composing world was divided were each to submit three works to the final in Vienna. Logically enough, Norway, Sweden and Denmark formed the Scandinavian zone (Finland, not being a part of Scandinavia, was included with Poland and the Baltic countries). By the deadline on 30 April 1928 (it was extended from 31 March when the change in the terms of the competition stimulated a rush of new entries), the scores of 35 orchestral works – submitted anonymously – had been received in the Scandinavian zone: eight Swedish, sixteen Danish and eleven Norwegian.

Torolf Voss (1877–1943) was nominated as the Norwegian member of the Nordic adjudicating committee.[9] The others on the jury were the Swedish composer Ture Rangström (1884–1947), and three Danish composers: Carl Nielsen (1865–1931), Hakon Børresen (1876–1954) and Ebbe Hamerik (1898–1951 – the son of the composer Asger Hamerik). In an interview given on his arrival home from Copenhagen, where the Nordic jury had met, Voss spoke about the jury's painstaking work and the difficult assessments

[8] The 'Weber sketches' were those for the opera *Die drei Pintos*, at which Weber worked between 1821 and 1824; in 1887 the 27-year-old Gustav Mahler realised the seven numbers that Weber had sketched and added thirteen more of his own composition, based on Weber's themes.

[9] Composer and conductor at the Central Theatre, and a sometime critic for *Aftenposten*; he was later a director of Norsk Musikforlag.

they had to make. Most of the works, he said, were quickly filtered out, but on the third day they were left with six pieces:

> We were already almost certain that the two best works were 'Symphony in C major' and 'Passacaglia', but we did not agree on which of these should have the first prize, nor which of the remaining four should have the third prize. We decided to sleep on it a little. On Saturday morning we continued with the last thorough read-through, with the result that, at lunchtime, we unanimously proposed 'Symphony in C major' as No. 1, 'Passacaglia' as No. 2 and 'Sinfonia per un orchestra piccola' as No. 3.
>
> The committee further proposed that it should be recorded that 'Passacaglia' as an artistic work was wholly on a level with 'Symphony in C major', but that it was thought that the first prize-winner kept more closely to the wording of the prospectus, as his work was a symphony.[10]

From this and other interviews (including one with Carl Nielsen[11]) it might seem that the jury was adhering to the spirit of the original 1927 terms of the competition – and yet there was no demand in the revised terms that the work should be a symphony; only a 'symphonic composition' was required.

As some members of the jury had guessed, it was the Swede Kurt Atterberg (1887–1974) who was the composer of 'Symphony in C major'. The third prize went to the Dane Jens Laursen Emborg (1876–1957) for his *Sinfonia per un orchestra piccola*. It had been very difficult to guess the composer of 'Passacaglia', but Carl Nielsen thought that he must be Norwegian. Voss was surprised to hear that the work was written by an unknown Herr Jensen from Norway, but when the whole name and address was taken from the sealed envelope, he knew straightaway who it was:

> The whole committee, with Carl Nielsen at its head, rose and congratulated me; in the enthusiasm I had to get up on a chair and make a speech for my distinguished countryman.
>
> There was great excitement. I could go to the magnificent closing celebration at Nimb [a restaurant] with a good conscience. The composer of 'Passacaglia' could not have been happier than I was, when, on behalf of Norway, I said thank you for the ovation which was accorded us on the occasion of the Schubert Competition's second prize.[12]

Voss also brought with him a calling card from Ture Rangström, on which he had written: 'Bravo, Irgens!' The rest of the jury had also written their greetings:

[10] *Aftenposten*, 12 May 1928 (evening edition).
[11] *Politiken* (Copenhagen), 8 May 1928.
[12] *Ibid.*

That was good! Carl Nielsen
Da capo. Hakon Børresen
Promises of something great. Ebbe Hamerik
I was happy when the envelope with your name was opened. Torolf Voss

The Norwegian legation in Copenhagen also followed the competition. The ambassador, Emil Huitfeldt, was himself a member of the presidium of the honorary committee and was present at the announcement of the result and the celebration afterwards. On 9 May 1928 he wrote to the Ministry of Foreign Affairs about the outcome:

> Both the Danish chairman of the adjudicating committee, Carl Nielsen, and the Swedish member, Ture Rangström, used many strong terms about Irgens Jensen's composition and were in agreement with the Norwegian member, *capellmeister* Torolf Voss, that within the committee there was much doubt as to whether the first prize should be awarded to the Norwegian or the Swedish composer.[13]

The letter enclosed two newspaper cuttings, in one of which, from *Politiken,* Carl Nielsen also spoke about the work of the jury and about the three compositions:

> As far as the prizes themselves were concerned, the placing of the two first prizes was in truth a matter of taste, for artistically and as regards content, both works were considered equal. We were all very glad that we encountered them and felt we were confronted with something not just relatively good but something really good. The Swede Kurt Atterberg's C major Symphony is a brilliant, beautifully crafted, large-scale work and splendidly orchestrated. It is interesting that, in some places, namely in the Finale, it is akin to Schubert's Great C major, whether or not Atterberg was conscious of it. The cohesion and flow is so vital that it nevertheless feels original. The Norwegian Irgens Jensen's Passacaglia is a very weighty, slightly Brahmsian-sounding work, although outwardly not so colourful, but perhaps of more gravity, one of those works from which with concentration one can draw more and more. It was so much more surprising, as four out of five of us judges did not suspect his existence at all. He appears to be a young man of 30 – he will be welcome among us.[14]

Atterberg received $750 and Irgens-Jensen $250; Jens Emborg had to be content with a diploma of honour.

The Oslo newspapers immediately gave much coverage to Irgens-Jensen's winning of the prize. *Aftenposten* even managed to snatch a conversation with the composer:

[13] J. no.07712UD/1928 (Foreign Office Journal).
[14] *Loc. cit.*

A SUCCESSFUL MUSICIAN

Composer Irgens Jensen on his Passacaglia

[...] 'Would you have taken part in the great Schubert Competition if the Americans had been allowed to offer it for a completion of Schubert's unfinished B minor Symphony?' we asked with journalistic irreverence the young composer, Ludvig *Irgens Jensen*, who has won second prize in the Scandinavian section of this great international competition.

Of course, we received the answer we had deserved: 'Do you really believe anyone other than the Americans would have anything to do with it?'

'And your Passacaglia, can you tell us a little about that?'

'It is basically classically constructed. I thought originally that it would be church music with organ, choir and soprano solo, but I have limited it to instrumental music.

'It is, as the name indicates, variations over a fixed bass. This is interrupted by a fugue, and framed by an introduction and coda. It is serious, "dense" music. Originally I thought I had gone beyond the assignment, because I have used more instruments than were used in orchestral music in Schubert's time.'

'And so now do you hope to be considered at the great decision in Vienna this summer?'

'No, not by any means. I am pleased I have come so far. Just think of the number of entries that were sent in, if here in Scandinavia there were 35. In Germany every single little kapellmeister has probably taken part.'

'Oh, Irgens Jensen's work will certainly become internationally known,' Odd *Grüner-Hegge* interjected. 'It is some of the most important Norwegian music that has been written in recent years.'[15]

The three Scandinavian compositions, together with the other winners from the nine other zones, were sent in to the 'World Final' in Vienna in June. Here Atterberg's Symphony again won first prize, $10,000, giving rise to its nickname, 'The Dollar Symphony'. The second prize went to the Polish-born Swiss composer, Czesław Marek (1891–1985), for his *Sinfonia*, and the third to the Austrian Franz Schmidt (1874–1939) for his Third Symphony. The Schmidt work is especially interesting in conjunction with Irgens-Jensen's style in this work. Nielsen was a member of the Vienna jury, too, where he offered an opinion on Schmidt's score:

The Austrian *Schmidt*'s symphony is extraordinarily proficient, but a little too much influenced by Brahms. It lacks the freshness of the other two compositions.[16]

The Passacaglia is dedicated to Irgens-Jensen's father, whom he described (in a note among his papers) thus:

[15] Issue of 7 May 1928.

[16] Quoted in the *Oslo Illustrerte*, 11 July 1928.

> My father was my best friend, enormously understanding and kind, well-meaning, strict with himself and gentle towards others, and not censorious. A character to look up to.
>
> (He was especially fond of Beethoven, and works with a large span).

In the draft of an answer to a questionnaire (which was probably never submitted) the composer described the Passacaglia as a sort of contrast to his *Tema con variazioni*:

> The work came into existence as perhaps a kind of counterpart to v.v. [the Variations]. The urge to express oneself with a stricter continuous span. I don't remember. In any case in the development there is something [illegible], a contrast to v.v. even though there are, naturally enough, points of resemblance. [...]
>
> I have certainly struggled more than most with form in my works.
>
> I think that what we like to call form ought rather to be called the formal pattern, so sonata pattern, rondo, passacaglia (var. schema).
>
> But in all comp. as in all art, there is something in common, namely the form.
>
> The form is the means through which the artist communicates and, moreover, it is a necessary part of the musical 'material'. [...]
>
> (Ey! I'm going mad with all this talk![17])

In the Passacaglia, then, he chose what he himself called a 'variation-schema' for the work. There is also a large form to this 'schema'. Sverre Lind[18] counts five principal sections both in this work and in the *Tema con variazioni*. In the Passacaglia these passages are quite clear: an introduction, a first section of the passacaglia, which is interrupted by a triple fugue, a second passacaglia section and a coda (Figure 1). Irgens-Jensen himself described the introduction as 'angular'.[19] There is both the 'chaotic' and 'improvisatory' presentation he imagined,[20] and one theme in particular, presented in the bass, which has a characteristically angular shape (Ex. 13). Other themes enter, among them the 'chorale theme', which becomes prominent towards the end. They generally fall into two categories: 'closed' themes (such as the passacaglia theme (Ex. 14), and to some extent the 'pastoral' theme (Ex. 16) and the chorale (Ex. 23[21])) and those where the material is developed further – and the latter, in contrast to the first group, have an asymmetrical construction, possibly a legacy from Brahms. Both

[17] A quotation from the Norwegian writer Ludvig Holberg (1684–1754).

[18] 'Ludvig Irgens Jensen som komponist. En skisse på grunnlag av tre orkesterverker'('Ludvig Irgens Jensen as Composer. A Sketch of the Foundation of Three Orchestral Works'), *Nordisk musikkultur*, Copenhagen, Vol. 3, 1953–54, pp. 111–14.

[19] In the draft of a letter found among his papers.

[20] *Ibid.*

[21] *Cf.* p. 124, below.

Figure 1
The Structure of the Passacaglia

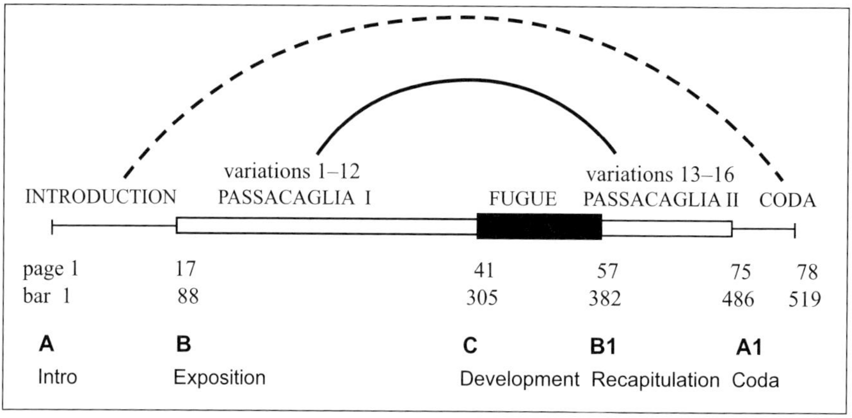

passacaglia sections build on the sixteen-bar bass theme: Passacaglia I has the presentation of the theme and twelve variations; Passacaglia II has four variations. Convention suggests that a passacaglia should be in $\frac{3}{4}$ time, with the theme in the bass. The theme should have an anacrusis and be in the minor key.[22] It should also be symmetrical, since it was originally a dance. Irgens-Jensen's passacaglia theme has all these characteristics.

Ex. 13

Ex. 14

[22] It is commonly assumed that the passacaglia and the chaconne are equivalent forms. Both, indeed, involve variations over a ground bass, conventionally eight bars in length. Initially, though, the passacaglia was in a minor key and in $\frac{3}{4}$, whereas the chaconne was in a major key and in $\frac{4}{4}$, but in practical terms the two forms soon became indistinguishable.

The theme is diatonic, in a Dorian-coloured minor and has much stepwise movement, together with many fourths and fifths; there is only one third. There are a few three-note motifs which constantly recur and give an impression of being sequences. The theme changes somewhat throughout the variations, either through simple changes of interval or through modal colorations, most often caused by use of the Dorian sixth.

The Passacaglia, like the *Tema con variazioni*, becomes a series of character variations which also create a dynamic form of development, or symphonic variation. The transitions between the variations are deliberately blurred by overlappings and shifting of the layers. Polyphony is emphasised from the very first variation, where the passacaglia theme has a traditional counterpoint with contrary motion and complementary rhythm (Ex. 15).

Ex. 15

By the second variation the counterpoint is developed to a 'faux-bourdon' theme, consisting of three different parts which form a common harmonic layer, where some exciting harmonic progressions arise, but which really functions as a broad band of sound that must be seen as a unified layer. This theme, too, is moulded to appear to begin and close in the middle of the variation, thus weakening the strict architectural form of a passacaglia.

In the following variations especial attention is given to the instrumentation and sound. But in the ninth variation an extension is heard: the first theme from the introduction is played as a counterpoint before the tenth variation introduces an important theme on the oboe (Ex. 16); Irgens-Jensen himself labelled it 'pastoral' in his notebook, and both

Sverre Lind[23] and Bjarne Kortsen[24] call it a 'folk tune'. It becomes important in the fugue and in Passacaglia II.

Ex. 16

The fugue develops into a triple exemplar in the Baroque manner, with three themes (the first two are given in Exx. 17 and 18) and a couple of counter-subjects and short toccatas (Ex. 20 is an example of the latter). The countersubject in the winds (Ex. 19), an important short, syncopated motive, presented in fugato, is an inversion of the first part of the first fugue theme. Indeed, if this countersubject is regarded as a distinct fugue theme, too, the fugue becomes a quadruple one. Each fugue theme is presented in the usual way, generally with transpositions of a fifth for the *dux* and *comes* – with the exception that the second theme is always presented in ascending seconds instead of fifths. This theme has already been presented in the introduction (then on cellos, too, as a continuation of the first angular cello theme). The third fugue theme is the pastoral theme (Ex. 16), formerly a countersubject to the passacaglia. The first and second themes of the fugue (Exx. 17 and 18) have most in common with Baroque equivalents, with a distinctive principal motif, a driving rhythm and further motifs which open them both to sequencing and to further development. The pastoral theme is inserted as a contrasting, more evenly balanced element in the overall impetus. Both the first two themes start on the beat and the third theme, too, often loses its anacrusis. In the toccata-like parts of the fugue, a *sforzando* is inserted where the new chain starts, and this syncopated accent contrasts subtly with the more even and on-the-beat principal motif from Ex. 17.

The development of the material is not so much thematic metamorphosis as a kind of germination of themes where new variants arise. Ex. 21, for example, shows how closely the opening of the first fugue (Ex. 21(b); the theme is given in full in Ex. 17) is related to bars 7–10 of the passacaglia theme (Ex. 21(a)).

[23] *Loc. cit.* p. 112

[24] *Loc. cit.* p. 63.

Ex. 17

Ex. 18

Ex. 19

Ex. 20

Ex. 21

(a) Passacaglia theme, bars 7–10

(b) Fugue theme

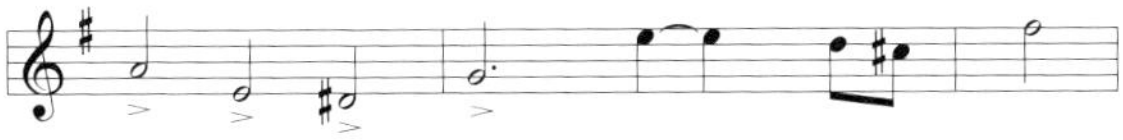

In the large *stretto* all the elements and themes are set against one another; for the most part the texture is a five-part presentation of the theme marked 1F in Ex. 17 plus the remaining themes and the countersubject (Ex. 19) as well as small fragments of other themes added to the contrapuntal weft. The pastoral theme, Ex. 16, is quickly silenced, because it is to have a special place in Passacaglia II, but the rest form a part of a 'contrapuntal knot'[25] where they are pared down to the principal motifs, and where the toccata-like theme, Ex. 20, now has an ascending outline and is both augmented and diminished in order to retain a strong forward movement, to which end a *crescendo* and *accelerando* are also employed.

Passacaglia II is not an anticlimax after this impressive fugue; it is really a continuation of Passacaglia I, the themes of which now appear here in a new perspective, so as to complete the symphonic variation. The passacaglia theme, of course, sits at the bottom of the texture and at the top is the light pastoral theme, Ex. 16. In the middle lies the faux-bourdon theme first

[25] Irgens-Jensen, in his broadcast interview with Torstein Gunnarson in 1969.

introduced in variation 2, the three parts forming one line, an undulating band (Ex. 22).

Ex. 22

Indeed, the four variations of Passacaglia II function as a double passacaglia when both the passacaglia theme (Ex. 15) and the faux-bourdon theme (Ex. 22) go steadily forward, albeit in a dislocated relationship intended to soften the transitions between the variations and avoid the 'chain' character of passacaglia form, abetted by the fact that the faux-bourdon theme appears to begin and end in the middle of the variation. Passacaglia II ends in a sort of transition where both these themes are 'destroyed' and the transition crescendos into a powerful chorale, where the organ enters (*ad lib.*) to strengthen the orchestra (Ex. 23). Here Irgens-Jensen introduces a striking shimmering layer of sound in the strings, almost suggesting Svendsen and the French late Romantics and Impressionists.

Ex. 23

The chorale is modal, harmonised in a homophonic way so that, from a tonal perspective, it underlines something of the unrest which occurs in large parts of the work and which has already been suggested in the introductory cello theme at the beginning (Ex. 14). The development has advanced towards clarification and simplification in the chorale. And the new light now thrown on the listener's experience of the many lines of the fugue and the tight, almost compact movement between the passacaglia theme and the faux-bourdon in Passacaglia II allows the chorale to signal a clear culmination.

But Irgens-Jensen wanted something more, and an ethereal coda follows. It is as if the music 'completely disappears into the blue'.[26] A solo violin and harp lay a characteristic light tone over the whole, under which both the chorale and reminiscences of the passacaglia theme move up in register. The work ends on a bright B major triad.

The inherent conflict between an architectonic form in small units and the dynamic form of the larger constructed units make the Passacaglia exciting as a large form. The tonal structure, with many different possibilities and in many forms, plays a vital part in this effect. As a whole, the work is tonal, that is, it has a central tonic for each section; it is dominated by different types of minor key: both harmonic and Aeolian minor are found, and some parts are coloured by the Dorian mode. In some places the music also sounds as if synthetic scales provided the basis of the music: variable tetrachords can appear. Some of the variations are tonally removed from the central tonic, E, but the tonal centre sometimes moves away from the initial key during a variation. In the fugue, the tonal centre is moved quite frequently and not always to the nearest note or key in the circle of fifths, which is most usual in the variations. In the more developmental parts (and also in the *stretti*) there appears to be a form of polytonality between the parts, which individually can be considered as free-tonal: each has a central note which does not coincide with that of the other parts.

As may be heard, at several of the rest points striking tonal functional cadences are applied, but in large sections the chords are a product of linear thinking. In more apparent note-against-note motion (as in parts of some of the variations) the harmony is modal, as it also is in the chorale. There is a generous use of false relations and of 'irregular' resolutions of dissonances, compared with the 'classical' voice-leading rules. Throughout the coda and in its closing cadence, too, there are non-functional progressions and, as in the chorale, the penultimate chord is a third away from the final chord. Then, as a surprising exclamation point, comes the decisive and closing

[26] *Ibid.*

major chord, which is anticipated only in very short major sections (as in the seventh and eighth variation).

This modally coloured tonality gives the work its distinctive sound. In addition to the characteristic, 'organ-like' instrumentation *à la* Bruckner, it is easy to see that in the sections which proceed note by note there is a rather 'fat', Romantic string-sound (dense and with spicy chords); in the contrapuntal parts and in the developmental sections, by contrast, the mobile, differential colours of the woodwind dominate.

Some of this division is also underlined by time-signature, tempo and rhythm. There is an advancing, sliding movement in the note-against-note parts, almost as in Renaissance *tactus*, where the distinction between duple and triple time is not always clear. This ambiguity also gives the note-by-note passages a peaceful harmonic pulse. The contrast may be found in the $\frac{9}{8}$ metre section of the introduction and particularly in those parts in the fugue where there is a faster pulse or more abrupt rhythms, which also strengthen the impression of the angular and asymmetric themes in the complicated contrapuntal texture. These elements become part of the construction of the form as a whole.

Several revisions to the score were made in 1934–35, before it was published: a few doublings of wind instruments were thinned out and tempi and expression marks were made more precise. There was more reworking when the work came up for publication in a more attractive edition in 1949–50. Irgens-Jensen thinned the texture considerably by deleting doublings. The lowest wind-instruments (bass clarinet, contra-bassoon and tuba) are omitted in many places or written as small notes for playing *ad lib.* A few of the most important melodies were also moved from the woodwind to the strings.

The most drastic change occurs at number 16 in the score, where a new theme appears for the woodwind, built on material from the strings. The new theme now appears as a kind of counterpoint. In the first printed edition the wind had the main theme against a constantly moving demisemiquaver movement in the first violins. The trombones play the passacaglia theme in varied rhythms in the first edition, but in the second edition they are in four even parts.

The Passacaglia, of course, had brought its composer new fame long before the work was first performed. There were plans to have it played at a concert with the Philharmonic Orchestra in Oslo shortly before Christmas 1928, but it was cancelled. Pauline Hall then had the original idea of hiring the whole orchestra for a private concert. She had made an arrangement with the Oslo Philharmonic Society to hold an evening of her own compositions before Christmas, but the concert was postponed until February the next year. Then, possibly because it was too high an economic risk for her alone, she invited Arne Eggen and Irgens-Jensen to take part with a work each and to cover some of the costs.

Hiring the orchestra was expensive: the Philharmonic originally demanded 1,200 kroner but eventually reduced the price to 1,000 – still a considerable sum, but cheap in comparison with what it would cost today. The composers could expect to make some kind of loss; it was more important that they become known and show their profile.

Arne Eggen chose the first two movements from his Symphony in G minor, which had previously been performed at one of the 'Young People's Concerts' on 4 March 1920. Pauline Hall wanted the whole of her *Verlaine suite* performed. Its second movement, 'Nocturne parisien', had also been heard at the Young People's Concerts before, on 30 April 1922. It was natural that Irgens-Jensen should choose the Passacaglia; in any case, he already had the parts ready. Eggen wanted to conduct the two movements of his Symphony himself; Hall and Irgens-Jensen chose Odd Grüner-Hegge to direct their works. The concert was finally fixed for Saturday, 19 January 1929, in the Aula of the University.

Many of the musicians in the orchestra were quite conservative and found Hall's 'French whims'[27] difficult to accept; they regarded Irgens-Jensen's work as radical. One of the wind-players was especially fractious, complaining that in one place his part was unplayable. Irgens-Jensen was able to point to an analogous place in a Bruckner symphony and the musician had to give in.[28]

There was extensive advance publicity in the press: it was something of a novelty that three young composers should dare such a risky economic and artistic venture. As usual, Irgens-Jensen was reticent, although a journalist managed to draw some comments from him:

> 'It is so difficult to speak about music. I well know what I have intended with my work, but if I put it into words I risk dragging it down.'
>
> 'Your "Passacaglia" is, in a way, classical music.'
>
> 'Yes, it has part-writing of the same sort as classical music. It creates a distinctive air. A stronger mood follows in such a form – no, that is not right, I don't want to say anything – just imagine if someone came to you and demanded that in front of a large orchestra you should explain the contents of your last portrait article.'[29]

Saturday was not reckoned to be a good day for concerts – it was rather for the family and the theatre – but the musicians' other engagements left

[27] Per Reidarson, *Arbeiderbladet*, 21 January 1929.

[28] Related by Dagny Irgens Jensen in an interview with the author in 1973.

[29] *Dagbladet*, 17 January 1929.

Pauline Hall, composer and critic, around 1940.

them no choice. As a result the Aula was barely a third full. 'Artistically the concert was a triumph, but the ticket sales only brought in 398 kroner', Hall reported.[30] As might have been expected, Irgens-Jensen's father covered the loss.

The critics were well-disposed towards both the Hall and Irgens-Jensen works and rather more reserved about the Eggen. Monrad Johansen was enthusiastic about the Passacaglia:

> Odd Grüner-Hegge deserves the warmest appreciation. He lent all his artistic will to it, and it was admirable with what convincing authority he elucidated this complicated work, which stylistically, formally and not least spiritually, had something of the loftiness of a cathedral about it.
>
> The performance of Irgens Jensen's 'Passacaglia' was a joyful triumph for all our young Norwegian talent, an encouragement and a light to those who have the fate of our own music close to their hearts.
>
> The spontaneous and sincere applause with which the work was greeted showed that the public, too, had the sensation of being faced here by a great work. The composer was recalled over and over again with the conductor. But do not now let the Passacaglia lie for a year or two before we hear it

[30] In a letter accompanying the accounting after the concert.

again. Our orchestral literature is not so excessive that that would be to our advantage. And here the Philharmonic has an obvious duty.[31]

Jens Arbo was no less receptive:

It is a weighty work and seems completely overwhelming; it must be reckoned amongst the most significant orchestral works that the younger generation of composers in our country has produced. [...] The deep, ethical character of the music is particularly manifested by the introduction of a chorale theme, which gives the coda its particular significance before the music is finally transfigured and rises up into high, light spaces.[32]

Elling Bang set the occasion in a wider context:

the strict rules of the form placed no stress on the listeners; one was swept away and overwhelmed by its imagination and deep spiritual content, which speaks through the notes.

[...] From all sides the concert looked so promising that one was tempted to say that, fundamentally, there is nothing wrong with our musical life, if we could just see to cutting ourselves free from the smothering thicket of dilettantism. The only regrettable thing was that the concert-givers have had to stand outside and knock at the door in all modesty to ask to be let in.[33]

Per Reidarson – widely known for his aversion to any music which smacked of the modern – was the only Oslo critic who was cool in his discussion of the Passacaglia:

One follows this work with interest, even if one is often torn away from the prevailing mood by sudden breaks in the line and abrupt tossings to and fro. Just as one thinks it has finished, it carries on again until it finally closes without any definite ending. In that respect the work remains in a modernist style, but elsewhere there is quite a lot which reminds one of good music. Now and then there are some bars which are absolutely beautiful, but then the composer seems to become frightened that he is not being original enough and retreats into the purely technical once again.[34]

Elling Bang mentioned dilettantes – a controversial theme at the time because of the stipend conflict, among other reasons[35] – and the fight to have new orchestral works performed. The losers from the conservative programming of the Philharmonic Society in Oslo were the young Norwegian and foreign 'radical' composers and the public, which accounts

31 *Aftenposten*, 21 January 1929.
32 *Morgenbladet*, 21 January 1929.
33 *Dagbladet*, 21 January 1929.
34 *Arbeiderblad*, 21 January 1929.
35 *Cf.* pp. 110–11, above.

for the indirect criticism in Elling Bang's and Monrad Johansen's reviews. This very criticism appeared in a reader's letter, signed 'E.', in *Dagbladet*:

> But what does one see these days? Three Norwegian composers, one of whom won a sensational prize in the great international Schubert Competition last year, have to *hire* the orchestra in order to have their works performed. One would have thought that the Philharmonic Society would have *rushed* to secure the prize-winning work for themselves.
>
> It would interest the general public to hear the reason why the Philharmonic Society has found such conduct appropriate.[36]

On 31 January, moreover, the Philharmonic held a purely Norwegian concert, with Johan Svendsen's *Zorahayda*, an occasional cantata by Karl Svensen (1859–1932), *Cavatine* and *Najadene* ('The Naiads') by Alfred Andersen Wingar (1869–1952) and Arne Eggen's *Mjøsen* ('The Mjøsa' – Norway's largest lake), to a text by Hulda Garborg. As a result, a number of critics accused the Philharmonic of helping to make sure that Norwegian musical life remained stuck in 'the quagmire of dilettantism', while 'the Society turns its back on works of high worth'.[37] It may not have been a coincidence that, despite protests from the manager of the Philharmonic Society, it was not many days before a decision was taken to perform the Passacaglia again, and it was heard once more on 7 February.

By then the Passacaglia had already been performed in Bergen, on 24 January; the audience was just as enthusiastic as in Oslo, and the reviews were effusive. The work was repeated three days later. Ture Rangström, one of the jury members in the Schubert Competition in Copenhagen, conducted it at a performance in Stockholm on 27 February 1929, writing to Irgens-Jensen afterwards:[38]

> With greatest sincerity I will tell you that this composition impresses as an expression of a new Norwegian spirit in music. You have, dear Mr. Irgens Jensen, much-prized values and cherished national monuments to clamber over! In your own way. I believe in your career as a composer.
>
> In the Passacaglia you have touched the innermost strings. […]

Kurt Atterberg, a critic on *Stockholmstidningen* as well as the winner of the Schubert competition, was glowing in his review, published the next day. The other critics were also equally positive, apart from the conservative Wilhelm Peterson-Berger, himself an esteemed composer, who referred to Irgens-Jensen as a Danish composer and complained of the Passacaglia:

[36] Edition of 24 January 1929.

[37] *Cf.* Huldt-Nystrøm, *op. cit.*, p. 247.

[38] Letter dated 28 March 1929

> It is lacking a definite plan, a purposeful intention. Much in it captivates the ears and promises spiritual experiences that never materialise.[39]

On 4 November – in a kind of settling of scores, so to speak, for the occasion in 1926 when the *Tema con variazioni* had been eclipsed by Honegger's *Pacific 231*[40] – the Passacaglia was played immediately after *Pacific 231*, the critics this time agreeing that Irgens-Jensen had outshone Honegger.

Grüner-Hegge had a run of outstanding successes with the Passacaglia in Germany. On 23 June 1929 he performed it in Kiel during a prestigious Scandinavian-German week. In another reversal of fortunes Irgens-Jensen this time carried the day over Atterberg, whose 'Dollar Symphony' was also played, with the Passacaglia receiving the critics' superlatives. On 14 November 1930 it was performed by the Berlin Philharmonic in Grüner-Hegge's debut with that orchestra, which he had hired (for 3,500 Deutschmarks) in order to present himself. It was a success for both conductor and composer, although Irgens-Jensen wrote to his father from Berlin a few days later:[41]

> I think myself that the performance was splendid, widely flowing and finely detailed, exactly according to my ideas. But the large and significant majority have scarcely been convinced by Passacaglia. There was none of the spontaneous enthusiasm from the public that we have become spoilt by from previous performances (recently).

The other conductor who helped ensure an international reputation for the Passacaglia was the chief conductor of the Oslo Philharmonic, Issay Dobrowen (1891–1953). Dobrowen was born in Russia and received his musical education in Moscow and Vienna. He was an outstanding pianist and made his debut with orchestra as a twelve-year-old. One of those who was captivated by Dobrowen was the slightly older Stravinsky. When Stravinsky began work on a concert piece for piano and orchestra in 1910, it was Dobrowen he had in mind.[42]

Dobrowen was professor of piano at the conservatoire in Moscow, appearing at the same time as conductor and composer. He emigrated in 1922 and became musical director at the opera in Dresden and later at the Grosses Volksoper in Berlin. When he came to Oslo in 1927, he also had a contract in Sofia.[43] For the Philharmonic Society orchestra and its audience, Dobrowen was a good catch. The conductor Øyvin Fjeldstad, then a

[39] *Dagens Nyheter*, 28 February 1929.
[40] *Cf.* p. 94, above.
[41] Letter dated 20 November 1930.
[42] This was the work that metamorphosed into the ballet *Petrushka*.
[43] *Cf.* Huldt-Nystrøm, *op. cit*, p. 231.

violinist in the orchestra, reported that Dobrowen directed the orchestra completely authoritatively, with a very firm hand, and was very efficient at rehearsals.[44] He showed himself to be adept at using the newspapers to call advance attention to particular works and composers, to the Society – and to himself. And on the platform he had a magnetism and audience appeal which also drew new groups (particularly ladies) to the Aula.

In his choice of repertoire he was quite conventional and preferred to conduct Classical and Romantic music. Naturally enough, he had a particular affinity for Russian music. But he also had a feeling for some contemporary composers. From his very first seasons he presented first performances of modern composers such as Bartók, Hindemith, Honegger, Křenek, Prokofiev, Scriabin and Stravinsky to the public, even enjoying a relatively warm reception, perhaps both because his performances were outstanding and lively and because the works were moderate and had been widely advertised beforehand. Dobrowen also started a series of 'Academic Concerts', where Bach and older music was presented as something almost new, in what contemporary accounts suggest were rather Romantic interpretations. As part of Dobrowen's cultivation of his audience, these concerts were preceded by talks about the works and their composers. But he does not seem to have had the most cordial relationship with new Norwegian music, and it is therefore something of an exception that he went in so whole-heartedly for the Passacaglia.

Dobrowen's hectic conducting career – he was active also on the Continent, in Britain and the USA – created problems for the Philharmonic Society and eventually he chose to resign as artistic director in 1931, although he continued to have Oslo as his home and was a frequent guest conductor; his family lived there, and he had become a Norwegian citizen in 1929. He also sought peace in Oslo to continue his composing activities, although they lessened as demand grew for his services as a conductor.[45]

In October 1931 Dobrowen set out on a long concert tour of the USA, taking with him the music of the Passacaglia. He had accepted an offer to take over as artistic director of the San Francisco Symphony Orchestra from 1931 (a post he held until 1935[46]) and performed the Passacaglia in his first season there. In order to create some publicity for himself, the work and the composer, Dobrowen gave the impression to the press that Irgens-Jensen was an unknown village genius he had discovered, and he took a couple of years off his age:

[44] In a conversation with the author in 1971 and in subsequent discussions.

[45] Dobrowen's output includes a piano concerto, three piano sonatas and a violin sonata.

[46] His successor was Pierre Monteux.

Issay Dobrowen around 1930. He conducted Irgens-Jensen's Passacaglia several times in Europe and the USA.

> It was three years ago that Jensen came to Dobrowen in Norway and submitted this work.
>
> 'I don't know whether it means anything or not,' he told Dobrowen. 'I have had no training in writing; I have taught myself what I know of music. But, if you would be so kind as to look it over I would be appreciative.'
>
> 'This is a remarkable case of genius,' said Dobrowen. 'Young Jensen is only 27 years of age and previous to the writing of "Passacaglia" evidenced no capacity for creative work along this line. He has since written an opera, an oratorio, a trio and a quintet, as well as more than a score of songs.'[47]

This false version of events soon spread to the American press, which responded positively to the Passacaglia.

The following year Dobrowen was scheduled to perform the Passacaglia several times in the USA. The Norwegian international copyright agency TONO and the Norwegian Society of Composers were working at that time to get payments from ASCAP[48] for performances of Norwegian works in the USA. They therefore asked their members to send in information about performances they had had in the USA in recent years. A draft letter from Irgens-Jensen to the Composers' Society gives some details:

[47] *The San Francisco Examiner*, 25 October 1931.

[48] The American Society of Composers, Authors and Publishers, a performing-rights organisation.

> In connection with the request to give information about Norwegian works in America, I would like to report that my orchestral piece Passacaglia (22 minutes) has been performed by Professor Dobrowen a number of times in the course of 1931–32–33. In an interview the professor said recently that he had performed it 20 times in America. To me he has said that it was played four times in the course of one week in New York and that it has twice been broadcast over there.
>
> As to time and place for these performances I only know what I have seen from the periodicals and notes in the music.
>
> 1931: 2 performances in S. F. [San Francisco]
> 1932: Performed in S. F. [18 and 19 November]
> and in New York (8/12 and 11/12)
> 1933: in Philadelphia in February
>
> Yours sincerely, L. I. J.

The concert by the New York Philharmonic on 11 December 1932 was broadcast over the entire United States by CBS and the work attracted some attention. On 23 January 1933 the American pianist Irvin Schenkman, who was on a European concert tour, was quoted by the Norwegian newspaper *Den 17de Mai*:

> And recently a great work by Irgens Jensen was performed in New York, as you well know. It received good reviews. In America they are expecting much from Irgens Jensen.

Two days before the radio transmission in the USA, the Passacaglia – under the baton of the composer-conductor Olav Kielland[49] for the first time – was also broadcast from Oslo to large parts of Europe in the 'Europe Concert Series'. This time, too, it attracted attention and received reviews from a number of countries: Austria, Denmark, Finland, Sweden and Switzerland. The majority were, as usual, positive. Grüner-Hegge conducted the Passacaglia again in Berlin in 1933.

Spring 1934 saw the birth of an international composers' society, the *Ständiger Rat für die Internationale Zusammenarbeit der Komponisten*, with Richard Strauss as president – which later became an element of Nazi cultural policy.[50] On 9 September of that year, at its festival in Venice, Dobrowen conducted a performance of the Passacaglia in La Fenice, at

[49] Kielland (1901–85) studied in Leipzig and Basel (conducting with Felix Weingartner). He was offered the conductorship of the New York Philharmonic in 1939, together with the English conductor John Barbirolli and Polish conductor Artur Rodziński, although the appointment was foiled by the outbreak of war. Orchestral music looms largest in his output, including four symphonies (1935, 1961, 1970, 1977), a *Concerto grosso norvegese* (1951) and concertos for violin (1940) and piano (1977).

[50] The *Ständiger Rat für die Internationale Zusammenarbeit der Komponisten* ('Permanent Council for the International Collaboration of Composers') was a German-Italian forum, launched on Strauss' initiative under the aegis of the *Reichsmusikkammer* and intended as a counterpart to the ISCM, which

an associated concert devoted to Nordic composers. *Aftenposten* gave a full account of this occasion, publishing a letter from the Italian singer Cesare Formichi to his wife, the Norwegian singer Grace Holst Formichi, whose enthusiastic telegram about the performance had also had some publicity:

> Heavens, what a success! The audience stood and waved. Dobrowen was called back again and again. After the concert we went to a restaurant called Taverne. Almost all the critics were eating there. The great music publisher Ricordi asked if he could publish Passacaglia and other things by Irgens Jensen. Dobrowen is to conduct Passacaglia in Rome.
>
> Corriere della Sera writes that Passacaglia is the fruit of an eminently lyrical and deeply impassioned musical nature with the talent to express the noblest and most sublime human emotions in great lines and with powerful strength. There followed a very detailed and to a great extent flattering technical analysis of the work, in which the composer's technical mastery and great wealth of ideas are particularly emphasised. The work attracted enormous enthusiasm in the crowded theatre, where all Italy's most famous musicians were present, together with many great musical figures such as Toscanini, Horowitz, Chaliapin.
>
> The very excitable Chaliapin led the audience's enthusiastic response to Irgens Jensen's work.[51]

By 19 September 1934 Dobrowen was back in Oslo and was met by family, friends and several journalists. *Dagbladet* made use both of pictures of the music director and large headlines on its front page:

> IRGENS JENSEN
>
> Proclaimed as world genius
>
> Three world publishers fight for Passacaglia.
>
> Dobrowen home again
>
> [...] 'I have with me no fewer than three contract offers to Irgens-Jensen. One from Ricordi, one from Förster and one from Senart. Personally, I would stick to Ricordi, the world's largest publisher. But the condition is that Ricordi will have the sole rights to all Irgens Jensen's works, just as every publisher insists on.'
>
> 'And what has this fantastic victory brought you personally, besides laurels and honour?' we finally asked the professor.
>
> 'I have had to promise to play *Passacaglia* everywhere. In November I will direct a series of concerts in Rome, afterwards I go to La Scala in Milan, Turin, Trieste etc. But first I shall be at home for a time, follow the Nordic

---

was held to be too radical; when it became clear that the German Ministry for Propaganda was financing its activities, several countries stopped attending.

[51] Edition of 18 September 1934.

music festival and write my third piano concerto, which I hope to finish soon.'[52]

Some sceptics suggested that Dobrowen must be exaggerating the enthusiastic reaction to the work, but the contemporary Italian reviews bear him out. Further confirmation came from a less welcome source, the notorious anti-Semitic musicologist Herbert Gerigk,[53] writing in *Die Musik:*

> Dobrowen is an admirable routine conductor, but as a Jew he was not exactly suited to conduct the Scandinavian music. – A '*Rhapsodie*' by the Norwegian *Bjarne Brustad* is misconceived folklore. A Romantic Norwegian native art that nowhere achieves great form, an art which becomes asthmatic if it breathes deeply. The echo of the beginning of the Siegfried Idyll was indicative of the whole manner of the work. On the other hand one gained the best impression from *Ludvig Jensen* (likewise a Norwegian). Here is an expert at the task. For all the classical touches he is also a Romantic. Out of the linear writing a harshness of sound is born, which is not disturbing. His *Passacaglia* is in any case brilliantly constructed. With a wind chorale, which since Bruckner is no longer difficult, he finally achieved a roaring success.[54]

One year after these successes, the pianist Vladimir Horowitz was interviewed on a visit to Oslo:

> *Toscanini enthusiastic about Irgens-Jensen*
>
> [...]
>
> 'Do you know any Norwegian modern composers?'
>
> 'No.'
>
> 'Definitely not?'
>
> 'I have only heard of one. Jansen. Irgens-Jansen or something like that.'
>
> 'Irgens-Jensen, where do you know him from?'
>
> 'My father-in-law, Toscanini, talked about him. That was at home in Milan; he had read through a "passacaglia" and was very taken with it. "A great talent," he said. I remember it quite clearly. I also had the feeling that he spoke about performing "Passacaglia" in New York. But I won't put my head on the block for it.'[55]

I have been unable to find out if Toscanini ever performed the Passacaglia. But the dualism in the work – with both French and German elements of style and expression – is matched by the contrast in approach between the

[52] Marie Fearnley in *Dagbladet*, 19 September 1934.

[53] Gerigk (1905–96) was the compiler, with Theo Stengel, of the *Lexikon der Juden in der Musik* (Hahnefeld, Berlin, 1940), the foreword of which claimed that 'The purification of our cultural, and thus also musical, life of all Jewish elements [...] has succeeded'.

[54] Herbert Gerigk, *Die Musik*, XXVII/1, October 1934, pp. 46–49. In the June issue of the previous year *Die Musik* had published a special issue entitled 'Das neue Deutschland', marking its conscription as the official musicological organ of the Nazi regime; Gerigk became its editor in 1937.

[55] '-m' (probably Hans Jørgen Hurum), *Norges Handels- og Sjøfartstidende*, 2 November 1935.

two conductors who were its early champions, Dobrowen and Grüner-Hegge. Although, unfortunately, no recording of the Passacaglia by Dobrowen seems to have survived, their many recordings show a difference in attitude towards music in general, which, according to the conductor Øivin Fjeldstad[56] and a number of commentators, was also reflected in their approach to the Passacaglia. Dobrowen, it seems, saw the passionate aspect of the music, the sacred elements and the Romantic intensity which, according to the sources, through him and the orchestra sounded brilliant and direct, whereas Grüner-Hegge brought out the lofty, perhaps somewhat aristocratic aspect and rather laid emphasis on the inner tension and construction which smoulders powerfully under the surface. And both were correct, each in his way – all that and more is to be found in this sterling work.

[56] In conversations with the author.

VI
Heimferd

Immediately after the first performance of the Passacaglia Irgens-Jensen began a huge undertaking which would attract at least as much attention: the cantata *Heimferd* ('Homeward Journey').

The Christianisation of Norway had begun in the ninth century, but it is the Battle of Stiklestad in 1030 – where Olav Haraldsson, king of Norway from 1015, defeated an army of local warlords – which is seen as the crucial event in the conversion of the country from Norse religious beliefs. Although Olav fell in the battle, his local canonisation a year later[1] ensured him a quasi-mythical status as the founder of Christian Norway.[2] In the later 1920s, as the 900th anniversary of Stiklestad approached, it was seen as an ideal opportunity to celebrate the Norwegian Church, and to view its growth and development in an historic perspective. Some commentators were anxious that this event should not be a purely internal matter for the church, arguing strongly that the St Olav anniversary should instead be a truly national affair, and so in June 1928 the Ministry of Education, Culture and Church Affairs therefore decided to hold a special cantata competition, to take place in two stages, the first to establish the texts to be set, the second for the music.

The competition for the text was announced in the press on 31 October 1928, with a tight deadline for the submission of entries – 15 February 1929; a total of 56 manuscripts was received nonetheless. The members of the cantata committee met in March to judge the texts, which were considered anonymously. A submission headed 'Gloria in excelsis deo' was chosen, although a draft labelled 'Eystein' also received many plaudits, the committee concluding that it 'deserved to be performed'; indeed, a minority preferred it, since it was more typical of a church cantata. 'Gloria in excelsis Deo' turned out to have been written by Olav Gullvåg, a well-known author born in Trondheim. 'Eystein' was written by the journalist Heming R. Skre[3] from Haugesund.

[1] Pope Alexander III confirmed the local canonisation in 1163.

[2] For more information on the St Olav myth, *cf.* pp. pp. 146–48, below.

[3] Skre, born in 1897, had worked as an organist near Haugesund, and in 1929 was a journalist on *Haugesunds Avis,* before he later moved to *Gula Tidend* in Bergen. He also wrote other literary works and translated the Old Norse lay, *Geisla*. During the Second World War, Skre was arrested and sent

Olav Gullvåg, who won the competition for a cantata text for the St Olav Anniversary in 1930

Olav Gullvåg (1885–1961) had wide experience as a newspaperman. He became editor of the left-wing newspaper *Norig* in Skien in 1912, turning it from a weekly into a daily paper, and in 1921 took over the editorship of *Gula Tidend* in Bergen, western Norway's leading outlet for the movement for New Norwegian[4] and a mouthpiece for the interest of rural communities. In 1929, though, he resigned the post: his editorial work had been exhausting and he wanted to have more time for his own writing. His work on the cantata text may have given him new inspiration, too, and the belief that he could win standing as a writer. In 1930 and 1931, indeed, Gullvåg received a

as a 'Nacht und Nebel' prisoner to Germany, where he was shot in 1943. (The 'Night and Fog' decree, issued by the Nazi authorities on 7 December 1941, ordered the arrest of 'persons endangering German security', who were not to be executed immediately; they simply vanished without a trace. Over 6,000 prisoners, largely from Belgium, France, the Netherlands and Norway, disappeared in this manner.)

[4] After the long Danish rule of Norway (until 1814) the dominance of the Danish language continued in print and on stage. In 1848 the philologist Ivar Aasen (1813–96) published a grammar and a dictionary systematising a rural Norwegian language. This 'New Norwegian', also known as *landsmål*, has the same roots as Danish and Swedish and was used and promoted by some radical intellectuals and politicians as a way of enhancing national awareness. It was accepted as one of two official languages by the end of the nineteenth century, gaining ground especially in schools and churches in rural areas. The other official form of Norwegian, *riksmål or bokmål* ('Book Norwegian'), moved away from its Danish roots and is used by 85 per cent of Norwegian schools today.

government stipend for authors and he and his family spent those two years in Italy and Germany.

Gullvåg's most important collection of poetry, *På viddene* ('In the Mountains'), came out in 1934 but it was a series of novels with subjects from the Norway of the 1700s onwards that brought him real fame. The first book in the series, *Det byrja ei jonsoknatt* ('It Began One Midsummer Night'), came out in 1937 and went straight into several editions. In 1939 the novel was translated into German and within five months the publishers had sold over 250,000 copies of the German edition – perhaps because folk-historic writing (especially from the 'Aryan' north) was fashionable in Germany at that time. In the same year *Det byrja ei jonsoknatt* was translated also into French and Hungarian.

On 3 April 1929 the cantata committee had the two winning texts published in a number of newspapers, immediately issuing an invitation to members of the Society of Composers, among them Irgens-Jensen, to compose music to one of them. For this competition a prize fund of 4,000 kroner was set up, which the committee could share out as it wished, 'unrestricted by the prizes in the literary adjudication already undertaken'. The deadline set for 10 January 1930 was later extended to 25 January, since it was held to be too tight. In spite of the little time available (nine months), seven large-scale works were entered, four to Gullvåg's text and three to Skre's.

While the composers worked at their drafts for the cantata (between April 1929 and January 1930), an aversion to both the selected cantata texts began to spread, in the country at large but especially in Trondheim. The opposition came largely from three groups: the speakers of standard Norwegian (*riksmål*) who opposed New Norwegian and saw a bias in the choice of two texts in New Norwegian (*landsmål*, from the rural districts) and none in *riksmål*; members of ecclesiastical circles who considered the cantata texts too dramatic and insufficiently religious, especially the section dealing with the Battle of Stiklestad in Gullvåg's text; and the fiercest opponents, a group of Trondheim citizens who were infuriated that Gullvåg should be one of the authors – he had written some harsh words about the language politics in the city of his birth, Trondheim, which he wanted to re-christen Nidaros, the old Norse name of the city and the medieval diocese covering all of Northern Scandinavia, Iceland, Greenland and the northern British Isles.

The conflict between the two forms of the language lies behind the dispute over the name of the city. In an official act of 14 June 1929 the national parliament – as a part of an ongoing process of Norwegianisation – had determined that Trondhjem, the official name of the city which had a Danish ring to it, should now be changed to Nidaros. But the overwhelming majority of the population of the city was against the change. An *ad hoc* group, the Trondhjem Society, was formed 'to rescue the city's name and reputation'; people met in mass gatherings and demonstrated against the decision. The organised opposition in Trondheim culminated in a large public meeting in June 1929 when 20,000 people, around sixty per cent of the population of the city, met to protest against the parliamentary decision, which indeed was revoked in 1931, when the city was named Trondheim.

Gullvåg had stepped into this debate on Saturday, 8 February 1930, with a stern article on the front page of *Dagbladet*, which argued that the entire anniversary in 'that city which has no name' should be cancelled. In another article in *Dagbladet*, 'St Olav's Day and the Norwegian Church', on 25 February 1930, Gullvåg emphasised Olav Haraldsson's historical role in uniting the nation and creating a strong state, and he attacked the church for trying to make the anniversary into a purely religious event.

Amid this controversy came the announcement of the winner of the music competition, the adjudication having been made by the cantata committee, reinforced by the organist and composer Eyvind Alnæs and the conductor Odd Grüner-Hegge, both nominated by the Norwegian Society of Composers. A third member was then added: the critic Jens Arbo. The composer Arne Eggen had withdrawn from the committee at his own suggestion: it later transpired that he was one of those who had submitted an entry.[5]

After several meetings the committee recommended awarding a first prize of 2,500 kroner for the entry with the motto 'Heimferd' ('Homeward Journey'), and a second prize, 1,500 kroner, for 'Tre prosesjoner'('Three Processions'), both to Gullvåg's text. When the envelopes containing the names of the composers were opened, it emerged that Irgens-Jensen was responsible for 'Heimferd' and Eggen for 'Tre prosesjoner', the oratorio which later became known under the name *Kong Olav*. The recommendation was dispatched to the Diocesan Board, which approved it at its meeting on 13 February and announced the result on 14 February.

The statement of the committee (written up by Alnæs, Arbo and Grüner-Hegge) on *Heimferd* is also enthusiastic:

> The cantata is a broad-scale work, through-composed in all sections, grandiose in construction, noble in form and in all its spirit of religious character. [...] In particular it should be emphasised that a deep, consistent perspective and an inner unity are attained because the important thematic elements and characterising motivic material are organically developed and combined in mutual regard to the text and the music, not only within the individual sections, but throughout all the movements. [...]
>
> One would not hesitate to characterise the cantata as the most outstanding that has been produced in our country in recent decades in the area of

[5] *Cf.* note 105, on p. 102, above.

epic-dramatic passion-like cantatas and to consider the work the obvious one to take first place at the religious musical celebrations at the St Olav anniversary this year.

[…] the composer has firmly kept a religious basic tone throughout the whole work and in a way which shows the composer's deep ethical and religious relationship to his subject very favourably. […]

The religious musical feeling is placed in a musical-historic perspective and recreated with a loyal sympathy towards our church by the pure style of church music. For example, the choruses 'Te Deum' (in the 1st section), 'Sanctus' (2nd section), 'Kyrie' and 'Gloria' (3rd section) and the use of the chorale in the various sections.

The composer has clearly delineated the national-historical character of the subject in the Norwegian character of the music and the striking treatment of the lyrical, epic and dramatic, which is illuminated by rich imagination. The part-writing is supported by simplicity and clarity, where masculine strength is no less well-drawn than the lyrical gentleness in the melodic elements. The composer, with his talent for illuminating the text by discreet illusion-awakening effects, has avoided every feature of theatricality, empty effects and lyrical banalities. Through a well-constructed crescendo in the last section, the poem is elevated to pure, bright heights and closes with the words 'lead us to Christ', by which the concept of the work is crowned in the most beautiful manner by a large-scale fugal hymn.

The value of the cantata beyond the generally short lifetime of an occasional cantata will certainly ensure it a monumental place in Norwegian music and make it, religious as it is – in our opinion – worthy to be performed at the first cantata evening on 29 July.[6]

The Diocesan Board recommended 'that the cantata with Irgens-Jensen's music be performed […] as a church concert during the celebrations'. The arguments over language, names, nationalism and the church continued nonetheless, and *Heimferd* was drawn into it all. On 27 February the Concert Committee for the celebrations in Trondheim sent a letter to the Diocesan Board stating:

[…] The Concert Committee considers the mood in the city so heated that we find we have to ask the honoured Diocesan Board to request the Ministry to abandon the performance of Irgens Jensen's cantata in Trondhjem. Irgens-Jensen's splendid composition is and will be, even for the more sensible Trøndelag people, solely Gullvåg's cantata [… and he] has exacerbated the already confused situation, to such an extent that in the opinion of the Concert Committee, in the event of a performance of the cantata, one would

[6] Quoted in Oluf Kolsrud, *Olavsfest 1930. Minneskrift (Norvegia Sacra*, Vol. X), Oslo, 1937, pp. 349–50. The style seems to be that of Jens Arbo; *cf.*, for example, his review of Irgens-Jensen's Passacaglia, quoted in part on p. 129, which contains almost the same use of words and imagery.

> have to be prepared not only for a passive demonstration on the public's part but also an active one.[7]

The very next day the Diocesan Board wrote to the Church Ministry, enclosed the Concert Committee's letter and recommended that a performance of Irgens-Jensen's cantata elsewhere should be seriously considered. The Minister of Church Affairs, Sigvald Hasund, wrote to Irgens-Jensen on 22 March to ask if it would be possible to arrange the cantata for a performance by limited forces. The composer replied two days later, writing that, after consideration of both the artistic and technical aspects, he found that he could not do so. On 31 March, therefore, Hasund concluded 'that any thought of the performance of Gullvåg's and Irgens-Jensen's cantata during the religious celebrations must – also with regard to the question of the expense – be abandoned'.[8]

> After a suggestion from the Diocesan Board it [the Ministry] gave its consent to there being on 29 July, instead of the cantata, a lecture by Professor Fredrik Paasche about St. Olav, suitably framed by choral music.[9]

This decision was incomprehensible to many people outside Trondheim. The Oslo newspapers immediately took up the debate, ridiculing the chauvinism of the citizens. Gullvåg's cantata was strongly defended in the New Norwegian newspapers and those of the Left. In Trondheim, though, there was a spontaneous outburst of joy when the decision became known: the citizens thought that they had won one of their skirmishes with the authorities in Oslo in the war to win back their 'own' city name. But battle continued: on 15 April *Dagbladet* was able to report triumphantly that the Oslo Philharmonic would perform *Heimferd* in Vår Frelsers kirke ('Our Saviour's Church') in Oslo in November.

The Oslo premiere should have been conducted by Issay Dobrowen, but there were changes to these plans: the venue was moved to the University Aula and the conductor was now to be Odd Grüner-Hegge; the date for the first performance was set as late as Monday, 1 December 1930, to allow as much time for rehearsal as possible.

Two days beforehand *Aftenposten* carried an article about *Heimferd* and the expectations that had been raised before the public dress-rehearsal. The paper reprinted a large picture of Irgens-Jensen and a flattering report on the 36-year-old composer and the enormous amount of work he had invested in the rehearsals before the first performance:

[7] Quoted in Kolsrud, *op. cit.*, pp. 357–58.

[8] Quoted in *ibid.*, p. 48.

[9] Quoted in *ibid.*, p. 48.

> For the composer, there has been a very great strain with the rehearsals of the work, in which he has taken part by playing the piano at choir rehearsals, attending orchestral rehearsals and at night correcting the parts, etc.

His reaction to the cancellation in Trondheim was quoted two months later:

> It was certainly best it happened as it did with the performance of the cantata in Trondhjem [...]. The rehearsal time was extremely short, and a less-than-good performance is worse than no performance [...].[10]

Tidens Tegn also picked up a few words from the composer and Grüner-Hegge. Interviewing Irgens-Jensen was clearly a difficult exercise. He was asked to describe this modern music:

> 'Modern...? No, not a bit!'
>
> 'It is distinctly linear music', the conductor Mr. Grüner-Hegge joined in, 'thematic, melodic music. Strong fare, naturally. We are served the whole Battle of Stiklestad in its full glory with the din of fighting and the well-known battle-song in strict time: Fram, fram kristmenn, korsmenn, kongens menn alle... [Forward, forward men of Christ, men of the king, soldiers all...], a battle between light and dark, paganism and Christianity.'
>
> 'Indeed, it was exactly that which struck me so strongly', says Irgens-Jensen in his quiet way. 'And as the background to this battle amongst the people, this powerful struggle between doubt and the need to believe, King Olav's powerful regal character appears clearly [...,] a figure, who is also full of contradictions and who is developing, but with the powerful peace and divinity which are associated with his character. The concluding fugue, the final note from Stiklestad for combined choir and orchestra, sounds: "for han berre vilde – no veit me det visst – oss føra til Krist" [for he only wanted – now we know for certain – to lead us to Christ].'[11]

On 28 November *Morgenposten* published another interview:

> 'I call the cantata a dramatic symphony with the title "Heimferd". The word modern I cannot stand. It is a catchword. Let us rather distinguish between good and bad, genuine or artificial music. And "Heimferd" is tonal, that is to say, a reaction against the modern. Fanaticism so easily goes in these so-called new directions, one becomes blinkered and so values are thrown out of the window.'
>
> 'Was Gullvåg's text so inspiring?'
>
> 'Yes, absolutely. It was clear, concise, straightforward, dramatic, and the conflict is brought to life in the characters. I have, of course, kept to the text and have tried to make a musical relationship with leitmotifs. Not so that the leitmotifs are contrived, they came by themselves, or', says Irgens-Jensen laughing ironically, 'from a lack of inventiveness. Of course, that's not what

[10] From an interview by Theo Findahl in *Adresseavisen*, 24 January 1931.

[11] *Tidens Tegn*, 29 November 1930.

I think. In short, I have tried to find my way to a unity, with the orchestra as the connecting link.'

'So this is your largest work?'

'Yes, at any rate that I have had time to finish, but it was a hard task as the time was short – only nine months.'

'Is it typically Norwegian?'

'I suppose the reviewers and all the others will decide that.'

The composer had no time for more. [...]

On Saturday, 29 November, *Dagbladet* presented a full preview of the work by its music-reporter Elling Bang and printed Gullvåg's text in its entirety. In addition it featured Irgens-Jensen as 'The Week's Profile', in an interview with Marie Fearnley – unarguably the best from the period, both in terms of revealing his personality and as a report of his music and career, and parts of it are reproduced elsewhere in this book.[12] He recounts his enthusiasm for Gullvåg's text:

> To begin with I had a few reservations [...]. But after I read it I was struck by the poem's humanity and tremendous dramatic form. What did it matter then if I was sometimes taken aback by a word I did not know. For me the atmosphere and the music were there.

But he dismissed the religious arguments against the work:

> 'What do you think about criticism of Gullvåg's text from conservative Christians?'
>
> 'I think it has been meaningless. Why should a dramatic conflict necessarily be un-Christian? Just think of the Passion Plays! They were dramatic enough and yet no one calls them profane. And think of all the image-symbols of evil powers of which we have such a wealth in Nidaros Cathedral. Are these un-Christian? No, the fact is that religious art today is paralysed by mannerisms, in our time we find it difficult to express religious feelings. We lack the naivety and perhaps also the contact with the church.'[13]

In addition, his sister recalled,[14] he drew parallels between parts of Gullvåg's text and the highly dramatic parts of Bach's *St Matthew Passion* and the dramas and church plays of the Middle Ages, which were not liturgical either but still had their place in the church.

It is King Olav's life – as described by Snorre Sturluson[15] – which forms the framework for the text. And, like Snorre, Gullvåg wanted to look at the events in a wider national perspective – not only as a political chronicle but

[12] *Cf.*, for example, pp. 261 and 273–74.

[13] Mais (Marie Fearnley), 'The Week's Profile', *Dagbladet*, 29 November 1930.

[14] In an interview with the author, c. 1975.

[15] Snorre or Snorri Sturluson (1179–1241), historian and writer of *Heimskringla*, the chronicles of the kings of Norway.

also as an expression of ideas and attitudes – with political consequences. In a long letter[16] to Irgens-Jensen after a performance of *Heimferd* by the Philharmonic in 1961, Gullvåg wrote that he was amazed that King Olav had been selected for a church anniversary:

> I wrote the cantata manuscript [...] almost as a protest against a conventional view. [...] It was King Olav who was the unifying point and who has become the object of the most we have of myth-building in the time from the year 1000 onwards, until we had our own great international writers. And I thought, as I still do, that this is a precious inheritance, that it was well worth all the St Olav's Day bonfires which are burned in this man's honour. And he deserves that his memory be upheld by Norwegian writers and artists. The times we are living through today are not kind to a cultural heritage of this sort. It is all the more important that those who see the danger in throwing overboard all the 'un-modern' know their duty: being a hero has a cost.

Gullvåg's text reflects the saga style in its monumental New Norwegian gravity, through his choice of form, use of words and rhyme-scheme. The opening male chorus offers an example of the literary style of *Heimferd*:[17]

Dagane dimmest	The days become shorter,
og døkkast kvart bil,	each moment grows dimmer;
råkalde rimast	bitter-cold hoarfrost
rustene til –.	clings to the branches.
Balder er burte,	Balder is gone,
på Ringhorn brend.	on Ringhorn burnt[18]
Nana hev vorte	Nanna[19] has been
åt Nåstrand send.	to Nåstrand sent.[20]
Gudane sit kalde	The gods sit shivering
kring Gagnråds bord, –	around Gagnråd's[21] table,
Idun åt Ivalde	Idun[22] returning to Ivalde,[23]
yver Iving fór.	crosses the Iving.[24]

16 Dated 29 April 1961.

17 The English translation here is by William H. Halverson for the CD recording on Simax PSC 3109.

18 I.e., cremated. Ringhorn was the name of Balder's ship.

19 Nanna was Balder's wife

20 Nåstrand is the shore of the dead.

21 Gagnråd was another name for Odin.

22 The goddess of spring.

23 Ivalde, a dwarf, was the father of Idun.

24 Iving is the river between Åsgard, the home of the gods, and Jotunheimen, the home of the giants.

Vesalt hev det vorte, –	Wretched has it become,
dagen er døkk.	the day is gloomy.
Balder er burte,	Balder is gone,
teken av Tøkk.	slain by Tøkk.[25]

The atmosphere and old-fashioned language which pervade these four strophes are as striking now as they were in 1930. But there were no fewer than eight words on this first page in the programme notes from that first Philharmonic performance which required an explanation. Some of the old Norse gods' names were – and still are – largely unknown and there were also many difficult New Norwegian words which even New Norwegian speakers found outdated and unfamiliar. In his writings Gullvåg normally used a conservative New Norwegian but here aspired to a 'saga flavour' by using many archaic, unusual words and having frequent recourse to Old Norse strophic forms which lay emphasis on, for example, internal rhymes through assonance and alliteration.

The contrast to this 'saga' tone lies in the use of Latin, the language of the church, which came to Norway with Christianity. The texts were selected from the Ordinal of the old Gregorian Mass, the 'Kyrie' and 'Gloria', and, from the Office, the 'Te Deum', which from the seventeenth century onwards had an important function as a hymn of thanksgiving after a military victory. In this Norse context the Latin texts have a subtle and exotic effect, but it is hardly liturgical.

Gullvåg also takes up the old idea of Olav as Norway's eternal king, 'Rex perpetuus Norvegiae' ('Konge skal du vera der i æva' – 'You shall be King there in eternity'), which was an important aspect of popular belief, writing and religious worship in Norway in the Middle Ages. Olav became a symbol, both of the new faith and of a new national feeling, the patron saint who could be worshipped and who could rally national forces. The text also has many other symbols, all of which hang together. Thus the sun becomes a symbol of the new faith; it brings new life (spring) – as also, for example, Demeter in ancient Greek mythology. But at the same time the figure of Balder, the 'white god' of the old Norse sagas, is alluded to as a sacrifice since he was killed through the intervention of the demi-god Loki. Balder, whom Gullvåg calls 'that good god', is perhaps a late addition to the corpus of myth, and it seems that the European Christ-figure may have influenced how he was viewed in Viking times. After Ragnarok (*Götterdämmerung* in Wagner's dramas), where the mythology describes the destruction of the world in a last conflict between the gods and the forces of evil, Balder will eventually rise again and lead the gods in the battle against evil. Olav's death

[25] Another name for the evil god Loki.

also stands out as a kind of sacrifice – even one of expiation – allowing Gullvåg to link him with Balder and, indirectly, with Christ.

Although Irgens-Jensen was faithful to Gullvåg's text, he was obliged to consider the overall span of the music. In his desire to avoid episodic construction, he created both form and line by responding to the large forms of the separate sections, at the same time creating unity by using short and pithy leitmotifs which fall into two clear main types: those of light and those of darkness – although, of course, 'light' motifs can be distorted to achieve a negative effect, to become an anti-motif. At times his handling of leitmotifs recalls Wagner's practice.

The most important of the few sources that offer guidance through these motifs is, of course, the composer's own incipits, found on the cover-sheet of a copy of the piano version preserved in the Norwegian Music Collection at the National Library in Oslo. The Collection also contains transcriptions of a contemporary interview with the composer and a radio talk, both by Jens Arbo. These three sources make it possible to draw up a 'catalogue' of some of the most important motifs with corresponding extra-musical connotations.[26]

Gullvåg's cantata text falls into seven sections:[27] 'Advent', 'Kongen' ('The King'), 'Fråfallet' ('The Desertion'), 'Kongen i utlæg' ('The King in Exile'), 'Heimferd' ('Homeward Journey'), 'Stiklestad' and Postludium.

The 'Advent' section is pervaded by an atmosphere of impending gloom. It is the time of pagan disintegration – now that Vegtam (Odin) and the white god (Balder) are both gone, there is confusion and uncertainty among men, despondency and doubt, a conflict between the new and the old, between the new and old faiths, between light and darkness. The sombre mood is dominated by a bass figure in the Phrygian mode. Yet the mood is transformed almost entirely when the tenor (representing good) enters with 'Hævare var Herren som Håkon og Olav sette oss til stemne' ('More splendid was the Lord with whom Håkon and Olav let us meet').[28] The music quietens down, the note-values become longer and a religious atmosphere is invoked, with the use of modal keys (a sort of A Lydian and C sharp Aeolian), and this part closes with a plagal cadence.

A tenor describes the sorry state of the old religion: 'there is no joy or life among the gods'. A pagan priest-chieftain, sung by a bass, responds with a call for a sacrifice to them and sings that 'Kanskje kjem Balder att' ('Perhaps Balder will return'), that is, if the old rites are honoured. The 'Christian' tenor continues his description of paganism with an impetuous

[26] *Cf.* Vollsnes, *Modernisme på norsk, op. cit.*, pp. 424–30.

[27] Irgens-Jensen omitted Gullvåg's prologue, 'Inngang'.

[28] Håkon (the Good) and Olav Tryggvason were earlier kings who failed to Christianise Norway.

ascending line accompanied by the ominous chromatic 'Ragnarok' motif (Ex. 24). Ragnarok was thought of as the final battle at the end of time when everything, including the gods, would perish. The 'Ragnarok' motif is heard in the brass, in glaring contrast to his description of the Lord who 'shone like the sun' (the 'sun' motif, Ex. 25) and thus marking the distance between the two religions. The bass takes up the ascending line, but here it is used to express his despair that Vegtam is gone and to invoke the Norns, the old visionary goddesses; one of them, Urd, could perhaps bring change. Instead, it is Urd's sister, Skuld ('that which will be/come', that is, the visionary), who enters. In a dramatically high register she prophesies the defeat of the old faith: 'Mundilfare's daughter' (the sun, the light and good, the new faith) will win and renew the world – a prophecy of the new, bright and warm religion which comes with a new spring. In the orchestra, the Sun motif (Ex. 25) – diatonically derived from the Ragnarok motif – is shaped into a complete form for the first time. Against Skuld's presentation of the Sun motif there is an obligato oboe solo as counterpoint.

Ex. 24

Ex. 25

The choir's 'Longing' motif, treated polyphonically, clears the way for the Yggdrasil motif (Ex. 26), Yggdrasil being the 'world tree' – always green – with its roots in the three worlds, its branches stretching out all over the world and its top above the heavens. But contrast comes with a homophonic call from the chorus to the terrible wolf, Fenrir, the son of Loki, and the use of the diatonic version of the Ragnarok motif (Ex. 24); after all, there is only a short distance between the sun and Ragnarok both in mythology and in this music. The chorus asserts that everything will rise again in Hodmimer's grove[29] and the Sun motif will be victorious, as can soon be heard in the music.

[29] The place in Norse mythology where a man and a woman survive Ragnarok.

Ex. 26

Here in the 'Advent' section the Sun motif changes to a fanfare motif (Ex. 27). It is further developed into Ex. 25, which also has a variation signifying the Yggdrasil ash-tree, and this sun-motif is developed further into a 'faith motif' in the 'Kyrie' section of 'Stiklestad'.[30]

Ex. 27

In 'Advent' Irgens-Jensen uses the orchestra – continuously accompanied by the choir – as a unifying element; the dark motifs representing paganism are dominant, but interspersed variants of the sun-motif predict that light will win through; and, indeed, final victory is won at the end of the work. In terms of construction, this section can be seen as a sort of double rondo, where the orchestral sections become a first ritornello, framing the whole, and the homophonic choral parts a second ritornello; the soloists then provide episodes of a sort.

The next section, 'Kongen' ('The King'), deals with Olav Haraldsson's arrival in Norway. Christianity is set against paganism and the power of darkness in dramatic manner when the King appears to the people, who acclaim him and praise his many good qualities. One who is loyal to the old ways stands against Olav for both political reasons and because of his new faith. He mocks the King's radiant vision and denounces him. He is revealed as King Canute's man[31] and Olav proclaims the hard punishments he will use against those who will not follow the new faith and who go against his power. One will shall prevail: mighty Canute's, or the 'real' king's. Olav then explains his visions of the strong but gentle God who comes with the light. Everyone is invited into the church. The section acquires a brighter, gentler tone as the bishop and the people celebrate mass.

'Kongen' is introduced by the orchestra, which presents the King as the sovereign, the earthly power (Ex. 28) – together with one of the pagan motifs. The King is acclaimed as a hero from his time as a viking, but the

[30] *Cf.* p. 153, below.

[31] King Canute (Knud) 'the Great' (995?–1035) was the Danish (and English) king who fought to be king of Norway as well. He conquered Norway in 1028, largely by bribing Norwegian noblemen.

Ex. 28

struggle between light and dark, Christianity and paganism, is intensified dramatically now that the King himself is finally appearing in Norway.

The music mirrors the harsh contrasts and juxtapositions of the text. The King is both 'gentle' and mighty, and so is God, in the bishop's summons to enter God's house. The King is also ruthlessly determined to win – by force, if necessary. While a kind of Mass sounds in the background – a Te Deum (Ex. 29) and Sanctus, together with the sun motif – the king explains his vision for the new land.

Ex. 29

In 'Fråfallet' ('The Desertion') the King, betrayed by his countrymen, has had to flee the country. It is Great Canute who prevails and Olav has become 'varg i veum' ('a wolf in the sacred places'), the Old Norse expression for an outlaw. There is unrest in the land.

In the introduction the most important light and dark motifs are presented again in a polyphonic orchestral prelude, including the Great Canute theme (Ex. 30). The tenor, King Olav's man, asks for the King. The

Ex. 30

bass answers with scorn and derision; quarrelling and fighting arise.

In 'Kongen i utlæg' ('The King in Exile'), the choir relates that King Olav is sitting in Gardarike (the Russian kingdom of Novgorod) in a depressed state of mind: 'Det gustar så gruste i Gardariket / um ein som i einsemd sit' ('Fierce gales blow in Gardarike / around one who sits in solitude'). The King asks that his icebound land may find the light and he is gnawed by doubt: 'Var eg for veik for verket, Herre?' ('Was I too weak for the task, Lord?'). He seeks support from God and in return has a vision of Olav Tryggvason.[32] He wakes again to belief in his task and in his Christian mission. Bjørn Stallare, the King's marshal, comes from Norway and asks on behalf of the people that he return to be victorious and give the land a new spring. Although he is troubled by doubt, God's goodness and the growth of light gain the upper hand and the music ends with a new form of the Sanctus in the choir.

'Heimferd' ('Homeward Journey') follows *attacca*. The King has raised a new and enthusiastic army and returns to Norway. The encounter with Norway, its people and its nature give him new confidence and faith; he has visions, with both lyrical and religious images. Jens Arbo described the music in an introduction to a printed version of the text:[33]

> The Homeward Journey is portrayed by a horn tune, a fiddle gently playing a *slått* [Ex. 31] leads us home to Norway, several instruments gradually fall in; one hears hoofbeats and the tramp of 'hundradtals hestar og kongsfolk hæve' ['hundreds of horses and the splendid king's men'] who appear, according to the description sung by the choir and the depictions of nature in the orchestra. The King is silent. He is thinking of the land as it often lay before him in the morning sun. The King's melody itself is gradually replaced by the march motif which now follows the choir, together with the nature depictions from the orchestra. Evening comes. The King sets up camp.

Ex. 31

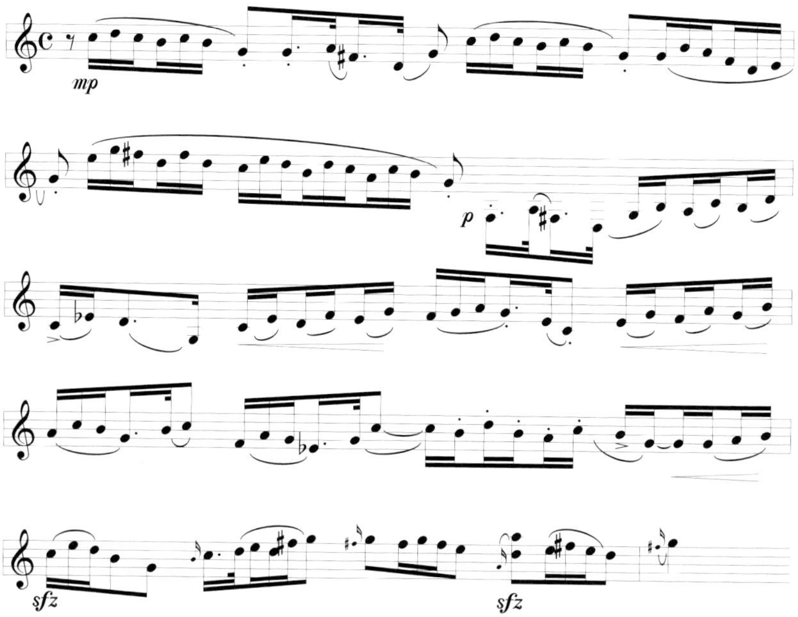

[32] Olav Tryggvason, king of Norway (995–1000), made the first real attempt to Christianise Norway.

[33] Manuscript in the Jens Arbo collection, Norsk musikksamling, National Library.

Outwardly, 'Stiklestad' is a description of the battle. It begins at dawn and follows the advance of the farmers' army, the call to action before the battle, the battle itself and King Olav's death.

Before dawn a Matins of a kind is celebrated (Gloria and Kyrie) before Tormod Kolbrunarskald greets the day and wakes the army with the old 'Bjarkemål':[34] 'Dag er på himlen komen' ('Day is dawning in the sky'). The final words of the ballad are repeated by the choir: 'upp til ljos og til liv' ('up to light and life'), and husky blaring horns from far away warn of the advancing mighty yeoman army. The battle begins and the war-cry (which is derived from the Sanctus motif) is heard: 'Fram kristmenn, krossmenn, kongsmenn alle!' ('Onward, Christ's men, men of the cross, king's men all!') The dark motifs of the farmers' army converge with the bright ones which characterise the King's army. Over the tumult of battle the King is heard singing: 'Fred vil eg lysa yver landet mitt / so langt eg kan. / Han som held vegen til himmelen open, / vil me skal vinna med reine våpen' ('I will proclaim peace over my land / as far as I am able. / He who holds open the way to heaven / wants us to win with pure weapons'). The dark and light motifs are set up sharply against one another as the orchestra depicts the battle. It ends with light motifs in the minor key, before the dark ones appear in the basses: the king has fallen.

The introduction to the Postlude give praise to the qualities of the King, which are only fully understood after his death. Then he is victorious. Through his death he finally was able to lead the people to salvation. Directly out of the din of battle and the King's death a simple folksong-like chorale rises: 'I blodet hans blømde' ('In his blood there blossomed': Ex. 32[35]). It closes in the major with what Olav wants: 'oss føra til Krist' ('to lead us to Christ'). In the fugue which follows, the chorale motif dominates interpolations of the dark motifs in the winds, and finally, in a texture of contrapuntal motifs from the lyrical section and the light motifs, the chorale is heard again with full choir and orchestra. The brass which had previously intoned the dark, minatory motifs, join in, both with motif fragments from the chorale and a 'Kongsdråpa' (a laudatory poem in honour of a king). Olav has been victorious through his fall. In the last bars, after the chorale, the King's great vision is sounded for the last time: he is triumphant in death.[36]

The music of *Heimferd* is completely tonal, even if it does not always adopt the usual harmonies and progressions of the conventional major-minor

[34] The 'Bjarkemål' is the 'Old Lay of Bjarki', an old-Norse poem, which Gullvåg presents in the version by Snorre Sturluson.

[35] *Cf.* p. 156, below.

[36] *Cf.* Irgens-Jensen's letter to Bishop Berggrav, pp. 162–63, below.

system. There are many phrases with church-mode characteristics, most frequently within the minor-mode tonal sections. Smaller areas dominated by the Phrygian mode are found; Lydian fourths are heard; and melodic phrases and chordal cadences coloured by the Mixolydian mode also appear. The use of such modally inflected phrases gives large sections of the composition a deliberately archaic character. Apart from the deliberate contrasts in 'Kongen', there are fewer abrupt modulations and transitions here than in Irgens-Jensen's earlier works.

The chordal material and chordal progressions are basically tonal, linked to a central tonality in their overall scheme. The concluding cadences in particular adhere to classical tonality, although there are more plagal and Phrygian cadences than is usual in major/minor tonal music. In general triads dominate the composition and are kept in diatonic progressions, but there is also some use of more compound chords and chords where the added notes do not accord with the passing notes or other standard types of dissonance of classical counterpoint; they thus add extra colour. There is also a moderate use of bare fifths and pedal points.

The entire work abounds with the well-formed melodies characteristic of the composer; they are to be found in all strata of the music, frequently connected to some of the leitmotifs. Indeed, it may be partially misleading to identify separate leitmotifs, since they rarely function alone; more often they are a part of a longer thematic context or of the counterpoint, and can contribute to melodic sequences in versatile, flexible lines. Most melodic lines are well balanced (except where, for contextual reasons, they are supposed to be hurrying or restless) although, perhaps because the light will win the final victory, they tend on the whole to ascend.

In general the second becomes the dominant melodic interval, although the ascending fifth is very frequently to be found, sometimes with additional notes filling out the interval. Sequences of fifths also frequently appear in association with modulations. Irgens-Jensen tends to keep the melodic fourth in reserve, perhaps to underline the Lydian when it finally appears. Thirds are very prominent in the 'sacred' parts. The 'Gregorian' melodies used here in the 'sacred' passages have not been traced to chants known in any of the traditional sources of Gregorian liturgical music; Irgens-Jensen appears to have devised them himself.

There is little use of chromaticism, but it can appear in the inner parts, most often in association with some of the dark motifs or warnings of some threat or other. False relations appear quite often because of sequences of chords in contrary motion.

As in Irgens-Jensen's earlier works,[37] there is ample use of polyphony, but the polyphonic passages in *Heimferd* are contrasted with more frequent, and longer, stretches of homophony. The use of homophony seems to be determined by the text; longer narrative sections with several performers and those where the text does not have a dramatic purpose are frequently written homophonically; on several occasions, indeed, Irgens-Jensen seems to write in a recitative style to get through the text as quickly as possible and resume the musical argument. There does not seem to be any demonstrable difference in his treatment of the light and dark motifs; both types are deployed in polyphonic and homophonic textures alike.

The chorale at the end is given twice, first as a soprano solo (Ex. 32(a)) and afterwards set for full choir (Ex. 32(b)), supported by the whole orchestra, which enters contrapuntally with the victorious light motif. The two versions are harmonised differently; in the second (in the lower of the two systems in Ex. 32, where it has been altered rhythmically to allow a direct comparison with the first) there is a degree of simplification, although with the addition of some obvious colourful chords.

In every episodically constructed 'scene', Irgens-Jensen tends to retain the time-signatures throughout a whole section, generally using predominantly symmetrical time-signatures, like $\frac{3}{4}$ and $\frac{2}{4}$ ($\frac{6}{8}$ in triplet form), although he will also use an asymmetric one, such as $\frac{5}{4}$, to characterise a complex situation. In some places he has interesting unexpected hemiolas, and there are constantly breaks or shifts through the use of syncopations and accents on normally unstressed beats.

There is a continuous pulse in most of the music: the metre is easily recognised, although the German bar-dominated phrasing and rhythms and understanding of tempo is not always present. In this mix Irgens-Jensen often uses feminine endings, weak cadences on the off-beat. It is not always as important that the accent immediately follows the bar-line as that it follows a natural declamation of the text.

Irgens-Jensen stated repeatedly that *Heimferd* was not a 'St Olav oratorio' or a cantata but a 'dramatic symphony'. And the work does attain symphonic form through its consistent development of motifs and themes, which give it a cyclic character. It is often the orchestra which articulates the dramatic turns of *Heimferd*, preparing or changing the mood, often at the entrance of a new character, but also suggesting both the dark (paganism) which rules and the light which wins, thus providing a kind of running musical commentary, as Irgens-Jensen himself acknowledged.[38]

[37] *Cf.* the *Tema con varizioni* and Passacaglia, pp. 86–98 and 119–26, above.

[38] *Cf.* the interview in *Morgenposten*, 28 November 1930, cited on pp. 144–45.

Ex. 32(a)

It is the orchestral sections which provide the setting for the drama, which create the moods and give the appropriate colour and, of course, present the leitmotifs of the different characters. The orchestra can also vary parts of the material in repetition, in contrast to the repeated material in the vocal sections, which appear mostly in connection with the building-up of larger forms (for example, in the construction of the two 'Mass' sections).

The choir has more of a function of 'the crowd', the turba in Bach's passions, which can comment on the action or impart a mood, though it

Ex. 32(b)

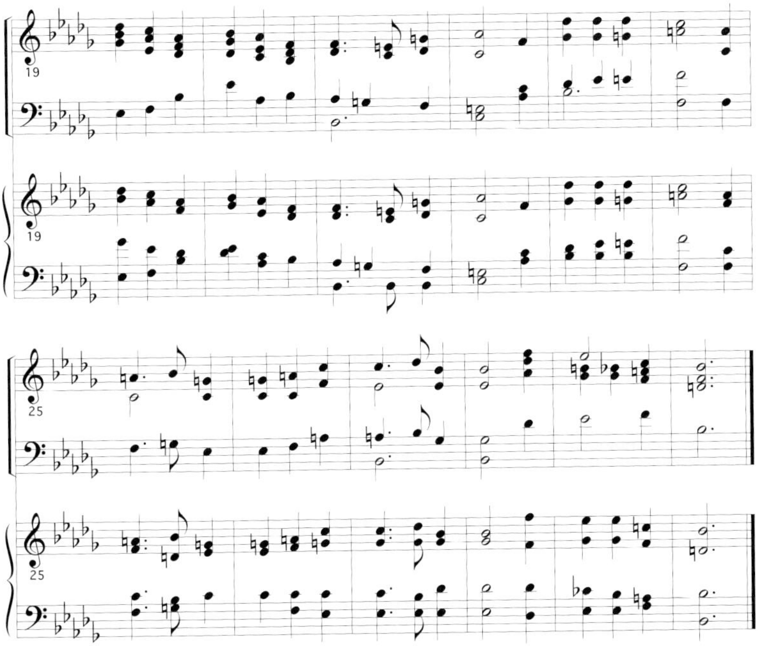

can also drive the action forward, especially in the 'Stiklestad' section. In general, the choir is used in two ways, according to the type of text: in the Latin sections (and in the closing chorale) there is a sacred atmosphere, both in the text and the notes, with more use of modal features in both melody and harmony; but in the Norwegian passages, the choir can often be used very dramatically, with excited interpolations and driving rhythms. The choir is usually used homophonically in the 'pagan' sections and in the most 'Gregorian' or 'liturgical' texts, while the polyphony is reserved for the context of religious motifs and the sun motif.

The characters of the soloists are drawn fairly concisely. As bearers of the leading leitmotifs, they represent attitudes, forces both within and outside human frameworks. In the first section it is the tenor who stands for good and light, while the bass represents the dark forces and the old faith; of the male soloists, the more important 'sceptics' and 'pagans' are put in the bass register. And Irgens-Jensen often has a harp sounding around the 'gentle' King.

The text has phrases that could directly suggest word-painting or pictorial depiction. But Irgens-Jensen, not wishing to call attention too strongly to the descriptive aspect of single words or phrases, does not follow these leads. Instead, his aim is to create a large symphonic context through variation, expansion, alteration and repetition. An example is the music to Skuld's visions of 'Mundilfare's daughter', the sun, whose music is transformed via the more sacred Yggdrasil motif and becomes, by way of the 'Kyrie', the 'folksong-tune' at the end. Thus he subtly demonstrates that there will be unity: Christ is musically associated with the best of the old faith, and the good, the new faith, is victorious in the end.

At the same time, the motifs and the different sides of the conflict become mutually illuminated through contrast. The tenor sings of Olav as the gentle ruler, 'Gjævare var herren' ('More splendid was the Lord'), against which immediately follows the bass's forthright 'Vålyndt det verte' ('Dangerous it will be'). A similarly striking contrast comes when the underlying dark motifs in the 'Battle of Stiklestad' feature as counterpoint and 'emblems' in the 'sacred' fugue. There is also a characteristic emblematic use of fanfares (and horn) both for the King and his forces, and threatening tritones which indicate disaster.

In *Heimferd* Irgens-Jensen achieved a masterly balance of strictness of form and style with expressive freedom. He mixes homophony with more freely linear counterpoint and contrasts this free counterpoint with a very strict fugue. He integrates a solemn church style with depictions of nature and a *slått*. In spite of these contrasts – or perhaps because he had succeeded in integrating such disparate material – Irgens-Jensen regarded the work as an indivisible unity. He allowed only the chorale of the closing sequence to be published separately. In a draft of a reply (dated 3 January 1939) to Professor August Werner at the University of Washington in Seattle, who had enquired about the possibility of excerpting out some sections for a church performance, he responded that he was very doubtful of the desirability of separating parts of *Heimferd*: he wanted to keep the large context and the overall symphonic construction, and so it would be wrong to prepare a short Mass from the score.

The Oslo Philharmonic usually gave its final rehearsal as an open matinée on the Sunday before its Monday concert. That given on Sunday, 30 November 1930, was completely out of the ordinary: it was highly unusual to find a report of a final rehearsal like that published in the morning edition of *Aftenposten* of 1 December.

> The hall was filled to the last seat. [...] And as the work proceeded the concert turned out to be a unique musical event. From section to section through the movements of the work, the atmosphere in the hall increased and made its effect felt time after time. And after the final great climax for combined choir and orchestra, where the text concludes, a storm of applause broke out so tremendous that rarely has anything like it been heard in the Aula. The audience rose spontaneously from their seats and clapped – the masterly

conductor Grüner-Hegge, the work's other participants, and especially the composer when he appeared on the stage. In this ovation to Irgens Jensen lay a warmth and spontaneity, which showed how strongly the audience was struck by his work. He had to appear before the audience time and time again.

The official first performance was at least as marked a success as the final rehearsal. Arne van Erpekum Sem wrote of the 'effusive reception' and 'storm of applause' which erupted, 'particularly towards the composer, who had to come forward countless times to receive for the tempestuous ovations. This was an unforgettable experience for everyone present on this remarkable day in Norwegian music history'.[39] Grüner-Hegge also received high praise, as did the soloists. The critics agreed that the premiere was a wholly special event in Norwegian musical life. *Tidens Tegn* carried pictures of Irgens-Jensen and Grüner-Hegge and a triple headline

A remarkable day in Norwegian musical history
Irgens Jensen's St Olav Cantata was performed for the first time yesterday
The most significant and profound work in our modern music

The review, which was written by van Erpekum Sem, is long and comprehensive and contains not a single adverse word:

> The day will remain as a memorable day in Norwegian musical history. Irgens Jensen's large-scale dramatic symphony signifies a high point in the output of young Norwegian composers and is without comparison the greatest, most significant, most profound work that modern Norwegian music has produced in recent years. [...]
>
> [...] At the first performance yesterday Irgens Jensen's dramatic symphony made an overwhelming impression. There is a richness in this music, a flight of fantasy, a holy inspiration, which thrills and inspires. Viewed purely technically, the composition is an unalloyed masterpiece. One does not know what one should admire most – the composer's great inventiveness in the choice of characteristic, vivid, valuable, beautiful themes or his superior technical mastery and the symphonic development of the thematic material. The composer works a lot with leitmotifs and already in the first section brings in many of the most important themes, with which he depicts the powerful contrasts and conflicts between paganism and Christianity, between old and new. [...]
>
> [...] in its unending richness and beauty and truth and genuineness it beckons with elemental power just as enthusiastically to the layman as to the expert. That was fully shown by the audience's effusive cheering both at the final rehearsal on Sunday and at the concert yesterday, which were both given to full houses.[40]

[39] *Tidens Tegn*, 2 December 1930.
[40] *Ibid.*

David Monrad Johansen also wrote enthusiastically:

> The performance yesterday, which was a sensational success, must be accounted a happy occasion in Norwegian music. [...] We were to encounter a work where separate talents and strengths somehow flowed together, where the rich material was placed under an overall vision and was gathered together with impressive authority. And why does one think the enthusiasm showed itself so spontaneously both at the final rehearsal and at the concert yesterday? Because everyone individually greeted its values with the secret joy of recognition. Country and people, history and nature, clarity and enrichment were in the music. And in this connection let me also mention the performance itself, which not least contributed to strengthen the happy expectations one can now have for a future for Norwegian music.[41]

He was not the only reviewer to sound a nationalist tone; so, too, did Sverre Hagerup Bull:

> And this music is entirely our own. It is Norwegian in every note. Not because of any mannerism or by virtue of any system. But the very spirit in it is Norwegian and makes every melody and every rhythm familiar and dear.
>
> For Irgens Jensen himself this work is something of a homeward journey. He has previously written brilliant works and he has also given us the joy of recognition that music with a Norwegian character gives us. But he has never so easily and so unaffectedly found himself and been able to give such direct expression to his personality. Nor has he previously in any large work been so thoroughly and genuinely Norwegian.[42]

Even the conservative critic Ulrik Mørk in *Nationen,* who had shown little fondness for Irgens-Jensen's radical tendencies around 1920, was especially struck by *Heimferd* and wrote a long panegyric review:

> But it is not just in the form that Irgens Jensen creates an epoch in our musical literature. He has used a fortuitous opportunity to write a work that points far, far beyond the single occasion, a monumental work that sparkles with talent, and which at several points elevates itself to brilliant heights, a work which shows us a 36-year-old Norwegian musician as a master of modern counterpoint. He has constructed the work on a wholly national basis, but has nevertheless not felt himself bound by any definite style. He uses leitmotifs at salient points in order to evoke this and that definite idea – e.g. the Ygdrasil-motif, which comes again later as an expression of the religious side of the King's task. His motifs often have unusual impact and he places them against one another in a masterly way and intertwines them to powerful contrasting effect. [...] But then we are led towards the sublime third movement, Stiklestad, with the magnificent morning mood in the orchestra,

[41] *Aftenposten*, 2 December 1930.
[42] *Dagbladet*, 2 December 1930.

the [solo] quartet's 'Gloria in excelsis', the choir's 'Kyrie eleison', the tenor's 'Bjarkemaal' and the interaction between these different groups. Afterwards, in sharp contrast, there follows a tone-picture of the yeomen army which gathers on the plain, and finally the clash and the terrible tumult of battle, which ceases suddenly at the fall of the King. And in immediate continuation thereof, the postlude with the hymn to the cathedral. Here all the motifs are encountered in the mighty fugue and all the forces appear together in a resplendent crescendo towards the ecstatically moving culmination in the final chord itself.

Irgens Jensen has orchestrated his work with Wagnerian splendour and with admirable knowledge of the value of the different instruments. Most of the solo parts are also excellently prepared; but he demands much too much of the baritone soloist. The choral movements sound superb, especially the 6- and 8-part 'Sanctus'. But he places very great demands on the capabilities of the choir, both in the many difficult entries and in the many chromatic passages; they are at times written quite instrumentally.

They themselves say that the rehearsing of this work has been a gigantic task for all the participants.[43]

In church circles, too, there was enthusiasm for the work. In *Norsk Kirkeblad* an editorial appeared after the first performance in Oslo:

The dramatic symphony by Irgens Jensen, with a text by Olav Gullvåg, is a large-scale work which we, from a religious point of view, have reason to be pleased about. The Christian substance in the work has been underlined by the music, so that in the concert hall it appears like a proclamation of Christianity, which powerfully leads to this 'For he only wanted, now we know for certain – to lead us to Christ.'

[…] We now ask, if this is a religious work, whether it would be possible for it to take root inside Nidaros Cathedral and inside the church generally. It would certainly be true of this work that, if it appears strongly Christian in the concert hall, then the paganism will appear more powerful in the church. It is a question of whether we are strong enough to let the paganism loose in the church without damage. It is a question of whether we in the church can accent the procession at the King's homeward journey from Gardarike, with the national flavour picked up by the fiddle tune. It is a question of whether we would like to hear the Bjarkemål in God's house.

The work as a whole has no religious style – neither the words nor the music, although there are parts that have a noble church style with a Norwegian tone. But if the work is honest and true, then, in my opinion, we should not be afraid to take it into the church. In a way it comes to us as a gift from outside, and it would be rather hypocritical to refuse the gift, as if we do not want to acknowledge our history inside the church. The main thing is its inclination; and that is not in doubt: it is decidedly Christian. It hardly

[43] *Nationen*, 9 December 1930.

> applies to our own time; but it is up to us to make something from what we have experienced in our church since the battle at Stiklestad.[44]

Bishop Eivind Berggrav showed a similarly positive attitude in an article in *Kirke og Kultur* ('Church and Culture'), written the day after the first radio broadcast of *Heimferd* in January 1931:

> Even on the radio, the experience of this work was so powerful and clear that one will never forget it. It must strike one that there, in the very emotion of St Olav's Day last year there was something that could really only be said in music. And here it is! If it had come in the middle of the anniversary celebrations, it would really have triggered a deep historical and religious sentiment in the minds all over Norway.
>
> The music was almost free of operatic jargon; it seems original and creative at precisely the most difficult points, the truly religious ones. Here the composer could afford to forsake all echoes of known religious melodic motifs, which would have been safe effects, and instead he everywhere gives a new spiritual and congenial tone to the words. The music was a contemporary experience in music of the past brought up to the present; it rose above what we are otherwise plagued by in all restoration work: the inhibited imitation lacking personality. And at the same time there was no 'modern' rush for effects – the whole was peaceful and natural.
>
> Indeed, that is how it sounded on the radio up here in the north to an anything but authoritative music-reviewer. [...] The composer has also simply rescued the poem.
>
> As a poetic work alone, this cantata on the whole would never have been anything great. Apparently, it may have been accepted in the belief that Olav Aukrust was the author. The mountain dialect and pine-root words in it point in that direction. But from now on the words will be one with the music and live in it. And the words deserve that; there is such a warmth and glow in them that flames leap up as soon as the music fans them.
>
> The whole – with or against the will of the Norwegian church – has become a splendid Christian opus, a folk-church monument which may live on for many generations.
>
> Tromsø 20.1.1931
> Eivind Berggrav[45]

This sympathetic and conciliatory stance from one of the church's bishops obviously pleased Irgens-Jensen. The draft of his answer was amongst his posthumous papers and here he expands on his own attitude to the work:

> Dear Bishop Berggrav,
>
> It was a great pleasure for me to receive your kind article on 'Heimferd'.

[44] *Norsk Kirkeblad,* Nos. 26/27, 26 December 1930, pp. 603–4.

[45] Eivind Berggrav, 'Olavs-Kantaten', *Kirke og Kultur,* Vol. 38, Oslo, 1931, pp. 120–24. Berggrav (1884–1959) was later celebrated for his refusal to obey the edicts of the Nazi occupiers of Norway.

Thank you very much!

That it came from a spiritual quarter was even more precious to me, as I have harboured an anxiety that my music could offend those who expected church music in the usual sense. It had of course to follow the dramatic conflicts in the text between old and new, paganism and Christian belief, and could therefore not have a sustained church style.

One thing I will touch on more closely: the end. My opus really closes at 'Oss føra til Krist' ['lead us to Christ']. After the soprano has sung the folksong-like hymn: 'I blodet hans blømde – ' ['In his blood there blossomed'], the orchestra begins a fugal passage which gradually brings in several of the earlier principal motifs. This section then runs into the hymn which this time is sung at full strength by the choir with the fugal passage as a counterpoint in the orchestra.

By this elaboration I sought to achieve a similarly monumental ending to that which the author had aimed for through the last section. The words 'Og myrkret rømde' ['And the darkness fled'] etc. were difficult for me to set to music – among other things because I think that there is still much to fight against in the world, inside the church, too. In the agitated fugato I have tried to suggest that the evil spirits of all time are present, and so must be fought anew. The fugue theme (a remodelling of one of Olav's motifs) continually cuts victoriously through the mass of notes. Suddenly there is silence. Then the 'varg-i-veum' ['outlaw'] motif warns from the distance, the 'darkness motif' appears once more, until Olav's great vision chases it away. Immediately afterwards the chorus comes in with the hymn, as everyone's affirmation of the soprano's bright announcement.

Finally, may I apologise for this lengthy explanation, which undoubtedly has most interest for me personally, but which I felt I ought to send you, since you have shown my work such rare great attention.

Yours respectfully and gratefully L.I.J.

The first performance was national news and reports from the first performance and summaries of or long quotations from the reviews were printed in newspapers all over the country, many as early as 3 December. On 8 December 1930 *Den 17de Mai* in Oslo, with barely disguised malice, printed a headline about the reaction of the people of Trøndelag:

'Some pages of black notes'

Grüner-Hegge, just you dare come to Nidaros with the cantata!

Indeed, *Heimferd* did not have a performance in Trondheim Cathedral until 1937. It was an outstanding success, both with the critics and the audience: the squabble over the city name and the language quarrel were by then a distant memory, and it was the artistic qualities that were assessed.

On 3 December 1930 M. M. Ulfrstad, the critic of *Morgenposten*, who had always been very well-disposed towards Irgens-Jensen's music, published this brief appeal:

> The St Olav Cantata will be performed in the Philharmonic on Thursday. I can do nothing more than earnestly urge everyone to go and hear Irgens Jensen's and Gullvåg's splendid work. Do not miss this opportunity.[46]

The public followed his instruction and flocked to secure tickets. Although it was the third performance in a week, *Dagbladet* wrote on 4 December that 'It looks like being sold out. Obviously!'

The following day, Friday, 5 December, the newspapers were able to report that the King and Queen and the Crown Prince and Princess had attended the performance in the Aula the previous evening. The public interest was unprecedented: people went two or three times to hear the work and more concerts had to be put on. The papers continued to recommend *Heimferd*, too; for example, *Nationen* on 6 December wrote: 'No-one can have a better reason for a bus trip. For one will be the richer for a great experience'. And *Morgenposten* on 5 December continued Ulfrstad's appeal: 'Go and hear it, all those who can'.

One of the few longer interviews Irgens-Jensen ever gave appeared on 5 December in *Oslo Aftenavis*:

> The composer with the great break-through: Irgens Jensen.
>
> A conversation about composing now and in the old days, and a warm defence of Oslo.
>
> Heimferd's composer on the move.
>
> [...] Today Irgens Jensen stood outside in his garden in Fastingsgate like a picture of living anxiety. It is certainly not the thought of Saint Olav's tragic end at Stiklestad which occupies him, but what he should do with all the flowers! For today he is moving to Nordstrand, but the removal vans do not have the everyday appearance with chests of drawers, laundry baskets and a waving palm on top. No, they are like a swaying procession of flowers...
>
> However, we sit down amongst the remains of his large drawing-room to talk music. But first inevitably it is about paintings. The walls are strewn with duly chosen items by Henrik Lund, Deberitz, Thaulow, Henrik Rom[47] and others. And with that little slanting and shy sideways look over his spectacles, Irgens-Jensen confesses that he himself has painted.
>
> 'Do you think there is any close relationship between music and painting?'

[46] *Morgenposten*, 3 December 1930.

[47] These names indicates Irgens-Jensen's taste for contemporary art: Henrik Lund (1875–1948) was especially famous for his portraits, Per Deberitz (1880–1945) was an Impressionist trained in Paris and Frits Thaulow (1847–1906) another Norwegian Impressionist, known especially for his landscapes; the short-lived Henrik Rom (1887–1919) was condemned to a sanatorium because of his tuberculosis.

'Basically no. Music is music. Other types of art can be imaginative and rewarding, like painting, like literature.'

'Like Gullvåg's St Olav cantata?'

'Yes, exactly. That had a power in it which simply drove me out of my laziness.'

'Was it terribly hard work?'

'Not at first. The music seemed to come by itself. I had it clear after a month, but the working-out was difficult. And nine months is quite a short time, because it has become more difficult to compose now than in the old days.' [...]

'Do you believe that the St Olav drama will be performed in Trondhjem?'

'I sincerely hope so, but nothing seems of any use. The conflict over the names Trondhjem and Nidaros, they are just the stools I have fallen between. One does not have any kind feelings about any of them. I am glad we have a large and broadminded city, where each and everyone can breathe freely. Olav Aukrust once wrote about Oslo as the "cess-pool". This is wrong and ungrateful. A great and distinctive talent brought up in a lonely country area risks being frozen in. In any case it is good to have the large town, with its responsiveness and gratitude to those who succeed and its conciliatory indifference to those who do not. The clever people in small cultural communities should be the first to understand that.'

Heimferd had no less a success after Christmas and the New Year than it had in Advent, with long queues of hopeful people building up before further performances.

The newspaper *Den 17de Mai*, which was prominent in the nynorsk (New Norwegian) movement, made much of the fact that *Heimferd* was to be broadcast live from the Aula on Monday, 19 January, at 8.00pm, preceded by an introduction by Jens Arbo. Broadcasting was still a relatively new medium in Norway; by New Year 1931, only 83,000 licenses for receivers had been bought, most of them in and around Oslo.[48] Around the country, technical equipment was quickly assembled so that communal hearings of this special concert could be arranged in meeting halls, much of the audience doubtless attracted as much by the chance to experience the new technology as by the music itself. A report in a Haugesund newspaper gives some indication of how the broadcast was received:

The broadcast of Irgens Jensen's and Olav Gullvåg's dramatic symphony 'Heimferd' which 'Haugesunds Avis' arranged yesterday in Totalen [the Temperance Hall] was received with great interest by the audience. By 19.15, people began to flock in and when the introductory lecture began at 19.30,

[48] Hans Fredrik Dahl, *Hallo – hallo! Kringkastingen i Norge 1920–1940*, Cappelen, Oslo, 1975, p. 369.

> the hall was more or less full. It was completely crammed when the broadcast in the university Aula began at 20.00.[49]

The technical quality of such broadcasts was generally poor. Interference, both atmospheric and from stronger foreign stations, was usual in places that lay any distance away from the few transmitters. Microphone technique was little developed, even though it had improved considerably around 1930. Most domestic receivers were still crystal sets equipped with poor earphones or simple valve receivers with weak loudspeakers. So the pronunciation of the text and the sensitive orchestral instruments, for example, could lose a good deal of the detail, and the printed text, which had been published ahead of the broadcast, could be of considerable help in making sense of the content.

On 22 January *Den 17de Mai* reported triumphantly:

> The streets in Nidaros were empty on Monday evening!
>
> When 'Heimferd' – Irgens Jensen's and Gullvåg's cantata – was broadcast from Oslo on Monday evening 20.00–22.00, the streets in Nidaros were empty of people, almost like Christmas Eve, they reported to 'Den 17de Mai'. So desirous were the Trondhjemmers to hear 'the despised cantata'.

The broadcasting company received many requests for another broadcast and so arranged to transmit the next performance on Monday, 2 February. On that day, *Dagbladet* carried a letter from Gullvåg, who was now living in Mori Borgata in Italy with his wife and three children. He had tried in vain to listen to the broadcast transmission on 19 January, but Norway had been 'drowned out' by German 'beery chatter' and he was now hoping for better listening conditions for the next broadcast.

At about the same time Irgens-Jensen received a letter from Gullvåg[50] which complained about the hopeless listening conditions:

> As ecstatic as people are about the music, there must surely be a chance for me too to hear the work. So in any case I will travel just as far as I have to, to be present. [...] a heap of letters and telegrams gave me a powerful sense of how this has been a coup for Norwegian music, Norwegian spirit in general. [...] I hope at the end of March when I pass through Oslo, that I may meet you and thank you personally for the great pleasure you have given not only those who are specifically musical, but many ordinary people. It will amuse you to read through the letters I have received. Captain Os, director of Noregs Boklag, an especially cold and materialistic chap writes thus:
>
> 'I heard the cantata yesterday. I cannot describe this event. I have never experienced the like. I felt myself forced to the floor and lifted to the roof.

[49] *Haugesunds Avis*, 20 January 1931.

[50] Sent from Mori Borgata and dated 25 January 1931.

I struggled in vain against my tears. But I console myself that harder chaps than me were just as bad. I and all my household were there together at Koht's (the professor's).[51] None of us could find words, as we went home. And on reaching home, we all sat and stared down at the table-top. Yes, that was an experience.'

That is the tone of all the letters I have received.

The *Heimferd* broadcasts were also the direct cause of a long article by Arne van Erpekum Sem,[52] where he discussed various aspects of such radio broadcasts and their importance for the 'thousand homes'.[53] The disadvantages were few, he thought, with the danger of a fall in concert-going in the larger towns offset by an increasing circulation of music countrywide.

For the transmission of the concert on Monday, 2 February, the whole of Parliament and the government met in the Aula to hear the work.

The ninth and final performance that season took place on 12 February, with the Oslo City Council as guests. Before the concert came the question:

'Is there any other work that has been played so many times in so short a time?' 'Den 17de Mai' asks manager Berckenhoff of the Philharmonic Society.

'No, this is a record', he answers. 'The most any other works have been played in one year has been 8 times. And only 'Voluspå' by Monrad Johansen and 'Olav Trygvason' by Grieg have done that, – oh, and the Ninth Symphony of Beethoven perhaps. The last work has certainly been played 35 times, but that is in 10–11 years. 'Heimferd' has been played 9 times in 10 weeks, and there has been a full house every time. Yes, that is a record!'[54]

One can thus calculate that in two months around 13,500 listeners had experienced *Heimferd* in the flesh and many thousands more had heard enjoyed the radio broadcasts. It is doubtful whether any Norwegian piece of music enjoyed a similar success before the age of television.

In the next concert season, too, the Oslo Philharmonic had to programme *Heimferd* again and so it was performed on 8 and 9 October 1931, with largely the same performers. This time the concert hall was unusual: the Colosseum, a large cinema which the Society wanted to try out, and there were reduced ticket prices. All these extra performances brought in much extra income and in fact saved the Philharmonic Society from a humiliating deficit.

[51] Halvdan Koht (1873–1965) was Norwegian foreign minister from 1936 to 1940, and was an eminent historian and writer.

[52] 'The Importance of the Radio for the Musical Life of the Country', *Tidens Tegn*, 7 February 1931.

[53] A reference to the description of Norway in the national anthem.

[54] *Den 17de Mai*, 11 February 1931.

The orchestra of the Oslo Philharmonic Society in the University Aula, with the conductor Odd Grüner-Hegge and Edvard Munch's decorations prominent behind them.

Irgens-Jensen had now become a celebrity and even minor matters in which he was mentioned were prominently reported in the papers, as in *Morgenbladet* on 21 February 1931:

> THE COMPOSER IRGENS JENSEN
> has bought from director Paul Launen a property on Vestre Sæter in Nordstrand for 46,000 kroner.

In this property, Kastellveien 20, he was to live for the rest of his life.

New performances of *Heimferd* were constantly demanded. But it was banned by the occupying Germans during the Second World War – for obvious reasons – and although a stage performance in 1947[55] brought a temporary revival of interest, it was, like much of the music composed in the 1920s and '30s, out of tune with the modernist aesthetics that prevailed after the War. Ironically, it was a series of performances in Nidaros Cathedral in Trondheim in the 1990s which signalled a revival of interest in the work, bolstered by the appearance, in 1994, of its only recording to date,[56] which was well received both in the Norwegian press and in music periodicals abroad.

[55] *Cf.* pp. 238–41.
[56] *Cf.* Discography, pp. 342–43.

Heimferd was conceived on a large scale, and it is a large-scale achievement; it was an occasional work which more than transcended its original purpose. With the gradual rediscovery of the music of Irgens-Jensen – a movement in which one hopes this book will play its part – *Heimferd* ought gradually to take its place not only as one of the gems of Norwegian music but as a work of world standing.

VII
The 1930s

No other Norwegian work of this period enjoyed a domestic success comparable to that of *Heimferd*, but it was the Passacaglia which had more success abroad. Irgens-Jensen was now constantly in demand, almost to the point where he had to contend with hero-worship. He received a steady flow of appreciative letters from the time of the celebration of the St Olav anniversary and the first performance of *Heimferd*, as also many from people asking for help, or trying to further their own interests. As a man of principle, he suffered pangs of conscience because he felt he ought to respond to all such approaches: he did not want to appear to be unwilling to do so, or to seem to give offence. Finally, though, he had to compromise, and took an unlisted telephone number.

Even so, he did not have enough peace to compose and, without a regular publisher, was obliged personally to supervise such mundane tasks as the copying of parts and the preparation of arrangements. With his dislike of the limelight, the problems surrounding *Heimferd*, all the publicity and fuss and, later, the very success of the work did much to wear him down. After the performances in spring 1931, indeed, he was so run down that he developed pleurisy and spent a short time in Ullevål, Oslo's major hospital, which put a pause to his composing activities once again.

Early that year a journalist sent him a questionnaire containing the question: 'What or who has annoyed you most in 1930?' His draft reply, unsent, reads as follows:

> Myself.
> Trivial matters.
> The emperor's new clothes.
> That the Philharmonic Society's work is not sufficiently appreciated by the public.
> That time runs away from me!
> You, Miss, who want me to answer such a difficult question.

For a while, it seems, he felt rather empty, perhaps even depressed and pessimistic. On a sheet of paper amongst his posthumous papers is the draft of the last part of what appears to have been intended as a longer poem.[1] The last few lines give an impression of his sentiments:

La stjernene tendes,	Let the stars be lit,
tiden er inne,	it is time,
du vandrer mot fredens helligdom	you wander towards the sanctuary of peace
som menneskehjertet	that the human heart
alltid søker,	is always seeking,
men aldri finner på jorden.	but never finds on earth.

The pressure on his time continued remorsely. His name was now so well-known that he was asked to serve on a number of committees, though he generally refused such requests. Even in connection with the controversy in the Philharmonic Society,[2] in which he was directly involved, he turned down an appeal to stand for election.

The success of the Passacaglia abroad led to invitations to travel. Thanks to the impact of the work in a Norwegian-German week in Kiel in June 1929, he received an invitation[3] from the city of Kiel to be part of the Ehrenausschuss (committee of patronage) a year later, during a *Bachfest* on 4–6 October 1930, but he turned it down. After the worst of the storms in the Norwegian Society of Composers had subsided, he was persuaded to join its board in 1930–31[4] and was elected as vice-chairman, but he resigned after the elective period of two years. He was later asked to rejoin the board by a number of people, among them Pauline Hall, who thought he would generate 'peace among many argumentative dispositions',[5] but only in 1946 did he allow himself to be re-elected, as a deputy member of the board for two further years, though he was later to sit on the board for ten more years, from 1951.[6]

In October 1931 the Ministry of Education, Culture and Church Affairs appointed Irgens-Jensen to the committee which made recommendations on artists' stipends. At the same time he served as a member of the State Expert Committee for authors' and artists' questions (an advisory board to the church and education ministry intended to settle questions on authors' rights to creative works and to act as arbitrator in the event of any disagreements). Later, in 1934, he was persuaded to sit also on the City of Oslo Committee, which likewise awarded stipends to deserving artists.

1 Its title would seem to be 'Høstens tid er nær' ('The Autumn Season is Near').

2 *Cf.* pp. 175–76, below.

3 Letter from a Stadtrat (town councillor) Gluck, dated 10 July 1930, preserved in Irgens-Jensen's papers.

4 Kristian Lange, *Norsk Komponistforening gjennom 50 år*, Norsk Komponistforening, Oslo, 1967, p. 134.

5 Letter dated 30 June 1936, preserved in Irgens-Jensen's papers.

6 *Cf.* p. 231, below.

Irgens-Jensen was an assiduous concert-goer and kept up with music in other ways, through reading books, periodicals and scores; he was attentive to radio broadcasts, too. At the beginning of the 1930s radio reception at his Nordstrand home was poor, but setting up an extra-long aerial improved matters and allowed him to receive foreign stations as well.

A bill for scores bought from Norsk Musikforlag in the period 1929–30, discovered in his woodshed by chance, throws much light on his interests:

9.9.29	Grieg: Sonata
	Grieg: op. 66 [*19 Norwegian Folk-Tunes*]
	Im Geschichte [?]
2.10.29	Sparre Olsen: Fjell-Norig
	" " : Tri Aukrustsongar [*Three Aukrust Songs*]
	Sandvold: Seks improvisasjoner [*Six Improvisations*]
17.10.29	Die Musik [periodical]
	Grieg: Lyriske stykker [*Lyric Pieces*]
30.11.29	Grieg: Op. 50 [*Olav Trygvason*]
19.12.29	Musik for hjemmet ['Music for the Home', a periodical which published scores]
23.1.30	Børnenes Musik ['Music for Children', an anthology of piano music]
24.1.30	Tekst til Børnenes Musik [Text of 'Music for Children', above]
7.2.30	Fartein Valen: Sange [Songs, Op. 6]
28.2.30	König David [Honegger]
22.3.30	Die Tonsprache [a periodical]
	Gramer: Op. 82 [Cramer?]
	Liturgisk musik [Liturgical music]
29.3.30	Eggen: Ciaconna
8.4.30	Bach: Trauerode [Cantata No. 198]
14.4.30	Reger: Op. 46 [*Fantasia and Fugue on BACH* for organ]
7.5.30	Reger: opus 46 [a second copy, a gift?]
	" : Op. 52, Nos. 1, 2, 3 [*Chorale Fantasias* for organ]
	" Op. 57 [*Symphonic Fantasy and Fugue* for organ]
2.6.30	" Op. 92, Suite for organ
12.6.30	Bela Bartok: Opus 17 [String Quartet No. 2]
	Respighi: Quartetto [*dorico*, 1924]
	Schoenberg: Op. 30 [String Quartet No. 3]
	Stravinsky: Les Noces
	Bruckner: Grosse Messe
20.6.30	Reger: Second Sonata Op. 60 [organ]
10.9.30	Niemann: Orchestrierung [Riemann, *Handbuch der Orchestrierung*, 3rd impr. 1919?]
17.9.30	Grieg: Bergljot
21.11.30	Knud Jeppesen [*Kontrapunkt*?]

Irgens-Jensen, Christian Sinding and Odd Grüner-Hegge in the early 1930s, on the veranda of Grüner-Hegge's summer house on the Oslo Fjord.

This list tallies with the notion of Irgens-Jensen as a man of broad taste and artistic curiosity. The large number of Grieg works he bought is perhaps surprising; some of them may have been intended as gifts. Although he was busy with *Heimferd* and its fate during this period, he maintained his awareness of new music, also indulging his interest in Reger and established masters such as Bruckner and Bach. Schoenberg's Third String Quartet is one of his finer and most 'systematic' twelve-note works – but it could hardly have been daily fare for any Norwegian composers of the day other than Valen and Irgens-Jensen. There are sketches, probably from his younger years, to show that he experimented with twelve-note exercises for a period the better to understand the technique.[7] He obtained the three Goethe settings that form Fartein Valen's Op. 6 even before the sensational first performance of 'Sakontala' in March 1930.[8] The other contemporary Norwegian composers whose music he bought – Sparre Olsen, Arne Eggen and Arild Sandvold – are all represented by works in a more Romantic vein, some stylistic distance from those of Bartók, Honegger, Respighi and Stravinsky.[9]

[7] *Cf.* also pp. 41 and 44, above.

[8] These songs by Valen evoked a heated debate in some of the Olso magazines and newspapers which lasted for more than three years.

[9] Bartók's Second Quartet was also a modern contemporary work; it had its first performance in Norway by the Philharmonic Quartet in 1931.

The final item, 'Jeppesen', is most likely Knud Jeppesen's famous textbook, *Kontrapunkt (Vokalpolyfoni)*, which had recently been published.[10] In it Jeppesen,[11] taking his starting point from his doctoral thesis of 1923, formulates a 'set of rules' for counterpoint after the style of Palestrina. This textbook was of crucial importance for many music-educational institutions over the whole world, not least because many of the ideas there could be used directly in modern compositional technique, even if one worked with extended tonality or atonal music.

In the Norway of the 1930s the aesthetic standpoint of a number of composers changed in a more nationalist direction. Like seeks like, they say, and Irgens-Jensen, who continued to hold onto his more European Neo-classical ideals, will doubtless have noticed that there were some friends whose views and output gradually became more peripheral to his own concerns. David Monrad Johansen, who had been best man at his wedding, was one of them. Monrad Johansen felt he deserved more influence in Norwegian musical life, but the two people who stood in his way, as he saw it, were Christian Sinding and Odd Grüner-Hegge, thanks to Sinding's status and Grüner-Hegge's importance as a conductor – and Irgens-Jensen was a friend of both of these men of many years' standing. Monrad Johansen may also have been piqued by the success of the Passacaglia and *Heimferd*, which became a direct rival to his own *Voluspå*.[12] The cordial relationship they enjoyed in the 1920s does not seem to have survived into the following decade, even though many hearty greetings from Monrad Johansen are to be found among Irgens-Jensen's papers from the time. They also worked together a good deal on projects for the Norwegian Society of Composers and sat together on the committee for the 'Society of Composers' radio concerts for the Norwegian radio in the spring of 1940, when music by contemporary Norwegian composers was performed – but the concerts naturally enough came to an end after 9 April, the day of the Nazi invasion.

During the 1930s Irgens-Jensen was in regular contact with Pauline Hall, often trying to cheer her up when she felt her efforts on behalf of modern music were not bearing fruit. In the summer of 1938 she went to London and obtained permission from the board of the International Society for Contemporary Music to form a Norwegian branch; she then asked Irgens-Jensen for financial support in setting it up, which he gave. Before she went to London, she asked for a copy of the Passacaglia, and managed to obtain a

[10] Wilhelm Hansen, Copenhagen, 1930.

[11] Knud Jeppesen (1892–1974) studied under Carl Nielsen, who encouraged his work as a composer. Although Jeppesen is remembered now chiefly as a musicologist who radically revised the appreciation of Palestrina and his contemporaries, his compositions include an opera, a symphony, several large-scale choral works and a number of weighty organ pieces.

[12] On *Voluspå*, *cf.* p. 112, above.

performance by the BBC that autumn. In a draft for a greeting on her 60th birthday in 1950 found in his papers, he wrote:

> At this moment I wish I were a skilful writer and could thank you properly for everything you have accomplished in our musical life. Thank you for your perseverance, courage, strength of character, perhaps that most of all. I imagine sometimes it has been exhausting!
>
> Thank you, too, for good friendship through all these years.

In the early 1930s there were two heated arguments over the position of the conductor in the Oslo Philharmonic Society; both involved a clash of personalities. The first dispute, in 1930, was a contractual one between the conductor, Issay Dobrowen, and the chairman of the board of the Philharmonic; the second arose from Dobrowen's absences – he was conducting elsewhere during weeks he should have been in Oslo. There were open discussions in the press, and in spite of an apparent reconciliation between the conductor and his critics, the atmosphere remained heated. Dobrowen withdrew as chief conductor in the spring of 1931, not least since he had been appointed conductor of the San Francisco Symphony Orchestra. The board then decided that the post should be divided between Olav Kielland[13] and Odd Grüner-Hegge from autumn 1931 to spring 1932: for the next season Kielland was solely responsible for the autumn term and Grüner-Hegge for the spring concerts. But then, on 12 July 1933, the board resolved that Kielland should be given sole responsibility – a decision of which Grüner-Hegge was not informed. Further debates ensued in the press and, for once, Irgens-Jensen took part. Together with Elling Bang and Hagerup Bull, he wrote an open letter to the board of the Philharmonic in support of Grüner-Hegge; co-signed by several other prominent personalities in Norwegian musical life (Johan Halvorsen, Arne Eggen, Pauline Hall, Per Reidarson and Arne van Erpekum Sem among them), it was published in several Oslo papers on 27 July 1933:

> Mr Grüner-Hegge placed himself at the Society's disposition without conditions, out of respect for the Society's difficult position, but was not appointed. [...]
>
> As precarious as the Society's position is at the moment, above all it needs forces which can and are willing to work together. But the board has chosen the one who rejected any thought of collaboration.

It soon became apparent that this debate was not only about the qualifications of the conductors: the issue was of wider 'national' interest, as Kielland was seen as the conductor who had done most for the 'national'

[13] *Cf.* note 49 on p. 134, above.

When Stravinsky visited Norway in 1931, Louise Irgens-Jensen took this picture of him, Christian Sinding and Siss and Odd Grüner-Hegge on Holmenkollen.

composers, such as Monrad Johansen and Groven, whereas Grüner-Hegge had more often taken a radical, 'European' line; Kielland was therefore the more 'Norwegian' conductor.

Soon after New Year 1934 matters came to a head. Grüner-Hegge wrote to the board on 3 January, severing all ties with the Philharmonic; he would not, therefore, conduct the concert on 19 February, when Irgens-Jensen's *Der Gott und die Bajadere* was to have been premiered.[14] Finally a council meeting was called at the Philharmonic on 26 January 1934, for which occasion Irgens-Jensen again supplied a letter in support of Grüner-Hegge. The board compromised by allowing Grüner-Hegge some concerts each season (while he took a full-time post with the National Theatre Orchestra) but retaining Kielland as chief conductor because of superior 'administrative experience'. Grüner-Hegge was thus a victim of the uncompromising campaign for 'nationalism' in Norwegian music.[15]

Up to this point all the performance of Irgens-Jensen's works from the 1920s had used manuscript material, since only a few short works had been published: 'Baanlaat' ('Lullaby', from *Fables and Children's Songs*)

[14] *Cf.* p. 180, below.

[15] *Cf.* pp. 106–13, above.

together with the *Siciliano* for piano in the periodical *Musik* in December 1924, and 'Die Debatte' (a German translation of one of the *Fables*)[16] in D. F. Scheuleer's *Gedenkboek*, published in s'Gravenhage in 1925. Several of the *Fables* immediately became very popular thanks to performances by leading singers around 1925 and, so as to meet the many requests for the music, Irgens-Jensen allowed a series of them to be hectographed (a simple and cheap technique for reproducing handwritten material) as single songs, whereby they achieved relatively wide distribution.

The Ministry of Church Affairs owned the rights to *Heimferd* and was supposed to take care of both copying scores and writing out the orchestral parts. But in practice it was the composer himself who had to do the work. The choral parts were printed by Norsk Musikforlag, but it was again Irgens-Jensen who had to take care of the orchestral parts after each performance of both *Heimferd* and the Passacaglia, supply any that went missing and see that the material was out in good time for the next performance, a job that was both tiring and time-consuming. All this administrative work drained his energy and his joy in creativity, leaving him with insufficient time to concentrate on new tasks in the early 1930s – his archive contains the drafts of several letters from these years where he complains about having too little time to compose.

It was probably the reputation of the Passacaglia in Europe and the USA that led to an offer, in May 1932, from Sven Wilhelm Hansen of Wilhelm Hansen Musikforlag in Copenhagen to publish the work. But it was not to be so simple: two years later, on 9 October 1934, *Tidens Tegn* reported that four foreign publishers – Wilhelm Hansen, Ricordi, Förster and Senart – were fighting for the rights, but the composer was sceptical about using a publisher abroad and so eventually chose Norsk Musikforlag as his publisher.

In January 1934 Irgens-Jensen had allowed his first choral song – *Til Norges Flag* ('To Norway's Flag'), with a text by Gunnar Reiss-Andersen, which had probably been composed as early as 1916 – to be published by Norsk Musikforlag. The score had previously been hectographed, thus becoming very popular. Later in 1934 Norsk Musikforlag wrote to the composer requesting that the song be included in a collection of choral songs intended for use in a nationwide choral competition, with an estimated print-run of 2,500–3,000 copies; it was published at Christmas 1934. In autumn 1934 he agreed to a general contract, which was signed in January 1935. The engraving of the orchestral works was immediately set in motion by Norsk Musikforlag and in mid-August 1935 they were able

[16] On these works, *cf*. respectively pp. 75–77, 79 and 71, above.

to send the first half of the proofs of the Passacaglia. Not many months afterwards, the *Tema con Variazioni* – the title he gave the revised edition of the Variations and Fugue in G minor – was also issued. Unfortunately these editions were not especially attractive; what's worse, they are full of mistakes.

Two years later the publisher Max Hinrichsen, who had recently heard Paul van Kempen's well-received performance of the Passacaglia during a Dresden music festival, wrote[17] on behalf of C. F. Peters in Leipzig, offering to consider it and other works for publication, but Irgens-Jensen felt obliged by the contract he had negotiated with Norsk Musikforlag and turned him down.

Der Gott und die Bajadere

Although *Heimferd* is in many ways a high point among Irgens-Jensen's compositions, his large-scale cantata *Der Gott und die Bajadere* ('The God and the Bayadere'), for contralto/mezzo soprano, baritone, choir and orchestra, displays a like talent for musical drama. The text is a ballad by Goethe presenting a dramatic legend from India, a story of love between a god and a 'bayadere', a temple dancer dedicated to the gods. The work had been with Irgens-Jensen for many years, having begun life in sketch-form as far back as 1920. His sister, Dagny, the dedicatee, heard some of it for the first time around 1921 and repeatedly nagged Ludvig to complete the score, but he seems to have hesitated, probably because he had so many other ideas he wanted to try out in new works. The score was finally completed in 1932.

The god Mahadö – master of the earth – descends for the sixth time to earth to live like a man in order to understand humans better before he judges them. In the shape of a young man he meets with a bayadere, who takes care of him, feeds him and entertains him, and gradually he becomes aware of her pure soul despite her low social position. She falls in love with him and wails bitterly when in the morning she discovers him dead by her side. He is carried away to be burnt and, when she hears the priests chanting, she makes her way to the fire. The priests will not allow her to be burnt with him: she is not his widow. But when she throws herself into the fire, a miracle is seen: the young man rises from the fire and ascends to the heavens with his beloved in his arms.

Irgens-Jensen 'stages' Goethe's long ballad using some simple dramaturgical effects. The use of a single male voice for different characters and the choir to represent the crowd and the priests may not be unusual, but in employing the female voice not only as bayadere but also as a commentator

[17] Letter dated 23 June 1937 preserved in Irgens-Jensen's papers.

describing the bayadere, he creates a narrative perspective which works on different layers. The composition is symphonically constructed. The main theme of the work (Ex. 33) is presented at the very opening, and is transformed when the choir delivers a moral commentary and again in the conclusion, when it takes the form of a hymn. This moving work anticipates both Irgens-Jensen's *Heimferd* and his later attempt at opera.[18] It is indeed a dramatic libretto, although Goethe's text might be seen to present stages in an operatic dramaturgical scheme, as arias and choruses do in an opera: it stops the flow of the action and the psychological development. But the music itself both illumines the words and carries forward the wordless story and the musical development, not least in the shifting moods and expression brought about by contrasts in modulation and tonality, the flux of different times, meter and rhythms, and the variety of layers in the polyphony of the music. Irgens-Jensen's dramatic flair is clearly audible in the musical characterisation of the two main characters, the male god set in vigorous textures, the female supplicant treated in a more subdued manner.

Ex. 33

On 11 November 1933 Grüner-Hegge wrote to Irgens-Jensen from Berlin, a day after he had conducted the Passacaglia there. After reporting on how the performance had gone, he revealed that *Der Gott und die Bajadere* had been scheduled in his programme with the Oslo Philharmonic for

[18] *Cf.* pp. 227–29, below.

19 January the following year, with the famous Danish-German contralto Emmi Leisner (1885–1958) as a soloist.[19] In the event, the performance was later postponed to 19 February and then again, because of the controversy over the conductors,[20] until 17 January 1935. In the premiere Grüner-Hegge conducted the soloists Anna Brekke Tibell (-Hegert) (1891–1981) – Leisner, unfortunately, was engaged elsewhere – and Morten Vatn (1908–70) and the Philharmonic Choir and Orchestra. Before the performance, the editor of *Tonekunst*, Klaus Egge, wrote two detailed articles about the work, its background and plot.[21]

The premiere was an unqualified success, both for the performers and the work itself:

> As is to be expected, the greatest interest was focussed on Ludvig Irgens Jensen's 'Der Gott und die Bajadere' to Goethe's well-known text, for soloists, choir and orchestra. Every single new work by this composer, who is on a sure road to world fame, is anticipated with excitement and the highest expectations. And it should be said straightaway that the new work is worthy of its predecessors, which already have added lustre to Irgens-Jensen's name, 'Heimferd', 'Passacaglia' and the great Variations for orchestra. Irgens-Jensen has clearly been strongly moved by the beauty and depth of Goethe's poem and, inspired by it, his powerful imagination has created music that is intimately bound up with the changing moods of the text. With intuitive strength the composer is able to match the right colour in the choral movement as well as in the strongly descriptive orchestral accompaniment, and the music often seems to stream out from and completely meld together with Goethe's immortal text.[22]

The interest in the music was so strong that the work was immediately rescheduled for Monday, 21 January, with the same performers. The draft of a letter reveals that Irgens-Jensen was well satisfied with it, especially after the first performance, since he had used a mosaic-like instrumentation which he thought made a good effect.

At the time of writing, *Der Gott und die Bajadere* has not had a performance for over two decades, although it is a stirring and moving work that audiences are sure to enjoy.

[19] Letter preserved in Irgens-Jensen's papers.

[20] *Cf.* pp. 175–76, above.

[21] 'Ludvig Irgens-Jensens Der Gott und die Bajadere', *Tonekunst*, 1935, No. 1, pp. 17–18, and No. 2, p. 31.

[22] Van Erpekum Sem, *Tidens Tegn*, 19 January 1935.

Irgens-Jensen with his father and son in the mid-1930s

Kong Baldvines armring

In 1935 Irgens-Jensen composed the incidental music to a children's comedy, *Kong Baldvines armring* ('King Baldwin's Arm-Ring'), by Helen Stibolt (1888–1975), a journalist with the newspaper *Tidens Tegn*. The plot takes an historical episode from the time of the medieval Norwegian king Sigurd Jorsalfar (literally, 'who went to Jerusalem', Jorsal being the old Nordic name of the city) who embarked on a crusade around 1110, visiting King Baldwin in Jerusalem.[23] In the play King Sigurd's arm-ring, which he had been given by King Baldwin, has been stolen on Sigurd's return to Norway. A clever and noble choir-boy uncovers the deceit, the swindlers are finally revealed and all ends well and in much joy. The play was accepted by the National Theatre for performance before Christmas 1935; the eminent female director Gerda Ring (1891–1999) was asked to stage it, and Irgens-Jensen was commissioned to write music both for the songs and individual instrumental numbers and dances, which were to be played by a small orchestra.

The play did not receive the best reviews, but one critic reported that 'Irgens-Jensen's imaginative and simple music can well stand being

[23] The reign of Baldwin I (1100–18) is summarised in Simon Sebag Montefiore, *Jerusalem: The Biography*, Weidenfeld & Nicolson, London, 2011, pp. 258–61.

mentioned alongside Grieg's'.[24] Another, Ulrik Mørk, felt that the music 'towered far above the type of music which is usually associated with a theatrical performance. Its character is strong, but always dignified'. Irgens-Jensen, he continued, had reconciled its disparate elements

> in a masterly way and has recreated them into a whole that has become his own, inspired by his rich artistic imagination and constructed with a brilliant talent for simplicity in lines and colours. There is something monumental in this music and it will live long after the theatrical work which inspired the composer has played its role out.[25]

The play was performed a total of 32 times that first season;[26] it seems that it was too cumbersome and costly a production for revival in later years.

Irgens-Jensen's music mostly takes the form of dances, songs and interludes. At the opening there is a Sami 'Bear Trainer', characterised by a rather monotonous Sami-like song before he dances with his bear in a wild scene. The theme sounds like an original Sami melody, although it is Irgens-Jensen's own invention. A monk then relates a legend about the birth of Jesus almost as a melodrama, where the music is given a sacred quality through the abundant use of modal scales, although there is also something Impressionist about its evocation of a fairy-tale; the mood is both mystical and occasionally threatening. The king enters to fanfares and shouts, a stark contrast to the more solemn music for Christmas Eve. The people's homage is presented in a choral song which, according to the programme, is supposedly built on a melody from crusading times, although it has not been identified. Some black men guarding the chest that contains a sliver of Christ's cross and other valuables dance a grotesque dance, styled 'in a manner of a Madagascar dance'.[27] In the bodyguards' room, a Faroese dance-song is danced before 'Deilig er jorden' ('Beautiful is the world', a familiar Christmas carol) is heard, archaically harmonised. There are also dramatic and comic scenes, one of which is strange and ominous, set on the Galgeberg (the gallows). There is an avaricious but anxious Turk who wants to buy the ring, and the pixies dance a lively dance in changing time-signatures, and with many syncopations, interrupted by a dance of elves.

Irgens-Jensen's score requires only ten players, but they are used to the full, many playing multiple instruments. Ulrik Mørk noted that

[24] 'E.S.' (Einar Skavlan), *Dagbladet*, 18 December 1935. In 1872 Grieg wrote incidental music to Bjørnstjerne Bjørnson's play *Sigurd Jorsalfar* which he then arranged into a suite, which was revised and premiered in Oslo in 1892.

[25] *Nationen*, 20 December 1935.

[26] Anton Rønneberg, *Nationaltheatret gjennom 50 år*, Gyldendal Norsk, Oslo, 1949, p. 309.

[27] Irgens-Jensen, in the programme.

> What they achieved, these ten proficient musicians under Mr Odd Grüner-Hegge's first-rate musical direction, surpassed all expectation. I presume that the composer will prepare a suite of 'Baldvine music', and that this will appear in the 'Philharmonic' under Mr Grüner-Hegge's outstanding direction.[28]

Yet it was to be four years before Irgens-Jensen extracted parts of the music, adjusted the orchestration for the personnel of the Radio Orchestra and fitted four movements together into a little suite, performed for the first time on the radio in 1939.

Driftekaren

Irgens-Jensen's major undertaking in 1937 was another commission for incidental music, this time for the poetic play *Driftekaren* ('The Drover') by Hans E. Kinck, who had died in 1926. The initiative for a staging of *Driftekaren* came from Hans Jacob Nilsen (1897–1957), then manager of Den Nationale Scene in Bergen; Irgens-Jensen's childhood friend, Finn Grüner-Hegge, the brother of the conductor, was asked to put the finishing strokes to his adaptation of the unwieldy play, making it better suited to theatrical presentation, and it was he who persuaded Irgens-Jensen to write the music. Halfdan Christensen, the stage-director of the National Theatre, had previously worked with Kinck in 1910 on his play *Agiluf den vise* ('Agiluf the Wise'), explained the theatrical shortcomings of his plays:

> Kinck was scarcely thinking of the theatre when he wrote his dramas. Or perhaps more correctly: he did not *want* to think of the theatre. The scenes formed themselves freely in his imagination; he has not adapted them to the narrow framework of the stage. [... It is the same with] 'Driftekaren', that great national monument which Kinck has erected over the Norwegian people's soul and Norwegian national character.[29]

At the centre of *Driftekaren* is the drover, Vrål, who as the action opens is returning to his village with only one bad horse: the rest of the herd has been sold, but he has squandered all the money he should be bringing home to his neighbours. The sparse action of the drama covers a long span of time, the importance lying more in the characterisation of Vrål. From the first scene one understands that he is a man of vision and a poet as well as a womaniser and a liar who has problems with genuine affection and who is nonetheless also tormented by the consequences of his betrayals. The mighty natural world of western Norway forms images of landscapes in Vrål's mind and dreams, and his monologue expresses these feelings, which are also coloured by his observations of the changeable weather and the

[28] *Loc. cit.*
[29] *Dagbladet*, 5 March 1938.

symbolism of different birds in the landscape. He arrives over the winter mountains to a narrow fjord (and narrow-minded people) and longs for the open ocean eternally glittering in the sun. Vrål is obviously conceived as a parallel to Ibsen's Peer Gynt, and Ibsen's ideal Solveig is similarly reflected in the young Bol, who may likewise bring atonement.

Irgens-Jensen had expressed his interest in Kinck's writing both in interviews and in the effort he put into the music to the drama *Bryllupet i Genua* ('The Wedding in Genoa'), from which he had intended to fashion an opera.[30] He met Kinck on only one occasion[31] and seems to have enjoyed the encounter, arranged by Finn Grüner-Hegge who, according to Dagny Irgens Jensen,[32] was almost obsessively interested in the playwright. Finn Grüner-Hegge claimed in an extended interview that

> Kinck is the most wonderful author in the world, clear in his depictions, logical in his train of thought. Kinck has absorbed me since I was a young boy, continues the violinist. One day I met a friend who knew Kinck; he took me with him to the writer and so the bond was tied. I asked and delved and discussed in a rather childlike way, but the wise master was never impatient or unwilling. One day I also dragged along my friend Ludvig Irgens-Jensen to see him. We were, as I said, lads and we hinted that we would like to throw ourselves into 'Bryllupet i Genua'. Ludvig would write the music. And we struggled with the plan for many years. Irgens Jensen had written a lot of music for the play, but now it has been abandoned.
>
> On the whole it is quite interesting to note that it is musical people in particular who have appreciated Kinck's greatness.
>
> – Kinck's production invites musical adaptation, says Grüner-Hegge, and here in 'Driftekaren' we get to hear Irgens-Jensen at his best. Never has the composer achieved more. As well as the prelude before each act and the entr'actes between the sections, we also hear music to large parts of the lyrical parts of the play. 'Driftekaren' is partly adapted as a melodrama, a good many snatches of song appear in the production, including Bol's song, but whether this is to be sung is still not clear. Because for that people who can sing are needed. [...]
>
> We also exchanged a few words with the composer. It has not been an easy matter to write music to 'Driftekaren'.
>
> – Melodrama is a very difficult art form, says Irgens-Jensen, especially when it is tied up with the theatre. One cannot order intervals, one cannot linger where it would be natural for the music if it does not also suit the speech. And then the music is never muted enough. Sometimes it is really tempting to increase the sound significantly but, as I said, the music must not

[30] *Cf.* pp. 69–70, above.
[31] *Cf.* p. 69, above.
[32] In a taped interview.

drown out the words. It should sound like a distant background, at the same time as it must not seem soporific.

– You have worked with Kinck's works for many years, did the writer himself ever get to hear the music?

– No, but he was very happy that music had been written to his works. He constantly asked about it; I worked for many years with 'Bryllupet i Genua', but the material was too intense for me – at that time.

– Is that to say that you intend to tackle the same task again?

– Yes, it is very possible. But first it is a question of finishing 'Driftekaren'.

– Can you describe the music? Have you especially emphasised the national aspect?

– I have underlined it through the rhythms, through the *slått*. But otherwise I am myself.

Irgens Jensen makes the last remark out of sheer modesty, but nevertheless he has inadvertently given the music the best recommendation that can be imagined. The orchestra has 21 musicians and he thinks they sound good, the orchestra is first class and the conductor Odd Grüner-Hegge is above banal eulogies.[33]

The premiere was transferred from Bergen[34] to the National Theatre in Oslo where on 10 March 1938 it had an enthusiastic response; Alfred Maurstad in particular was praised for his interpretation of the drover, Vrål. *Aftenposten* published a double review on 11 March 1938, the first part written by the theatre-critic Anton Rønneberg:

Ludvig *Irgens Jensen* composed the lovely and atmospheric music to 'Driftekaren'. Seen both literally and theatrically, the task ought to have been limited to a matter of preludes and entr'actes. Now again and again the music breaks disturbingly into the action at exactly the most beautiful lyrical parts of the work. However, the performance shows that precisely where the word reigns alone and sovereign, the poetry comes most finely into its own. [...]

In a performance full to the brim with freshness, emotion and imagination, the National Theatre has recreated Kinck's national masterpiece on the stage. On such evenings the theatre wins a central place in Norwegian cultural life.

Anton Rønneberg

The music to 'Driftekaren'

It has certainly not been an easy task for Ludvig Irgens Jensen to write the incidental music to 'Driftekaren'. The poetry does not immediately invite musical treatment; it could lie both in the idea of the piece and also have its foundation in the special way Kinck expresses himself. But these were difficulties which could have been conquered if only the composer had had more *freedom*; if, for example, he could have taken the material out for use

33 *Dagbladet*, 7 March 1938.

34 H. J. Nilsen's contract there had come to an end, and he moved to Oslo.

Alfred Maurstad (right) as the drover Vrål, in the staging of Driftekaren *at the National Theatre in 1938*

> by soloists, choir and orchestra. In this case, however, where he had to place his art in a wholly subservient position to the poem, and especially when the very dangerous melodramatic form has become the principal task and has received much too large and dominant a place. If the melodramatic form is to succeed, then the composer must have far more command of, and freedom with, the poetry and the poetry, too, must have reduced its demands; then the two art forms would perhaps meld together and form a third, namely true melodrama. [...]
>
> The music made the strongest impression when it accompanied Vraal's great monologue in the third act. Here the music had a touch of warmth, of temperature, somehow it began to sprout and grow, possibilities opened... It did well, because it gave us an insight into the subtle artistic character that we know from the concert hall and whom we value so highly, that we therefore demand the best from him.
>
> David Monrad Johansen

Rønneberg later repeated his view that 'Ludvig Irgens Jensen's lovely music exactly matched the poetry, but took up rather too large a place'.[35] In *Tidens Tegn* on 11 March 1938 Arne van Erpekum Sem wrote:

> Inspired by Kinck's fantastic poetry, Ludvig Irgens Jensen has created wonderful music, which is intimately linked to the action and the mood.
>
> In the opening prelude to the opening sections, he captures with intuitive strength the essential aspects of the theatrical action and his music prepares, enhances and deepens the changing moods.

[35] *Nationaltheatret gjennom femti år, op. cit.*, p. 334.

> Where the music joins the words as melodrama, it seems to stream out from the stage picture and to go on speaking when the words are silent.
>
> [...] In the concert hall, in the form of a suite for large orchestra, it will show itself to be of everlasting value.

The production was given a total of nineteen times that season and Alfred Maurstad's interpretation of the main character, the drover Vrål, became part of Norwegian theatrical history. In a letter of 10 May 1938[36] Kinck's daughter, Eli Kinck Lie, thanked Irgens-Jensen for contributing to the success of *Driftekaren*: 'Because you agreed to the plan, we were heard'.

Partita sinfonica

Encouraged by the many compliments he received from professionals and public alike – and under a little pressure from Odd and Finn Grüner-Hegge – Irgens-Jensen selected six sections of the incidental music, reworked and re-orchestrated it, assembling it 1938 in a suite which he entitled *Partita sinfonica*. The programme note (probably an adaptation of Irgens-Jensen's own words) for the first performance, on 20 February 1939, gives an idea of its first version:

> The *Prelude* [*Allegro con brio*], which is in sonata form, tries to express the driving unrest of the drover Vraal. He swings between aggressiveness and a shy need for affection.
>
> *Bol's Vise* is a song about restrained longing. The song comes back as a refrain running through the poem and the music.
>
> In the third movement, *molto vivace*, *slått* rhythms can be heard; this is a scene from folk-life in a farm-yard.
>
> The fourth movement, *largamente funebre*. Vraal judges himself. He has suffered a setback.
>
> The next movement, *presto con fuoco*, is formed as a scherzo. Vraal throws himself into wild visions to overcome his gloom. *The Epilogue* [*Andante tranquillo*] expresses the resignation and peace that the drover attains.

But before a performance in 1945 the ever-critical Irgens-Jensen removed the third and fourth of these six movements, so that the final version consists of three preludes together with 'Bol's Song,' none of which is directly linked to the text of the play. The lovely and expressive 'melodramatic' sections – such as, for example, the part with Vrål's visions and experiences of nature when he finally sees the fjord after having come over the mountain – were obviously judged less well suited to the concert hall. Nor did the preludes and the song demand much alteration to the material; only the scoring was changed.

36 Found in Irgens-Jensen's papers.

A draft of a letter dated '4/9 1954' from Irgens-Jensen to the conductor Finn Audun Oftedal in Trondheim, who was evidently intending to perform the suite, offers some further comments:

> The suite consists of
>
> I the prelude to the first act
>
> II Bol's Song, which is hummed on stage in the 1st and 2nd acts and is found elsewhere in a couple of the melodramas. It is played at the final curtain.
>
> III prelude to the 3rd act. The introductory theme is taken from the place in the 2nd act where Vrål, in desperation, suddenly starts to sing:
>
> 'Dugg falder skyr / og ørn går i å – '
>
> [Magpies fall as dew, / and eagles swim in brooks][37]
>
> IV prelude to the last act. (The music here appears first as background music in the 2nd act and depicts the sensitive mood Vrål is in when he has to renounce Bol. (See Driftekaren from the middle of page 81 to the top of page 82.))
>
> But all this is something which at most can be of interest to those who know the text very well, and therefore I don't think it is something to emphasise.

I. Prelude

The tonality of the first movement has a modern ring in that, avoiding traditional major or minor mode, it uses a central tone as a fixed tonic, in the manner of Hindemith and other German composers of his generation. Polyphony, also as imitation, occasionally breaks the theme up between lines and instruments. There are the clear articulations of sonata-form: exposition, development and recapitulation. There is also the expected contrast both in expression and tonality between the first and second subjects (Exx. 34 and 35), a contrast lessened in the recapitulation – another hallmark of Classical sonata practice. Rhythmically and structurally, the main theme (Ex. 34) is formed like a stylised *halling* with a characteristic Scotch snap ('Lombard rhythm') right at the start. Melodically, the 'Grieg motif' (tonic–leading

Ex. 34

[37] A 'bakvendt-vise', backwards song, where all the images are reversed.

note–dominant) introduces the theme, which is otherwise dominated by a diatonic stepwise movement and some broken triads. The key is G minor Aeolian, but there is an intriguing alternation between the sharpened and flattened leading note. Ostensibly the theme arranges itself into eight-bar phrases. Against the theme Irgens-Jensen, typically, has set his very typical stamp with a flexible and striding bass line.

Against the rhythmic insistence of the main theme, the second subject (Ex. 35) is more lyrical, its syncopations offering a contrast to the solid, on-the-beat *halling* rhythms that dominate the first subject. The change of key brings in two sharps as a fixed key-signature, not heard as the dominant, but starting after the strong pedal point on E in A Mixolydian. The harp accompaniment sounds more pentatonic, bringing a further small contrast in tonality. The second-subject section is otherwise dominated by a constantly ascending register in the melody.

Ex. 35

The end of exposition resembles the end of the first movement of Brahms' Fourth Symphony, and there is no doubt as to the point at which the relatively short development begins, during the course of which the lyrical second subject now appears *agitato*.

Viewed tonally, the recapitulation is 'correct' in following the convention of moving the secondary theme tonally in the recapitulation: back in the principal key of G minor, the first subject recovers both its first form and orchestration, and the second subject moves down a fifth to D major Mixolydian. The change in instrumentation and movement-structure between incidental music and symphonic suite means that there is no longer a stark contrast between the sections of this movement; even so, Irgens-Jensen here has surely taken into account that the two sides of Vrål do not remain constant through the drama. Isolated from the spoken drama, a movement must rest on a firmer structure, and so here it takes a more conventional sonata-allegro form. Regarded as a part of a larger wordless drama, this movement presents the untamed Vrål.

II. Bol's Song

The second movement consists of two differently coloured versions of 'Bols vise' ('Bol's Song') (Ex. 36 gives the first), plus a little coda. 'Bol's Song' is sung in its final form, with the text 'Sveinen han lye på kvednå, han' ('The lad, he listens to the sound of the mill'), at the end of the play. Bol is a young woman with whom Vrål is very much taken, but whom he does not dare try to win. In the incidental music, parts of the song appear as a recurrent theme, almost a kind of leitmotif, in all the acts. In one of the manuscripts the song is called 'Song i gjelet' ('Song in the ravine'), as in the play.

Ex. 36

It is a simple and lovely melody, with an AAB form, which is also found in the overall form of the movement. Tonally, the melody moves in changing variants of D minor, mainly diatonically stepwise movement; only a few thirds give spice to the line, and so it can be said to have a connection to some Norwegian folk-tunes in both melody, contour and time. The rocking movement in the accompaniment, which goes over the barlines (Ex. 37), can be considered to reflect both Bol's soothing effect on Vrål and the monotonous rotation and humming of the mill. As in the first movement, the independent bass part does not always serve as the foundation of the chord; it can also have notes foreign to the harmony.

'Bols vise' immediately proved very popular: Irgens-Jensen prepared almost unaltered versions for voice and orchestra, for violin and orchestra and for violin or voice with piano accompaniment. It has retained its popularity over the years and, along with the song *Altar*,[38] is his most performed work.

[38] *Cf.* pp. 198–201, below.

Ex. 37

III. *Presto con fuoco*

The third movement has the agitated rush that Irgens-Jensen describes in his programme notes. This unrest is foreshadowed as early as the introductory main theme, *Allegro,* which has a dualism about it and an abrupt change of time-signature (Ex. 38). This principal motif undergoes rhythmic change throughout the movement; the first triplet subdivisions are soon simplified. The motif becomes an important part of what develops into a scherzo, as Irgens-Jensen mentions in his programme notes. With its recurrent motif and clear sectional subdivisions, the movement could perhaps also be described as a rondo-scherzo. The driving, insistent expression is underlined by several longer spans with asymmetrically changing time-signatures and changes of tempo.

Ex. 38

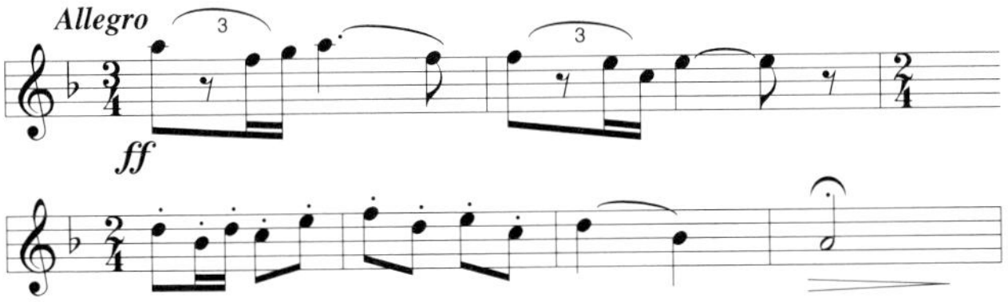

IV. Epilogue

The fourth movement sums up elements from the preceding three, although the *Partita* can't quite be called cyclic: fragments of motifs appear, both obvious and hidden. The main theme of the Epilogue (Ex. 39) has the diatonic stepwise motion and the thirds from 'Bol's Song'. The main motif also has something of the rocking rhythm from the accompaniment of 'Bol's Song', but with repeated notes instead of the tied notes which created the gentle syncopations in the second movement. Here a 'broken-theme' technique of both parsing and expanding the theme through various instruments extends the line to considerable length, where it is decorated by a number of simple counter-subjects. Fragments of 'Bol's Song' re-appear to conclude the work.

Ex. 39

The *Partita sinfonica* differs from Irgens-Jensen's earlier works on a number of points. First, it is more clearly tonal in its functional harmony. Modality is also found here both in the melody and the harmony but is not as dominant. To that extent it seems as if he has gone in a rather more conservative direction. Second, the *Partita* has a more explicitly Norwegian tone, with traditional dance-forms and *slått* rhythms, folksong melodies (not least the dominating, folksong-like 'Bols vise'), open fifths and pedal points. In Kinck's play, Vrål represents both the national and the individual. Einar Skavlan, writing in *Dagbladet* on 11 March 1938, expressed these characteristics in a manner typical of the time:

> In the drover Vraal, Hans E. Kinck has portrayed a genuine Norwegian figure – a man with the great characteristics of the race and with its weaknesses. But Vraal is not just any allegorical figure: he is a living man, unruly in his way of life, because he has strong passions and instincts which control him.

In his book on Kinck, Edvard Beyer explained the author's relationship to the 'two cultures', the Danish (European) and the Norwegian, setting it in a wider perspective:

> He [Kinck] carries the conflict between the two cultures in his own mind; therefore he also experiences it very strongly, and with his ambivalent attitude and his mercilessly sharp view of both quarters he is in a place of his own in his relation to this central theme in our history and writing. [...]
>
> The deepening of nationalism for him – and so many others at the time – stands as a release from the individualism which ends in emptiness. But at the same time he is very strongly attached to – and bound by – the individualist tradition and so ambivalent in his relationship to every common experience – also on purely personal grounds [...] – that to an exceptional degree he becomes the representative of the break between individualist and collectivist trends at the beginning of the twentieth century and onwards.[39]

Irgens-Jensen undoubtedly had a clear understanding of Kinck's drama as a part of both Norwegian and European tradition: Norwegian in its relation to the environment and nature, European in form and psychological depths. So the music must also reflect the psychological conflict in the main character, Vrål – a characteristic which is passed directly into the *Partita sinfonica*.

In the theatre version Kinck required the offstage singing of a psalm in the Fourth Act. Irgens-Jensen chose the text of an old Danish psalm, 'Det er saa svært, det ene Punkt' ('This point is so hard'), by the Danish priest and author M. N. Schmidth (1801–40)[40] but composed an archaic melody to the words himself. And towards the end of the Second Act there is a small dance-scene (later made into a version for string quartet, probably for a performance in Bergen in 1963) for which he found no room the *Partita*.

With its four movements, the *Partita* has an external similarity to the traditional 'European' symphony; the individual movements likewise have a form and an inner relationship which justify the designation 'sinfonica'. The tonal choices, polyphony, orchestration and the sound are similarly a part of a European tradition. Other Norwegian composers were then straining to give a more Norwegian cast to these elements, among them Sparre Olsen, Klaus Egge and Eivind Groven. But such aims were of little interest to Irgens-Jensen: his primary concern was fidelity to the tensions and conflicts of the play itself.

During the Second World War Irgens-Jensen withdrew all his works: he did not want any public performances, either at home or abroad. But the *Partita sinfonica* soon re-appeared, being performed in Bergen as early as autumn 1945. Sigmund Torsteinson, the curator of the Grieg Museum at

[39] *Ibid.*, Vol. II, pp. 64–65.

[40] From Schmidth's collection *Bibelske Sange til Kirkeaarets Søn- og Festdage*, Copenhagen, 1839, p. 44 (information from Arne Holen, National Library, Oslo, and Anne Ørbæk Jensen, Royal Library, Copenhagen).

Troldhaugen and a good friend of the composer Harald Sæverud (who had also withdrawn his music from performance), wrote to Irgens-Jensen:

> Even though several days have already gone since it [the suite] was played, its atmospheric power has not loosened it hold on me. It sparkles on the blue fjord, on mountain lakes, glaciers and birch leaves. The cold concert hall became a piece of the Hardanger fjord, thanks to you!
>
> To tell the truth, I believed only the Westlanders were able to tackle the challenge of Hardanger music, and then you come and kick the feet from under all the theory and show that it is not the place where one sits that is the deciding factor, but the affinity of the mind, the dream of the Norwegian, which remains eternally the same, wherever we are in the country. [...]
>
> Give Sæverud my best wishes if you see him. Believe me, his Salme [Symphony No. 7] and your Driftekaren went well together – two great visions on one and the same evening![41]

The *Partita sinfonica* was performed also in the 1946 spring season in Oslo and Bergen, and later that year in Sweden and France. It was well-received in Norway; abroad the response was mixed. On 29 April 1946 there was a concert of Norwegian music in Paris with L'Orchestre National which was broadcast over the whole country. It formed part of a series, featuring Norwegian, Belgian and American music, whereby Manuel Rosenthal, then director of the music department of the ORF (the French national broadcaster), would travel and conduct in other European countries while conductors from the co-operating countries came to Paris. On this occasion Odd Grüner-Hegge conducted Klaus Egge's First Symphony, Irgens-Jensen's *Partita sinfonica* and Sæverud's *Sinfonia dolorosa* and *Kjempeviseslåtten*. The critic René Dumesnil wrote in *Le Monde* on 7 May:

> The programme included a Symphony by Klaus Egge, of which the slow movement is of a delicate poetry, a Suite by Irgens Jensen, of which the four varied movements, as one would wish, are also finely coloured, and two pieces by Harald Sæverud, a Sinfonia Dolorosa and a Dance of the Giants,[42] full of warmth and vigour. M. Grüner-Hegge showed himself to be an excellent conductor.

Edmund J. Pendleton, writing in the European edition of *The New York Herald Tribune* (published in Paris), was rather less enthusiastic:

> Not all the colors are brilliant, however, or even bright. The Norwegian concert given in the Champs-Elysées Theatre, directed by Gruner-Hegge, was characterized by 'Nordic nostalgia' with, here and there, timid reminiscences of Grieg. Worn-out scholastic procedures were too often apparent in the

[41] Letter found among Irgens-Jensen's manuscripts.

[42] Sæverud's *Kjempeviseslåtten* is usually known in English as *The Ballad of Revolt*.

> Symphony of Klaus Egge, in the Suite by Jensen and in the Sinfonia Dolorosa of Sæverud. The latter's Dance of the Giants terminated the concert with a picturesque note somewhat in the manner of Borodin.[43]

In truth, it was something of an honour for Irgens-Jensen to have been selected by the ORF, and the *Partita sinfonica* was later chosen several times to represent Norway at festivals and special concerts. The work was also picked to be on the first gramophone recordings (78rpm records, nicknamed 'stone-cakes' in Norway) produced by the Norwegian Society of Composers and the Ministry of Foreign Affairs in 1950; these recordings were transferred to LP in 1955 for distribution in the USA. Egge, Eggen, Fliflet Bræin, Groven, Monrad Johansen, Sparre Olsen, Sæverud and Valen were among the other composers selected. The records were given a good deal of air-time on American radio stations, but the music drew less attention than had been hoped. One well-known critic, R. H. Hagan, wrote about the work:

> As it turns out Jensen's *Partita Sinfonica*, a concert version of music originally written for 'The Drover,' a dramatic poem by the Norwegian poet Hans Ernst Kinck, is quite the most impressive work in the set. All Norwegian composers *since* Grieg seem to have been involved in a complicated struggle to reconcile the tunes and the rhythms of Norwegian folk music with the formal structures of 19th century romanticism. And, in the case of post 19th century composers this struggle has been further complicated by new developments and innovations on what can be called, I suppose, the central European musical scene. Somehow, Jensen's music, in its rugged emotional rhythms, its warm lyricism, and its echoes of Norwegian folk melody, has managed to synthesize that struggle in music that has both power and originality.[44]

The Suite was published in 1951, at about the same time as Norsk Musikforlag completed new editions of the Passacaglia and the *Tema con variazioni*. It was also distributed abroad with help from the Ministry of Foreign Affairs. These publications were reviewed only patchily, although one American critic evidently preferred the Variations to the Suite:

> Ludvig Irgens Jensen's 'Symphonic suite' for full orchestra, is in four movements, the last of which is a dramatic and quite moving Grave. The melodic writing is obviously strongly influenced by Norwegian folk music.
>
> The theme of the same composer's 'Tema con Variazioni' is very quiet and chorale-like. The succeeding variations are worked out with great skill and

[43] Undated cutting in Irgens-Jensen's papers.

[44] In the Sunday supplement, 'This World', to *The San Francisco Chronicle*, 28 August 1955.

> imagination, one or two having an almost Elgarian breadth and dignity. The scoring is brilliant. This is a work that should be heard over here.[45]

The *Partita sinfonica* has remained popular in Norway. Since parts of the work might seem to have an illustrative character, the music was used in the 1960s in a number of Norwegian short films about Norwegian nature, and also in a few foreign film productions, including the BBC TV film *Wuthering Heights* (directed by Rudolph Cartier in 1953) and the BBC's *The Grandeur that was Rome* (1963, director Kim Mills). In 1992 the Bergen ballet company Nye [New] Carte Blanche made a television ballet to the music, which was transmitted as part of the annual summer concert in Holmenkollen the same year.

Barnebilleder and other songs

During the late 1930s Irgens-Jensen wrote a number of songs which became very popular. On 19 October 1937 the soprano Elisabeth Munthe-Kaas premiered twelve (of seventeen) of his *Barnebilleder* ('Children's Pictures') to texts by Marie Hamsun (1881–1969), the wife of the Norwegian Nobel laureate author Knut Hamsun.[46] These charming songs are quite unpretentious and continue the line from *Fabler og barnerim*, although without the ambiguities of the latter. This was the last occasion on which Irgens-Jensen appeared in public as a pianist, accompanying his own songs.

The music was published at much the same time, drawing the following encomium from Klaus Egge:

> The songs are borne aloft by the composer's fine lyrical form. His melodic expression is, for all its simplicity, very clear and personal. Irgens-Jensen has a distinct talent for summing up an atmosphere in a fine circuit, where no hint of disturbance is allowed to appear. His greatest talent is to create a sustained melody. Where one might perhaps expect a daring use of the material, one encounters the composer's strict principle: part-writing first and foremost. This principle gives his music a Neoclassical form in Norwegian composition. The atmosphere that underlies these children's songs is very warm and rich. The rhythm is very supple and easy, and the lyricism really sparkling and masterly.[47]

The pianist Elisabeth Reiss, who in 1926 had taken part in the first performance of Irgens-Jensen's Violin Sonata, travelled around Norway in the late 1930s and for several years after the War, presenting various forms

[45] Harry Dexter, 'Pick of the Publications', *The Pianomaker*, September 1953, Vol. 41 (cutting found in Irgens-Jensen's attic).

[46] Before the War Marie Hamsun wrote four collections of children's stories under the collective title of *Bygdebarn* (1924, 1926, 1928 and 1932) as well as *Barnebilleder* (1935) and a collection of poems, *Vintergrønt* (1925).

[47] *Tonekunst*, 27 September 1937.

of music in a mixture that might almost be called cabaret: she played, read and sang, presenting her programme in an entertaining manner. Around 1938 she asked Irgens-Jensen for help in enlarging her repertoire and so he wrote her some humorous songs, including *Kokkedrengen* ('The Cook's Lad') to words by the popular poet Jakob Sande and music to some of Gustaf Fröding's Swedish poems. Unfortunately, most of the music has been lost; fortunately, a recording has been preserved in which she performs some of these songs.

A letter in Irgens-Jensen's archive from an American, Marshall Bartholomew,[48] dated 24 July 1937, reveals that he had given permission for three of his children's songs to be printed in a collection in the USA: 'Ola og Kari', 'På tunet' ('In the farmyard') and 'Hvem er det som rider' ('Who is that riding'), which had been written for Reiss. Irgens-Jensen signed a contract with the New York publisher Silver Bendett on 28 January 1938, but it has been impossible to verify whether the collection reached publication.

The end of the 1930s saw a rise in Irgens-Jensen's interest in writing for chorus: between 1936 and 1939 he composed no fewer than 46 choruses – nineteen for male-voice choir, seven for female voices and twenty for mixed chorus. Many of them were published at the time, too, and thus form a substantial part of his total published output. Most of the male-voice choruses arose from requests from his friend Sigurd Torkildsen, the conductor of the Oslo University Students' Choral Society (the official male chorus). Irgens-Jensen also composed for the choir of the Håndverkersangforening (Craftsmen's Choral Society) and for the Arbeidersangforening (Workers' Choral Society), among them the highly prized *Dagvise* ('Day Song'), to a text by Arnulf Øverland. During these years he wrote both nature-lyrical and ballad-like male-voice choruses, most of which became popular, many of them being performed during national singing competitions, often as repertoire for the 'Felleskoret', when all the choirs sang together at the end of the event. On 14 December 1952 Øverland wrote to him:

> The other day I heard on the radio your composition to my Dagvise. It was absolutely lovely music. I must thank you for it. You don't have any piano music for it?
>
> Should we not see each other sometime in this life?

During the 1930s Irgens-Jensen corresponded with the priest Dagfinn Zwilgmeyer (1900–79) and composed seventeen fine hymns to his texts.

[48] Bartholomew (1885–1978) was a conductor, composer and arranger; he conducted the University Glee Club of New York City from 1922 to 1927 and the Yale Glee Club from 1921 to 1953, much expanding the scope and standard of its concerts.

Only seven of these settings were published.[49] One of the published hymns, *Skrifte* (Ex. 40), shows the major characteristics of these songs, most prominently among them the recurrent use of a single note in on of the parts to form an organ point that allows the music to linger like the contemplative character of the text, and at the same time creating interesting harmonic combinations.

In 1939 P. M. Jensen, Ludvig's father, fell ill and was taken to hospital, where he later died a couple of weeks later. In the interim Ludvig wrote the song *Den gamle* ('The Old One') to a text by Finnish poet Johan Ludvig Runeberg[50] – a leave-taking worthy of a chieftain. For the funeral he arranged the choral song *Rosa* ('The Rose', with words by Olav Aukrust) for string quartet as a *Pastorale religioso*; the quartet also played the chorale 'I blodet hans blømde' ('In his blood blossomed'), from *Heimferd*. The same pieces were performed on the occasion of the burial of his mother six years later; indeed, the *Pastorale religioso* was heard at Irgens-Jensen's own funeral in 1969, as was the song *Altar*.

Altar (the word is the same in Norwegian and English) was also composed in 1939.The text, by Halldis Moren Vesaas, was published in a collection of poetry, *Lykkelege hender* ('Happy Hands'), in 1936. The soprano Ina Blom premiered *Altar*, together with *Fiskerens aftensang* ('The Fisherman's Evening Song', to a text by Arnulf Øverland) and *Den gamle*, at a concert in Rjukan in Telemark county in the spring of 1940; in June she sang the same songs at the University Aula and later in the year on the radio. After the broadcast Blom received a letter from Moren Vesaas:

> We sat by the radio yesterday evening and were very pleased by it – I of course by 'Altar', which you sang so beautifully. It was also nice that a prominent man like Irgens-Jensen could get music out of my poems.[51]

During the War copies of *Altar* were smuggled to Sweden and often performed for the expatriate Norwegians there. The pianist Robert Levin, who usually played the accompaniment on these occasions, once told Irgens-Jensen's son Olav that in Sweden at the time they believed the song was written after the first executions of Norwegian patriots by the German

[49] In 1980 Valdis Zwilgmeyer had a selection of her husband's lyrics published (*Dikt og salmer* ('Poems and Hymns'), Cappelen, Oslo). The 1997 edition of the state church hymn-book includes several poems and translations by Zwilgmeyer – but none of Irgens-Jensen's settings, perhaps because they were considered to be too demanding for congregational singing.

[50] Runeberg (1804–77) was a writer much favoured by Sibelius, of whose hundred solo songs no fewer than 27 set Runeberg poems (the connection was personal, too: Runeberg had taught Sibelius' father Latin). Irgens-Jensen, by contrast, set only one other Runeberg text, the 1870 poem 'Lutad mot gärdet' ('Leaning on the Fence'), which tells of the loss of a childhood sweetheart: composed in 1938, *Lutad mot gärdet*, was to become one of Irgens-Jensen's most popular songs.

[51] Cited in a letter (undated) from Ina Blom found among Irgens-Jensen's papers.

Ex. 40

occupiers at the castle of Akershus in Oslo in 1941. From the serious character of the text this supposition is perhaps not so far-fetched.

In October 1949 the contralto Kathleen Ferrier and her accompanist, Phyllis Spurr, were in Oslo to give a recital for NRK. On the morning of the performance Ferrier asked the programme secretary, Torstein Gunnarson, if she could see some Norwegian art-songs. Among those she was shown was Irgens-Jensen's *Altar*; she immediately fell for it and included it in the evening recital. Although Ferrier herself was not entirely satisfied with the technical side of the recording,[52] Irgens-Jensen was very enthusiastic both about the performance and Ferrier herself. The NRK recording

[52] Winifred Ferrier, *The Life of Kathleen Ferrier*, Hamish Hamilton, London, 1955, p. 22.

was later issued commercially; over the years it has been re-issued in a number of different incarnations, and *Altar* duly became the best-known of Irgens-Jensen's works outside Norway: many music-lovers know the melody without being aware of the identity of the composer.

Ferrier took the song home with her and tried to get it published in English. On 29 June 1951 Norsk Musikforlag wrote to the author of the poem, Halldis Moren Vesaas, and to Irgens-Jensen to say that Novello in London was prepared to publish *Altar* and so asked the copyright-holders for permission to obtain an English translation and to set up an arrangement for the rights. The translation was duly prepared by Ragnar Christophersen, a lecturer in English at Oslo University, and *Altar* was then published in London. Later another translation was made by Birger Huse in collaboration with Guri Vesaas, daughter of Halldis Moren Vesaas:

> Here is a sacred altar for all those who wish to pray.
> Many have come before it and knelt in their quiet way.
> We too come forward, our heart is full,
> we turn where the others turn.
> We can only wish for people who pray:
> Oh God, exist for them!
>
> They must not believe in you vainly.
> Grant that their hopes prove right.
> Grant they will meet with the loved ones they lost
> in death, the deepest night.
> Grant it exists, the peace that
> they hope in the end to attain,
> may it embrace them every one
> who prayed for it time and again.
> Yes, there must be an open door
> for all those who want to turn home!
>
> The heart is full of prayer tonight
> for every human's faith!

In a box of old papers discovered in the composer's loft was a questionnaire from a Norwegian paper, *A-magasinet*. He wrote 'unanswered' on it but had nevertheless scribbled down a few ironic suggestions for answers to some of the questions:

1. *Your motto in life*: 'It is just a passing phase, said the fox'.[53]
2. *Which month of the year do you like best?* 'A rainy July at Nordstrand'

[53] Norwegian saying: 'It's just a passing phase, said the fox, as he was being skinned'.

3. *Your opinion of youth today?* 'A beneficial lack of respect'
4. *In what age would you have most liked to have lived?* 'None'
5. *Which nation would you most like to belong to if you had not been born in Norway?* 'None'
6. *What sportsmen have impressed you most?* 'The hunger fakirs'
7. *What is your favourite food?* 'Potatoes'

In the same box there was a piece of paper with an answer to a question from the venerable German periodical *Der Norden. Monatschrift der Nordischen Gesellschaft* ('Scandinavia. Monthly Publication of the Scandinavian Society') asking if he would say a few words about Jean Sibelius, who was going to be 70 on 8 December 1935. Irgens-Jensen's answer was: 'Jean Sibelius – primitive strength, originality. Symbol of a people. Understood by a world. LIJ'.

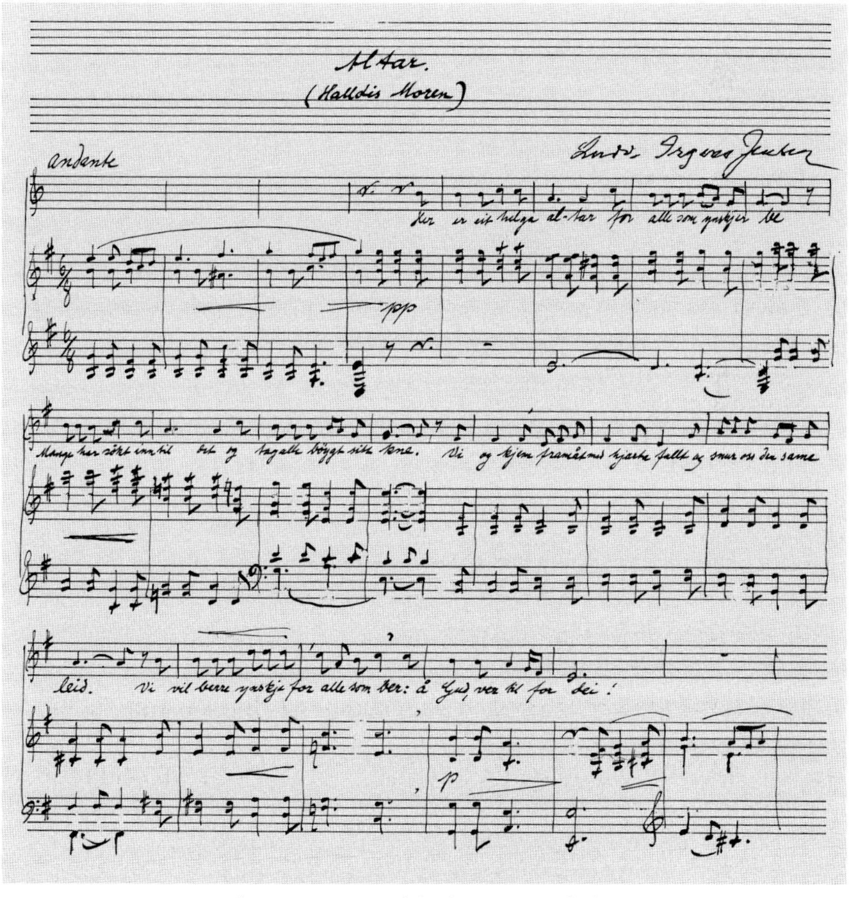

The manuscript of the beginning of Altar

He also received a commission for film music. A letter from the producer Alexander Markey[54] thanks him for agreeing to write the score to a film based on the novel *Den siste viking* ('The Last Viking', 1921) by Johan Bojer (1871–1959). The production was to take place through a large Hollywood company, a prospect which attracted respectful comment in the Norwegian newspapers and film milieu. But probably because of the impending hostilities, the film was never made and so the music was not written.

During the 1930s it was difficult even for the better-known Norwegian composers to make a living from their compositions. Irgens-Jensen could still rely on the independent means of his family. He was rather impractical, very modest and absolutely undemanding. It is thus hardly surprising to find that the prize money for *Heimferd* was eaten up by expenses – which should have been covered by the Ministry for Church Affairs – as a note of his on the back of a bill from Norsk Musikforlag indicates:

re. Heimferd		
Prize money		2500.00
Corrections, music paper, binding etc.	236.25	
To first correction	346.00	582.25
expenses not included		1917.75

written out piano arrangement of Heimferd
108 pages – 216 kroner
(not included the colossal work with parts and score which I took care of myself, minimum estimate 500 kroner)
income through Tono 146.50 (?)

There was not very much to be earned through TONO in the initial years of the existence of the organisation (it was set up in 1927). In 1936, for instance, he received only 1.68 kroner; he received more from TEOSTO, the Finnish authors'-rights society, that year: 8.68 kroner for a performance of the Passacaglia in Finland. But the Passacaglia does seem to have made some money that came through the TONO accounting system: on 9 July 1934, for example, TONO sent a cheque for 350 kroner (approx. £35) as an addition to the annual settlement for performances of the work in the USA.

In 1939, after a board meeting on 14 September, Irgens-Jensen's colleagues in the Norwegian Society of Composers applied to the Ministry of Church Affairs for an honorary yearly grant for him, along with Eivind Groven (1901–77) and Halfdan Cleve (1879–1951). But on 9 April 1940 war came to Norway, and the new Nazi rulers had other favourites to consider.

[54] Dated London, 18 August 1937.

VIII
The War Years

German troops began their invasion of Norway on 9 April 1940, and by 9 June the entire country was under German control. In Narvik, in northern Norway, the Germans first suffered two naval setbacks in April, largely at the hands of the British navy, and a further defeat followed on land in May thanks to an Allied force working with the Norwegian army; but after the military collapse of France, official Norwegian military resistance was terminated. The elected Norwegian government decided to evacuate to Great Britain and continue the fight from there and, together with the king and crown prince, they left the country on 7 June 1940 on the British cruiser HMS *Devonshire*.

But the Norwegians were conquered in name only, and anti-German and anti-Nazi feelings soon developed into both an open cultural resistance and an active underground movement. The Germans were surprised by the resentment with which they were met and the many acts of resistance they encountered from the start, and the occupation soon became brutal and oppressive. After the German attack on the Soviet Union in July 1941 in particular, the existing policies of occupation – already requiring harsh punishment for disobedience and retaliatory measures for resistance – were intensified. To begin with, for example, the president of the University of Oslo was removed from his position and the university nazified; but when that proved insufficient to subdue the students and employees, more than 700 students were sent to concentration camps in Germany and the university was closed.

The hardening of German attitudes had the opposite effect to that intended, strengthening the general scorn in which the occupiers were held and reinforcing the attitude of non-collaboration within the education system, the churches and other larger cultural organisations. Gradually, musical life also became more deeply involved in this struggle. Some leading artists collaborated with the German and the Norwegian Nazis, the most prominent composer among them being David Monrad Johansen. But the overwhelming majority withstood all efforts to nazify cultural life. Some composers – like Pauline Hall – also took an active part in forming the strategy and tactics of resistance, through the central underground leadership, Hjemmefrontens ledelse ('The Home Front leadership'), which was supported by the Norwegian government-in-exile.

The 'Hjemmefront' organised its own information network as an alternative to the Nazi-controlled newspapers and broadcasting. Illegal information leaflets were distributed, and in *Kulturfronten – Oversikt oktober 1943* ('The Cultural Front – Survey October 1943') the following order was issued and printed in the underground newspapers:

> No good Norwegian artist will give public concerts. He will not perform as a soloist at orchestral concerts. [...] The public will not go to solo recitals. The public will not go to the Philharmonic concerts, nor to subscription concerts. Soloists will not appear. This is an order. This cannot be discussed, only followed. You are warned against all attempts to create confusion.[1]

Irgens-Jensen began a personal boycott before the 'official' orders came from the Home Front in 1943. In the first years of the war he was unhappy that some of his larger orchestral works were being performed at home and abroad: the *Partita sinfonica*, for example, was played in Copenhagen (also under German occupation) in January 1941 under Grüner-Hegge's direction; and the Passacaglia was performed there immediately afterwards and again in Italy in the summer of 1941 with Dobrowen[2] as conductor and, in September in the same year, by the Oslo Philharmonic and Grüner-Hegge. The Passacaglia was performed also in neutral Sweden in 1941, 1942 and 1943; and the *Tema con variazioni* was heard in November 1942 from the Oslo Philharmonic under Grüner-Hegge. Irgens-Jensen was acutely conscious of the struggle against Nazi efforts to influence Norwegian cultural life and made up his mind that for the rest of the war there were to be no further performances of his larger works.

Before he had decided on his self-imposed ban, *Heimferd* was proposed for performance by the Philharmonic in spring 1941, but first the music had to be submitted to the new Nazi 'Directorate for Cultural and Adult-Education Affairs' (commonly called the Theatre Directorate) for approval – such were the rules. The board of the Philharmonic received a message on 21 February 1941 from the Directorate that a performance of *Heimferd* could not be countenanced:

> The public mood for the time being is so agitated that one cannot take the responsibility for the consequences a performance of this sort could have. It is a question of the text. Excellent though it may be in itself, the public would

[1] Similar orders were printed in other illegal leaflets: *cf.* Hans Jørgen Hurum, *Musikken under okkupasjonen 1940–1945*, Aschehoug, Oslo, 1946, pp. 136 and 158.

[2] Dobrowen (a Jew) was then a Swedish (i.e., neutral) citizen – and Fascist anti-Semitism in Italy was far less systematic than that of the Nazis.

> doubtlessly read current circumstances into this poem about King Olav and will demonstrate in an extremely unfortunate way.[3]

This evaluation of the situation was surely correct.

Irgens-Jensen faced a real dilemma when the German board of the annual festival Nordic Music Days decided to perform his Violin Sonata in Kiel in 1941: the application appeared more of an order than a request and he did not know how he could get out of it. He did not want his music played in Germany and used in Nazi cultural propaganda, but he could not directly refuse the request without coming under suspicion of contempt for the authorities. It was his sister Dagny who came up with a Solomon-like suggestion – that he should write to the organisers in Kiel, regretting that for the time being the Sonata was being reworked and that unfortunately it would not be finished in time for the rehearsals for the music festival.

In 1942 he received a request to write a wind quintet for Waldemar Wolsing and his colleagues in the group Blæserkvintetten af 1932 in Copenhagen, who wanted to perform the work in De Unge Tonekunstneres Samfund (The Young Musicians' Association), which before the war would have been a prestigious event. But he again turned the offer down as he did not want to contribute to an official event.

The Concert Society in Stockholm had put the *Partita sinfonica* on the programme for the 1944–45 season, and so in a letter of 31 August 1944 to the Concert Society Irgens-Jensen expressed his regret that the performing material could not be obtained: 'Various circumstances, over which I do not have a complete view, have led to this inconsistency, which will be explained on a later occasion'. He certainly did not want a performance in Stockholm: the authorities in Norway could have used it in their propaganda to 'demonstrate' that everything was 'normal' in the relationship between occupied Norway and neutral Sweden.

The boycotts of official concerts led, *pari passu*, to the establishment of a private, 'underground' concert system.[4] Paradoxically, musical life blossomed: with national self-expression severely circumscribed, at least in public arenas, there arose a deeply felt yearning for culture – and for Norwegian culture in particular. More and more people sang in church, in their workplaces and in the few cultural organisations which were permitted. They gathered in churches, in meeting-houses or in private homes to hear leading artists present music or literature. These concerts were often camouflaged in the advertisements as some other event – 'prayers', for example.

[3] Quoted in Hurum, *op. cit.*, p. 106.

[4] For more information, *cf.* Hurum, *ibid.*

The newest widespread 'institution' in musical life during the war was the 'house concert' – an unofficial small concert in a private home. These events began as early as autumn 1940 but blossomed in particular after all radio sets were confiscated in 1941. When the unofficial concert boycott began to have an effect, from late autumn 1942, house concerts were already established as an important underground form of cultural life. Information about these concerts spread by word of mouth, and they were often oversubscribed.

Within Irgens-Jensen's circle of friends, Leif and Esther Bruun (who was a cousin of Louise Irgens-Jensen) in particular put on house concerts for close friends and acquaintances. Leif Bruun himself played viola in a quartet with the violinists Ernst Glaser and Robert Andersen and the cellist (and composer) Karl Andersen,[5] and it was for these musicians that Irgens-Jensen brought along the *Pastorale religioso* and some violin duets. At one of these concerts, too, his Piano Quintet from 1927[6] was performed, with Kari Aarvold Glaser at the piano, as were several of his songs.

A brief anecdote from this time is revealing. Like Irgens-Jensen, Leif Bruun was interested in the pictorial arts and he had bought various pieces of art in the 1920s, among them Edvard Munch's two lithographs from around 1912–14 of the singer Cally Monrad and the composer Christian Sinding. Both of these musicians were embraced by the National Unity Party (the Norwegian Nazi party) and so the lithographs were banished to hang in the lavatory. 'That is where they belong', Bruun said. David Monrad Johansen – who was later revealed to have been a member of the National Unity Party at the time – took part in one of these concert evenings, saw the prints in the lavatory and complained of the *lèse-majesté* to Leif Bruun. 'Do you want them?' Bruun asked. 'Yes, please', said the composer and took both pictures home with him when he left.

Long before the war and the German occupation, Irgens-Jensen understood the real essence of Nazism. On 20 January 1937 the author Nordahl Grieg wrote to him to ask if he would take part in a protest against a possible Norwegian recognition of the Franco government in Madrid. This he did. In the draft of his reply, he wrote:

> If recognition of Franco implies recognition of his moral right, I am very much against such a decision. (But sooner or later we shall certainly be forced to recognise his power if he is victorious).

[5] Andersen (1903–70) was a member of the Oslo Philharmonic Orchestra from 1924 and its solo cellist from 1932 to 1962. His music includes a symphony for chamber orchestra (1936), a suite (1937) and *Festspill* (1951) for orchestra, and two string quartets (1934 and 1962).

[6] *Cf.* pp. 103–5, above.

At the end of the 1930s, along with Odd Grüner-Hegge, Irgens-Jensen tried to get their mutual friend Christian Sinding to understand the danger that threatened from the Nazis. Sinding paid little attention to what was happening and, especially after his wife, Augusta, died in 1936, the old man had little contact with and understanding of the outside world. After the occupation of Norway, the two again tried in vain to prevent Sinding from letting himself be used by the National Unity Party. Sinding could not understand what was happening around him; after all, the Germans had been so generous towards him and his music. As Gunnar Rugstad put it, Sinding lacked political discernment:

> His belief in, reliance on and admiration for German culture was so firmly established that all bad, inhumane sides of Nazism paled. Not even when one of Nazism's worst excesses, the persecution of the Jews, was demonstrated to him did he react.[7]

It ought to be noted that Sinding died in 1941, before the Holocaust itself was launched.

It was not always so simple in those war years to be able to identify those who were acting in the occupiers' interests – an uncertainty which tainted all of musical life. Irgens-Jensen, like so many Norwegians, saw close friends and colleagues being subjected to persecution and sent to the Nazi concentration camps in Norway – Grini, near Oslo, and to Kirkenes, in the Arctic far north – or to Germany. A number of other musicians also disappeared from musical life when they escaped over the border to Sweden.

Both before and during the war Irgens-Jensen sought to put down some impressions in verse and fable intended only for himself, not least in two poems from 1936: *Sultanfest* ('Sultan's Feast') – which seems to be an ironic commentary on Hitler's mass rallies in Nuremberg and his secret police – and *Anekdote (om tygget mat)* ('Anecdote about chewed food').[8] The martial Nazi youth was dealt with in a little march, which also had its own music (Ex. 41).

One unpretentious poem was written while the invasion of Norway was underway and the Germans were eager to capture King Haakon. German propaganda abused the king for cowardice and dishonour because he had fled from their bombs.

[7] Gunnar Rugstad, *Christian Sinding 1856–1941. En biografisk og stilistisk studie*, Cappelen, Oslo, 1979, p. 265.

[8] Both texts can be found in Appendix 2, pp. 330–31, below.

Ex. 41

Ulveære (juni 1940)

'Det var engang en ulv!' –
nei han er ennå på færde
og glammer vilt om sitt jegerkall,
om rett og om ulveære.

Kraft ja!
og kjeft ja!
det har han nok av –
men er han så lur som han tror?

Her nylig fikk killingen berget seg unna
oppetter stupet i nord,
Med hopp og med sprett,
ja på lette killingvis.
Nå står han så frekk og glor.

'Hei, du feige, usle kje!
Hør nå den rette lære:
Hver den som flyr fra ærlig strid,
ødet har han sin ære.'

Men killingen ble hvor han var –
så fikk en friste med annet slag:
'Kom ned og la oss være venner
og glemme gammelt nag.'

Det mekret der oppe:
'Det vilde være greit om du var vennen min.
Men først får du se å få brynet unna
den stygge tandgaren din.'

Wolf Honour (June 1940)

'Once upon a time there was a wolf!' –
no, he is still on the prowl
and howling wildly about his hunting vocation,
about right and about wolf honour.

Strength, yes!
and abuse, yes!
that he has plenty of –
but is he as cunning as he thinks?

Recently the kid goat saved himself
up along the cliff in the north,
with a hop and a bounce,
yes, in an easy kid-like way.
Now he stands boldly staring.

'Hey, you cowardly, miserable kid!
Now listen to the proper teaching:
Everyone who flees from an honourable fight
has ruined his honour.'

But the kid remained where he was –
the wolf tried in another way:
'Come down and let us be friends
and forget old grudges.'

It bleated up there:
'It would be nice if you were my friend.
But first you must grind away
that ugly row of teeth of yours.'

Irgens-Jensen also set this poem to music.

Irgens-Jensen portrayed by Gøsta Hammarlund in 1943 – the first of a long series of composer-portraits by Hammarlund, who was to become one of Norway's most famous illustrators

Some of his earlier patriotic choral pieces became very popular during the war; one was the song for male-voice choir *Til Norges flagg* ('Det fødtes i en alvorsstund' – 'To Norway's Flag: It was born in hard times'), first performed in 1928.[9] Gunnar Reiss-Andersen's text was so general that it was a while before the authorities realised its seditious power.

Another male-voice choral work from the 1920s, *Norge* ('Norway'), with a text by Øverland, was also revived, and parts of it performed illegally. Early in the war Irgens-Jensen also set to music two poems which, distributed illegally in stencils and in underground newspapers, had an especial appeal to people's emotions and stiffened the will to resist. He spoke of them himself in a radio programme in 1946:

> At the beginning of the war I composed melodies to two of the most well-known illegal poems, Nordahl Grieg's 'I dag står flaggstangen naken' ['Today the flagpole is empty'] – 17. mai 1940[10] and Arnulf Øverland's 'Til Kongen' ['To the King']. The latter was smuggled over to Sweden and recorded there. It was sent to London and played on the King's birthday [3 August 1944], but of course without the composer's name being mentioned.[11]

[9] *Cf.* p. 177, above.

[10] 17 May being Norwegian Independence Day.

[11] Einar Haugen, 'De brente våre gårder', manuscript of a national radio programme in 1946 on Inger Hagerup's poem and Irgens-Jensen's music (p. 4). The manuscript is with Olav Irgens-Jensen.

When the war was drawing to its close, several choirs began to prepare songs in readiness for performance with the advent of peace. One of these was *Til Kongen*. So that it could be rehearsed without its real contents becoming known by the authorities, Irgens-Jensen himself wrote a new, innocuous, text, 'Natten og stjernene' ('The night and the stars'), and assumed the pseudonym Paul Jerndal as the source. Paul was his own middle name; Jerndal he took from his paternal grandfather's family name from Østfold.

<table>
<tr><td>Til Kongen</td><td>To the King</td></tr>
<tr><td>Ditt løfte, 'Alt for Norge'
det har du trofast holdt.
Om vi stod frem på torget
og ropte på revolt,
om våre ord falt krasse,
dig ledet ingen vill.
Du hørte ingen klasse,
men hele folket til.</td><td>Your promise, 'All for Norway'
you have faithfully kept.
Whether we stood on the square
calling for revolt,
whether our words fell coarsely,
no-one led you astray.
You belonged to no class,
but to all the people.</td></tr>
<tr><td>Natten og stjernene
(av Paul Jerndal)</td><td>The Night and the Stars</td></tr>
<tr><td>Al dagens glede sluknet
det skumrer på vår jord.
Nu springer frem små stjerner
i evig blomsterflor.
Det er i dype netter
at drømmene blir til:
De løfter seg på vinger
mot lys og hellig ild!</td><td>All the day's happiness dies,
it is dusk over our land.
Now small stars appear
in an eternal profusion of flowers.
It is in the deep nights
that dreams are made:
They raise themselves on wings
towards light and blessed fire!</td></tr>
</table>

The choral song with the substitute text was performed illegally several times during the war and, immediately after the end of hostilities, the text by 'Paul Jerndal' was replaced by Øverland's words and the song performed on the University square in Oslo, where important national celebrations traditionally were held. In June 1945, when the king returned from his exile, the Oslo Philharmonic Orchestra gave a celebration concert (on 12 June) with music of Grieg, Svendsen, Halvorsen and Irgens-Jensen (the Passacaglia) conducted by Odd Grüner-Hegge. The next day the Royal family was greeted on the Royal Palace Square in Oslo by over 8,000 singers who stood in front of the palace, 'a living carpet of gleaming white choir caps'.[12] The opening item was 'Kongesangen' ('God save the King'), and

[12] Hurum, *op. cit.*, p. 65. All the male-voice choirs and a substantial proportion of the women's had their own distinctive caps for performances or competitions.

then the male choirs, some 3,300 singers, performed Irgens-Jensen's and Øverland's *Til Kongen*. The conductor was the leader of the Oslo University Students' Choral Society, Sigurd Torkildsen.[13]

A month earlier some 3,000 mimeographed copies of *Til Kongen* had been printed and distributed around the whole country. Norsk Musikforlag immediately offered to take the work for normal sale and, in accordance with a suggestion from Irgens-Jensen, he and Øverland were each to share a commission fee equally (it would normally have been split 33 per cent to the author and 67 per cent to the composer). This publication has probably been the most widely sold choral work in Norway over the years since then.

The final patriotic poem for which he wrote a melody was *De brente våre gårder* ('They burned our homes) by Inger Hagerup (1905–85), in memory of the German reprisals against Austvågøy after the Norwegian-British raid on Lofoten in 1941.[14] Both Hagerup and Irgens-Jensen spoke about this work on a 1946 Norwegian radio programme presented by Einar Haugen (1906–94), then the cultural attaché of the United States in Oslo.[15] The composer explained:

> It was very late during the Occupation, I think it was a month before the liberation. It was really a rather amusing illustration of how cultural life had been kept up during the dark times. You see, I received a commission to write a melody from Norwegians in Sweden. One day a friend of mine rang and said there was a lady who would like to speak to me. We arranged where I should meet her, and when I arrived, she was doling out soup for the evacuees from Finnmark. The unknown lady [Gunvor Ingstad Trætteberg] and I went out onto the University square and talked while we walked. There were both Germans and Norwegians walking around us, but it was still safer than within four walls. She told me that the Norwegian lads who received military training in Sweden were very enthusiastic about the poem and they asked if I might write a melody to it.
>
> I thought I had the poem at home amongst the illegal things I had hidden away in a sofa. But when I went to look for it, it was not to be found.
>
> I had to call my new friend again and explain what it was about. She was incautious enough to send it to me by post. But when I did receive it, it went unexpectedly fast. I believe I have seldom written anything in so short a time. My wife said she believed I had written it in three-quarters of an hour. I orchestrated it straightaway. The lady I had spoken with then sent out her

[13] Øverland's text was performed again later during this event, this time in a roughly contemporaneous setting by Pauline Hall for mixed choir (*Aftenposten*, 14 June 1945).

[14] British and Nowegian commando troops were engaged in a raid on Austvågøy in Lofoten. The mission failed, and the Germans executed several men and burned down a score of farms as reprisals and to discourage future collaboration by the local population in any new attacks.

[15] *Cf.* note 11, p. 209, above. Haugen later served as professor of Scandinavian language and literature in Madison, Wisconsin, and at Harvard.

> brother, who incidentally was Helge Ingstad, the well-known hunter and polar scientist, to me to fetch it, and he had it delivered by secret courier to Sweden. It was just the music, without the words – we had to be that careful.[16]

Shortly afterwards *De brente våre gårder* was rehearsed with the Student Choral Society in Oslo, but without the text. When peace came, the student singers sang the composition with Inger Hagerup's text during the programme which re-opened the free Norwegian broadcasting service. The text was translated into Russian and several other Slavic languages, hand-written into the music and then copied so that the song could be performed in Moscow, Prague and Belgrade.

When the Norwegian Student Choral Society made a guest appearance in Copenhagen in August 1945, Irgens-Jensen's old friend Knudåge Riisager wrote to him:

> Your songs were received by everyone with great interest and in particular, naturally, the brilliant work 'De brente våre gårder', which engendered a deep and moving silence and afterwards a storm of applause, so that it was repeated. It is also a very strongly inspired work which is both absorbing and remarkable and which will remain as a lasting monument of this time.

Another song by Irgens-Jensen had special appeal during the war, both because of the music and its patriotic – but universal – text. This was *Ei malmfuru* (literally, a pine-tree rich in core wood/heartwood pine) with words by Hans Henrik Holm (1896–1980). This powerful text is now sculpted into Holm's tombstone:

I storskogen hogg dei ein mastetall;	In the forest they cut a mast-pine;
han tungt på bakken fall,	it fell heavily onto the ground,
kvasst rydja dei honom kvistine av,	fast they got rid of its branches,
gnura han glatt og hard,	rubbed it smooth and hard,
alt veikt for sin store skyldnad han gav.	everything it gave up for its great duty.
Men bratt gjenom brim og sjodande hav	But through surf and boiling sea
i storm han skuta bar.	in storms it carried the vessel.

The last two lines of the poem may refer directly to King Haakon as a symbolic pine-mast.

After a NRK peformance of *De brente våre gårder*[17] Cecil Collin-Hansen – a prominent lawyer and choral conductor in Trondheim – wrote to Irgens-Jensen:

[16] Haugen, *loc. cit.*, p. 4.

[17] Perhaps at the Student Choral Society's jubilee concert in November 1945, or the NRK programme in January 1946 (Irgens-Jensen marked the letter 'answered 19.1[.46]').

> Your Malmfuru was our secret national anthem in our secret concerts during the Occupation. I think I took away all the choir's breath with the number of times I have performed the song – and it also took the breath from the public. Thank you for that!

The first page of the manuscript of Irgens-Jensen's Ei malmfuru

During the war Irgens-Jensen's friend Sverre Hagerup Bull had amused himself by writing *Robin Hood*, a puppet play for children, and asked the composer to write the words and music for a few brief songs. It was originally conceived as an unpretentious trifle on the Robin Hood legend, but when Hagerup Bull was forced to remain in hiding for a while at Irgens-Jensen's home (some parts of his resistance network were about to be disclosed to the Gestapo), the project evolved out of the nursery. It ended up as a children's comedy at the National Theatre, with eleven performances around Christmas 1945. The subject of Robin Hood and his Merry Men – fighting against their oppressors in Sherwood Forest – had an obvious parallel to the times that Norway had just lived through. The best-known song from the play is 'To svaler' ('Two Swallows'), with which Bokken Lasson, a famous cabaret singer then 75 years of age, was so taken that she performed it many times to her own lute accompaniment and on NRK (Ex. 42).

In 1943 Irgens-Jensen's son Olav was confirmed, for which occasion his father wrote the song *Til de unge* ('To the Young'). The melody, to his own text, was taken from incidental music he had written ten years earlier to *Hannemor* (a translation of a Gerhard Hauptmann play, *Hanneles Himmelfahrt*) which had never been performed – and later was partly included in the music for the Wergeland celebrations in 1945.[18]

[18] *Cf.* p. 229, below.

Ex. 42

Irgens-Jensen celebrated his 50th birthday on 13 April 1944. Among the many greetings was a telegram from Bergen:

Lat idag mine toner ta sig frem over fjellene
med fart og med futt,
så de kan bli patroner som kan øke smellene

til en høvelig salutt
for dig, gjeve femtiårsgutt.
Harald Sæverud

Today let my notes go forth over the mountains
with speed and sparkle,
so that they can become firecrackers that can increase the bangs

for a proper salute
to you, my fine fifty-year-old lad.

Til de unge

Like most Norwegians, Irgens-Jensen naturally suffered a number of privations during the war. In 1943 the magazine *Alle kvinners blad* ('All Women's Review')[19] asked a series of prominent personalities the question: 'What is the first thing you will do when the war is over?' The actress Wenche Foss and other celebrities expatiated on travelling out into the

[19] No. 4, 23 January 1943.

world or consuming the best food and drink. Irgens-Jensen's answer was by far the shortest: '"The first thing I will do is to smoke myself to death", says composer *Ludvig Irgens-Jensen* without considering for a second'. Like many of his generation Irgens-Jensen smoked a good deal; in his early years, he was almost a chain-smoker. But the shortage of tobacco became critical during the war. Olav Irgens-Jensen relates that his father could not wait until the tobacco plants from the garden were dried and treated: when his craving became too strong, he simply ate the leaves raw. On one occasion, at a party, one of his friends said he had read that eating a cigarette would be fatal. 'Do you want to bet a pack?' Irgens-Jensen asked, and enthusiastically ate his cigarette.[20]

A little time after the war, he was sent some cigars by his brother-in-law in Copenhagen, who was a doctor. In the draft of his letter of thanks, Irgens-Jensen wrote:

> Herr Doktor was so considerate as to send me his patent medicine: the packet of wonderful cigars. I will, of course, be economical with them, but not so much that I am not already able to demonstrate a significant improvement both spiritually and bodily. The arteriosclerosis has strongly subsided, my breathing is easier. I leap up the hill like a goat and in the mornings I jump happily out of bed in expectation of what the new day will bring. Thank you very much!

Symphony in D minor

One of Irgens-Jensen's most powerful reactions against the war and the oppression it brought was not heard until the advent of peace: his Symphony in D minor, which was probably completed in 1941 or early in 1942.

In 1942 the Norwegian Society of Composers announced a secret, internal competition to mark the 25th anniversary of its foundation; there was no public announcement so as not to support the authorities in their efforts to maintain an ostensibly normal musical life. The deadline for entries was 1 March 1943. The juries for the different categories were chosen strictly from those members who were not *stripete* ('striped', that is, inclined to collaborate with the Nazis). Irgens-Jensen was a member of the jury for works within the categories 'Large-scale chamber music' and 'Small-scale instrumental vocal works'; in the class for 'Large-scale orchestral works' the jury members were Arne Eggen, Odd Grüner-Hegge and Karl Andersen. Nine works were entered in this latter category; the first prize was awarded to Irgens-Jensen for his Symphony in D minor and second prize to Klaus Egge for his First Symphony.

[20] Information from the composer's son.

Irgens-Jensen at the end of the 1940s

The board of the Society of Composers naturally understood from the start that they could not present a performance of the winning works as long as the war continued. Instead, they became a way of marking the Liberation and were presented in concerts during a 'Norwegian Music Week' at the beginning of October 1945, which was the first substantial music festival after the restoration of peace. Many composers from the rest of Norway and from the other Nordic countries attended, and two Soviet composers – Vissarion Shebalin, president of the Moscow Conservatory and board member of the Union of Soviet Composers, and Yury Shaporin – arrived unexpectedly in the middle of the festival. So soon after the war, it was difficult to find hotel rooms and the Society had to resort to private hospitality. Thus Harald Sæverud stayed at Irgens-Jensen's home, as did, for some days, Knudåge Riisager and the Swede Hilding Rosenberg.

During the festival week, seven concerts with almost exclusively Norwegian contemporary music took place in Oslo; there were concerts also in Bergen, Trondheim and other places the length of Norway. At the time there was some enthusiasm for the idea that this festival week should become an annual event, perhaps even as the first national festival, but in those difficult days there was not enough support for such ambitious plans.

Irgens-Jensen had been considering a symphony before the war but did not begin work until 9 April 1940, the day of the German invasion. In a draft of a letter he wrote later: 'That poem (which you mentioned) I wrote down (10 April 1940) just as I had the plan of the symphony clear to myself. I had had most of the musical material for a long time'. In an interview with *Dagbladet* on 28 September 1945, in connection with the first performance, he discussed the Symphony briefly:

> 'I worked a lot during the war', he says, 'but I must say that from time to time it was difficult to concentrate. [...] When the plan [of the symphony] occurred to me, I scribbled down a few lines I called "Dragsug" ['Maelstrom'] and which give the content of the symphony. It has therefore become something of a superstition with me that there is an inner relationship between the symphony and the poem. That was how it was for me. But in that case it is a relationship which lies mostly in the atmosphere, less in the details. One should not try to make the notes cover the words or vice versa – it is not intended like that.'
>
> 'Will you let me have the poem?'
>
> 'I do not know if it is right to influence the public with a programme for a musical work like this. People should rather feel what I wanted to give without having it explained in words.'

Dagbladet still received permission to publish the splendid poem:

Dragsug	Maelstrom
I. *Glimt av skavler langt der ute* *skumdrev i lange flak.* *Du går i fjæren – og foten trår* *i rester av gamle vrak.*	I. Glimpses of breakers in the distance, Foam driven in the wind. You walk on the beach – and your foot treads in the remains of old wrecks.
Flom fra fjellene, skred mot dalene *– ondt er alt som skjer.* *Her lå en grend og søkte ly* *– du finner den aldri mer.*	Floods from the mountains, avalanches to the valleys – everything that happens is evil. Here was a farm seeking shelter – you will never find it again.
Ja skred må løsne, vil mot dypet *– ungt er jordens blod!* *Hører du kreftenes ville hymne:* *Aldri eide vi ro.*	Yes, avalanches must break loose, roll into the abyss – young is the earth's blood! Listen to nature's savage hymn: Never we had any peace.
II. *Da fatter du menneskehetens smerte.* *Gjennom sekler i gravkoldt mørke* *holdt den en hellig kjerte:* *Drømmen som tendtes i knuste sinn,* *drømmen som flammet da slektene led,* *drømmen som trosser livet, –* *drømmen om fred.*	II. Then you will grasp mankind's pain. Through centuries in grave-cold darkness it held a holy candle: The dream which is lit in broken minds, the dream which blazed as generations suffered, the dream which defies life, – the dream of peace.

III.	III
For det er en drøm – men er det mer?	For it is a dream – but is it more?
Se deg da om, vår gode bror,	Then look around you, our good brother,
og si oss hva du ser:	and tell us what you see:
De gamle krefter trives godt,	The ancient powers are thriving,
de er våre trofaste mødre.	they are our faithful mothers.
Bølger i hav,	Waves on the sea,
storm i fjellene,	storm in the mountains,
flom og skred	flood and avalanche
ser du her,	you see here,
ser du her hos deg, hos meg.	you see here, in you, in me.
Vold og drap og sjelemord	Violence and killing and murder of minds
ser du hos dine brødre.	you see amongst your brothers.

This is a stark vision of mankind's bleak fate and of impending catastrophe – but the second movement suggests something of the optimism required for survival, and that was how the music was understood when it was first performed.

It was Odd Grüner-Hegge and the Orchestra of the Philharmonic Society who were to premiere the work – the first in the first concert of the Music Week. The other works performed were Klaus Egge's *Fjell-Norig* ('Norway, Land of Mountains'), written in 1941 and described in the score as a 'Symphonic Song of Praise[21] for dramatic soprano and orchestra' to a text by Aukrust, and Thomas Beck's 'Stiklestad-slaget' ('The Battle of Stiklestad') from the 1937 oratorio *Arnljot Gelline,* based on a poem by Bjørnstjerne Bjørnson.

The title of Irgens-Jensen's new work was given in the programme for the first performance as Symphony in D minor, but at later performances it alternates between that and *Symphony in re*; the title-page of the score has *Sinfonia (Re minore).* When Sverre Hagerup Bull gave a radio lecture about the work – with the composer at the piano to provide the musical examples – before a performance in Oslo (on 12 September 1946), it was referred to simply as 'Symphony'.

For a performance in Brussels in 1957 Irgens-Jensen drafted a short text about the work, later found amongst his papers:

> The work was written during the war and is marked by that. The first movement is sombre and, with its desolate, monotonous sounds, can give an idea of elements at peace and in revolt, sea and breakers. [...] The variation theme in the second movement has a sacred quality about it, and the mood gradually becomes light; it is as if something warm, something human wins through.

21 The Norwegian word is 'Høgsong', which is taken from the Song of Songs.

In his various statements over the years in connection with performances of the Symphony, fearing that the relationship between it and his poem might be over-interpreted, he expressed the view that the work should not be considered programmatic in any way. Conceptually, he contended, it had nothing directly to do with the wartime struggle even though the war and the events which led up to it probably contributed to his preoccupation with universal problems while the music was being sketched; the events in the 1940s became, in a way, a sort of confirmation of his pessimism.

In its original version, the work had three movements and lasted some 55 minutes. After his second performance Grüner-Hegge suggested cutting the third movement in its entirety and making some other minor adjustments. In his interview with Øystein Gaukstad, Grüner-Hegge recalls the argument he had with the composer: 'Ludvig complained, saying: "You are cutting into my flesh!" "No, only into the fat!" I replied'.[22] In the end Irgens-Jensen agreed to shorten the work and in 1952 took the brutal but straightforward expedient of excising the final movement.

The first movement is a sonata-allegro with a concentrated recapitulation. The second, which like the first bears no tempo indication, is in variation form with interludes (ending with a fugue), the variation theme being derived from what is in effect the second subject of the first movement. Some of the thematic material of the third movement was taken from both the first and second movements; here, too, Irgens-Jensen was thinking cyclically.

The introduction to the first movement presents a motif which is developed into one of the principal themes; its core intervals are given in Ex. 43.

Ex. 43

In this hesitant, lingering section the theme then appears in its proper form (Ex. 44):

Ex. 44

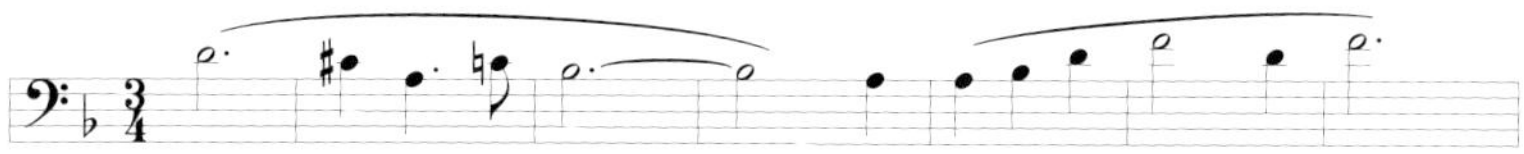

The main thematic section also has an important *Agitato* section with a restless theme (Ex. 45), where rhythm, contour and direction become as important as the intervals in the melody:

22 *Loc. cit.*

Ex. 45

There is also a little motif (Ex. 46) which is used in a fanfare-like manner familiar from earlier works such as the *Passacaglia* and *Heimferd*:

Ex. 46

There is also another characteristic Irgens-Jensen wants to bring out through the lyrical second subject, which develops into Ex. 47, presented by solo violin. It is this theme which appears most modal because of its context: it draws its colour from the counterpoint in which it finds itself and from the general sound and harmonies of this section.

Ex. 47

In the development these themes are combined polyphonically, with Irgens-Jensen allowing the lyrical second subject (Ex. 47) to influence the main theme (Ex. 44), when it is scored for gentler and brighter instruments than the low strings and winds of the introduction. Similarly, this principal theme becomes modally coloured, slowly gaining an *agitato* character; by contrast, the initial *agitato* sections become more peaceful. The gradual convergence of these themes gives the movement a special construction and weight which concentrates its expressive power.

The second movement is a sort of variation-set, with three variations and interludes – but it is not an architecturally strict chain: it is at the same time a development form, an asymmetrical wave which culminates in a triple fugue. Indeed, both the theme of the variations and the first subject of the fugue are derived from the secondary theme of the first movement (Ex 47). Ex. 48 shows the variation theme and the first fugue-subject, with its two different endings, one open and one closed.

Ex. 48

The fugue has three different subjects, and indeed Irgens-Jensen described it as a triple fugue on several occasions.[23] Each of the subjects has its own formal section with a presentation and development, and in the concluding stretto all three themes are set against one another, although in a more concentrated manner than in other fugues by Irgens-Jensen (as, for example, in the Passacaglia).

Rondo Marziale

The third movement cut from the Symphony is now performed separately under the title *Rondo marziale*. It sounds a more pessimistic tone, chiming well with Irgens-Jensen's background poem. The poem closes with the lines 'Violence and killing and murder of minds / you see amongst your brothers'. The human element loses, the destructive wins. This movement, which bears the tempo and character indication *Andante lugubre*, is in rondo form with an introduction and a concluding coda, and is relatively long in relation to the two movements which precede it. There is a degree of ambiguity in the introduction in the use of motifs and tonality, caused by its roaming through some of the motifs from the first two movements. In the ritornelli a martial aspect appears clearly: it turns into a war march that constantly returns with a distortion of a 'warm' theme from the second movement. The war march increases in intensity each time it returns so that the redeeming chorale cannot break through.

The transitional episodes, too, derive motifs from both the first and second movements, and the coda brings back material from the introduction to the first. As in the poem, it is the humans themselves who are the destructive elements; in the coda it is as if catastrophe has obliterated everything. The sea is left peaceful once more, unchangeable; the strong tide has taken everything with it.

With the motivic unity found through all the movements and the return in the coda of the introductory motifs of the first movement, this symphony

[23] For example, in the 1957 draft referred to on p. 219, above.

is plainly cyclic. But does the recurrent use of this material unify the work as a whole, or does it over-egg the pudding? After a couple of years the composer himself took the latter view.

The third movement lay unperformed for many years after Irgens-Jensen excised it from his symphony. It was only after his death that it was played as an independent work as *Rondo marziale*, a name bestowed by the composer's son: in 1972 it was heard for the first time since 1952, played by the Philharmonic Society Orchestra under Øivin Fjeldstad. More recently the *Rondo marziale* has been performed several times by Norwegian orchestras, but it was a British one, the Bournemouth Symphony Orchestra, which recently recorded the three-movement version of the Symphony, conducted by Bjarte Engeset.[24]

The reviews of the first performance, during the Norwegian Music Week in 1945, were enthusiastic, some almost effusive. As so often, Pauline Hall combined her positive report with a technical review and drew some interesting comparisons:

> Irgens Jensen's musical language is exceedingly sophisticated. In this new symphony, as elsewhere, he always works on a tonal foundation. As simple and clear as his themes are, they are nonetheless never ordinary; something pure, severe pervades them and a decisive hand directs and shapes. The melody has something remote about it, at times showing some pathos, but at the same time it is easy to grasp and easy to follow through the symphonic texture even when the texture becomes rather variegated.
>
> If we consider the form, we might ask whether the sonata-form is developed enough to defend the title *symphony*. The first movement, the decisive one in this instance, somehow falls apart in various sections; the movement is constructed, the material is worked up to a powerful crescendo, then the music subsides, it comes to a stop – and then begins again! Because of that, the movement loses its character of unity – which sonata-form demands above anything else – and has more similarity to free composition. On closer acquaintance with the work one could, of course, come to other conclusions. One can certainly dare to assume that it will be repeated. The composer has the right to expect that.
>
> A wealth of fine and characterful features is contained in this music and one will surely gradually discover more. One example in passing is the bright motif in the first movement, 2–3 triads which follow one another; how stirringly it is transformed from its optimistic mood, darkening in sound and character until it is nothing but sombre.
>
> For Irgens Jensen is particularly melancholy in this work; it fights within itself and even the victory is tragic. He does not leave us much hope of a better

[24] With the *Air* of 1958 (*cf.* p. 253, below) and the Passacaglia, on Naxos 8.572312, recorded in 2009 and released in 2011.

> world. The cold and sinister atmosphere which strikes one in some parts of the last movement, leads one's thoughts to Čapek's 'Salamander War',[25] something inevitable threatens, behind the notes one glimpses an eternal struggle. The orchestration of these sections helps underline this impression. To a large extent, Irgens Jensen commands an orchestral language which is closely related to his own in 'Passacaglia' and 'Heimferd'; one finds purely musical reminders, too, but the little reminiscences of Wagner, of which 'Passacaglia' cannot be said to be entirely free, are blown away in the work we heard yesterday. Both in the first and second movements the orchestra can seem overtaxed and it is possible that both the first movements would gain by some limitations, which would benefit the whole.[26]

Other critics took a rather different approach:

> The evening began with a first performance, Ludvig Irgens Jensen: Symphony in D minor. A gigantic work – completely overwhelming. The symphony was written in 1943 – which explains everything. It explains the expressive – the eruptive – the latent *maestoso doloroso*. It was a symphony with a wealth of brilliant details – a symphony which, regardless of how many times one hears it, will constantly have something new to say. The first movement's pithy principal theme and the second movement's powerful fugal development seemed the strongest to me. This symphony will – if there is any justice – always remain as a landmark of the time and the circumstances under which it was created.[27]

Pauline Hall's call for a repeat performance was evidently supported by its enthusiastic reception by the public, and so the Philharmonic programmed the Symphony again at an ordinary subscription concert on 9 October 1945, only a week after the premiere.

On 16 January 1946 the Symphony was performed in Stockholm by the Concert Society, conducted by Odd Grüner-Hegge, together with Grieg's Piano Concerto and Sæverud's *Kjempeviseslåtten*, and the reviews again were encouraging:

> First came a symphony by Ludvig Irgens Jensen. Its dimensions are on a Nibelung-Ring scale, and moreover in several places displays moods of primeval mists and natural catastrophes. [...]
>
> It is very rewarding to listen to Irgens-Jensen's music. He is a born symphonist and he spins his symphonic lines in curves as long and powerful as a Bruckner or a Mahler. His means of expression is always cultured and his craftsmanship eminent.[28]

[25] The famous satirical science-fiction story (*Válka s mloky*) written in 1936 by the Czech writer Karel Čapek (1890–1938).

[26] *Dagbladet*, 2 October 1945.

[27] Poul London, *Friheten*, 3 October 1945.

[28] Kurt Atterberg, *Stockholmstidningen*, 17 January 1946.

'Hl' in *Dagens Nyheter* mentions that the concert was broadcast and adds:

> What one was first struck by yesterday was Jensen's impressive technical ability, instrumental and contrapuntal; he seems to have decided to keep up with the old masters in this piece. One finds with ever-increasing admiration that this lavish exterior by no means existed in order to conceal anything lacking in invention and musical feeling. The melodic material leads at least my thoughts to Brahms – with a scent of Norwegian folk music about certain themes, for example, the first movement's song theme. In any case, Jensen seems to find himself on something like the same spiritual wavelength as the Hamburg master. He is one of humanity's armour-bearers, but as such deeply pessimistic. For those who should not hear it from the music, there was included in the programme a poem from his own hand to clarify the symphony's atmospheric content: 'Violence and killing and murder of minds you see amongst your brothers'; the blessed flame, the dream of peace, are nothing other than a dream.
>
> Is there, then, nothing new to be found (because pessimism and counterpoint are as old as the hills)? Yes, the harmony was naturally considerably bolder than the old ones had allowed. Jensen's 'modernism' appears on the scene in the last movement in particular, which was perhaps the most interesting of all.[29]

Later that year, the Symphony was performed in Gothenburg:

> With this, his first symphonic creation, he has pulled himself up into the foremost rank of the symphonists of our time in the whole of Scandinavia.
>
> [...] The only thing which in the reviewer's mind hardly fits into the ideology of the whole was a fugue included in the second movement. That appeared to be, so to speak, musico-psychologically unwarranted. It appeared rather as a sort of musical confession: a modern composer *must include* a fugue![30]

> [...] this symphony is an extraordinary piece of music, a thoroughly sterling and mature work of art, created by a man with a refreshingly serene and natural temperament and with an ability which approaches perfection. In Scandinavian music, Irgens Jensen's name has always been imprinted on the common musical consciousness.[31]

In the autumn of 1946, the Symphony was broadcast both in Switzerland and at a Philharmonic concert, and it was played (and broadcast) in Copenhagen in winter 1947.

On all these occasions it was played in its original three-movement form. Grüner-Hegge premiered the shortened version on 12 September 1952 with

[29] 17 January 1946.

[30] K. R. (Kajsa Rootzén), *Göteborgsposten*, 13 December 1946.

[31] G. N. (Gösta Nystroem), *Göteborgs Handels-Blad*, 13 December 1946.

the Philharmonic, together with Barber's *Essay* No. 1, Bach's 'Brandenburg' Concerto No. 3 and some songs and arias performed by Todd Duncan.[32] Irgens-Jensen's drastic decision won praise from the critics, Hall among them:

> [The Symphony is] a work which enriches one anew each time one hears it and gets to know it more closely, a musical creed that never leaves one unmoved. In the shortened form the Symphony now has, the release of the forces at work in the material becomes more convincing. The last great crescendo is felt as a proper conclusion to the dramatically constructed music.[33]

One critic – in *Dagens Nyheter*[34] – made an added observation: he remarked that there was something of Norwegian folk music about the 'singing theme' (second subject) in the first movement. This folk-music tinge is very clear in the pastoral oboe theme, which gradually develops into the diatonic fugue theme in the final section of the fugue. Are there other features in this Symphony that can be considered typically Norwegian? Opinions are divided. In a letter to Irgens-Jensen,[35] the composer Sverre Jordan wrote about his difficulties with 'great and small prophets in music', adding:

> Therefore it was lovely this afternoon to listen to your excellent D minor symphony, a sterling work and so Norwegian in tone. (One becomes so tired of listening to Norwegian colleagues' attempts to speak internationally; after all it only becomes just an unnatural mixture).

There are indeed aspects of the Symphony which might be considered 'Norwegian' as the term is commonly understood: some passages use rhythmic and/or metric elements found in Norwegian folk-music; some also Aeolian or Dorian melodic outlines. But, again, this interpretation depends a good deal on the listener's focus. By contrast, it is easy to point to features which are more universally European: there are rather coarse harmonies with parts that struggle against one another, and frequent, rapid modulations and transitions which, together with the rhythm, help create the restless character and produce a special effect when they occur in the darker orchestral instruments. But there is not only gloom: there is also 'en drøm om fred' ('a dream of peace') both in the poem and in the music, a dream which cannot be crushed.

[32] Duncan (1903–98) was best known for his creation of the role of Porgy in Gershwin's *Porgy and Bess* in 1935, a part he performed over 1,800 times. Since Anne Brown (1912–2009), who created the role of Bess, settled in Oslo in 1948 and, first as singer and then as a teacher of voice, became an important figure in Norwegian musical life, it was probably she who recommended him for this concert.

[33] *Dagbladet*, 13 September 1952.

[34] 'Hl': *cf.* p. 225, above.

[35] Dated '2nd Easter Day' (that is, Easter Monday), though no year is given.

Operatic Projects

Heimferd, Der Gott und die Bajadere and *Driftekaren,* together with the children's comedy *Kong Baldevines armring,* all bear witness to Irgens-Jensen's considerable talent for music-drama. In his youth he strove to express himself in opera. It is therefore rather touching to read the draft (probably from the mid-1920s) of a reply to Gerhard Schjelderup, himself a composer of operas, in which he wrote:

> The opera is for me, for the time being, rather far away as a means of expression, probably it is beyond my talent. But I wait with suspense for the development (and solution) of the opera question[36] in Norway and wish you, its loyal champion, fortune and joy in your endeavours.

The operatic project of his youth was *Bryllupet i Genua* ('The Wedding in Genoa'), to a text by Hans E. Kinck, some of which he himself played for Kinck.[37] 'Fra unge år' ('From my youth') he later wrote on the music. These sketches also preserve sections entitled 'Den olme hjort' ('The angry stag') and 'Alatiel' (a seabird) – two pieces which seem practically finished and partly orchestrated.

In the interview with *Dagbladet*[38] where he discussed the Symphony, Irgens-Jensen also mentioned that he had done a good deal of work during the war. Among other things he had undertaken a large project with the author Peter Egge (1869–1959), who had contacted him in October 1940 to ask him to write stage music for his drama *Hevnen* ('Vengeance'), a fairy-tale in verse, published by Gyldendal in the spring of 1941. Egge was interviewed in *Aftenposten* on 28 March 1941:

> 'So it will be performed?'
>
> 'Yes, that is the intention. At the National Theatre. And with music by Irgens-Jensen. – Let us talk a little about the music', says Egge enthusiastically. 'It will not be finished and written out before around New Year. However, he has played for me everything that he has finished. And that is not a little. It is at the same time simple and rich. He has amongst other things a choir, the heavenly hosts, from the fairy-tale heaven. It is movingly beautiful. Unforgettable. That choir grows on reflection; every day it takes a larger place in my mind. He plans to make a suite of the music to "Hevnen"'.

Egge and Irgens-Jensen signed a contract for this production on 30 May 1941, but the drama never reached performance because of the boycott of the National Theatre, and the war meant a lack of further interest. Since

[36] After the closing of the Opéra Comique in Oslo in 1921, opera was rarely performed in the city. The commercial theatres performed mostly operetta, and Schjelderup wanted the Parliament to grant money for a regular opera company.

[37] *Cf.* p. 69, above.

[38] 28 September 1945; *cf.* p. 218, above.

there were no performances in 1942, Irgens-Jensen was released from the contract. He had hardly finished all the music that the correspondence with Egge suggests he was required to write. Later some of the music was used in the music to *Mennesket* ('Mankind') at the National Theatre in July 1945, as part of the centenary commemoration of the death of the poet Henrik Wergeland (1808–45).[39]

Later Irgens-Jensen worked periodically on another operatic project,[40] but that, too, was destined to remain incomplete. It was initiated in 1941 when Magnus Grønvold, a teacher at the Oslo Handelsgymnasium (Business High School), tried in 1941 to interest Irgens-Jensen in a libretto he had written on the Danish folksong 'Ebbe Skammelsøn', a dramatic mediaeval ballad.[41] This proposal might have resulted in a sort of dramatic 'folksong-opera', which would indeed have been out of the ordinary. Initially, Irgens-Jensen liked the subject and they drew up an agreement on 23 July 1941. Grønvold reworked his text and finally sent his draft libretto for printing on 20 June 1943. But when the composer read the entire text, he was no longer happy with it. In particular, he thought that the characterisation was not strong enough and that with an unsatisfactory text it would be difficult to create anything of value. He worked at the libretto himself to make it more suitable for musical-dramatic treatment, asking permission for every single correction from Grønvold – who was so eager and over-enthusiastic that Irgens-Jensen gradually came to regard him as something of a nuisance and eventually abandoned the whole project.

[39] *Cf.* p. 229, opposite.

[40] *Dagbladet*, 25 August 1947.

[41] In 1925 the open-air play *Ebbe Skammelsen* by the Danish playwright Harald Bergstedt had attracted incidental music by Carl Nielsen.

IX
The First Years after the War

It was not only his choral songs that brought Irgens-Jensen's name to national attention upon liberation in May 1945: his Passacaglia was chosen, together with music by Johan Svendsen, Edvard Grieg and Johan Halvorsen, for two 'liberation concerts' presented by the Philharmonic in the National Theatre on 12 and 14 June, at which the royal family had place of honour.

A month later, on 12 July, the National Theatre celebrated the centenary of the death of the Norwegian poet Henrik Wergeland. The manager of the theatre, Axel Otto Normann (1884–1962), asked his stage manager, Stein Bugge, to select parts of Wergeland's great dramatic poem *Mennesket* ('Mankind') and stage them with the leading actors of the house. Irgens-Jensen was asked to write the music, which had to be produced within a month; he worked hard, writing out the parts himself.

The single performance was an unqualified success, much of the credit for which was given to the music. Typically enough, given the mentality of the time, Irgens-Jensen was not paid for his work. Nor was it the first time Normann had let him down: late in 1934 he had asked him to write incidental music to *Hanneles Himmelfahrt* ('Hannele's Ascension'; in Norwegian, *Hannemor*) by the German Nobel laureate Gerhart Hauptmann (1862–1946). The intention was that Bjørn Bjørnson would stage the piece, and in January 1935 Odd Grüner-Hegge, then conductor at the National Theatre, indicated[1] that he expected the production to be staged in a month or so – but nothing came of it. From the surviving sketches it seems that Irgens-Jensen intended to expand it all into an opera, but only one song from the incidental music is known: it was used at the confirmation of his son, Olav,[2] who recalls that a small part of the music for *Hannemor* was included in the music for Wergeland's *Mennesket*.

Another happy event occurred in the first year after the war. Back in September 1939 the Norwegian Society of Composers had applied to the Norwegian Parliament for composer's stipends for Irgens-Jensen, Halfdan Cleve and Eivind Groven.[3] Only a few composers had previously received this honour; those alive at that time were Christian Sinding, Iver Holter,

[1] In a letter to Leif Bruun, dated 31 January 1935, preserved by his family.

[2] *Cf.* p. 213, above.

[3] *Cf.* p. 202, above.

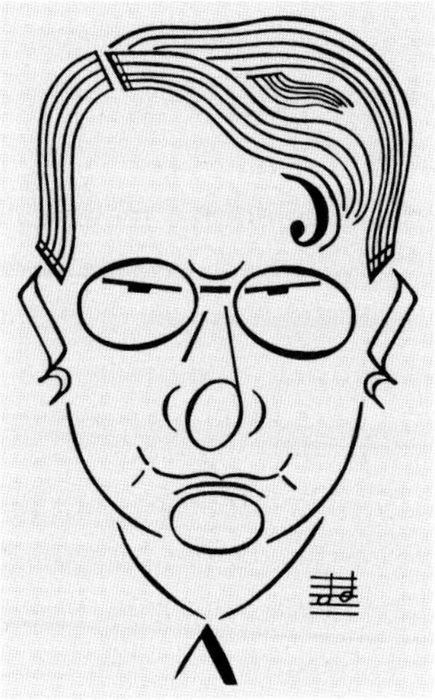

Irgens-Jensen drawn in musical signs by Axel Haugen for Verdens Gang

David Monrad Johansen, Arne Eggen, Fartein Valen, Carl Gustav Sparre Olsen, Marius Ulfrstad and Per Reidarson, the last six having received state grants through applications put forward by friends and supported by politicians. It is clear from some of these choices that the parliamentarians had taken account of regional politics and considered who represented a 'national' line; they bore in mind also who might require economic support. The critic Torvald Engjadal had ventured into print as early as 1936 to say that Irgens-Jensen deserved a state grant, stating the widely held opinion that his music was far more worthy than that of Ulfrstad or Sparre Olsen, the two composers who received a grant that year.[4] When the Society of Composers made its application in 1939, it was the first time it had taken such an initiative, the aim being to bring about a more 'artist-led' cultural life by letting the artists' own organisations evaluate candidates for grants and other forms of recognition. But parliament had not acted on this application and then, of course, the war had come and with it the nazification of cultural life. Sinding and Holter died in 1941, and the composer Geirr Tveitt and an outsider, Signe Lund Skabo, a minor composer who had a strong connection to the National Unity Party (the Norwegian Nazi party), received the state grant from the Nazi government.

Soon after the war, four of the composers (Lund Skabo, Monrad Johansen, Reidarson and Tveitt) and a singer (Cally Monrad) were deprived of their

[4] Undated cutting from *Den 17. Mai* in Norwegian Music Collection.

grants because of their collaboration with the occupying forces. Parliament was therefore able, on 21 May 1946, to grant – unanimously – an artist's stipend to someone in musical life who was very strongly associated with 'a true national temperament': Irgens-Jensen. He was then 52 years old. The award brought him a permanent annual income of 2,000 kroner per year, plus a cost-of-living supplement of 1,100 kroner – more than an ordinary worker's yearly income, but somewhat less than that of a minor clerk in the courts.

After the war, too, the Society of Composers was re-organised and there was a fresh election to evict those who had held Nazi sympathies. Irgens-Jensen was voted onto the 'Expert Committee,' an influential organ within the Society: it advised the board on professional musical questions, evaluated the music of applicants for membership and for the grants the Society had at its disposal and recommended the music for various festivals and works to be chosen for publication or recording. Irgens-Jensen was repeatedly re-elected, eventually sitting on the Committee continuously for eighteen years, from 1946 to 1964. Among his fellow committee-members, also of many years' standing, were Odd Grüner-Hegge, Karl Andersen and Arne Eggen; later, around 1960, David Monrad Johansen and a number of younger composers – among them Knut Nystedt, Egil Hovland and Johan Kvandal – also joined.[5] Irgens-Jensen was also persuaded to sit as a deputy on the board of the Society from 1947 to 1951 (with a break in 1949), and he sat as a full member of the board from 1951 to 1961. He was also a member of the board of TONO in the years 1944–45 and 1951–57. In 1946 he was elected to the programme committee of the Philharmonic Society, which wanted to secure the services of a composer with an open mind; he remained a member for nine years, until 1955.

With these tasks came honours. He was appointed Commander of the Order of the Norwegian Student Choral Society in connection with its centenary celebrations in 1945, and shortly afterwards he was dubbed a knight of Bel Canto Merituoso, the order of the Female Students' Choral Society, for his kindness to the choir and for his compositions *Spurvekor* ('Sparrow Choir') and *Den lange reglen* ('The Long Story'), two pieces he had written, to his own texts, for the choir during the war at the request of its conductor, Agnes Brevik. The title was conferred at the anniversary of the Choral Society in December 1945, when both compositions were on the programme.

In 1947 he was elected to the Kungliga Musikaliska Akademien (Royal Swedish Musical Academy) for his work as a composer – no small

[5] Kristian Lange, *Norsk komponistforening gjennom 50 år*, Norsk komponistforening, Oslo, 1967, pp. 74 and 136.

recognition: he was the only Norwegian to hold such a position at the time, and the first since Johan Halvorsen in 1924. Among the other musicians elected at the same time were Ibert, Prokofiev and Vaughan Williams and the conductors Malcolm Sargent, Bruno Walter and Albert Wolff.[6]

In the years after the war Irgens-Jensen's large-scale orchestral works were performed a good deal, abroad as well as at home. His *Partita sinfonica* was chosen for a concert of the French Broadcasting in Paris in April 1946 and the following month the Passacaglia was one of the selected works at the Scandinavian Music Days in Copenhagen. From Stockholm came a letter, dated 15 January 1946, from the composer Moses Pergament revealing that he had orchestrated some of Irgens-Jensen's songs and had them performed.[7] Pergament had heard Dobrowen's performance of the Passacaglia in Stockholm in October 1945, he explained, and now he was looking forward to a performance of the Symphony there – which duly took place on 16 January 1946. The Symphony was also performed in Switzerland and Denmark in 1946 and 1947 respectively.[8]

In a letter of 11 June 1946 Sven Wilhelm Hansen of the music publisher Wilhelm Hansen asked Irgens-Jensen to arrange Grieg's 'Våren' ('The Spring', No. 2 of the *12 Melodies to Poems of A. O. Vinje*, Op. 33) for strings; Wilhelm Hansen held the Scandinavian rights and, according to their contract with the Grieg estate, were allowed to publish their own edition for that region. The request was rather strange – since Grieg's own arrangement is so good – and Irgens-Jensen turned it down. He was nonetheless awarded Wilhelm Hansen's prize of honour in 1947, a mark of respect for his music.

Immediately after the war many of Irgens-Jensen's songs and choral works were published, as was a set of variations for piano on the folksong 'Falkvor Lommanson' – only the second of Irgens-Jensen's works for piano (after the *Siciliano* of 1924) and destined to be his last. On 24 April 1947 the publishers Norsk Musikforlag proposed that the Norwegian composer and conductor Johannes Hansen should orchestrate *De brente våre gårder* for symphonic band and male-voice choir if Irgens-Jensen did not want to undertake the task himself. They obviously believed that such an edition would sell well, but it seems never to have been published. In 1949 Norsk Musikforlag issued the revised version of the *Tema con variazioni* and brought out a new version[9] of the Passacaglia in 1951.

[6] Four years later, five other foreign composers were accorded this distinction: Hindemith, Honegger, Kodály, Schoenberg and Stravinsky. Two further Norwegian composers, Harald Sæverud and Klaus Egge, were elected in 1952 and 1953 respectively.

[7] Which songs, and the date of performance, have not been possible to discover.

[8] *Cf.* p. 225, above.

[9] *Cf.* p. 126, above.

In the years after the war there was, hardly surprisingly, strong antipathy towards anything that smacked of Germany and towards artists who had acted in the Germans' interests or been inclined to collaborate in different ways. Through no fault of his own, since his behaviour during the Occupation had been exemplary, Irgens-Jensen proved to have been particularly unfortunate with some of his associations in the 1920s and '30s: he had set music to words by Goethe and to Bethge's German translations of oriental poetry and had written some choral pieces to texts by Åsmund Sveen and Dagfinn Zwilgmeyer, who had both become Nazis. Works by such authors were boycotted for some years after the war, and Irgens-Jensen's compositions were silenced with them.

That enforced absence may be one of the reasons that some of his songs have not passed into the standard Norwegian repertoire: the cycle *Barnebilleder*, which he wrote in 1935 to texts by Marie Hamsun,[10] the Nazi wife of the author Knut Hamsun, is one obvious example of a work which one might expect to enjoy frequent performances but which all too quickly disappeared from recital programmes. Irgens-Jensen was sensitive to such questions, too, even when the text in question was by no less a figure than Goethe: when, not long after the war, he received an enquiry from Hugo Kramm, then head of the music department at NRK, about performing *Der Gott und die Bayadere*, he wrote back and requested that the work should not be performed. And when, early in 1946, he received an enquiry from Harald Wiksø of the Stavanger Handelsstands Sangforening (Stavanger Businessmen's Choral Society) asking how he felt about a possible performance of one of the male-voice choral songs with a text by Åsmund Sveen, Irgens-Jensen replied on 16 February:

> It is an awkward dilemma I am in – for Sveen's texts are excellent and I am still fond of my own 'children'. But that is no help! For the time being, Sveen is excluded by the Norwegian Society of Authors and I think their line must be followed, as far as performances of song-texts are concerned as well, at any rate for the present.

From the mid-1930s onwards Irgens-Jensen and Harald Sæverud met with increasing frequency and, in spite of the differences between their personalities (Sæverud being much more of an extrovert), they became good friends. Irgens-Jensen's drafts include one for a celebratory telegram, written in April 1947 for Sæverud's 50th birthday:

[10] *Cf.* p. 196, above.

Harald Sæverud
Råda. Fana

Aldri i strider *vek den vrange.* *Seir vant han omsider!*	Never in fights did the stubborn one yield. He won the victory at last!
Rumslig er riket *han legger til landet.* *Viking og skald tillike!*	Great is the empire he adds to the country. Viking and skald alike!
Løft ham i kjete *til heders-pallen.* *Magre Harald skal ete!*	Hoist him in joy to the place of honour. Thin Harald shall eat!
Fyll hans krus. *Må venners fryd* *skjenke ham fullgod rus.*	Fill up his jug. May his friends' joy make him pleasantly drunk.

Louise, Ludvig, Olav

The poem describes Sæverud well; it is elegant in its language, and its author has also contrived both the alliteration and end-rhymes of skaldic verse.

Irgens-Jensen and Monrad Johansen also made contact again after 1950. In one of Irgens-Jensen's boxes of papers was a telegram from Monrad Johansen from 1955:

> Dear Ludvig.
> I am deeply moved and thank you most sincerely. It was such a lovely proof of your friendship.
>
> David.

Further, for Monrad Johansen's birthday on one occasion (perhaps in 1958), according to the notebooks, these greetings were sent:

Er det toner i vær og vind, *sanger – glemt under muld?* *Og kan vi fange tonene inn* *når strengen er spunnet av guld?* *Herr David slår sin harpe.* *Nu spiller han sorg og glede.* *Nu synger han for til dansen!* *Det er det glemte kvede.*	Is there music in the air and wind, songs – forgotten under the earth? And can we capture the notes when the string is spun from gold? Lord David plays his harp. Now he is playing sorrow and joy. Now he is singing for the dance! That is the forgotten ballad.
Hilsen fra Ludvig	Greetings from Ludvig

From a reception for Klaus Egge's 50th birthday in 1956, at his home at Ljan near Oslo: from the left, Irgens-Jensen, Egge and Odd Grüner-Hegge

Similar greetings also went to other friends, usually on birthdays or at Christmas. And his friends were largely the same as before the war: he spent time with Klaus Egge and met Knudåge Riisager in both Denmark and Norway.

It is not known who persuaded Irgens-Jensen to agree to an operatic version of *Heimferd*. According to newspaper reports around the time of its premiere, at Det Norske Teatret (The Norwegian Theatre in Oslo) in 1947, confirmed in the programme notes, it was Sverre Hagerup Bull who initiated the staging of *Heimferd* and worked on the realisation of such a production. After Hagerup Bull had been in hiding at Irgens-Jensen's home,[11] he ended up as a fugitive in Sweden where he met another refugee, Hans Jacob Nilsen, the well-known theatre-manager,[12] who also appeared to be interested in trying to get *Heimferd* performed on the stage. Hagerup Bull and Nilsen then contacted Issay Dobrowen and the three together planned to present *Heimferd* at the Stockholm Opera.

In February 1945 Irgens-Jensen received a reduced-sized letter, copied from a microfilm brought across the border by illegal courier. The letter was from an enthusiastic Hagerup Bull, who wrote in slightly coded language:

[11] *Cf.* p. 213, above.

[12] *Cf.* also p. 183, above.

Up to now I have not bothered you too much with letters, but I am almost convinced that you are pleased about that – so you can also avoid filling your note-book. […]

So as you know, Lillemor's brother [Hans Jacob Nilsen], Alex's father [Issay Dobrowen] and I have together made a plan: the great work from 30 must rise! There is every reason for this:

1. At home it will be excluded for a long time. Think how many of those from last time who have disappeared. Moreover: if someone in Harlem's society [the harpist Oscar Harlem, i.e., the Philharmonic Society Orchestra] gets rid of all those who do not have pure grain in their sacks any longer or who are of enemy nationality, the assembly will become unfit for work (says Alex's father). Moreover, rehearsals and everything like this will take an eternity. […]
2. Here everything is very much ready. First I will mention Lillemor's brother and Alex's father. And then the opera's brilliant, truly European ensemble which will make everything possible. […] Accordingly one will be able to obtain an epoch-making performance.
3. A moment of great value is one that relates to foreign affairs. Here they would very much like to make this beau geste for Norway. […] The matter has been submitted to the Ministry for Foreign Affairs here and both the press office and His Excellency have expressed their warm approval of the matter. One thinks it is of importance for the attitude on the peninsula. […]
5. One important point is naturally the possibility of a guest performance in Oslo immediately after liberation. An important point, but not a condition. That question is first and foremost dependent – naturally – on how it will be accepted at home. […]
7. I must urge you that this matter is of *great* importance, not only for you, but for us and – not least – for inter-Scandinavian relations. Great store is laid by this on both sides here and it has simply been mentioned that possible necessary large expenses might be covered officially. So you understand that this is meant seriously.
8. You must therefore immediately see to the piano edition and score. […]

If you send it *straightaway!*, then you can avoid writing a letter!

Irgens-Jensen seems to have been sceptical about the project: it was hardly realistic given the political realities and attitudes of the day, and the plans were abandoned.

But others saw the potential of *Heimferd* as a stage-work. Olav Gullvåg wrote to Irgens-Jensen on 26 September 1945 to say that he had prepared an operatic draft of *Heimferd*, which he wanted him to see before he had it duplicated (it is possible that he already had been contacted by Hans Jacob

Nilsen). A couple of weeks later a further letter, dated 15 October 1945, came from Olav Gullvåg, who for once wrote in *riksmål*:

> [...] I send you herewith an attempt at making an opera text from Heimferd with the Ingegjerd motif interwoven. The work is not easy. First of all the libretto form is rather unfamiliar to me. Second, one is bound by the cantata form. I have thus not dared to alter anything of the final cantata movements. There if necessary the director can deal with the matter. [...] It would be a good idea if we had Hans Jacob Nilsen's opinion, too. Can you, when you have time and opportunity, confer with him?

The 'Ingegjerd motif' must be an attempt to include a feminine element, most likely connected to King Olav's sister-in-law, Ingegjerd, married to Prince Jaroslav of Gardarike (Russia), as narrated in the Snorre Sturluson sagas. But Irgens-Jensen was not interested in making a new opera based on his old music. So when *Heimferd* had its stage premiere at Det Norske Teatret (Oslo) on 27 August 1947 Gullvåg's suggestions for an opera were not taken into consideration: the operatic edition was constructed directly from the version of 1930 with only minor changes. Hans Jacob Nilsen had taken over as manager of Det Norske Teatret after the war and his ideas both about repertoire and on the use of music in plays were unconventional – but largely successful: after *Heimferd*, for example, he put on his New Norwegian, anti-Romantic version of Ibsen's *Peer Gynt*, with a new score commissioned from Harald Sæverud.

Some of the critics found *Heimferd* only partly successful as music-theatre, although their views may have been jaundiced by incautious advance publicity from the theatre which came close to promising a new national opera; what they encountered was certainly not the conventional opera they had anticipated. Pauline Hall wrote in *Dagbladet* on 28 August 1947:

> It is difficult to imagine that there can be divided opinions about the musical worth of this work. In pieces of such large dimensions one is already prepared to encounter weaker episodes beside the stronger ones; that is almost the rule. But where 'Heimferd' is concerned, all the time one has the feeling of an unbroken connection between the composer and the thoughts behind the text. And never does Ludvig Irgens-Jensen write merely technically; the music has a tone which never loses its noble sound, its intensity and its deep gravity. Not least, one has to admire the firmly formed choral movements with the elastic part-writing. Or the wealth of fine and pithy musical motifs and ideas. 'Heimferd' is one of the great achievements in Norwegian music in the last generation, that we can surely all agree on. [...]
>
> The music to 'Heimferd' will survive this theatrical assault without any trouble and, for the music's sake, the event deserves the warmest welcome.

> One should simply not believe that it is a question of an opera, but rather a series of tableaux with marvellous music.

And on the same day Olav Gurvin wrote in *Verdens Gang*:

> one cannot escape from the fact that this staging smacks a little of the old national-romantic and Meyerbeer-like operatic extravaganza. Should we not have finished with that kind of theatre? Would it not be possible to give the national-romantic a form which belongs to our time?

Sverre Bergh,[13] in *Arbeiderbladet* on 28 August, was less sceptical about the staging, putting more weight on the music:

> there is every possible reason for repeating the superlatives on this occasion and even add to them.
>
> 'Heimferd' is and will always remain one of the great works in Norwegian music and this new way to perform it underlines that fact.

In the Communist paper *Friheten* ('Freedom'), Tore Sinding reacted positively but, perhaps predictably, put another perspective on the drama:

> It is not Christianity's victory over paganism which is so great in this saga; one religion is as bad as another where barbaric superstitions are concerned. Seen from a moral point of view, one comes to realise that Christianity has encouraged mankind's talent for sympathy and mutual helpfulness, but at the same time it causes us a heavy burden of guilt and angst, which have done great damage, and it has without doubt killed a great deal of healthy happiness and made us considerably untruthful and hypocritical. The open primitive and barbaric cruelty in pagan times was, under Christianity, modified to sadism and more hidden malice, and if there has been any particular gain from it, God knows.

It is the music in this work that the critics liked, as evidently the audience did, too. The staging was not an opera in the usual sense, but more a theatrical version of the dramatic symphony, of which the combination of several well-known singers, the conductor Odd Grüner-Hegge, a good choir and a very good orchestra produced fine performances. Audience numbers increased strongly after word spread through Oslo and the theatre tried to extend the run. Regretfully, Nilsen had to abandon the attempt: the theatre and several of the artists were bound by earlier contracts.

NRK mobilised its very best technicians and managed to get a radio transmission direct from the theatre, a considerable undertaking at that time, when music had to be sent directly through a battery of static microphones. The musicians also found it difficult. Grüner-Hegge recalled:

[13] *Cf.* also note on p. 301, below.

From Det Norske Teatret's staging of Heimferd *in 1947: scene from the First Act with 'The Sacrificial Priest' in front of the image of the god.*

> I think it was a fabulous presentation by Hans Jacob Nilsen, and we played it at that time in Det Norske Teatret. With the small orchestra pit it was frightfully difficult. But we squeezed ourselves in [...].[14] In any case we played it as it was and in this fantastic production by Hans Jacob Nilsen. I think it was splendid and I heard there were many who said so. [...] He was exceptional. Nobody else could be found who could do it like him. He was, so to speak, a musician himself.[15]

In Dagny Irgens Jensen's view,[16] the parts which worked least well on the stage were the long 'Catholic' sections, where the music, though beautiful, now seemed too static; conversely, the battle itself was chaotic since there was too much happening on that constricted stage at the same time. Many of the scenes which required fewer singers were quite striking, she remembered, and King Olav's inner drama and his struggle with himself made a strong impression.

[14] The first two rows of seats in the theatre were removed so that the orchestral pit could be enlarged.

[15] Grüner-Hegge, interviewed by Øystein Gaukstad *(loc. cit)*

[16] In a taped conversation with the author (*cf.* note 28, p. 127, above).

X
The 1950s

At the 900th anniversary of the city of Oslo in 1950[1] a music competition was arranged for the inauguration of the new Rådhus (Town Hall), the building of which had started in 1933. In 1938 the Society of Composers had suggested that a cantata be written for the opening ceremony. But taste and fashion had changed since the war, and audiences now wanted to hear festive orchestral music. In announcing the competition in 1949, the City Anniversary Committee invited works only from a selection of Oslo composers, each hand-picked by the board of the Society. This restriction aroused such opposition that the competition was opened up to any composer with a strong connection to Oslo (residence or birth-place) and who had had an orchestral work performed by the Philharmonic in the past ten years.[2]

The winner of the competition (and the first prize of 10,000 kroner, a huge sum for a music competition) was Irgens-Jensen with his *Canto d'omaggio*, ahead of Eivind Groven with *Hjalarljod,* and Karl Andersen with *Allegro festivo e canto solenne norvegese,* each of whom received 5,000 kroner. Irgens-Jensen's score carried the motto 'Vår egen by' ('Our own town'), since the *Canto d'omaggio* consists of variations on a song he had composed in the 1920s to the poem 'Vår egen by' (Ex. 49), also called 'Til Oslo' ('To Oslo'), by Nils Collett Vogt (1864–1937).

Before a performance in Bergen in 1956, Irgens-Jensen wrote in the draft of a letter to Jan Lampe-Olsen, the manager of the Bergen Philharmonic Orchestra:

> there was a 'programme' at the basis of the work during its creation, something I have not previously mentioned. First the royal command: 'Here will the city stand'.[3] Then the growth from the idyll in the little fjord town through hardship and tyranny – to freedom and the feelings released by it. I am otherwise sceptical about the value of such 'programmes'; perhaps they

[1] The first reference to the city – then called Viken – was then to be found in the saga 'Harald Hardråde' by Snorre Sturluson, but later research has unearthened older sources and archeological evidence, enabling the city to celebrate its millennium in the year 2000.

[2] Lange, *op. cit*, pp. 70–71.

[3] A command from King Christian IV, who moved the centre of the city westward and renamed the city Christiania.

> hinder personal contact with the music for some listeners. But it was this 'programme' I had in mind when I wrote it.

Another draft contains the following elucidation:

> The composition consists of a series of character variations, all of which have a connection to the main theme. *At the same time* the aim of the composition – the celebration of Oslo's 900th anniversary – makes it natural that the development should have a certain narrative character. The mood in the different variations can therefore be expressed by *titles*.

The score of *Canto d'omaggio* therefore offers a kind of programme music, with historical allusions, something rather unusual for Irgens-Jensen.

A sketch by Øyvind Sørensen of the opening ceremony of the new Oslo Rådhus during the first performance of Canto d'omaggio

The Town Hall had also had a carillon installed, and Grüner-Hegge and Irgens-Jensen were asked to choose music that might be suitable for it; in October 1952 they therefore went to Strasbourg with the engineer Olaf Platou to study the famous carillon in the cathedral there. For several days Irgens-Jensen sat 'with mittens on'[4] in a shed by the cathedral in foul and raw weather. He wrote down all the music – the melodies and harmonies – that

[4] From Dagny Irgens Jensen's memoirs ('Erindringer', *loc. cit.*)

Ex. 49(a)

was used each day, gaining some insight into the potential of a carillon. His idea was that the music heard from the carillon in Oslo would take the function of the old watchmen's songs; it would therefore appear as the 'Guardian of Time'. When he came home, he chose which folksongs and other Norwegian music might be suitable for the different times of the day, to be sounded on the hour. Thus in the morning, for example, the hymn 'Se dagen bryder frem' ('See, the day is dawning') was played, followed by other 'morning' music. At noon 'På solen jeg ser' ('I look at the Sun') from *The Herdgirl's Sunday*) by Ole Bull was played, and at 6pm *Baansull* ('Lullaby'), a well known Norwegian folksong (also used by Delius in *On Hearing the First Cuckoo in the Spring*) was heard. At 9pm the bells played a folktune,

Ex. 49(b)

used by Grieg in the *Album for Male Chorus*, Op. 30, with the text: 'I'll go out one evening, find a friend, I'll certainly want to drink'. Other times he used folk material from different parts of Norway. During the rest of the evening there would be a melody from the mediaeval ballad *Draumkvedet*, an evening hymn and the beginning of Grieg's 'Vektersang' ('Watchman's Song') from the *Lyric Pieces*, Op. 12 would round off the day.

Irgens-Jensen arranged a number of the melodies in unison, but most of them are in two-part harmony, which is difficult to bring off on a real carillon: the bells have a long resonating time and the tones or overtones can clash disagreeably. The work seems to have been much more complicated than had been foreseen and so took rather longer than expected. The music was finally punched onto a paper tape that automatically controlled the playing of the bells on the hour. In 2001 a new carillonier was appointed and given full responsibility for the instrument. He chose new music for the hourly presentations, retaining only a few of Irgens-Jensen's arrangements.

Irgens-Jensen's choral songs were much in use in the 1950s. He had still close associations with the male-voice choirs in Oslo and wrote some songs for them, including *To Holberg-epigrammer* ('Two Holberg Epigrams') for Oslo University in connection with the memorial of the 200th anniversary of Ludvig Holberg's death in 1754. Also for male-voice choir, he wrote *En hustavle* ('House-rules') to a text by Øverland, *Skjærgårdsvise* ('Song of the Skerries') with a text by Gabriel Scott (1874–1958), and *På jorden et sted* ('Somewhere on earth') to words by André Bjerke (1923–85), all of which met with real success.

Only five of Irgens-Jensen's larger works were recorded on gramophone records during his lifetime. In 1950, the *Partita sinfonica* was one of the works chosen by the Society of Composers (together with music by Valen, Egge, Sæverud and others) to be on the first records issued by the Society itself, in a series of ten-inch 78 rpm records, issued by the company Nera in Norway between 1950 and 1952.[5] The recording was made by the Oslo Philharmonic and Odd Grüner-Hegge. In 1954–55 the 78s were transferred to LP for distribution in the USA by Mercury.[6] In 1959, an agreement was made between the Norwegian Composers' Society and Norsk Musikkproduksjon (Egil Monn-Iversen A.S.) to issue the Passacaglia (also with the Oslo Philharmonic and Grüner-Hegge, and with Sæverud's Seventh Symphony, *Salme*, on the second side) on the Triola label. In May 1961 the Oslo Philharmonic Orchestra with Grüner-Hegge conducting made a recording of the *Tema con variazioni* for Philips.

Shortly before Irgens-Jensen's sudden death in 1969 – only a few days before his 75th birthday – a recording was made of the Symphony in D minor and *Japanischer Frühling* with Øivin Fjeldstad conducting the Oslo Philharmonic and with Karin Langebo as soloist in the song-cycle, the

[5] *Cf.* p. 195, above.

[6] Lange, *op. cit.*, p. 121.

Øivin Fjeldstad, who conducted several of Irgens-Jensen's works at home and abroad in the 1960s and '70s

intention being that the recording should be issued to mark the composer's 75th birthday. In the event, the recording appeared only in 1971.

Altar (in 1947[7]), *Til Kongen* (probably in 1958; the date has proved difficult to confirm) and 'Bols vise' (1968) were also issued on record during the composer's lifetime. So, too, was a recording of the *Partita sinfonica*, performed by the Moscow Radio Symphony Orchestra conducted by the Finnish conductor Harald Andersén, and issued as an LP on the Soviet label Melodiya in 1957.[8] But Irgens-Jensen never heard it, since nobody sent him a copy (it was never released in the West), nor did he receive any payment for it.

Although Irgens-Jensen stayed out of the public eye, he did enjoy meeting his fellow composers. Among his colleagues on the board of the Society of Composers Klaus Egge, the chairman, a man with a powerful and insistent personality, was one of the most influential. He was also an international spokesman for composers, succeeding Arthur Honegger as chairman of the European Composers' Association. Among the other fellow composers were Johannes Rivertz (also a lawyer of the Supreme Court and later a presiding judge), Erling Kjellsby (chairman of the board of TONO) and Grüner-Hegge, all of them also strong and capable organisers. One might wonder whether the cautious and discreet Irgens-Jensen would or could

[7] Recorded by Eva Gustavson, mezzo soprano, and Amund Raknerud, piano. *Cf.* also pp. 199–200, above.

[8] Catalogue number d-004902-03.

Drawing by Pedro (Salo Grenning) from 1955.
The text reads: 'A happy inner trio from our musical life. Intimate encounter at the Christmas table of the Composers' Society'.
From the left: Karl Andersen, Irgens-Jensen, Harald Sæverud.

assert himself in such company but, as Eivind Groven, who sat on the board for many years, recalled: 'Ludvig Irgens-Jensen was mostly very quiet. But when he did say something, it was worth listening to and everyone knew that'.[9] (Egge said something similar in his tribute at Irgens-Jensen's funeral in 1969.[10]) Irgens-Jensen and his well-formulated and -founded points of view were always held in respect. He was also the composers' representative on the state music-stipend committee for many years, and he continued to sit on the board on the Friends of the Norsk musikksamling (Norwegian Music Collection). In 1960 he was also appointed a member of the consultative board of The Norwegian Opera.

Irgens-Jensen also received requests to teach composition but did not feel he was able to do so. He made an exception for Edvard Hagerup Bull (1922–2012), the son of his friend Sverre, who received lessons in harmony. Arnljot Kjeldås (1916–97) and Oddvar S. Kvam (b. 1927) also received occasional lessons.

Among his youngest colleagues Irgens-Jensen had a special relationship with Egil Hovland (1924–2013). They sat together on the advisory committee of the Society of Composers and on a couple of smaller committees. They

[9] Conversation with the author.
[10] *Cf.* p. 259, below.

gradually became good friends as the older composer came to value the younger one both as a person and as a composer; he felt they were on the same wavelength and he enjoyed discussing musical questions and new musical directions with him. They often travelled from town on the same train, and Hovland recalled[11] that sometimes Irgens-Jensen almost forgot to get off at Nordstrand because he was so involved in the conversation.

Irgens-Jensen regularly went to Philharmonic concerts; when a colleague's work was to be performed, he used to attend the rehearsals as well. On such an occasion, a first performance of a work by Klaus Egge (his Symphony No. 3 in 1959), there was such confusion in the music of one movement that he offered to help Egge with the writing-out of new parts. It took them all night, but it saved the premiere.

Japanischer Frühling

The last large-scale work Irgens-Jensen was to complete was *Japanischer Frühling*. This song-cycle was, as earlier mentioned, originally published with piano accompaniment as his Op. 2 in 1920 and was performed a number of times, even after he withdrew all the stock only a year after the publication.[12] After 1924, though, the song-cycle was not performed complete; a few separate songs were occasionally performed up until 1931, after which he refused to allow further performances.

It seems he never felt himself to be finished with these songs: there are some drafts for orchestration to be found from the late 1930s, and he worked with the songs again also in 1950 and in 1954, but only in 1956 was the whole cycle ready, 'simplified and orchestrated', as he put it in a draft programme note found among his papers.

As so often before, it was Odd Grüner-Hegge and the Oslo Philharmonic who took charge of the first performance, with the soprano Eva Prytz (1917–90) as soloist. Immediately before the first performance, on 11 January 1957, Irgens-Jensen and Grüner-Hegge were interviewed by 'Arco' in *Verdens Gang*:

> VG tried to question the composer a little in advance about the work being premiered, but whoever believes that the floodgates of communication will open at the first turn does not know Irgens Jensen well. No Norwegian composer is as shy and reserved as he when it comes to talking about himself and his compositions, and it is with considerable resignation that he confides the following to VG's journalist:
>
> – As a young man I was passionately interested in poetry from many countries, among them Japan. I read Hans Bethge's paraphrases of old

[11] In conversation with the author, 1979.

[12] *Cf.* p. 63, above.

Japanese poetry; they affected me strongly and I wrote 9 songs as a cycle for voice and piano. They were also performed in the concert hall, but since then they have been left. Perhaps not so strange, however. They are hard to sing and to play. So I took them up again, and thought that the piano perhaps ought to be replaced by the orchestra, at the same time that certain alterations ought to be made in the form, and that the work ought to have a broader and simpler character. The work now appears in a new, revised version – for the first time. Most of the poems are from around 900, a couple from the 18th century.

– And now you are looking forward to being present at the first performance on Friday?

– Looking forward? I'm dreading it! […]

[Odd Grüner-Hegge:] The more I immerse myself in 'Japanischer Frühling', which in my younger days I knew in its original form, the more strongly this work affects me. It is such a characteristic and finely felt work, so sophisticated in its material and preparation that I become more and more enthusiastic about it the deeper I delve into it. And I would think that the same will happen with our musical public.[13]

That autumn, on 24 October, the work was again performed, by the same musicians, at an Aula concert marking the fortieth anniversary of the Society of Composers.[14]

The title of the work is taken from the title of a poetry collection published by Hans Bethge in 1911.[15] Of course, a European tradition of translations or paraphrases of oriental poetry existed long before Bethge, and the translations of many earlier German writers (among them Goethe, Schiller, Chamisso, Rückert and Klabund) were already an accepted part of German literature. But it was Bethge, despite enjoying only mediocre success with his own poems and short stories, who attracted especial attention as a German paraphrast of oriental poetry in the period 1907 to 1924. His first collection was *Die chinesische Flöte* ('The Chinese Flute'); later, in 1910, came *Hafis* (mystic Sufi texts by the Persian poet Hafiz-e Shirazi, *c.* 1320–89/99), *Japanischer Frühling* in 1911, *Arabische Nächte* ('Arabian Nights') in 1912 and *Die indische Harfe* ('The Indian Harp') in 1913. Irgens-Jensen used poems from all these collections except the Arabic paraphrases. Later Bethge published poems from Turkey, Oceania, China and Armenia, and paraphrases of Omar Khayyám.

Bethge was educated as a philologist (with a doctorate in theatre history from Erlangen in 1899). He never mastered an Asiatic language and had

[13] *Verdens Gang*, 11 January 1957.

[14] The other works were the Suite No. 1 from Geirr Tveitt's *100 Tunes from Hardanger*, Klaus Egge's Second Piano Concerto and Harald Sæverud's Seventh Symphony, *Salme*.

[15] *Cf.* p. 54, above.

to base his 'Nachbildungen' on English, French and some German texts, especially translations by Sir William Jones and Edward FitzGerald. Criticism has been levelled against him for his many factual, linguistic and stylistic errors: he did not have a sufficiently strong background in the outlook and culture of the countries and traditions concerned to produce 'correct' translations. In his (German) doctoral thesis the Chinese scholar Chuan Chen writes of Bethge's 'Das Mädchens Klage' (from *Die chinesische Flöte*):

> Hans Bethge's paraphrase is [...] a complete transformation of the original text, a Europeanisation, through which all the essential Chinese elements have been lost [...]. Everyone with a knowledge of China will smile when he reads the delightful exclamation 'süsser Freund'. Such an exclamation would never pass a Chinese girl's lips. Moreover, the plaint is too passionate and therefore un-Chinese. One does find passionate plaints in Chinese poetry, especially in 'Schi-King', but these are not so direct and spontaneous. [...]
>
> These poems give us a deep insight into the inner nature of Chinese passion. That is something Hans Bethge certainly has not seen; he has written poetry which has nothing of this Chinese spirit in it. One must regard his poetry as Bethge-esque poetry and not Chinese. And Bethge-esque poetry is sometimes very beautiful.[16]

In spite of the objections that Bethge lacked knowledge and linguistic understanding, his collections became enormously popular and sold in very large numbers from 1907 up to the 1930s, when interest declined. Many composers – most obviously Mahler[17] – have been inspired by Bethge's paraphrases.

Irgens-Jensen, in his usual manner, sketched various motifs in his own editions of Bethge's poems, setting music next to far more verses than he later used. There a clear correlation between these first, spontaneous musical ideas and the songs that were included in the Op. 2 cycle. In the orchestral version he altered the music of the piano version published in 1920; in particular, he simplified some difficult melodic lines, rearranged the rhythm of the text in some places, and thinned out the textures in the dense piano part. The lines became far clearer when they were orchestrated. The order of the songs was also changed, to effect a more flexible transition between them, both atmospherically and tonally. In the orchestral version he chose the following order:

1. 'Heute' ('Today') (Ôshikôchi no Mitsune, d. 924)

[16] Chuan Chen, *Die chinesische schöne Literatur in deutschen Schrifttum*, doctoral thesis, University of Kiel, Glückstadt, 1933, pp. 102–3.

[17] *Cf.* p. 54, above.

2. 'Der Blütenzweig' ('A Branch of Blossoms') (Fujiwara no Hirotsugu, eighth century)
3. 'Die Weide im Wind' ('The Willow in the Wind') (anon., eighteenth century)
4. 'An einen Freund' ('To a Friend') (Ôshikôchi no Mitsune)
5. 'Der Liebeslaut' ('The Sound of Love') (Segawa, eighteenth century)
6. 'Betrachtung' ('Reflection') (Ise, *c.* 900)
7. 'Nichts leichter' ('An Easy Game') (anon., eighteenth century)
8. 'Einsam' ('Lonely) (Ono no Komachi, 834–80)
9. 'Dauer im Wechsel' ('Permanence in Change') (Ki no Tomonori, 845–905)

A number of the interludes were substantially altered, especially noticeable in 'Heute', 'Die Weide im Wind' and 'An einen Freund', all of which are lengthened, and the introduction to 'Nichts leichter' is completely re-composed. He also expanded some of the interludes, particularly in 'Heute' and 'An einen Freund'.

Harmonically and melodically, the two versions are very similar. An exception is to be found in 'Der Liebeslaut', where the first part of the vocal line is changed a little but in the second part the melody is completely altered, though the harmony of the ending is retained.

Ex. 50

In many cases he transposed phrases up or down a third or a second. The most marked changes are in the song ‘Betrachtung’ (Ex. 50, where the upper stave gives the 1957 orchestral version and the lower that of Op. 2 from 1920). The second time the phrase ‘mit kleinen Spannen’ (etc.) comes around, the vocal line is transposed down a third. From ‘Gelehnt’ the melody is tonally ‘in place’ again, with small alterations. The vocal line is back in register, but somewhat altered in the section ‘Ob ich wohl leben’; from ‘Die aller kleinste’ the melody accords more closely with Op. 2. The orchestral version is almost pentatonic, but the melody is lengthened and rhythmically simplified.

‘Nichts leichter,’ too, has undergone a major alteration: Ex. 51 shows the melody from the orchestral version in the upper stave, with that from Op. 2 in the original key in the middle stave, and transposed in the bottom one. The key-change was undoubtedly to prevent too stark a contrast with the surrounding songs. The extended introduction is newly composed, and the vocal line is altered. The postlude, too, is new. There are no major alterations in the introduction of the vocal part here, but the small changes, both rhythmic and melodic, are important. The melody has become tightened by altering the intervals, excluding the large leaps.

Ex. 51

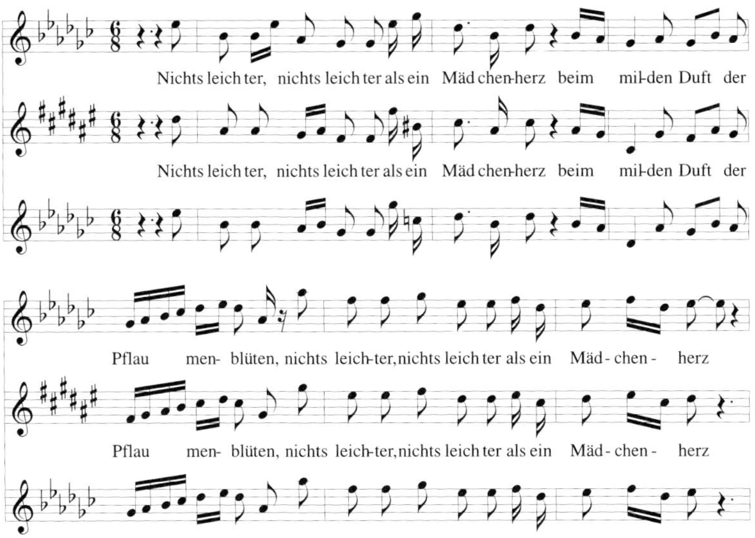

In this song and in the others there is more of an effort to retain the rhythm of the declamation of the text in the orchestral edition. Fewer sophisticated interpretations of the rhythms of the text are transferred to the music, something which gives the orchestral songs a more peaceful, less nervous, character. The Japanese poems are full of imagery, particularly from nature, which might invite simplistic word-painting. Irgens-Jensen avoids the kind of trap this sort of text might have set for him:

Heute	Today
Bald wird der Sturmwind durch die Fluren heulen	Soon the stormy wind will howl through the fields,
Und Laub und Früchte von den Bäumen schütteln	And fruit and leaves are shaken from the trees
Und Blumen knicken, wo er immer weht.	And blossoms break, wherever it blows.
Drum, willst du Blüten pflücken, – tu, es heute!	Thus, if you want to pick flowers – pick them today!
Vielleicht, vielleicht, ist's morgen schon zu spät.	Maybe, maybe, tomorrow will be too late.

The songs are colourful both in form and in detail. The forms are more through-composed, and more complex than is usual for Irgens-Jensen: the text has taken precedence. His orchestral palette here is both bright and light. The use of high registers in the strings together with high woodwind is not unusual, but when in addition he brings in the harp (also employing harmonics), celesta and apposite percussion, the atmosphere becomes shimmering and brilliant.

Something of the same orchestral colour is found in Mahler's song-cycles, especially in *Das Lied von der Erde* where, of course, Mahler also used Bethge's paraphrases of Chinese poetry. Both works have a particular 'oriental' sound in the orchestra, both in chosen instruments and the combinations they produce. Irgens-Jensen's 'exoticism' similarly has an Impressionist element, which does not seem to conflict with the Germanic influence. He was also easily able to work in elements of pentatonic and whole-tone scales in his music without losing the fundamental aspects of expression or line and reverting to Impressionist 'ribbons of sound'.

Some critics considered the song-cycle *Japanischer Frühling* a return to Romanticism, the expression of a rather conservative attitude. Indeed, they saw the work in the light of Mahler, who was not in fashion at that time. It is essentially an expression of Irgens-Jensen's basic attitude of authenticity and individuality, and it was quite radical to present such a work in 1957, in the face of prevailing trends and taste. The work also anticipated the subsequent revival of interest in Mahler's music.

In his obituary of Irgens-Jensen in *Dagbladet* on 12 April 1969, Arne Nordheim wrote:

> In 'Japanischer Frühling' we encounter unobtrusive musical reflections of the basic tone of the text. There is no tone-painting imposed on these words, but a fine and thought-through musical structure which lives its life on the same level as the narratives in these atmospheric poems. A sustained discretion in the relationship of the music and the words makes 'Japanischer Frühling' an enchanting piece of music.

After his success with the orchestral version, Eva Prytz tried to persuade Irgens-Jensen to make a piano version of the new cycle which she could perform at solo recitals. At first he refused, but in an undated draft of a letter to her he is found to relent:

> I must see to arranging this, but *if* I can do it and *when*, I cannot say for certain. The transcription must be playable, indeed, lie passably well for the piano, without the music changing its fundamental character. Probably I ought to sacrifice one or more of the orchestral interludes; without the orchestra's colour and dynamic contrasts, I am afraid they will diminish the effect of the work.

Prytz did get her piano version, a version with shortened interludes, and gave the premiere in Paris on 11 September 1959.[18]

The orchestral version has now been performed many times, in recent years especially by young Norwegian singers, who also have made CD recordings.[19] It may well be that *Japanischer Frühling is* one of the works which takes Irgens-Jensen's music to a wider international audience.

In 1958 Irgens-Jensen added a delicate miniature to his orchestral output. With the public interest in his *Japanischer Frühling* the Norwegian Broadcasting Radio Orchestra wanted to include some of this music in their weekly programme *Meloditimen* ('Melody Hour') – probably an initiative from the producer Sverre Bergh, who had attended the premiere of the cycle. Irgens-Jensen complied with a version of the song 'An einen Freund' scored for chamber orchestra. This piece was announced as *Air*, which established its title.

[18] This version was recently recorded on CD, by the soprano Isa Katharina Gericke and pianist Sveinung Bjelland (Simax PSC 1231).

[19] Details are given in the Discography on p. 343, below.

XI
The Later Years

In the last ten years of his life Irgens-Jensen spent much time trying to recast musical material from his younger days. He worked amongst other things with a *Fransk suite* ('French Suite') for orchestra in four movements, built on songs he had written to French texts soon after the First World War: Verlaine's 'Gaspard Hauser chante', 'Femme et chatte' and 'Colombine', and Verhaeren's 'Les deux enfants de roi'. 'Gaspard Hauser chante' and 'Les deux enfants de roi' were complete and practically fully orchestrated; the other two are almost completely composed but not orchestrated. Their 'French' tone rather sets them aside from the rest of his works. There is a private tape-recording of Irgens-Jensen himself playing through this suite; it makes for fascinating listening.

In these years he also worked on some smaller orchestral pieces: *Liten ouverture* ('Little Overture'), *Vetle hjuringen* ('The Little Shepherd') and *Processione Infantile*. The last builds on the song from the play *Hannemor*.[1] These small pieces are almost complete but are only partly orchestrated, perhaps because he was not entirely satisfied with some of them and so left them unfinished. *Processione infantile* is the most nearly complete; having it completed and performed would doubtless be a rewarding experience.

Indeed, he did not start work on anything completely new during these years. He mentioned to his son that he could imagine writing a work for choir and orchestra to Latin texts, but the score was never begun. Odd Grüner-Hegge thought that there were several reasons that Irgens-Jensen had fallen silent as a composer in the last years of his life.[2]

> He was so despondent, crushed to such a degree. Like the fine person he was, he had no strength. It was purely private things. [...] It may also have weighed heavily on him that he could not – or I would rather say – would not keep up the pace of the rapid development of music. [... He mastered all new trends] but due to his conscience, he could not leave the path he had chosen, and this was deeply rooted in the classical.

Like a number of other composers of his generation, he seems to have felt little contact with the experimental music which was setting the tone in

[1] *Cf.* pp. 213 and 229, above.

[2] From the 1972 interview with Øystein Gaukstad; *cf.* p. 43, above.

Europe after the Second World War, and looked with a degree of suspicion on many of the new works that appeared. Unlike many other composers he did not want to change his style simply to keep up with the times. The former radical had become more conservative; in common with many other tonal composers faced with the modernist hegemony (Berthold Goldschmidt in England and Einar Englund in Finland, for example), he may even have believed that his music no longer had any appeal in what seemed to be a new age.

Yet Irgens-Jensen was not prejudiced against new music in general: he listened with interest to works by composers like Egil Hovland and Arne Nordheim, in whom he saw real talent. And although he saw too much that went in an 'unmusical' direction, the draft of an answer to a letter from Geirr Tveitt in May 1959 contains a comment which reveals his basic open-mindedness: 'It could well be that even the more doubtful experiments could lead to something useful – if they fall into the right hands'.[3]

Another reason could be that he simply had run dry; 'burned out' was the expression Grüner-Hegge used.[4] He felt he no longer had anything to say, and so he might just as well be silent. In a draft reply to a greeting on his 70th birthday, he wrote: 'I myself am still well, but there is not much music getting done any more – and that is not pleasant'.

His poetry, too, indicated that he felt he was growing old. After some pressure he allowed a poem, 'By the Shore', to be printed in a Christmas album, *Julefest*, in 1962. The concluding lines of the poem, which is concerned with the dreams and visions of a child, are as follows:[5]

Siden gikk leken ofte i stå.	Later the game often came to a standstill.
Det ble ikke flere borger av sand,	Finished the building of castles of sand,
skyer seilte bort, og så –	the clouds sailed away, and then –
var han en gammel mann.	he was an old man.

Not long before he died, Irgens-Jensen again took out the manuscripts setting 'Le Voyage' in Baudelaire's *Les Fleurs du Mal*.[6] He arranged a section from Part III of the work as a song for soloists, women's voices and piano for his sister's birthday in 1968 (Ex. 52 gives the opening), with the greeting 'Til minne om gamle dager' ('In remembrance of old days'). When he died, he was working on adapting the end of the poem (Part VIII), which has the text:

[3] The exchange is quoted more fully on pp. 277–78, below.
[4] Gaukstad interview, *loc. cit.*
[5] The poem in its entirety may be found in Appendix 2, p. 334, below.
[6] *Cf.* p. 45, above.

O mort, vieux capitaine, il est temps ! levons l'ancre !
Ce pays nous ennuie, Ô Mort ! Appareillons !
…
Au fond de l'Inconnu pour trouver du nouveau !

Oh death, you old captain, it is time! let's weigh anchor!
This land wearies us, oh death! Let us get under sail!
…
To the depths of the Unknown to find something new!

Ex. 52

Irgens-Jensen photographed by Aftenposten *in connection with his imminent 75th birthday. In his hand he is holding a newly completed reworking of a section of his early setting of* Le Voyage, *by Baudelaire.*

In 1969, some of Irgens-Jensen's friends and the Society of Composers jointly began to plan the celebration of his 75th birthday. The family commissioned the sculptor Kjeld Rasmussen (1917–99) to model a bust of him, a bronze cast of which now stands in the Oslo Konserthus, peering down a little shyly, while Klaus Egge stands on the opposite side, staring self-consciously at Irgens-Jensen and the many listeners who go to and from the concert hall.

Irgens-Jensen was invited to NRK to be interviewed by Torstein Gunnarson, who was making a programme about him. The interview proved difficult and did not go at all well. The composer, profoundly shy, would rather not have entered the studio; when he sat down in the chair in front of the microphone, it was almost impossible to get him going and he soon wanted to abandon the hesitant interview – Gunnarson almost had to take hold of his jacket to keep him in the chair. Bit by bit, he delivered a few sentences which were later spliced together into a more fluent whole. This interview, parts of which have been already quoted here,[7] is an important source for understanding Irgens-Jensen as a person and some of his views.

To avoid the excitement around his 75th birthday, he and his wife went to Sicily – and here, in Piazza Armerina, he died of a heart attack on 11 April, two days before the date itself; NRK had to transform its planned tribute into a memorial programme. He was cremated in Italy, and the urn was flown home to Norway by his son and wife; later it was interred in the Cemetery of Honour ('Æreslunden') in Oslo. A sturdy and modest stone from the Jotunheim mountains marks the grave – a fitting and proper symbol.

At the interment Klaus Egge, the chairman of the Society of Composers, spoke movingly of him:

> In a spiritual sense, every single human being also leaves behind his footprint. We sense the weight of their personality through the imprint of a step.
>
> It is exactly this that we feel so strongly at this moment, when we are to take our farewell of our dear Ludvig Irgens-Jensen. Being with him gave us all the feeling of knowing a creative man with a distinctive peace and inner balance.
>
> He was unassuming. Comfortable with words he was not. But when he did say something, one often felt that it came from a person with unusual spiritual perspectives. He was highly gifted. Not only as a creative artist, but also with poetic talents; indeed, he even painted in his time. He had a rare overall view of all the arts, literature, painting and music.
>
> Irgens-Jensen seemed to be a wise philosopher, something one senses in certain visionary parts in a number of his works. But then there was this remarkable thing, that he carried his wisdom so unassumingly with him. He

[7] *Cf.* pp. 26, 30, 37, 82 and 123, above.

Irgens-Jensen's grave-stone in Vår Frelsers ('Our Saviour's') graveyard

> was not obtrusive in speech, but even he could momentarily light up and get excited, and then the words came with weight. [...]
>
> Such a long span of time has gone by, and his works have been performed for decades, so we know we can say: his music is timeless, and the timeless quality of art will always have its time throughout the changing epochs.
>
> In this connection I remember some words I picked up, something he said about ten years ago, but which was not said directly to me. 'My time will come', he said. It was, of course, an outburst of thoughts about current artistic principles. But it also betrays something else, namely that the natural and real modesty he undoubtedly possessed arose from understanding what the demand for quality really consists of. His conscious, strong will is the counterpart of this inborn humility. [...]

In an obituary in *Arbeiderbladet* on 14 April, Egge filled out the picture:

> Irgens-Jensen's impressive contribution to Norwegian symphonic music is of an innovative, constructive kind within our own national music. He was one of the pillars that marked the *real* development of symphonic music in this country in the 20th century. Therefore, in our awareness, he is amongst the greatest we have.

Øistein Sommerfeldt[8] used a telling quotation from Irgens-Jensen in his obituary in *Verdens Gang* on 15 April: 'There are no short-cuts in

[8] Sommerfeldt (1919–94) was a leading Norwegian composer in the generation after Irgens-Jensen.

art'. Sommerfeldt also touched upon Irgens-Jensen's many ascents of the mountain Store Skagastølstind in the western part of Norway, which he found noted down in the guest book in the mountain hotel Turtagrø and wrote that this composer was 'a genuine climber of spiritual summits'.

Hans Jørgen Hurum, too, in *Aftenposten* on 12 April, drew a comparison between the composer's life and his works:

> He has not written one piece that defiantly shouts, clear the way for here is something new coming, original caprices, effects that no-one has dreamed of. There are not many musicians who have so totally lacked the need to attract attention.
>
> And yet his music is so powerful that it is counted amongst what we will be most reluctant to dispense with. It shines, but only by virtue of its inner glow, for it never dazzles.

XII
Irgens-Jensen as a Person

In December 1934 the operetta *Jomfruburet* ('The Maiden's Bower'[1]) by Heinrich Berté was performed at the National Theatre in Oslo;[2] the plot is based around the life of Schubert and the music is largely his. The main role was to be played by Tore Foss who asked the director Bjørn Bjørnson at the outset of the rehearsals how Schubert should be played. 'You know Irgens-Jensen?' asked Bjørnson. Yes, Foss said: he knew him from a collaboration with the Student Choral Society. 'Make Schubert like Irgens-Jensen,' the director said, 'a little distant and withdrawn, an impractical, romantic and dreamy artistic type.'[3] Such was the general image of the composer at that time.

Several of Irgens-Jensen's friends and relations described him as a typical artist: absorbed by his art, unworldly, always behaving with reticence and caution. These characteristics can also be noticed in the interviews he gave. Marie Fearnley wrote[4] of him:

> Irgens-Jensen's shyness borders on morbidity. Just a newspaper wanting a comment from him brings him to pure despair. He wrings his hands like an unhappy schoolboy and begs to be spared. What would he have to say to people, he who never in his life has published a note and yet is the country's best young composer.
>
> That is the way he is. Free from all prima donna whims and altogether as modest as a person can be.

And in a later interview in *Norsk Musikkliv* ('Norwegian Musical Life'),[5] Jens Arbo confessed that

> it is not easy to carry out an interview. Irgens-Jensen is shyness itself and to begin with he is reluctant to express himself. Often he withdraws into himself and with a 'noli me tangere' expression, which is both charming and shy at the same time. But when I ask him to play a little for me from his children's rhymes, male-voice choir songs, hymns and canons he does not refuse.

[1] Composed in 1916, it bears the title *Das Dreimäderlhaus* in the original German and is known as *Lilac Times* in English.

[2] Rønneberg, *op. cit.*, p. 281.

[3] Recounted to the author by Odd Grüner-Hegge and Dagny Irgens Jensen.

[4] 'This Week's Profile', *Dagbladet*, 29 November 1930.

[5] 1943, No. 1, pp. 6–9.

In a draft from the 1930s responding to a request for an interview, Irgens-Jensen wrote:

> In connection with your kind enquiry may I inform you: the rather unfortunate comments which on many occasions are put into my mouth in the newspapers, possibly because of my own ineptitude as an object for interviews, have finally decided me not to let myself be interviewed, a principle for which I hope no-one will reproach me. Yours respectfully L.I.J.

That attitude was hardly moderated by age: a quarter of a century later, the journalist who spoke to him before the premiere of *Japanischer Frühling* ran into the same reserve.[6]

Even if he was sparing in talking about himself, the best interviews are nonetheless revealing. It is obvious that he detested talking about private matters and he was careful with comments about his own works and views. In his youth he could at times be very outspoken about his own music, although he could never be persuaded to say anything negative about his colleagues:

> 'You only talk about those you admire. Say something about what you find poor in Norwegian music at present.'
>
> 'No, one becomes so cowardly, living in a small country,' says Irgens-Jensen, smiling genially. 'And *peace* is still the best thing....'[7]

His sister Dagny contended that he was not really shy and that in his youth he could be extraordinarily free and witty. But gradually, as he became an artist and a 'public' person, his reserve increased. In the beginning he felt frustrated that journalists failed to communicate what he thought was important and that he was accorded opinions he did not hold. He therefore became more reserved when talking about his own compositions and tried to avoid the public light. Nor was it his way to make a fuss to have his works performed. As Odd Grüner-Hegge put it, he had 'on the whole an over-modesty which has done him real harm. Imagine if he had had a little of the others' boldness!'[8]

In spite of his reserve, it is clear both from statements and from interviews and reports that Irgens-Jensen had distinct authority as a person. He was reliable and dependable, by reason of both his knowledge and his wisdom, and he was elected again and again to represent his colleagues in the Society of Composers and TONO, the Norwegian organisation for composers' rights.

Very few of Irgens-Jensen's letters are preserved – compared, for example, with those of his contemporary Fartein Valen, another deeply reserved

[6] *Cf.* pp. 247–48, above.

[7] From an interview by Theo Findahl in *Adresseavisen* on 24 January 1931.

[8] *Loc. cit.*, p. 5.

personality. The majority of them are found only as drafts, preserved among his other papers. Indeed, he strongly disliked writing letters. 'I cannot write, have never been able to,' he wrote in the draft of a letter to the publishers Gyldendal, who wanted him to write some words for a *Festschrift* in honour of Harald Sæverud's 70th birthday. But the drafts that have been preserved show that he was a fine stylist with a real talent for formulating words – and the fact that he did prepare drafts of his letters and public comments (an obvious boon for a biographer) indicates how much care he devoted to such statements, even when intended for an audience of one.

As far as is known, he never wrote a diary, but in some of his many sketchbooks – particularly those from his youth – there are a number of notes both about his works and about everyday matters. Among them is a quantity of quick sketches, pictures in pencil or coloured chalk, which say something about his experience of nature and people. In the sketchbooks much of the text is written in a sort of shorthand, undoubtedly not only because it would be fast but also because these were personal notes. Even if there were nothing contentious or dangerous in the text, such a procedure at least shows considerable caution – and this singular, personal shorthand has so far resisted all attempts to transcribe it.

Irgens-Jensen was a man skilled in languages and much of the literature he read was in the original. His library included much of the best of foreign literature: poetry, prose and drama, although it is clear that his predilection was for poetry. In his youth he particular enjoyed modern or 'exotic' poetry in French or German, as well as poems by his friend Arnulf Øverland. Indeed, he owned an unusual amount of Norwegian literature, from the Old-Norse sagas to the generation of writers of the 1960s. During the 1930s he became more and more preoccupied with Norwegian poets, those who wrote in *bokmål* and *nynorsk* alike – as his many songs to such texts bear witness.

He also had a large library of music, scores and literature on music. He kept up with what was happening internationally, and he obtained almost everything in print by contemporary and younger Norwegian colleagues. He had a taste for art, too: right from his early youth he bought drawings and prints, both Norwegian and foreign, later adding paintings to his collection. He was particularly enthusiastic about Edvard Munch and early in life managed to buy some lithographs and woodcuts by him. At exhibitions and auctions in the 1920s he also bought paintings by among others Ludvig Karsten, Arne Kavli and Jean Heiberg, who all later became well-known Norwegian painters. He had a good eye for many of the younger artists from that time.

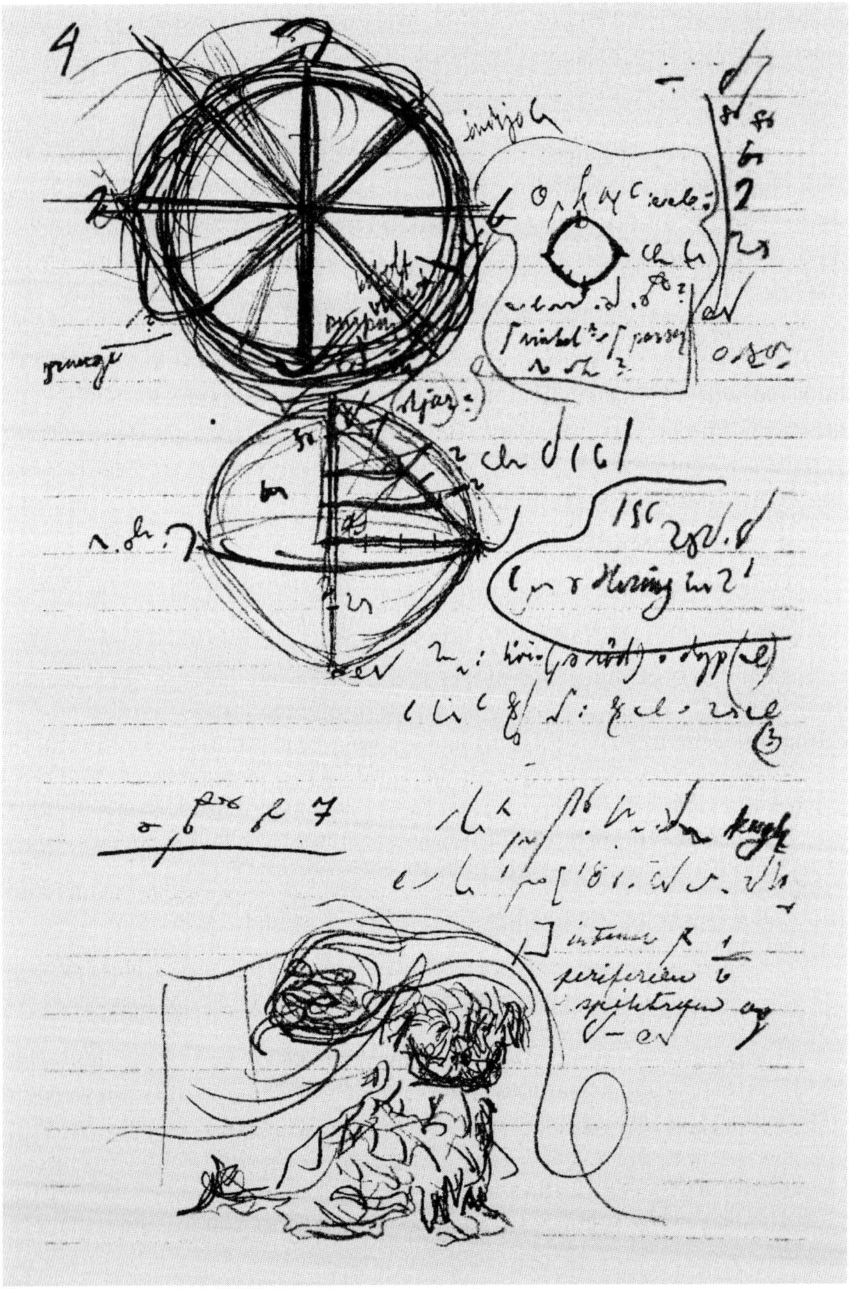

A page from one of Irgens-Jensen's sketchbooks around 1915

Dagny Irgens Jensen introduced her biographical sketch[9] by quoting Goethe: 'Edel sei der Mensch, hilfreich und gut'.[10] She explains: 'This Goethe quotation could well have been his motto for his life, for he was exactly that, noble, thoughtful and considerate in all his activities'.

Virtually every description of Irgens-Jensen mentions his noble character and appearance. According to his son Olav, he was kind to everyone, understanding and helpful, modest and grateful towards others. There was no self-importance about him; instead, he regarded his own person with abundant irony. He knew the art of listening, giving others his time and never saying anything disparaging about anyone else. Odd Grüner-Hegge recalled that: 'He never wanted to offend anyone. I cannot remember one moment when he spontaneously spoke harshly about others. Never'.[11] At the same time he was lively and interested in the world around him: being with him was never boring, says his son. He always got on very well with his son's friends, both at parties and on various mountain trips. One of these friends, Birger Huse, writes:[12]

> I remember my friend's father – whom I had the pleasure of knowing from when I was four or five years old and for as long as he lived – as a good friend with a genuine interest in what I was doing. And the interest never appeared strained, but was always genuine, often a little demanding: he took us seriously both as children and later as young men. Later I understood that the enjoyable conversations and reading aloud were also a deliberate mentoring activity in the Socratic spirit: he wanted to teach us things and give us a part of his experiences, books, history and not least nature. I also remember 'Olav's father' as an enthusiastic comrade on mountain trips and an eager instructor in the art of sailing.

Another of his son's friends, Johannes Øhrn, recalls:

> I met Irgens-Jensen for the first time when I was 15–16 years old, and I must say that it was the first time I had met an adult I felt completely at ease with. [...]
>
> I must also mention an episode from the cold winter of 1947. Irgens-Jensen, his son and I had been to the concert by a young woman pianist we knew well and after the concert we went home to Irgens-Jensen's with her to celebrate a little. Irgens-Jensen had a heavy rucksack with him, and it proved to be full of lobster and white wine. It was a very cheerful and, for me, a rare memorable evening, but it was so cold in the room where the grand piano

[9] *Cf.* note 4, p. 24, above.

[10] These are the first two lines of Goethe's poem *Das Göttliche* of 1783.

[11] From the interview with Øystein Gaukstad, *cf.* p. 43, above.

[12] Undated letter to the author.

was that Irgens-Jensen had to keep his overcoat on and play in gloves. [...] He was so very much alive and a very likable person.[13]

Even if, by nature, Irgens-Jensen was generous and helpful and was usually quiet and well-balanced, he could on rare occasions become agitated and indignant if he saw that a real injustice had been committed, as when he protested against the shameful treatment of his friend Grüner-Hegge by the board of the Philharmonic.[14]

Irgens-Jensen was both sensitive to the lyrical aspects of life and nature and a sceptic and rationalist. As such he had a typical analytical bent (in music, too), but his impulsiveness and spontaneity (both in his music and his life) were well-known and never surprised his best friends. He had the ideal combination of intelligence and wisdom – and yet he was impractical, though not in the sense that he couldn't use his hands; rather, it seemed as if he felt himself unsuited to share the assertive and competitive life of society.

He was very industrious. In his youth he had sustained a pressure of work that seems to have been almost too harsh. With a researcher's thirst for knowledge, he studied psychology, philosophy, English, French, Greek and more; he played, drew and painted – and composed. He has been characterised as a 'thinker', philosopher, a critical and reflective person, questioning and open. 'I am working all the time,' he said to his son, 'even when I go for a walk or lie on my sofa.'[15] He used to work far into the night – but it must be admitted that he did not get up very early. And he did have tasks other than his music. The visiting Knudåge Riisager once observed: 'I don't understand how you compose anything, with everything that has to be done in such a big, old house.'[16]

Irgens-Jensen's music bears witness to his strong and rich inner life. Here were experiences that had to find expression – a drive that must have been particularly strong to overcome his reserve and modesty. Strong emotions, indeed passions, are found in his music. One of his drafts put it simply:

> In spite of all clever talk about 'Neue Sachlichkeit' and 'pure music', I still believe the majority of composers also wish to express something they can put into their musical progressions, something 'outside music' – they simply cannot let it be!

Even if Irgens-Jensen was in no way religious in the usual conventional sense and had no direct association with Christianity, there seem to be religious – or, at least, existential – features in parts of his music, especially

[13] Undated letter to the author.
[14] *Cf.* pp. 175–76, above.
[15] Related by Olav Irgens-Jensen.
[16] Related by Olav Irgens-Jensen.

perhaps in the Passacaglia and *Heimferd.* And it is no accident either that both the 'Psalms' (to Zwilgmeyer's texts) and *Altar* were written very quickly and with commitment.

The recollections of his friends and colleagues in the Society of Composers reveal a man who liked a good party. He was generally conservative in his consumption of alcohol, but at parties he could take a generous amount and liked to sit with his cigar until early morning. And if there were not too many in the gathering, he could contribute sharp, subtly humorous observations and ironic comments on the current situation in cultural life. He was able to express humour and an understanding of people also through his music and his texts, as in his *Fabler og barnerim*, and in his many occasional poems.

The most conscientious of men, Irgens-Jensen took all his responsibilities seriously. It is striking how thoroughly he worked on each task for the committees and boards on which he sat. For example, with the evaluation of the music of colleagues as part of his work on the expert committee of the Society of Composers, his drafts show the thorough comments he made both on the works as a whole and on their details. Afterwards, as with his letters, he polished the language of these comments before they were presented to others.

But he was not only the reflective intellectual, the composer, the humorous-serious man in a suit. He enjoyed himself just as much in sports clothes: life in the open air, on the mountains, in the forest and by the sea meant much to him, as his verses and pastels and water-colours confirm. He was evidently as much taken with the simplest small flowers as with the desolate drama of the mountains.

In his villa at Nordstrand, with its wooded grounds and lovely view over the Oslo fjord, he had daily contact with nature and its changes. But best of all he liked to go walking in the mountains, and he particularly liked climbing. As a very young man he went on a climbing trip in the Skagastølstinder every summer,[17] but after he finished school gradually the trips became fewer. After the Second World War he again often went to the mountains, generally at Easter and in the summer, and preferably with his son and his friends. He also liked to be driven around the countryside, especially in the west of Norway, but he himself never had a car or a driving licence.

Throughout his life art in its various forms and genres was a strong passion. Early in life he was conscious of his many talents and tried, almost as a duty, to develop the possibilities he had of becoming an artist. Art thus became a necessity for him, both as a person and as a member of society – but

[17] *Cf.* pp. 34–36, above.

it also became a scourge for someone so idealistic and self-critical: the pressure of having to produce something of artistic value was constant. His sister Dagny wrote that when he was still living at home as a young man, he sometimes felt depressed if he did not have any musical ideas: he would stay in bed or, in such 'empty periods', he might turn to drawing and painting – operating, she felt, a kind of crop rotation.[18]

Later in his life, too, there were difficult periods where the ideas failed to materialise and he felt empty and uninspired. And he was self-conscious enough to think ahead to what might happen to his music: On a large envelope amongst his papers from the end of the 1920s is written in a large, strong hand:

> I want *all* my effects to be burned after my death, all drafts and notes, in words, music and (of course!) colours.
>
> Except the Violin Sonata in B flat major.
> The Variations
> The Passacaglia
> The Quintet
> (Rosenstaden, the best children's rhymes and fables and the songs in the *selected* pile)
>
> Ludvig Irgens-Jensen

According to his son, his wife did not always understand the special difficulties and the doubt and uncertainty artists can have when they constantly have to dig into their innermost selves to find new material. She had a rather difficult temperament and, unfortunately, was little support to him in his artistic work – perhaps a factor in the relative paucity of his output. But he never complained.

Immediately after the first performance of *Der Gott und die Bajadere* on 24 January 1935, he wrote regretfully to his friends Leif and Esther Bruun:

> Dear Leif and Esther!
>
> Now I have got the Bajadere out of my head, so now I can begin to be normal again, which means that one answers nice letters and says thank-you for generous gifts. So: Many thanks for the lovely present; music is the best thing I can receive. The posthumous organ work appears to be genuine Carl Nielsen like everything else I know of him;[19] I look forward to enjoying it in peace and quiet, for as long as a performance is being prepared – with choir rehearsals, rehearsals with the soloists, correcting the parts and all kinds of problems with the work itself, I can never concentrate on anything outside.

[18] *Op. cit.*, p. 6.

[19] Presumably *Commotio*, which was first performed on 6 October 1931, three days after Nielsen's death.

Irgens-Jensen climbing in West Jotunheim in his later days

The view from Irgens-Jensen's home at Nordstrand, in a water-colour from late in his life

In his younger years he was supported to a large degree by his prosperous father; even in the 1920s, he was regarded by colleagues and friends as having more money than most of his friends and acquaintances. By the same token, since he was also very kind, he was certainly exploited from time to time. He gave funds to good causes, both on his own accord and when someone came and asked for help for a good reason. He also gave away money (often anonymously) to colleagues who needed a helping hand and he lent money when someone was in a dilemma. One colleague wrote out a promissory note with his piano as security. Another asked for years to put off the repayment of a lesser sum – a debt which was evidently waived, as often happened. Dagny Irgens Jensen reported[20] that in the middle of the 1920s David Monrad Johansen came to her brother and said of the poet Olav Aukrust: 'This man could save Norway's culture if he could get 500 kroner' (a good deal of money at that time). Irgens-Jensen decided he could not allow Norwegian culture to go to ruin and gave him the money.[21]

Later in his life he had less to spare, even though there was no reason to be sorry for him economically. Among his pieces of paper and notes was the following little verse:

[20] *Loc. cit.*

[21] A receipt from Aukrust was amongst his posthumous papers.

Pluto

Penger, er det prosa bare,	Money, is it only prose,
blottet helt for fantasi?	completely without imagination?
Penger som kan rulle, løpe	Money, let it roll and run,
falle, stige, faen spare!	fall and rise, who cares!
Har jeg penger er jeg fri!	If I have money, I am free!
Har jeg penger kan jeg kjøpe	If I have money I can buy
lugtevand og poesi.	perfume and poetry.

Although Irgens-Jensen kept well informed of the divergent artistic trends of his time, he did not want to make himself conspicuous by a public expression of opinion: he never became a weather vane. Instead, there is artistic integrity in everything he did.

Grüner-Hegge said of Irgens-Jensen and his music in the 1920s:

> He was far more radical then. But he abandoned this, he thought it was a false way, a wrong way, he didn't want it. He went the other way, became conservative from being the direct opposite. That is quite remarkable. […] He could sit and think up things that they would accept – take to heart these great trend-setters of our day. He already knew all that. Nothing was difficult for him. But in any event he never wanted to put it down on paper or go that way. […] He really was a strong personality, I must say, a strong, strong personality.[22]

[22] *Loc. cit.* (transcription of the taped interview of 1972), p. 5.

XIII
Irgens-Jensen's View of Music and his Musical Style

The institutions supplying music education in Norway around the time of the First World War provided a limited number of courses and teachers, and Irgens-Jensen consciously chose to become an autodidact instead of turning to one of the established teachers of composition. The absence of a regular teacher (his piano lessons apart) may have made it easier for him to keep an open mind than was the case for some other young composers, who were clearly influenced by their teachers (as Monrad Johansen was by Alf Hurum, for example). This independence allowed Irgens-Jensen to find his own way and cultivate his own opinions. His journeys abroad, not least those to Berlin and Dresden, and the longer stays in Copenhagen and Paris, brought him into contact with new aesthetic outlooks and contrasting stylistic directions, and so it is hardly surprising that the first phase in his own stylistic development was exploratory and radical. But only a few years after his debut in 1920 there was clearly a synthesising phase, as in *Tema con variazioni,* where old and new met to form his mature, reflective position.[1]

One of the general, almost existential, questions asked of a composer is why he has to compose. Irgens-Jensen never answered it directly, but something can be learned from his interviews, however reluctantly given and guarded the tone (if, indeed, the opinions voiced in the interviews accurately reflect his views). In the first edition of the popular Norwegian encyclopedia *Musikkens verden* ('The World of Music') in 1951, for example, he was quoted as follows:

> On the question of 'musical belief' or general artistic views, Irgens-Jensen replies:
>
> a) I feel akin to the view of musical problems that Carl Nielsen has expressed so clearly.
>
> b) I will quote Carl Nielsen's words: '...an interval of a third should be regarded as a gift from God, a fourth as an experience and a fifth as the greatest happiness'.

[1] *Cf.* particularly pp. 95–96, above.

c) The singability of vocal music lies first and foremost in our 'inner ear' grasping it. It is my opinion that such singability, such a musical core, should also be present in instrumental music.[2]

Irgens-Jensen's reference to Carl Nielsen cites ideas presented in Nielsen's collection of essays *Levende Musik* ('Living Music') from 1925.[3] In the article 'Musical Problems' in particular, Nielsen offers something of a creed. He wanted the 'musical' grasp of music to be preserved; music must be music; the art must not become too artificial. Music must not become too descriptive or fall into sentimentality, though it can still retain elements of subjectivity and symbolism. Composers should look back to earlier times when importance was attached to form, vitality, polyphony and modality – and yet they must also avoid writing music in 'the old style', which becomes too stifling – a clear rejection of the fashionable historicism of the day. Nielsen preferred a 'young' classicism, a contemporary classicism, wanting at the same time his music to be perceived as distinctively Danish. Irgens-Jensen's identification of 'singability' as a product of inner perception can be related to the theories of cognition popular today; his awareness of tradition brought him into contact with ideas that have become current in the early 21st century, although from completely different standpoints.

When in the 1969 NRK radio interview Torstein Gunnarson tried to broach the personal side of composing, he was on thin ice: Irgens-Jensen would have preferred to leave the studio immediately.[4] But Gunnarson did manage to ask some questions:

> TG: Then I would like to ask you, for I have not asked about musical development and such elementary questions: has it been difficult or easy for you to avoid the trends and directions which were of current interest?
>
> LIJ: I did not think very much about it, I believe. I did not. It was certainly difficult then, too, for those who wanted to find themselves. I struggled and laboured with getting something together and formulating it, I remember, in my youth. Then gradually there were some songs and things, and they satisfied me. After all, I kept up quite well with what music I could get hold of […].[5]

In an interview in *Dagbladet* on 29 November 1930, in connection with the first performance of *Heimferd*, the interviewer Marie Fearnley asked:

> 'When will the world get to hear from you again?'

[2] Sverre Hagerup Bull (ed.), *Musikkens Verden*, Musikkens Verden forlag, Oslo, 1951, p. 1061.
[3] Martins Forlag, Copenhagen, 1925 (Norwegian edition *Levende musikk*, Gyldendal, Oslo, 1948).
[4] Told by Gunnarson to the author.
[5] National Library, Oslo/Norsk Musikksamling Tape: lyd/b194-195: transcription p. 2.

> 'I have a quintet finished. But the delight and value for a composer consists of scribbling down the work, not getting it performed.'
>
> How many composers are content with such meek and modest delight? [...]
>
> [Irgens-Jensen:] 'And the excitement of composing consists of the happy moment of inspiration, where one gathers, kneads and scribbles down the impressions in deadly anxiety that they will disappear. That is what music consists of; the further working-out interests me far less. I am almost inclined to call it office work, but a very necessary office work.' [...]
>
> 'What do you allow yourself to be inspired by in particular?'
>
> 'One does not let oneself be inspired; one becomes inspired. And inspiration can come quite independently of one's own state of mind. It has often been in tired and despondent times that bright melodies have fluttered towards me.'[6]

In an interview with *Nationen* on 21 September 1934, he gave a different side of the issue:

> In my questions I [the interviewer] touch on the great feelings that must underlie a work of art, but he answers that it was the Romantics who inflated artists to be visionaries who would carry all the world's weighty problems in their hearts. It is proficiency and form that he values the most.
>
> I take out my notepad and pencil to write down his words, but he stops me and says:
>
> 'You must not write this, for I don't mean it. Other people maintain other things, which are also human thoughts.'

In *Musikkens verden* in 1951 he was reluctant to expose his thoughts:

> To 'M.V.''s question about what he would say if, before a performance of his works, he had the opportunity to comment, for example in the programme, Irgens-Jensen answers:
>
> I would prefer not to say anything and let the music speak for itself. But I wish that we could all keep clear of the 'mass' suggestion that publicity and whims of fashion force upon us, that we could retain the talent to listen with our own ears.[7]

And in the 1943 interview with Jens Arbo he also goes indirectly into one aspect of the essence and function of music:

> Irgens-Jensen is of the opinion that music ought to be used more in the theatre as melodrama and 'priming' [literally, undercoating]. Here the theatre can take a lesson from French film.[8]

[6] *Dagbladet*, 29 November 1930.

[7] *Loc. cit.*, p. 1061.

[8] *Loc. cit.*, p. 7.

In an interview in *Aftenposten* published on 1 April 1924, he was asked directly if, with his modern songs, he had become influenced by French trends after his stay in France:

> 'I hope not.'
> 'Hope not?'
> 'I do not sympathise with the direction music has taken there. But I heard a great deal of interest.'

It seems strange perhaps that he did not find any trends in France that he was prepared to endorse: there were so many, and of course Stravinsky and a contingent of other eastern- and central-European composers added to the variety. But one must not forget that the best and most interesting 'modern' French works after Debussy and (in part) Ravel – by 'Les Six', for example – had not been written at the time he was in Paris.

From early in his career Irgens-Jensen was regarded as considering inherited tradition a good thing, as Marie Fearnley observed as late as in 1930:

> Ludvig Irgens-Jensen's musical language stands on a firm classical foundation. He has not lapsed into becoming some contemporary modernist.[9]

But in the interview which followed he did not approve of an uncritical acceptance of what had gone before, nor of a pursuit of modernity:

> 'It is so easy to make a slogan of everything,' he remarks. 'Some work with polytonality and some with other particularities. I think one ought to make the music as natural and good as one can. If one cannot be distinctive except at the expense of naturalness, it is no good. Much new music is fabricated and studied.'
> 'Do you fear the Romantics?'
> 'It is not a question of fear. I have my heroes Bach and Palestrina, Chopin and Brahms, all of whom have provided outstanding music.'[10]

And in the first draft of his replies for the questionaire from *Musikkens verden* in 1951, he wrote: 'I have always been very enthusiastic about literature, perhaps Ibsen and Kinck most of all'. Of music that has made a strong impression on him he mentions Bach and the 'old vocal polyphony', besides a number of Norwegian folksongs, and then adds:

> In my youth in particular I was captivated by Reger who was certainly important to me. Where the music of our time is concerned, with all its trends and conflicts, I think it is difficult to have an overview that would justify singling out individual composers.

[9] *Dagbladet*, 29 November 1930.
[10] *Ibid.*

In his mature years he seldom talked about contemporary music, and when he did it was in vague and general terms. When he was younger he was more outspoken, as in Theo Findahl's interview in *Adresseavisen*, on 24 January 1931:[11]

> 'Are you yourself a lover of ultra-modern music?'
>
> 'No. A great deal of it bores me—both the atonal and the polytonal experiments. It can be especially irritating when the music is monopolised by arrogant aesthetics and quasi-theoretical devices. Moreover, I believe that the fundamental defect of artistic life in our time – despite all talk of objectivity and collectivism – is the individualistic mentality: the need to assert one's own dear self at any price. If only each would do his best, honestly, in all modesty, without wanting to add to his stature with programmes and slogans and new devices! The need for originality has become too conscious. One searches for one's physiognomy and puts a mask on it – again authenticity is in danger. What can have made possible the unbelievable artistic blooming of earlier times, Palestrina, Bach? I wonder if it were not a different *mentality*, where humility and the need to serve were deeper realities. The artist had no "I" to display, but a glorious duty to the honour of the Almighty – a perpetual grace and joy which frees him from "himself" and gives his work beauty, a wealth of riches – true originality.
>
> 'On the whole I am against everything unnatural, everything strained in art', continues Irgens-Jensen. 'Art cannot be forced, it must grow organically. Art is always slow, requires a long preparation time. The sap must collect for a long time in the stem before the flower unfolds.'

The sectarianism he criticises was also in evidence in the music-criticism of the time, sometimes in highly politicised language, partly because of the power-struggles between competing aesthetic positions. He addressed this issue in a draft for a letter to the composer Signe Lund Skabo from around 1931:

> The more I think about the question of critical and factual evaluation of art, the more difficult I think the matter becomes. In the course of a few decades, there has been created a series of essentially different means of expression (Neoromantic, Impressionism, Neoclassical, atonality) whose representatives are foreign to one another and would prefer to deny one another both talent and good will. [...]
>
> This with new and old, of course, ought not to be a factor in the evaluation of the quality of the art; nevertheless it happens constantly, especially in a restless and sensation-hungry time like ours.

[11] The same interview was also printed in *Nordisk Tidende* (Brooklyn, New York), 12 February 1931, and in *Tonekunst*, No. 5, 1931 (where it was slightly shortened).

He was also aware of the practical dangers of shifting fashions, as an interview from 1934 reveals:

> About the ever new trends, he says that they can appear life-giving, but they have their drawbacks, for no sooner has one entered on a new issue than it is overturned as an otherwise natural reaction, and the performers don't attain enough proficiency. Something else which is also dangerous for 20th-century art is the desperate hunt for individuality. He takes out an album and reads aloud a fable of his own about his struggle. It was like a piece of a wonderful fairy-tale to hear him read the flawless poem.[12]

In his draft letter to Signe Lund Skabo in 1931, he also wrote about his own situation in relation to thoughts of originality:

> For my own part I cannot flatter myself that I bring anything new, anything 'noch nie dagewesenes' into the music. I try to do as well as I can and ought then confidently to entrust it to others and to the future to decide if there is a need for my contribution.

Almost thirty years later, Irgens-Jensen received a letter[13] from the composer Geirr Tveitt which touches (perhaps in harsher terms than Irgens-Jensen would have used) on the same thoughts on contemporary modernism:

> Unfortunately I cannot deny that in art (and particularly the 'contemporary') there is much too much nonsense, yes, often more than nonsense, there is deceit, indeed, lying. The music then sets out contentions for which there is no backing in any way. There are bizarre lines and harmonies and rhythms which just shriek: 'Look at me!' 'Buy from me!' 'Aren't I original', 'Aren't I much better' etc. In short, advertising and boasting. If all humanity is not to perish in humbug, then I can do nothing other than believe that the judgement of the future about the art of our time must be crushing, – indeed, more than that: it will be laid in the darkness of oblivion.
>
> Our so-called leading aesthetes only emphasise which 'ism' music has; they don't give a damn about its intrinsic value. They are children of that same time that does not bother about humanity's intrinsic value and personality, but only respects it if it belongs to a certain political system.
>
> Fortunately, however, there are exceptions to the rule. And you are one of the great exceptions. In the end and for the future, the truth of the art can depend only on posterity, just as finally will the truth in all the political jumble of deceit and propaganda.
>
> Your music is free of deceit and the hunt for false originality. It is modest and objective in the so-called external means, but it has greatness in its *inner* being. It is personal without being ballyhoo, and it is Nordic and Norwegian without making a song and dance.

[12] *Nationen*, 21 September 1934.
[13] Dated 14 May 1959.

Irgens-Jensen drafted a reply where, even if he agreed with Tveitt in some regards, he is far less categorical in rejecting the new:

> What you write about the art of our time I agree with. But it could be that even the more doubtful experiments can lead to something useful – if they fall into the right hands. It would be interesting some time to hear your opinion about the reasons for the artistic situation of our time and about the ways out of 'the crisis'.
>
> Finally, I wish you undiminished strength for your future work, you who still have the inventiveness and possibilities for development.

When he was most often in the limelight, around 1930, he also had a broad understanding of both the new trends and the distinctiveness of individual composers he found in Norway:

> 'Which trends are particularly striking in European music at the moment?'
>
> 'Generally we can say that there is – and has been for a long time – a reaction against the exaggerations of Impressionism: looseness of form, the one-sided cultivation of sound and the literary trickery in music, all the painting, all the illustrations. Stravinsky in his later works, Hindemith in Germany, Honegger in France – to mention a few of the leading names – are all searching for strict forms, clear lines, strong rhythms – music for music's sake.'
>
> 'And in Norway?'
>
> 'Yes, here we are somewhat behind. There is more of a widespread flow in different directions. One cannot talk of any strongly characterised common trend. We are each occupied with our own according to our good old Norwegian custom. Eggen, Monrad Johansen, Groven and others have a strong interest in folk music, from many different points of view. Norway also has a subtle and refined atonalist in Fartein Valen, a soulful talent who is very much alone here. That bold and uncompromising symphonist, Harald Sæverud, also avoids those places where any foot has trodden before. Since we are really talking about the main trends in the music of our time, I am thinking of the Dane Carl Nielsen. For a generation this master has maintained the strictness of form and the intrinsic value of musical elements. His magnificent works have been like a prophecy of what is stirring most powerfully at this time.'[14]

It was probably to Nielsen's anti-Romantic, unsentimental and musicianly attitude that he was most strongly attracted.

In his youth Irgens-Jensen wrote a little 'fable' about the modern music of the time:

> *A fable about the new things*
>
> The fox really has in many respects a very bad reputation. But the perception that the fox has no higher interests and only stagnates in materialism is not

[14] *Adresseavisen*, 24 January 1931.

correct, according to later investigations. Reynard is at any rate ambitious and, for example, does not like to be regarded with condescension in cultural questions.

The birds have the bad habit of cackling and laughing when they hear the fox snarl or screech down in the bushes. They well know that it is his form of singing, but, as mentioned, they cannot help enjoying themselves. It seems so amusing.

This is one of the fox's greatest sorrows. But one morning he thought up something.

Suddenly the birds hear a frightful commotion down in the forest. Was it murder or an epidemic?

There sat the fox with his neck straight up, emitting the most curious, raucous sound that was ever heard in the forest.

'Well, help and save us, what is the matter?'

'I am practising,' said the fox with dignity.

'Practising – what?'

'I am expressing myself. Don't you understand, little ones, that there are so many remarkable things to express here, that one must first acquire a completely new voice. It can no longer be done the old way. Think about it – then you will understand.'

Yes, they thought about it and understood a whole lot, for little by little they began, the thrush and the finch, large and small, to make strange sounds. They searched very seriously for their new voices. For they all had so many remarkable things to express.

And there is therefore no longer such fine birdsong in the forest as before – at any rate, so the old people think.

But now the fox is lying under the birch root wagging his tail. For of these new things he is the master. And the times when someone laughed as the fox broke into song are at an end.

Irgens-Jensen often praised his Norwegian colleagues, but the question of the position one should take towards the heritage of Norwegian folk-music and its use in art-music (an important, even burning, issue for many cultural commentators in the period between the two World Wars) he mentioned by implication only a few times – most cautiously, of course, after World War II – as in an interview with the Dane Knud Wissum in 1946:

'Is Norwegian music too Norwegian? Can there, in the long run, be a danger in drawing so one-sidedly upon folk-music sources?'

'Both yes and no. Our folk-music sources are almost inexhaustible. It should be admitted that certain composers' excessive use of bare fifths and Lydian modes at times have a touch of mannerism. However, if one uses the material with respect, without making pastiches, and if one confines oneself merely to allowing oneself to be inspired by the folk music atmosphere, this can only be a strength for Norwegian music.'[15]

Irgens-Jensen seems to have been enthusiastic about folk-music itself, recording the following views in an interview in 1931:

'Those skilled in writing are considerably divided in their views on fourths,[16] correct methods of notation (folk music is still being noted down) and on the connection with Gregorian church music', he says. 'But *one* thing everyone can agree on: the marvellous folk-music itself. We Norwegians feel that it gives a powerfully and at the same time finely *nuanced expression of Norwegian nature and national character*, and that really is the most important thing.'

'What do you value most highly in Norwegian folk music?'

'The marvellous ballads from the Middle Ages.'

'Which for example?'

'There is a whole host of them. To single out a few would be unfair to others. One day they may be known all over the world.'

'What is particularly characteristic of Norwegian folk music?'

'One can say about Norwegian folk-music the same as one can say about Slavic, even about English and French, that – fortunately – it has not been used as intensely as the German. Both melodically and rhythmically it can exhibit highly distinctive features, something that has made it more difficult to popularise as intensely has been the case with German folk-tunes, and it has been very unmanageable when it comes to forcing it into the strait-jacket of the harmony and form of later times. Norwegian folk-music was born in the open air!'

'And this folk music is still a source of inspiration for Norwegian composers?'

'Yes, of course. But I do not think that one should be content to copy. One must infiltrate its spirit. It is no use just wanting to be as extremely Norwegian as possible – authenticity will then suffer.'[17]

In a draft reply to a letter from the Danish composer Knudåge Riisager before 1928, Irgens-Jensen penned some thoughts both about his own understanding of some of the modernism he saw at the end of the 1920s, and what could be a positive side:

[15] Knud Wissum, 'Ludvig Irgens-Jensen', manuscript for an article prepared for the Danish magazine *Levende musik*, Copenhagen, 1946. The manuscript is in the possession of Olav Irgens-Jensen and was corrected by his father.

[16] The use of a sharpened fourth in the transformation of Norwegian folk-music into art-music was, together with the flattened seventh, an attempt to emulate the non-tempered intervals rather than 'nature scale' intervals produced by the *lur*.

[17] *Adresseavisen*, 24 January 1931.

> It has been difficult for me to answer, first and foremost because I am no letter-writer, but further because my understanding of the modern trends in music, despite my good intentions, is poor.
>
> I see how one after the other develops or drifts towards a musical radicalism with – so it seems to me – an often familiar or problematic foundation in relation to earlier times. Unfortunately, one gradually becomes very sceptical – do you not think there is a remarkable amount of bluffing and chasing after effects in the music of our time? [...] But if you think that modern music first and foremost ought to aspire to a renewed, thorough concentration on all formal values, lines, counterpoint, movement technique, then I am with you. Consequently, a very natural reaction to both dull programmaticians with their need for cheap effect, the subtle Impressionists' artificial 'refinement' and this intolerable misalliance with literature, which produces so much trickery.

And in various interviews he touches upon some of these stylistic features, as in the 1946 interview with Wissum:

> A characteristic feature in his production is polyphony. Quite naturally my first question runs:
>
> 'You have a predilection for polyphonic writing. Is this something typical of the time?'
>
> (Long silence) 'It may be. Abroad we encounter a strong and natural reaction to the excessive homophony in Impressionism. But Impressionism almost passed our door; only one single composer, *Hurum*, developed into a full-blooded Impressionist but did not form a school. Incidentally, he has had a remarkable fate. One fine day he took to oriental painting and now lives, as far as I know, in Hawaii.[18]
>
> 'For me there was an early need for polyphony and I eagerly studied Palestrina and Bach. I feel akin to Carl Nielsen's view of music, and I have very much enjoyed Knud Jeppesen's books.[19] A young composer up here in my young days said, "Polyphony is dead". Many young musicians thought the same around 1915. If one was interested in it, one was an eccentric. Now, on the contrary, everybody writes polyphonically. The question is certainly not either or, but both and.
>
> 'Personally I love to sit and potter about with polyphonic part-writing. There is repose in that work!' [...][20]

[18] Alf Hurum (1882–1972) moved from Oslo to Hawaii, where he founded and conducted the Honolulu Symphony. In the early 1930s he stopped composing and devoted his energy to the pictorial arts. Hurum is generally credited as being Norway's first Impressionist composer. His works include a Symphony in D minor (1927) and five orchestral suites, chamber and piano music and songs.

[19] *Cf.* pp. 172 and 174, above.

[20] Wissum, *loc. cit.*, p. 1.

> 'You have just had a *Symphony in D minor* premiered at the Norwegian Music Week in October. You don't think, then, that symphonic form is outdated.'
>
> (Pause. Large thick clouds of smoke). 'No, why? For us the course of the single movement is perfectly compatible with the thought and emotional make-up of the time. Sonata-form, so multifaceted and alive – as in the time of the Viennese classics, [it] could never become outdated because it has so many possibilities, at the same time as it gives the composition a backbone without restricting the composer. Later people tried to make the form into a pattern, so it has become a coat of armour which hinders the freedom of movement.
>
> 'In my perception, symphonic music calls for polyphony. Every new section is so tremendously stimulating. A movement that culminates in a fugue gains greater strength, can give a greater nobility than anything else. The fugue is indestructible, and the symphony as a form is still far from outdated.'[21]

As a result, he would appear to be saying, these complicated forms and textures should impose a unity which contributes to real simplicity. That is, of course, a generalisation, but it shows something in common with the thinking of other European composers in the years between the Wars, and which became the foundation for much of Nadia Boulanger's aesthetics and her teaching of the younger generations in Paris. Irgens-Jensen shared another ideal with her, too – that good workmanship is the foundation, not an end in itself:

> 'Is new Danish music little known in Norway?'
>
> 'At any rate not known enough. Of course we know Carl Nielsen up here. He has been a guest conductor with us quite a few times, including conducting several of his symphonies. Incidentally, that was a big success and attracted much attention in our musical life. But of other Danish music, especially the completely new, we do not know enough. What strikes us when we hear the newest Danish composers is their proficiency. They know their trade.'[22]

He had said something in a similar vein three years earlier, in 1943:

> Irgens-Jensen comes out with a declaration of love for the polyphony in his music. 'For me at any rate it is quite natural to write polyphonically', he says. 'Of course it demands a lot of work and concentration, but it is work which delights. Moreover, I work just as hard on my small things. But polyphonic or not – is immaterial! It is the *means*. If one can express what one wants to in homophonic movement, that perhaps is the best of all! Think of Grieg.'

[21] *Ibid.*, p. 2.
[22] *Ibid.*, p. 3.

> He continues: 'Every bird sings with its own beak – and it should be allowed to. No over-aesthetic person should come and exclude it by reason of its means of expression. Now, at a later time, polyphony is constantly called for. A generation ago it was said to be dead. Presumably it was the same judges of taste who shouted then, too. [...]
>
> 'And one more thing, which perhaps some people may not know: polyphony is not synonymous with something complicated, just as little as homophony in itself is simple. Not necessarily so, if anything, the opposite, in so far as polyphony with its concentration of lines looks towards an "ascetic" simplicity in its method of expression. The homophonic style naturally has recourse to colouring and contrasts, and listeners can run the risk of confusing the essential and inessential because of this intricate way of expression. Moreover, it really is that the homophonic style as a rule is used to express more complex and changing moods and perhaps also lends itself best to that.'[23]

This statement gives a complicated picture of Irgens-Jensen's attitudes to texture and its role in expression – one which does not completely correspond to statements he made elsewhere. But he did not want to criticise his colleagues or their music. As he wrote to Signe Lund Skabo in 1931:

> That there should exist hidden forces which, for personal reasons, seek to hold you and many others down, I have difficulty in understanding. Rather, I could imagine that the very stylistic character of your music does not seem striking enough at this precise moment. Therefore I beg you to remember that every age has its view and that no one shows less understanding than youth towards the previous generation.
>
> In a few years, who knows, there will perhaps be a reaction, the tide will turn and the values you regard as the highest in music will again have a hearing?
>
> You invited me to give my opinion of your things. But on second thought I feel that I ought not to embark on this because I am a very bad critic. Instead of underlining the good qualities in your compositions, I have therefore allowed myself to offer the preceding little argument.

Again his caution shines through, and he is careful to be diplomatic. But at the same time it is clear in the light of the earlier quotations that his aesthetic ideals lie more in a 'radical' Neoclassical direction than in Lund Skabo's conservative attitudes.

Musical Style

Like so many other composers, Irgens-Jensen modified his musical expression and style throughout his life: each work has its own character

[23] Arbo, *loc. cit.*, p. 6.

and distinctive quality. He worked single-mindedly, constantly trying to improve whatever he was working on. He was not a Mozart who could finish everything in a moment; instead, he was more of a Beethoven, someone with a good idea onto which he had to hold firmly, a thinker and critic who constantly sketched new possibilities, rejecting and altering until the score satisfied him – or had to be sent off. This approach is evident early on in his sketches. The long-term evolution of his style and expression takes place slowly, carefully and through a degree of struggle to master the musical material. Throughout his life, even in his mature years, he worked on his own 'further education'.

Irgens-Jensen's publicly acknowledged output was not voluminous, and the types of work performed were characteristic: orchestral works first and foremost, though not many in number, and songs, several with orchestra. He evidently also gave priority to the incidental music he composed: in such instances the personnel of an entire theatre might come to a standstill if the music were not finished. It is possible that these commissions (together with the songs and other works with a textual basis) were particularly rewarding for him. His chamber music encompasses only two large works of any significance. He did have an impressive number of choral pieces performed, but it is striking that he, a proficient pianist, left just two piano works, of which one is only a little *Siciliano*.

In everything Irgens-Jensen wrote, he set much store by solidly constructed form, a fact reflected in the titles of many of his works. Their forms can be architectonic or dynamic, or be a kind of mixed form (the most common, as in the Passacaglia and the Symphony) where development is an essential element, one with an inner dynamic that can run contrary to the architectonic framework. His music is ambitiously conceived from the outset. Themes, motifs and their reworking and development are the pillars of his structures, although they can often spring from a very few elements. Variation form is very important, perhaps the predominant idea in the larger works, requiring the use of almost all forms of variation. In some of the largest orchestral works – not least the Symphony, *Tema con variazioni* and Passacaglia – he uses cyclical principles. Movements or other clear sections have a thematic and motivic dependence which is developed throughout the work, sometimes also with a very clear idea of metamorphosis. That in its turn becomes a special form of variation. In the larger works (the Piano Quintet, Violin Sonata, the Symphony, even *Heimferd*) he also makes much use of sonata and rondo form.

The musical texture is almost exclusively dominated by clear lines that are 'tonal' – that is, with a fixed tonal axis, or at the very least free-tonal with less dominant hierarchy towards the tonal axis. The texture most often encountered is a line-against-line polyphony and counterpoint – 'old fashioned' and true to the old models in its outlines and in its complementary rhythm. Yet the lines are absolutely representative of their time in their tonality and individual rhythmic development. Fugue or fugato is incorporated into the large forms: a large fugue often crowns a movement or a whole work, as in the *Tema con variazioni*, Passacaglia and the Symphony; it can be developmental, but does not necessarily appear in the development section.

There is a clear dichotomy between the two main types of melodic lines Irgens-Jensen writes. Many of his themes are simple, a carefully balanced blend of stepwise movement and small intervals, which echoes music from the sixteenth century and folk-tunes. The other type of line is less balanced; if anything, these lines are asymmetrical and more abrupt, both in their jagged outlines, in the lesser degree of development to which the motifs are subjected, both melodically and tonally, and in the rhythm. This kind of line is used both in the development themes within a fugue and in the first subject in sonata-form. And he can construct entire movements on the contrasts formed by the dialogue between these two styles.

In some choral works and songs there is an almost pseudo-homophony with note-against-note movement. The clearest examples are found in the Psalms for mixed chorus. Even there, the frequent use of pedal points and suspensions plays a part in shaping more individual lines. The harmonies here will be 'thinner' than in more clearly polyphonically conceived works; in these homophonic sections there is often a predominance of pure triads or triads with an added note. Sometimes there are also more 'neutral' chords like the 'gender-free' fourths and fifths, and even tritones or seconds. Even though Irgens-Jensen is very conscious of the treatment of dissonance and obviously knew his tonal counterpoint, he allows himself to jump, not take a stepwise walk, to and from dissonance. In the middle layer, a resolution takes place through the part-writing, even if sometimes in a different part. Because of the linear writing, six-four chords, for example, frequently occur. When they are linear, they do not sound as archaic and hollow as when they have their own weight – as found in the more vertical chordal textures in some of the compositions of his Norwegian contemporary 'six-four-chord composer', David Monrad Johansen.

With Irgens-Jensen, the harmonic pulse and rhythm in such pseudo-homophonic sections will often be quite serene. The completely developed harmonic progressions (then seen in a middle or background layer) will rarely follow the functional tonal cadential formations. The progressions become ever more modally coloured and it is not rare for a quite distinctive false relation to appear. Even if the progressions at the cadences at the ends of sections come to be dominated by perfect or plagal cadences, many examples of progressions of a third from the penultimate to the final chord are also to be found.

In the polyphonic play of a relatively high number of lines, dense textures can at times be created – a feature particularly striking in his earlier works, even in many songs. The extensive use of pedal points also plays a part in forming the sometimes heavily loaded texture. Often it is the instrumentation that makes the more elegant of the individual lines noticeable: he is thinking of colour in every single line, even in the densest piano part in the early songs. Indeed, there are often suggestions for instrumentation noted in the manuscripts. His orchestration is brilliant and richly coloured, often Bruckneresque and organ-like (that is, emulating the manuals and pedals) in its division into layers. His use of woodwind in different combinations is particularly characteristic and gives some of the earlier works, especially the first variations of the *Tema con variazioni*, a fine shimmer. In later scores, from the Symphony onwards, the sound often seems confined to a darker register both in the wind and strings, in combinations where even the brightest nuances no longer have this glow. Indeed, the dark qualities of Irgens-Jensen's orchestration are characteristic enough to mark out his works as distinctively his.

With regard to metre, too, there is a degree of difference between his younger and more mature styles. All through his life he seems to have had a predilection for a tripartite division of the time, either as a triple time-signature or as a triplet subdivision. Like Brahms, he loved the simpler forms of polyrhythm, such as two against three. Duple or quadruple time-signatures were more frequently found in his earlier works; in his mature years it is as if he could not allow such 'correct' time-signatures to run for too long: they had to be broken up by various interpolations of triple time. He became fond also of breaking-up patterns by placing accents across the basic rhythm he has established, and it is not unusual for him to allow the contour of a line to reach its high point on an unaccented beat. Similarly, there is a frequent use of feminine endings to the lines.

The rhythm of individual lines can at times become tortuous, with accents and high points across the given time-signature. Seen in relation to an ongoing pulse and the surrounding lines, it appears neither special nor strange; instead, it is only part of the forward movement, which at times can be powerful. It can also be used to generate an exciting fluctuation in tempo, like the 'elastic time' used by Impressionists such as Debussy and, in part, Ravel in the first decade of the last century. Even though Irgens-Jensen seldom writes a *ritardando* or *accelerando*, they can be implicit, in that the line has to be able to breathe with a degree of organic liberty within the tempo specified. Grüner-Hegge's performances, which can generally be regarded as authoritative (they had the composer's sanction), show the flexibility this organic breathing requires.

The majority of Norwegian critics (and also many musicians) regarded the young Irgens-Jensen as a modernist, someone who writes difficult music. The critic Reidar Mjøen called him 'our youngest musical *enfant terrible*'.[24] That was, of course, relative to the musical environment then found in Norway: he was hardly radical when set against many of the trends then current elsewhere in Europe – something he himself understood more clearly than some contemporary critics, as an interview given in connection with the performances of *Heimferd* in 1930–31 makes clear:

> Now Irgens Jensen is certainly known for being so very modern, that one might have some difficulty in understanding him. However it is not possible to avoid this question [...].
>
> Astonished and definite comes the answer:
>
> 'Modern...? No, not a bit!'[25]

Another interview from around the same time drew the same sort of response:

> And still Irgens Jensen is not universally known as a composer. In the first place this is because only a negligible part of his large production has been printed and, second, that what he writes is rather difficult. His musical reputation says that he is modern, so ultra that one needs to be a specialist to understand his musical imagery. And when after much searching we met him (Irgens Jensen is very modest, almost hides himself away) that was of course the first thing we wanted to ascertain.
>
> 'I call the cantata a dramatic symphony with the title "Heimferd". The word modern I cannot stand. It is a catchword. Let us rather distinguish between good and bad, genuine and artificial music. And "Heimferd" is tonal, that is to say a reaction against the modern. Fanaticism so easily goes in these so-called new directions, one becomes blinkered, so that values are thrown out of the window.'[26]

Stylistically, the younger Irgens-Jensen was indeed radical in relation to the Norwegian milieu, showing a line of evolution parallel to that of

[24] *Dagbladet*, 11 April 1924.
[25] *Tidens Tegn*, 29 November 1930.
[26] *Morgenposten*, 28 November 1930.

Fartein Valen, with a point of departure in Bach, Beethoven, Brahms and Bruckner, together with Reger and other 'modernists' of the time. He had his free-tonal and quasi-atonal songs published before Valen had finished any atonal work. But after some years of searching, he found his way to his main features in a clearer style around 1924 in the Violin Sonata, *Fabler og barnerim* and *Variasjoner og fuge (Tema con variazioni)*.[27] It is nonetheless interesting to note that he did not completely reject the songs he first allowed to be performed, and at the end of his life he returned to some of the compositions from his youth which had been considered particularly radical.

His chief interest, though, was in polyphony, as well, of course, as in form; it encompasses both contrapuntal principles like fugue and multi-layered, line-against-line polyphony, and it was here that his contemporaries and younger colleagues found scope for further investigation. He himself seems to have worried that his textures might be too polyphonic and so he had recourse, perhaps as a contrast, to chorale-like melodies and harmonisations as the basis for the variation sections in his larger works.

He was also open to the modality that had already been used in some of his early songs and which, from *Fabler og barnerim* onwards, became a characteristic feature of his music. At that time modality had a double function: in melody and part-writing. Using the modally coloured melodic material was considered a modern stylistic element, but it could also be seen as a continuation of a national, specifically Norwegian line. But especially when modality was not nationally coloured by other stylistic elements, it became regarded as modern. And, not least, when modality tinted a part of non-functional harmony, it was a means of expression for the younger generation.

Modality, indeed, provides an excellent example of the role of style in different contexts. Those musical features which are generally regarded as Norwegian, either rhythm or melody or even the 'sound' characteristics from folk-music or from Grieg, for that reason gained status as explicitly Norwegian and thus acquired national association; paradoxically, in other contexts those same stylistic features could be regarded as modern – for example, as when used by Maurice Ravel. Irgens-Jensen's extensive use of modality perhaps owes something to this triple association with Norwegian folk-music, its modernity and its connection with pre-Baroque music – although in the event he found modality in different forms in much music, including Brahms and the more recent Neoclassicists like Stravinsky and Hindemith. But his attitude to tradition did not in any way lead him into

[27] *Cf.*, respectively, pp. 82–83, 73–77 and 86–98.

historicism: he did not, like Reger or Sinding, write a *Suite in the Olden Style* or anything of that nature.

'Impressionism' was one of several terms Norwegian commentators – through their lack of terminology and understanding – used to describe musical modernism around the time of the First World War. In the event, there is not much direct Impressionism in Irgens-Jensen's music. In the songs up to about 1924 he occasionally tried out a sort of Impressionism through his choice of chordal material and, of course, the texts, and there is an Impressionistic use of sound-colour in several scores, not least in the early *Tema con variazioni*. But the Impressionist approach soon seemed too formless for him, and on several occasions he declared himself against Impressionism. This reservation probably applies to French Impressionism as well as its influence on Norwegian composers such as Brustad, Hurum, Kleven and Monrad Johansen – a form of Impressionism which is in any case slightly superficial – though probably not to Pauline Hall, whose emphasis was on form. The characteristics of French music have to be sought elsewhere in Irgens-Jensen's output: in clarity, form, texture, moderation and, not least, in expression – he wanted to get away from the bombast and sentimentality he found in some Romantics who dressed in Impressionist clothes. His choice of French symbolist literature is telling, too.

Irgens-Jensen was not regarded as a modernist for very long, either by the public or the critics: in the 1930s, after *Heimferd*, *Der Gott und die Bajadere*, many choral songs and the incidental music for *Driftekaren*, there are fewer and fewer, and finally no, references to modernism in the reviews of his music. Indeed, it was Fartein Valen who was then composing the more radical music, but even his unfamiliar atonal note-rows were tolerated and received good reviews. Others among the younger composers managed to surprise in their own ways; thus a radical nationalist like Geirr Tveitt could attract media attention – whereas Irgens-Jensen was certainly not sorry to be out of the limelight.

Was he, then, a 'national' composer, either in his own eyes or in others'? In the Norwegian debate on modernism, which lasted almost a century (from the presentation of Grieg's late works shortly before his death until around 2000 when the 'pling-plong'[28] generation tried to assert themselves in a different international modernism), national characteristics were long considered to be the enemy of modernism. But the substance of these

[28] Not a term of disparagement: in 1995 eight young Norwegian composers – Mark Adderley, Ragnhild Berstad, Henrik Hellstenius, Gisle Kverndokk, Jon Øivind Ness, Rune Rebne, Helge Havsgård Sunde and Peter Tornquist – chose 'to embark on their composition careers by making a CD together', as Lasse Thoresen's booklet essay explained; the double album in question (Hemera HCD 2909) was entitled *definitely pling-plong*. Thoresen further explained that 'The composers have chosen the title for this recording with an ironic eye on the response they expect from the general public'.

two concepts changed strongly over time: in the 1920s it was difficult to appear both modern and Norwegian, but by the 1930s a position which incorporated the two was regarded as almost honourable as some composers in the public eye (Monrad Johansen, Tveitt, Klaus Egge) both in their music and in their writings. Similar tendencies are also found in Norwegian pictorial arts in this decade.

As the musical meaning of 'Norwegian' had changed its substance over that period, it was not exclusively the use of folk-music or the incorporation of stylistic features from the folk-heritage and from Grieg that was acceptable as Norwegian. In the 1930s, moreover, more importance was laid on the attitudes behind the music, which emerged, explicitly or otherwise, through titles, commentaries, reviews and the like. As now, political or ideological statements from composers could influence the reception of their music with public and critics alike. For some, it was of real importance that music should express a strong desire to be Norwegian; many wanted music that was as close to its national roots as possible. Irgens-Jensen thought this narrow concentration dangerous: it could compromise authenticity and 'Norwegian-ness' could be misused. But even though his music had no kind of nationalist sentiment, there is something which sounds inescapably Norwegian in it, even if he rarely used a Lydian mode, bare fifths and *slått*-rhythms – stock-in-trade Norwegian hallmarks for a number of other composers such as Eivind Groven and Sparre Olsen in those years.

The critics and public nonetheless often described his music as 'Norwegian'; it had a 'folk music atmosphere'[29] or was 'an expression of the Norwegian psyche'.[30] Many even interpreted *Heimferd* as more a symbol of Norwegian style in music than the music itself could warrant, even with a broad interpretation of what Norwegian style could mean. Where the listener wants to hear something Norwegian, he will concentrate on a few particular features and suppress others. Since Grieg was an icon of national cultural identity, so his music became normatively 'Norwegian'. Something similar happened with *Heimferd*, which acquired a national resonance, even though it has the same form of counterpoint, melodic writing, tonality and so on as other works by Irgens-Jensen. The subject itself, St Olav and the Christianisation of Norway, could scarcely be more Norwegian and so the musical style of the work was also perceived to be 'Norwegian'. *Slått*-rhythms and folksong-like melodies are certainly to be found in *Heimferd*, but they constitute only small parts of the whole and their use is naturally connected with the text. The textual origin of *Driftekaren* means that the same is true of Irgens-Jensen's incidental music, and thus the *Partita sinfonica*: Kinck's

[29] Olav Gurvin, 'Ny norsk musikk', *Musikrevy*, No. 2, 1959.

[30] Klaus Egge, in Arne Østvedt, 'Intervju med Klaus Egge', *Norsk musikkliv*, No. 8, 1945, p. 8.

Kjeld Rasmussen's bust of Irgens-Jensen, cast in 1968

text, the theme and the action almost invite the use of folk-music features. But it is far more difficult to find Norwegian features in Irgens-Jensen's many choral songs and solo songs, even if reviewers sometimes argue to the contrary. His music does not necessarily need to be 'national', even if he does make use of a number of New Norwegian poems.

Irgens-Jensen's Symphony in D minor has rarely been described as 'Norwegian' by local critics, and yet in it, too, he makes use of many of the same effects as in other scores; moreover, it inhabits the large-scale symphonic form that comes from a classical approach. *Canto d'omaggio* is also an expression of the same classicism, but here the quasi-programmatic depiction of everyday life naturally mean that some folk-music elements emerge more clearly.

Japanischer Frühling cannot be described as 'Norwegian': it is a manifestation of something both new and old in Europe. That is, on its first appearance, in 1920, it was regarded as something new; by the time of the revision, in 1957, it seemed to be behind the times. In the event, when the work is seen in relationship to the later wave of enthusiasm for Mahler's music that arose when modernism was gradually forced aside for a broader plurality, *Japanischer Frühling* may even have come too soon.

Throughout his composing career Irgens-Jensen preserved a special strength of expression, a genuine substance. In addition to the spontaneous musicality which permeates all his works and makes it directly appealing, a deeper character can be perceived in his music through his honest striving for a 'clean' expression. He was 'a humanist and philosopher', as Klaus Egge put it.[31]

Irgens-Jensen wanted his means of expression to be direct and unsentimental, in manner and in form – for him, two sides of the same coin. In most of his music he strives for balance and emphasis on lucidity of form, free tonality and flexible lines which form an elegant polyphonic texture. If his refined artistic taste sometimes seems to put an aristocratic stamp on him or his music, it is not as something distant or elevated but as an expression of a nobility and sophistication that was, simultaneously, personal and genuine and universal.

Many commentaries on Irgens-Jensen's music have stressed its elegiac air. Some writers found a certain thoughtfulness, others an almost Grieg-like melancholy. But, although such statements have some validity for the majority of his larger works it is only one side of his expression and sensitivity: much of the music also radiates humour and warmth. And instead of impressive piano pieces or virtuoso violin pieces, such as Christian Sinding's 'Rustle of Spring' or Halvorsen's 'Norwegian Bridal March', he wrote intimate, almost 'anti-virtuoso', pieces like 'Bol's Song' and *Altar*, which found a wide audience nonetheless. He reached his audience best through the polyphonic orchestral works. The Passacaglia, one of the greatest of all Norwegian orchestral works, is justifiably his best-known score. It is in the orchestral works, indeed, where this introverted man is at his most extravert; here such an intimate and strongly personal mood arises that his melancholy and pessimism becomes not only accepted but even loved.

What was Irgens-Jensen's legacy for Norwegian music? Though the three most important 'modern' composers in Oslo in the 1920s – Pauline Hall, Fartein Valen and Ludvig Irgens-Jensen – did not even belong to the same group, each had an effect on new music further afield in Norway, as did Harald Sæverud in Bergen: all of them had vision, knowledge and critical sense, and the will to go their own way. Irgens-Jensen's aesthetic attitudes and his style stimulated the development of Norwegian music, bringing incentives to rethink the 'ruling' style and import new music and ideas into the country without making any fuss. The style he created became a model for younger composers by opening the door to modern traits – not least

[31] *Ibid.*

the generation born some twenty years after him – although he could also be cited as supporting something archetypically Norwegian. Klaus Egge's obituary[32] crystallised Irgens-Jensen's historical position:

> Irgens Jensen's impressive contribution to Norwegian symphonic music is of an innovative, creative, constructive kind within our own national music. He was one of the pillars which signified the *real* development of symphonic music in this country in the 20th century.

Irgens-Jensen was an important figure also in the propagation of Norwegian music abroad. Many of the previous generations of conductors, with leading figures such as Odd Grüner-Hegge, Øivin Fjeldstad, Karsten Andersen, Finn Audun Oftedal and Sverre Bruland, had a genuine feeling for his music and frequently conducted his works for foreign audience.

Indeed, interest in Irgens-Jensen abroad has been growing since his death, and for obvious reasons. The British writer on music, Martin Anderson, reviewing the Norsk kulturråd/Simax CD recording of *Heimferd*, pulled no punches when he described Irgens-Jensen as 'to my mind Norway's finest composer ever' and *Heimferd* as 'a national glory. [...] There is barely anything finer to boast about in all Norwegian music'.[33]

[32] *Arbeiderbladet*, 14 April 1969.

[33] *Tempo*, No. 191, December 1994, p. 59.

Appendix 1
LIST OF WORKS

Most of Irgens-Jensen's manuscript scores and sketches are now in the National Library in Oslo. The manuscript scores have been scanned and some of the published scores will be included in the works featured in the 'Norwegian Musical Heritage Project'[1] and made accessible online if some copyright considerations can be met.

This list[2] presents those Irgens-Jensen scores that are available in final form in performance editions and those of his manuscripts that would seem to be playable with a minor amount of editorial intervention. The huge output of songs that Irgens-Jensen generated in his late teens and early twenties in his search for a style[3] – there are almost 300 of them – is so voluminous that recording them here in the same detail as his mature output would risk unbalancing this worklist; since they are now catalogued in detail on the website of the National Library along with the rest of his manuscripts (at www.nb.no), the reader keen to explore further is recommended to turn there.

This worklist is arranged chronologically by genre, although the dating of the compositions may refer either to the year of finished composition or, where that date is unclear or unknown, its performance or publication. First performances (FP) are indicated only when documented by reliable sources.

The scoring of orchestral works given here is limited to the minimum number of players and does not indicate doublings (as when, for example, a flautist is expected also to play piccolo or an oboist cor anglais). Thus 3222/4331/harp/cel/perc/timp/str indicates an orchestra of three flutes, two oboes, two clarinets, two bassoons; four horns, three trumpets, three trombones, one tuba; harp; celesta; percussion; timpani; strings (violins, violas, cellos, double-basses).

Durations are estimates or based on recordings.

Publishers' sigla are as follows:

NMO = Norsk Musikforlag (www.norskmusikforlag.no)
NMIC = Norwegian Music Information Centre (www.mic.no)
NMS = National Library, Music Collection (www.nb.no)
O.By = Oluf By musikkforlag (later part of NMO)
MS indicates that the published score is a reproduction of the composer's manuscript.

[1] National project for the conservation and republication of selected Norwegian scores.

[2] Thanks to Jorid Nordal Baumann at the National Library for her careful corrections.

[3] *Cf.* p. 46, above.

I. Orchestral Music

1. Works for Orchestra

Variations and Fugue in G minor
1925
3122/4331/harp/cel/perc/timp/str
FP: Oslo Philharmonic Orchestra, cond. José Eibenschütz, 29 November 1926
Revised 1934 and 1948 as *Tema con variazioni*
2122/4331/harp/cel/perc/timp/str
Duration: 23'
Publisher: NMO

Passacaglia
1927; revised 1934 and 1952
3222/4331/harp/cel/perc/timp/str (organ *ad lib.*)
FP: Oslo Philharmonic Orchestra, cond. Odd Grüner-Hegge, Oslo UniversityAula, 19 January 1929
Publisher: NMO
Duration: 21'

Partita Sinfonica: Symphonic Suite (from the play *Driftekaren*)
1938
2222/4331/harp/cel/perc/timp/str

1. Prelude
2. Bol's Song
3. *Presto con fuoco*
4. Epilogue

Two more movements were included in the first performances – *vide infra Two pieces from the incidental music to the play Driftekaren*
FP: Oslo Philharmonic Orchestra, cond. Odd Grüner-Hegge, 20 February 1939
Publisher: NMO, 1951
Duration: 18'
Cf. also 3. Incidental Music, p. 320, below.

Two pieces from the incidental music to the play Driftekaren
1938
2222/4331/harp/cel/perc/timp/str

1. *Molto vivace*
2. *Largamente*

FP: Oslo Philharmonic Orchestra, cond. Odd Grüner-Hegge, 20 February 1939
Publisher: NMS
Duration: 5'/4'
Cf. also 3. Incidental Music, p. 320, below.

Kong Baldvines Armring ('King Baldwin's Arm-Ring')
1935, arr. 1939
Suite for small orchestra from the music to Helen Stibolt's children's comedy
2221/2110/harp/pf/perc/str
1. Scherzo
2. Intermezzo
3. Galgeberget ('Gallow Hill'): *Andante misterioso*
4. Ballet

Publisher: NMIC (MS)
Duration: 13'
Cf. also 3. Incidental Music, p. 320, below.

Sinfonia in re (Symphony in D minor)
1941
3233/4331/harp/cel/perc/timp/str
I. *Allegro – Moderato – Allegro agitato – Molto moderato – Allegro agitato*
II. *Andante – Allegro moderato*
III. *Andante lugubre – Allegro, alla Marcia – Lento*
The third movement was excised in 1952 to form a separate work, the *Rondo marziale* below
FP: Oslo Philharmonic Orchestra, cond. Odd Grüner-Hegge, 8 October 1945
Publisher: NMIC
Duration: 42'

Rondo Marziale
1941
3233/4331/harp/cel/perc/timp/str
FP: Oslo Philharmonic Orchestra, cond. Øivin Fjeldstad, 15 October 1972
Publisher: NMIC (MS)
Duration: 15'

Pastorale Religioso
1943?
1111/2220/harp/timp/str
Orchestration of SATB choral song *Rosa* (*cf.* p. 315, below)
Publisher: NMIC (MS)
Duration: 6'

Canto d'omaggio: Festival Overture
1950
3222/4331/timp/perc/harp/org/str (choir *ad lib.*)
FP: Oslo Town Hall, Oslo Philharmonic Orchestra, cond. Odd Grüner-Hegge, 15 May 1950
Publisher: NMIC (MS)

Duration: 9'

Air
1958
Orchestral version of 'An einen Freund' from *Japanischer Frühling* (*q.v.*)
1111/2000/str
Publisher: NMO
Duration: 3'

2. Works for Solo Instrument and Orchestra

Bols vise ('Bol's Song'), arr. from the incidental music to *Driftekaren.*
1938
violin, string orchestra
Publisher: NMO
Duration: 3'

Altar ('Altar')
1963
violin, string orchestra
Publisher: NMO
Duration: 3'

3. Works for Voice(s) and Orchestra

Le flambeau vivant ('The Living Torch')
1920
voice, 2222/4331/harp/perc/timp/str
Text (French): Charles Baudelaire
Publisher: NMIC (MS)
Duration: 4'
Withdrawn by the composer

Skumring ('Twilight')
1922
voice, solo violin/2222/2000/harp/str
Text (Norwegian): Einar Solstad
Publisher: NMIC (MS)
Duration: 4'
Withdrawn by the composer

Chrysantemum
1922
voice, 2222/4331/harp/perc/timp/str
Text (Norwegian): Einar Solstad
Publisher: NMIC (MS)

Duration: 3'
Withdrawn by the composer

Das Mädchen auf der Brücke ('The Maiden on the Bridge')
1922
Text: anon., Chinese (c. 900), German paraphrase by Hans Bethge
soprano, 2222/4100/harp/cel/perc/timp/str
Publisher: NMIC (MS)
Duration: 3'

Hägring ('Mirage')
1924
Text (Swedish): Bertel Gripenberg
Opening song of the 1924 song-cycle *Rosenstaden* ('The City of Roses'): *cf.* III. 1. Song-Cycle, pp. 306–7, below
voice/2111/2100/harp/cel/perc/timp/str
Publisher: NMIC(MS)
Duration: 3'

Ökenridten ('The Desert Ride')
1924
Text (Swedish): Bertel Gripenberg
From the song-cycle *Rosenstaden*: *cf.* III. 1. Song-Cycles, pp. 306–7, below
voice, 1011/2100/harp/perc/timp/str
Publisher: NMIC (MS)
Duration: 4'

Heimferd ('Homeward Journey'): Dramatic Symphony
1930
soprano, mezzo soprano, three tenors, two basses, SATB chorus, 3222/4331/harp/cel/org/perc/timp/str
Text (Norwegian): Olav Gullvåg (*Olav-oratorio*)
FP: Oslo Philharmonic Orchestra and chorus, cond. Odd Grüner-Hegge, Oslo University Aula, 1 December 1930
Publisher: Score: NMIC, choral score: NMO
Duration: 90'

I blodet hans blømde ('In his blood blossomed')
1930
Text (Norwegian): Olav Gullvåg, from *Heimferd*
soprano, 3222/4331/org/perc/str (first version), strings (second version)
Publisher: NMIC (MS)
Duration: 3'
Der Gott und die Bajadere ('The God and the Bayadere')

1932
Text (German): Johann Wolfgang von Goethe
mezzo soprano, bass, SATB chorus, 2222/4331/harp/perc/timp/str
FP: Anna Brekke Tibell (mezzo soprano), Morten Vatn (bass), Oslo Philharmonic Orchestra and Chorus, cond. Odd Grüner-Hegge, 17 January 1935
Publisher: NMIC (MS)
Duration: 27'

Bols vise ('Bol's Song')
1938
Text (Norwegian): Hans E. Kinck
Arr. from the incidental music to *Driftekaren.*
Soprano, 1111/2000/harp/cel/str
Publisher: NMIC (MS)
Duration: 3'

Altar ('Altar')
1941 (orchestration of 1939 song with piano accompaniment)
Text (Norwegian/English): Halldis Moren Vesaas
Voice, strings
Publisher: NMIC (MS)
Duration: 3'

Lutad mot gärdet ('Leaning on the Fence')
1941
Text (Swedish): Johan Ludvig Runeberg
soprano, 2111/2000/cel/str
Publisher: NMIC (MS)
Duration: 3'

Til Kongen ('To the King')
1945
Text (Norwegian): Arnulf Øverland
SATB chorus, 2222/4231/harp/str
Publisher: NMIC (MS)
Duration: 4'

De brendte våre gårder ('They burned our homes')
1947 (orchestration of 1945 choral song with piano accompaniment)
Text (Norwegian): Inger Hagerup
male-voice (TB) chorus, 1112/2221/perc/timp/str
Publisher: NMIC (MS)
Duration: 4'
Japanischer Frühling ('Japanese Spring')

1957

Orchestration and revision of *Japanischer Frühling*, Op. 2 (1920), for voice and piano

Text (German): paraphrases of Japanese poetry by Hans Bethge

soprano, 2133/2200/harp/cel/perc/timp/str

1. 'Heute' ('Today'); text: Ôshikôchi no Mitsune (d. 924)
2. 'Der Blütenzweig' ('The Branch of Blossom'); text: Fujiwara no Hirotsugu (eighth century)
3. 'Die Weide im Wind' ('The Willow in the Wind'); text: anon. (eighteenth century)
4. 'An einen Freund' ('To a Friend'); text: Ôshikôchi no Mitsune
5. 'Der Liebeslaut' ('The Sound of Love'); text: Segawa (eighteenth century)
6. 'Betrachtung' ('Reflection'); text: Ise (c. 900)
7. 'Nichts leichter' ('An Easy Game'); text: anon. (eighteenth century)
8. 'Einsam' ('Solitary'); text: Ono no Komachi (834–80)
9. 'Dauer im Wechsel' ('Permanence in Change'); text: Ki no Tonomori (845–905)

FP: Eva Prytz (soprano), Oslo Philharmonic Orchestra, cond. Odd Grüner-Hegge, Oslo University Aula, 11 January 1957

Publisher: NMO

Duration: 23'

4. Orchestral Arrangements of Irgens-Jensen's Music by Other Composers

Das Meer erstrahlt ('The Sea is Shining')

Orchestration (1928?) by Arvid Kleven[4] of 1919 song (*cf.* III.1. Song-Cycles, *Gedichte von Heine*, Op. 3, pp. 304–5, below)

1010/1100/str

Publisher: NMIC (MS)

Hägring ('Mirage')

Orchestration (1928?) by Arvid Kleven of opening song of *Rosenstaden*: *cf.* III. 1. Song-Cycle, p. 306–7, below

1010/1100/str

Publisher: NMIC (MS)

Tanz

Orchestration (1928?) by Arvid Kleven of 1922 song (*cf.* III.2. Voice and Piano, p. 310, below)

1010/1100/str

Publisher: NMIC (MS)

[4] The short-lived Arvid Kleven (1899–1929: he died five days before his 30th birthday) earned his living as a flautist. The handful of works he composed, which move from Impressionism to Expressionism, put him at the forefront of Norwegian music in his day; his death, from rheumatic fever, extinguished what would probably have been a major voice in twentieth-century Norwegian music.

Siciliano
Arr. (1948?) for strings by Sverre Bergh[5] from the 1924 piano piece (*cf.* II.2. Instrumental Music, p. 303, below)
Publisher: NMIC (MS)
Duration: 3'

Partita sinfonica
Arrangement (1981?) for military band by Ole Henning Johannesen
Publisher: NMIC (MS)

Arrangement (2012) for military band by Lars-Thomas Holm
1. Prelude
2. Bol's Song
4. Epilogue
Publisher: NMIC

Passacaglia
Arrangement (2003) for wind band (+harp, cb) by Bjørn Mellemberg
FP: The Norwegian Wind Ensemble, cond. Bjarte Engeset, Sarpsborg Church, 12 November 2003
Publisher: NMIC

Arrangement (2011) for military band by Lars-Thomas Holm
FP: Sarpsborg Janitsjarkorps, cond. John Philip Hannevik, Trondheim, 24 March 2012
Publisher: NMIC

Japanischer Frühling: three songs
Arrangement (2009?) for soprano and wind band (+harp, cb) by Bjørn Mellemberg
1. Heute
2. Betrachtung
3. Nichts leichter
Publisher: NMIC

[5] Sverre Bergh (1915–80) studied with Fartein Valen and in Vienna. His compositions are generally in a Neoclassical style, often laced with a buoyant sense of humour, but he was also active as an arranger of music in a wide range of styles. He was also an important music administrator and organiser.

II. Chamber and Instrumental Music

1. Chamber Music

Violin Sonata in B flat major
1924
violin and piano
I. *Allegretto – Molto vivace – Allegro moderato – Tempo I*
II. *Andante serioso*
III. *Vivace*
22'
FP: Arve Arvesen (violin), Elisabeth Reiss (piano), Oslo, 8 October 1926
The Rondo for violin and piano (*q.v.*) was initially intended as the finale of this Sonata.
Source: NMIC (MS)

Rondo
1924
violin and piano
Publisher: NMIC (MS)
Duration: 7'

Piano Quintet
1926
I. *Allegro moderato*
II. *Andantino (quasi allegretto) Moderato*
III. *Allegro. Adagio.*
FP: Ivar Johnsen (piano), Oslo Philharmonic String Quartet, Oslo University Aula, 2 February 1932
Publisher: NMIC (MS)
Duration: 26'

Bol's Song
1938
violin and piano
Publisher: NMO
Duration: 3'

Dance Scene from the incidental music to *Driftekaren*
1938
string quartet
Publisher: NMIC
Duration: 4'

Altar
1939
violin and piano
Publisher: NMO
Duration: 3'

I blodet hans blømde ('In his blood blossomed')
1939
chorale from *Heimferd*; *cf.* III. 3 Works for Voice(s) and Orchestra, p. 298, above
string quartet
Publisher: NMIC (MS)
Duration: 2'

Pastorale religioso
1939?
string quartet
Publisher: NMIC
Duration: 3'

Duo
1943?
two violins
Publisher: NMO
Duration: 4'

2. Instrumental Music

Siciliano
1924
piano
Publisher: NMIC (MS)
Duration: 2'

Falkvor Lommanson – Variations on an Old Norwegian Ballad
1942
piano
Publisher: NMO
Duration: 6'

III. Voice and Piano

Irgens-Jensen's first published songs for voice and piano were printed by the music publisher Oluf By. Irgens-Jensen withdrew them all. But several of the songs were performed later, some in concerts with Irgens-Jensen playing the piano part. Some of these were then re-edited, and these edited versions may be found at NMS. Where apposite, details are given below.

1. Song-Cycles

For voice and piano

I Mørket ('In the Dark'), Op. 1
1920
Text: Arnulf Øverland
1. 'I mørket' ('In the Dark')
2. 'Vuggevise' ('Cradle Song')
3. 'Et barn' ('A Child')
4. 'Utopi' ('Utopia')
5. 'Den siste nat' ('The Last Night')
6. 'Landevei' ('Highway'); published in Aksel Schiötz and Gerd Schiötz (eds.), *Anthology of Nordic Solo Songs*, Vol. 4: Norway, Edition Egtved, Copenhagen, 1984
7. 'Sne' ('Snow')

FP: Hildur Øverland (soprano), Pauline Hall (piano), Kristiania, 4 October 1920 (No. 1 only); Margit Aarberg Rom (mezzo soprano), unknown pianist, Kristiania, 9 June 1920 (Nos. 2 and 7)
Publisher: O.By; later withdrawn by the composer

Japanischer Frühling ('Japanese Spring'), Op. 2
1920
Text: Japanese, paraphrased by Hans Bethge
1. 'Heute' ('Today'); text: Ôshikôchi no Mitsune (d. 924)
2. 'Die Weide im Wind' ('The Willow in the Wind'); text. anon. (eighteenth century)
3. 'Der Blütenzweig' ('The Branch of Blossom'); text: Fujiwara no Hirotsugu (eighth century)
4. 'Nichts leichter' ('Nothing easier'); text: anon. (eighteenth century)
5. 'An einen Freund' ('To a Friend'); text: Ôshikôchi no Mitsune
6. 'Der Liebeslaut' ('The Sound of Love'); text: Segawa (eighteenth century)
7. 'Betrachtung' ('Reflection'); text: Ise (c. 900)
8. 'Einsam' ('Solitary'); text: Ono no Komachi (ninth century)
9. 'Dauer im Wechsel' ('Permanence in Change'); text: Ki no Tomonori (845–905)

FP: Margit Aarberg Rom, mezzo soprano, unknown pianist, Kristiania, 9 June 1920 (Nos. 1, 5, 6, 7 and 9 only)
Publisher: O.By; this version was later withdrawn by the composer and a new version prepared in 1958 (*vide infra*)

Gedichte von Heine ('Poems of Heine'), Op. 3
1920
Text (German): Heinrich Heine
1. 'Nimm mich auf, uralte Nacht' ('Receive me, ancient night')
2. 'Herz, mein Herz' ('Heart, my heart')

3. 'Es ragt ins Meer der Runenstein' ('The runestone rises in the sea')
4. 'Das Meer erstrahlt' ('The sea is shining')
5. 'Es war ein alter König' ('There was an old king')

FP: Hildur Øverland (soprano), Pauline Hall (piano), 4 October 1920 (No. 4 only)

Publisher: O.By; later withdrawn by the composer. 'Das Meer erstrahlt' was published in *Ludvig Irgens-Jensen: Sangalbum (17 sanger)*, Norsk Musikforlag, Oslo, 2002.

Gedanken – Schwermut – Blüten ('Thought – Melancholy – Blossom'), Op. 4
1920
Text: Saigyó, 1118–90?, paraphrased by Hans Bethge

1. 'Gedanken' ('Thought')
2. 'Schwermut' ('Melancholy')
3. 'Blüten' ('Blossom')

Publisher: O.By; later withdrawn by the composer

Digte av Øverland ('Poems by Øverland'), Op. 5
1920
Text: Arnulf Øverland

1. 'Besværgelse' ('Conjuration')
2. 'Alrunen' ('The Mandrake')
3. 'Ballade'
4. 'Zigeunersang' ('Gypsy Song')

Publisher: O.By; later withdrawn by the composer. 'Besværgelse' and 'Ballade' were published in *Ludvig Irgens-Jensen: Sangalbum (17 sanger), op. cit.*, and 'Alrunen' ('The Mandrake') published in Aksel Schiötz and Gerd Schiötz (eds.), *Anthology of Nordic Solo Songs*, Vol. 4: Norway, Edition Egtved, Copenhagen, 1984.

Slaviske Digte ('Slavic Poems'), Op. 6
1920
Text: Slavic poetry, paraphrased in Danish by Thor Lange

1. 'Tre søstre' ('Three Sisters')
2. 'Guldskyen' ('The Golden Cloud')
3. 'Hvorfor vil de røde flammer spille' ('Why do the red flames play')
4. 'Intet ly' ('No Shelter')
5. 'Du og jeg' ('You and I')

FP: Hildur Øverland (soprano), Pauline Hall (piano), Oslo 4 October 1920 (selection)

Publisher: O.By; later partly withdrawn by the composer. 'Tre søstre' and 'Guldskyen' were published in *Ludvig Irgens-Jensen: Sangalbum (17 sanger), op. cit.*

Fabler ('Fables')
1924
Text (Norwegian): Ludvig Irgens-Jensen

1. ‘Grevlingen og lerken’ (‘The Badger and the Lark’)
2. ‘Småpus’ (‘Kitten’)
3. ‘Haren og reven’ (‘The Hare and the Fox’)
4. ‘På tunet’ (‘In the Farmyard’)
5. ‘I regn og blest’ (‘In Rain and Wind’)

Publisher: NMIC. ‘Grevlingen og lerken’ was published in *Ludvig Irgens-Jensen: Sangalbum (17 sanger), op. cit.*

Fabler og barnerim (‘Fables and Nursery Rhymes’)
1924
Text: Irgens-Jensen
Vol. 1:
1. ‘Bamse-Brakar’ (‘Bruin the Bear’)
2. ‘Bånlåt’ (‘Lullaby’)
3. ‘Storebjørn og Veslebjørn’ (‘Big Bear and Little Bear’)

Vol. 2:
1. ‘Gås og gasse’ (‘Goose and Gander’)
2. ‘Katten og musen’ (‘Cat and Mouse’)
3. ‘Debatten’ (‘The Debate’)

FP: Margit Aarberg Nergaard (mezzo soprano), the composer (piano), Kristiania (Oslo), 9 April 1924 (selection)
Source: NMO. A German translation of ‘Debatten’ was published in D. F. Scheuleer (ed.), *Gedenkboek*, s`Gravenhage, 1925, pp. 177–80.

Rosenstaden (‘The City of Roses’)
1924
Text (Swedish): Bertel Gripenberg
Part 1:
‘Hägring’ (‘Mirage’)
‘Rosenstjärnan’ (‘The Rose Star’)
‘Femton år’ (‘Fifteen Years’)
‘Livstråderna’ (‘Threads of Life’)
‘Lindagulls namn’ (‘Lindagull’s Name’)
Part 2:
‘Visa i lustgården’ (‘Song in the Garden of Pleasure’)
‘Vindens visa’ (‘Song of the Wind’)
‘Så kom du’ (‘Then you came’)
‘Och ägde jag’ (‘If I owned’)
Part 3:
‘En skugga’ (‘A Shadow’)
‘Ökenridten’ (‘The Desert Ride’)
‘Vid dammen’ (‘At the Pond’)
‘Serenad’ (‘Serenade’)
‘Lindagulls tårer’ (‘Lindagull’s Tears’)

'På himlen stå planeterna' ('Planets in the Sky')
Part 4:
'Önskestunden' ('The Moment of Wishing')
'Hjärtat' ('The Heart')
'Ännu en gång' ('Yet Once Again')
'Ormen' ('The Snake')
'Förbannelsen' ('The Curse')
'Till häst' ('On Horseback')
Part 5:
'Intermezzo'
'Korsväg' ('Crossroads')
'Den förlorade sonens återkomst' ('The Return of the Lost Son')
FP: Elisabeth Munthe-Kaas (soprano), the composer (piano), Gamle Logen, Kristiania, 2 April 1924 (excerpts)
Source: NMS (MS). 'Så kom du' and 'Ännu en gång' were published in *Ludvig Irgens-Jensen: Sangalbum (17 sanger), op. cit.*

Barnebilleder ('Children's Portraits')
1937
Text: Marie Hamsun
Album 1:
1. 'Per'
2. 'Randi',
3. 'Bestemor' ('Grandmother')
4. 'Vesle Ottar' ('Little Ottar')
5. 'I slåtten' ('In the Field')
6. 'Ottars katt' ('Ottar's Cat')

Album 2:
1. 'Randis vise' ('Randi's Song')
2. 'Barnesorg' ('A Child's Sorrow')
3. 'Ottar og far på fisketur' ('Ottar and Father on a Fishing Trip')
4. 'En liten gjest' ('A Little Guest')
5. 'Søndag' ('Sunday')
6. 'Middag' ('Dinner')

Album 3:
1. 'Trehesten' ('The Wooden Horse')
2. 'Små potetopptakere' ('Little Potato Diggers')
3. 'Livets gåter' ('Life's Mysteries')
4. 'Blomsterdun' ('Flowery Down')
5. 'Bekken' ('The Stream)'

FP: Elisabeth Munthe-Kaas, soprano; composer (piano), Oslo, 19 October 1937 (excerpts)
Publisher: NMO

Japanischer Frühling ('Japanese Spring')
1958, revised version
Text (German): paraphrases of Japanese poetry by Hans Bethge
1. 'Heute' ('Today'); text: Ôshikôchi no Mitsune (d. 924)
2. 'Der Blütenzweig' ('The Branch of Blossom'); text: Fujiwara no Hirotsugu (eighth century)
3. 'Die Weide im Wind' ('The Willow in the Wind'); text: anon. (eighteenth century)
4. 'An einen Freund' ('To a Friend'); text: Ôshikôchi no Mitsune
5. 'Der Liebeslaut' ('The Sound of Love'); text: Segawa (eighteenth century)
6. 'Betrachtung' ('Reflection'); text: Ise (c. 900)
7. 'Nichts leichter' ('Nothing Easier'); text: anon. (eighteenth century)
8. 'Einsam' ('Solitary'); text: Ono no Komachi (834–80)
9. 'Dauer im Wechsel' ('Permanence in Change'); text: Ki no Tonomori (845–905)

FP: Eva Prytz (soprano), Tasso Janopoulo (piano), Paris, 11 September 1959, Salle Chopin-Pleyel.
Publisher: NMO
Duration: 23'

2. Individual Songs

For voice and piano unless otherwise indicated
Several of the songs that were withdrawn by Irgens-Jensen were reworked and presented in new versions.
NMS has the personal scores of these songs of such singers as Hildur Øverland, Margit Aarberg Rom, Elisabeth Munthe-Kaas, Elisabeth Reiss and Dagmar Wittrup.

Ein Fichtenbaum ('A Spruce Tree')
1913
Text (German): Heinrich Heine
Source: NMS

De elskendes vin ('The Lovers' Wine')
1917
Text: Charles Baudelaire; Norwegian paraphrase by Irgens-Jensen
Source: NMS

Femme et chatte ('Woman and Cat')
1918
Text (French): Paul Verlaine
Publisher: NMIC (MS)

Qu'as-tu fait ('What have you done?')
1918
Text (French): Paul Verlaine

Publisher: O.By; also published in *Ludvig Irgens-Jensen: Sangalbum (17 sanger), op. cit.*

Den hellige Birgittas salme, later known as *Den hellige jomfrus salme* ('St Birgitta's Psalm'/'The Holy Virgin's Psalm')
1919–20
Text (French orig., Norwegian translation by the composer): Maurice Maeterlinck
Publisher: O.By; also published in *Ludvig Irgens-Jensen: Sangalbum (17 sanger), op. cit.*

Vaarregnen ('The Spring Rain')
1919–20
Text (Danish): Thu-Fu, paraphrased by Aage Matthison-Hansen
FP: Margit Aarberg Rom (mezzo soprano), unknown pianist, Kristiania, 9 June 1920 (Nos. 2 and 7)
Publisher: O.By

Der blinker ei Stjerner ('No stars shine')
1920
Text (Norwegian): Sigbjørn Obstfelder
Publisher: O.By

Seifenschaum ('Foam')
1920
Text (German): Richard Gerschow
Publisher: O.By

Sang for mor ('Song for Mother')
1921
Text (Norwegian): Ludvig Irgens-Jensen
Publisher: NMIC (MS)

Das Mädchen auf der Brücke ('The Girl on the Bridge')
1922, rev. 1950
Text: Anon., Chinese (c. 900), German paraphrase by Hans Bethge
FP: Dagny Constanze Knutsen (soprano), Waldemar Alme (piano), Kristiania, 8 December 1922
Publisher: NMIC; also published in *Ludvig Irgens-Jensen: Sangalbum (17 sanger), op. cit.*
Duration: 3'

Der schönste Tod ('The Most Beautiful Death')
1922
Text (German): Hans Bethge: translation from Hafiz

Publisher: NMIC (MS)

Tanz (‘Dance’)
1922
Text: Hafiz; German paraphrase by Hans Bethge
FP: Elisabeth Munthe-Kaas (soprano), the composer (piano), Gamle Logen, Kristiania, 2 April 1924
Source: NMS

Kulden (‘The Cold’)
1922
Text: Einar Solstad
FP: Elisabeth Munthe-Kaas, soprano, the composer (piano), Gamle Logen, Kristiania, 2 April 1924
Publisher: NMIC (MS)

Bøn (‘Prayer’)
1923
Text (Danish): Thor Lange
Publisher: NMS (MS)

Trädens sus (‘The Murmur of the Trees’)
1925
Text (Swedish): Anders Österling
Publisher: NMIC (MS)

Die Drei Prinzessinnen (‘The Three Princesses’)
1927?
Text: Chinese; paraphrase by Hans Bethge
Source: NMS

I blodet hans blømde (‘In his blood blossomed’)
1930
Text (Norwegian): Olav Gullvåg, from *Heimferd*: *cf.* I. 3. Works for Voice(s) and Orchestra, p. 299, above)
Publisher: NMIC (MS)

I blodet hans blømde (‘In his blood blossomed’)
1930
contralto, organ
Text (Norwegian): Olav Gullvåg, from *Heimferd*: *cf.* I. 3. Works for Voice(s) and Orchestra, p. 298, above)
Publisher: NMIC (MS)

Narrens ballade om vismannen ('The Fool's Ballad about the Sage')
1933?
Text (Norwegian): Svend Prås (i.e., Elling Bang)
Source: NMS (MS)

Barnevise ('Children's Song')
1934
Text (Norwegian): Ludvig Irgens-Jensen
Publisher: NMIC (MS)

Småguten ('Small lad')
1936?
Text (Norwegian): Åsmund Sveen
Source: NMS

En nyårslåt ('A New Year Song')
1937/1951
Text (Swedish): Gustaf Fröding
Source: NMS

Bol's Song
1938
Text (English): translated from Hans E. Kinck, probably by the composer
Publisher: NMIC (MS)
Duration: 2'

Bols vise ('Bol's Song')
1938
Text (Norwegian): Hans E. Kinck
Publisher: NMO
Duration: 2'

Det er så svært, det ene punkt ('It is so difficult, this single thing'): psalm from the incidental music to *Driftekaren*
1938
Text (Danish): N. M. Schmidth
Publisher: NMS (MS)

Lutad mot gärdet ('Leaning on the Fence')
1938
Text (Swedish): Johan Ludvig Runeberg
Publisher: NMO; also published in *Ludvig Irgens-Jensen: Sangalbum (17 sanger), op. cit.*
Duration: 3'

Hjuringsull ('Shepherd's Lullaby')
1938
Text (Norwegian): Ludvig Irgens-Jensen
Publisher: NMIC (MS)

To sanger av Hans Henrik Holm ('Two Songs of Hans Henrik Holm')
1938?
Text (Norwegian): Hans Henrik Holm
1. Farktausi ('Travelling Girl')
2. Surrefluga ('Buzzing Fly')
Publisher: NMIC

Hjemløs ('Homeless')
1938?
Text (Norwegian): Olaf Schou
Publisher: NMS (MS)

Harens rätt ('The Right of the Hare')
1938?
Text (Swedish): Gustaf Fröding
FP: Dagmar Wittrup?
Publisher: NMS (MS)

Ved mor si grav ('At Mother's Graveside')
1938?
Text (Norwegian): Hans Henrick Holm
Publisher: NMS (MS)

Huldrelok ('The Call of the Hulder')
1938?
Text (Norwegian): Peter Egge
Publisher: NMS (MS)

Jäntblig ('A Maid's Glance')
1938?
Text (Swedish): Gustaf Fröding
Source: NMS (MS)

Ola og Kari ('Ola and Kari')
1938?
Text: Norwegian folksong
Source: NMS (MS)

Hvem er det som rider ('Who is that riding')
c. 1938
Text (Norwegian): composer
Publisher: NMS

Kokkedrengen ('The Galley Boy')
c. 1938
Text (Norwegian): Jacob Sande
Publisher: NMS

Altar ('Altar')
1939
Text (Norwegian/English): Halldis Moren Vesaas
Publisher: NMO (Norwegian)/Novello (English); also published in *Ludvig Irgens-Jensen: Sangalbum (17 sanger), op. cit.*
Duration: 3'

Den gamle ('The Old One')
1939
Text (Swedish): Johan Ludvig Runeberg
Publisher: NMO; also published in *Ludvig Irgens-Jensen: Sangalbum (17 sanger), op. cit.*
Duration: 2'

Fiskerens aftensang ('The Fisherman's Evening Song')
1939
Text (Norwegian): Arnulf Øverland
Publisher: NMO; also published in *Ludvig Irgens-Jensen: Sangalbum (17 sanger), op. cit.*
Duration: 2'

Til Kongen ('To the King')
1940
Text (Norwegian): Arnulf Øverland
Publisher: NMO

Ulveære ('Wolf Honour')
1940
Text (Norwegian): Ludvig Irgens-Jensen

Publisher: NMIC (MS)

To svaler ('Two Swallows')
1941
Text (Norwegian): Ludvig Irgens-Jensen
Publisher: NMIC (MS)
From the incidental music to *Robin Hood*; *cf.* also p. 321, below.

Til de unge ('To the Young')
1943
Text (Norwegian): Ludvig Irgens-Jensen
Publisher: NMIC (MS)

De brendte våre gårder ('They burned our homes')
1945
Text (Norwegian): Inger Hagerup
Publisher: NMO; also published in *Ludvig Irgens-Jensen: Sangalbum (17 sanger), op. cit.*
Duration: 3'

Vårbekken ('The Spring Brook')
1950
Text (Norwegian): Ludvig Irgens-Jensen
Publisher: NMS; also published in *Ludvig Irgens-Jensen: Sangalbum (17 sanger), op. cit.*

Ludvig Irgens-Jensen: Sangalbum (17 sanger), op. cit., contains: 'Ännu en gång', 'Altar', 'Ballade', 'Besværgelse', 'Das Mädchen auf der Brücke', 'Das Meer erstrahlt', 'De brente våre gårder', 'Den gamle', 'Den hellige Birgittas salme', 'Fiskerens aftensang', 'Grevlingen og lerken', 'Guldskyen', 'Lutad mot gärdet', 'Qu'as-tu fait', 'Så kom du', 'Tre søstre', 'Vårbekken'
2002
Publisher: NMO

IV. Choral Songs

1. Mixed Chorus

I blodet hans blømde ('In his blood blossomed')
1930
Text (Norwegian): Olav Gullvåg
NMI

Den klare sol ('The Bright Sun')
1935
Text (Norwegian): Dagfinn Zwilgmeyer
Publisher: NMO

Kirken ('The Church')
1935
Text (Norwegian): Dagfinn Zwilgmeyer
Publisher: NMO

Kom due hit ('Come here, dove')
1935
Text (Norwegian): Dagfinn Zwilgmeyer
Publisher: NMO

Pinse ('Whitsun')
1935
Text (Norwegian): Dagfinn Zwilgmeyer
Publisher: NMO

Rosa ('Rose')
1935
Text (Norwegian): Olav Aukrust
Publisher: NMO

Skrifte ('Confession')
1935
Text (Norwegian): Dagfinn Zwilgmeyer
Publisher: NMO

Under korset ('Under the Cross')
1935
Text (Norwegian): Dagfinn Zwilgmeyer
Publisher: NMO

I dag står flaggstangen naken ('Today the flagpole stands empty')
1940
Text (Norwegian): Nordahl Grieg
Publisher: NMO

I dag står flaggstangen naken
1940
choir (unison), piano
Text (Norwegian): Nordahl Grieg
Publisher: NMO

Til Kongen ('To the King')
1940
Text (Norwegian): Arnulf Øverland
Publisher: NMO

Natten og stjernene ('The Night and the Stars')
1943
Text: Paul Jerndal (i.e., Irgens-Jensen)
The music is the same as *Til Kongen*
Source: NMS

2. Songs for Women's Chorus

Le voyage ('The Voyage')
1917
choir, piano
Text (French): Charles Baudelaire (excerpt)
Publisher: NMIC

Spurvekor ('Sparrow Choir')
1936
Text (Norwegian): Ludvig Irgens-Jensen
Publisher: NMO

Den lange reglen ('The Long Story')
1943
Text (Norwegian): Ludvig Irgens-Jensen
Publisher: NMO

Klokkene ('The Bells')
1944
Text (Norwegian): Ludvig Irgens-Jensen
Publisher: NMO

Senhøst ('Late Autumn')
1944
Text (Norwegian): Ludvig Irgens-Jensen
Publisher: NMIC

Jul ('Christmas')
1947
Text (Norwegian): Arnulf Øverland
Publisher: NMO

3. Songs for Men's Chorus

Norge ('Norway')
1924
Text (Norwegian): Arnulf Øverland
Publisher: NMIC

Elsker du landet ('Do you love the land')
1927
Text (Norwegian): Gunnar Reiss-Andersen
MS in NMS

Til Norges flagg ('To Norway's Flag')
1928
Text (Norwegian): Gunnar Reiss-Andersen
Publisher: NMO
Duration: 2'

Dyr og folk ('Animals and People')
1936
Text (Norwegian): Åsmund Sveen
Publisher: NMO

Græsset hvisker om natten ('The grass whispers during the night')
1936
Text (Norwegian): Arnulf Øverland
Publisher: NMO

Hvite tind ('White Peak')
1936
Text (Norwegian): Arnulf Øverland
Publisher: NMO

Ingers-Jon
1936
Text (Norwegian): Åsmund Sveen
Publisher: NMO

Puken ('The Devil')
1936
Text (Norwegian): Åsmund Sveen
Publisher: NMO

Tre rømlinger ('Three Fugitives')
1936
Text (Norwegian): Ludvig Irgens-Jensen
Publisher: NMO

Barken på Stadt ('The Ship at Stadt')
1937
Text (Norwegian): Jakob Sande
Publisher: NMO

Elvira
1937
Text (Norwegian): Jakob Sande
Publisher: NMO

Senorita
1937
Text (Norwegian): Jakob Sande
Publisher: NMO

Sur dag ('A Bad Day')
1937
Text (Norwegian): Jakob Sande
Publisher: NMO

Studentersang ('Student Song')
1938
Text (Norwegian): Nils Collett Vogt
Publisher: NMIC (also published in Georg Brochmann (ed.), *Studentene fra 1913*, Bokkomiteen for studentene fra 1913, Oslo 1938)

Ei malmfuru ('A Pine-Mast')
1939
Text (Norwegian): Hans Henrik Holm
Publisher: NMO
Duration: 2'

I dag står flaggstangen naken ('Today the flagpole stands empty')
1940
Text (Norwegian): Nordahl Grieg
Publisher: NMO

Natten og stjernene (same music as *Til Kongen*)
1940
Text (Norwegian): Paul Jerndal (i.e., Irgens-Jensen)
Source: NMS

Til Kongen ('To the King')
1940
Text (Norwegian): Arnulf Øverland
Publisher: NMO

På knarrar i gamal tid ('On merchantmen in olden times')
1944
Text (Norwegian): Hans Henrik Holm
Publisher: NMIC (MS)

Dagvise ('Day Song')
1945
Text (Norwegian): Arnulf Øverland
Publisher: NMO

De brendte våre gårder ('They burned our homes')
1945
Text (Norwegian): Inger Hagerup
Publisher: NMO

Vårt hjem ('Our Home')
1948
Text (Norwegian): Arnulf Øverland
Publisher: NMO
Duration: 6'

To Holberg-epigrammer ('Two Holberg Epigrams')
1954
1. 'Lykkens dage'
2. 'Sindets ro'
Text (Norwegian): Ludvig Holberg
Publisher: NMO

En hustavle ('House-Rules')
1955
Text (Norwegian): Arnulf Øverland
Publisher: NMO
Duration: 4'

Skjærgaardsvise ('Song of the Skerries')
1955
Text (Norwegian): Gabriel Scott
Publisher: NMO
Duration: 3'

På jorden et sted ('Somewhere on Earth')
1960
Text (Norwegian): André Bjerke
Publisher: NMO
Duration: 3'

V. Music for the Stage

1. Incidental Music

Kong Baldvines Armring ('King Baldwin's Arm-Ring')
1935
Music for Helen Stibolt's play,
FP: Nationaltheatret, Oslo, 17 December 1935
Printed score (209pp) in NMS

Driftekaren ('The Drover')
1937
Music for Hans E. Kinck's play,
FP: Nationaltheatret, Oslo, 10 March 1938
MS in NMS

Hevnen ('Revenge'): Music to Peter Egge's drama
1941

Robin Hood
1942–45
Music to a children's comedy, Nationaltheatret, (text: S. Hagerup Bull/Irgens-Jensen)
FP: 19 December 1945
MS in NMS

Mennesket ('Mankind')
1945
Music to dramatised texts of Henrik Wergeland, produced on the centenary of his death
FP: Nationaltheatret, Oslo, 12 July 1945
MS in NMS

2. Opera

Heimferd
1947
Opera version, Det Norske Teatret
FP: 27 August 1947
Publisher: NMIC

Unfinished Works

1. Orchestral Works

Fransk suite ('French Suite')
1950s?
Suite in four movements, based on songs written to French texts soon after the First World War:

1. Verlaine: 'Gaspard Hauser chante' – almost fully orchestrated
2. Verlaine: 'Femme et chatte' – composed in full but not orchestrated
3. Verlaine: 'Colombine' – composed in full but not orchestrated
4. Verhaeren's 'Les deux enfants de roi' – not fully orchestrated

Source: NMS

Liten ouverture ('Little Overture')
1950s?
Almost complete; only partly orchestrated
Source: NMS

Vetle hjuringen ('The Little Shepherd')
1950s?
Almost completely composed; only partly orchestrated
Source: NMS

Processione Infantile
1950s?
Built on the song from the play *Hannemor* (*q. v.*)
Almost completely composed ; only partly orchestrated
Source: NMS

Opera
Bryllupet i Genua ('The Wedding in Genoa')
Libretto: Hans E. Kinck

Ebbe Skammelsøn
1951
Libretto: Magnus Grønvold

Canons, childrens' rhymes and songs in arrangement are found in abundance.

Appendix 2
Irgens-Jensen as Poet

To shed light on all sides of Irgens-Jensen's multi-talented artistic activities, a selection of his poems and verses are included here in addition to the verses cited in the body of the book and the examination of his literary interests in chapter II.[1] In his sketchbooks musical ideas, short verses and rapid drawings are all mixed together, jotted down side-by-side as aide-memoires in case his brilliant memory failed him. His interest in poetry is evident both through the disproportionate number of his musical works which have poetic texts and through the number of collections of poems found in his library. Here one encounters most of the Norwegian traditions, a broad selection of other Scandinavian poets and dozens of books of French, German and English poetry, among them translations of Asian originals. Both classical and contemporary poetry were important to him.

His collection of poetry was a source of both experience and inspiration. His own creative literary output is substantial, but most of the verses and poems seem to have been written more on the spur of the moment, including occasional verses for celebrations and anniversaries. In general he did not have the same ambition for his literary efforts as he had for his music, which was much more thoroughly worked. His poetic output was mostly private, something which provided him with pleasure, and not intended for other's eyes, except some, perhaps, for an inner circle of family and friends. It was an outlet for his sentiments, both personal and political. But he was a master in his formulations both in the quick four-liner and in the longer narrative. His published poems were filed and honed in rhyme and rhythm during longer periods, both to be more exact in wording but also to be best suited to music and its demands – by, for example, avoiding certain vowels on the highest notes of a soprano *tessitura*.

Many of his poems are thus traditional, with strict form in both rhyme and rhythm. But his interest in modern French poetry around World War I encouraged him to write in a freer style, both then and later in life, without traditional end-rhymes – although this modern form did not change his rather conservative language and orthography.

Nature in all forms and the forces it displays are the favourite subjects of Irgens-Jensen's poetry – man's response to nature, his experience of its manifestations – and he uses the multitude of animals that nature provides to express human behaviour and peculiarities in his fables: political statements, satire and war-protest are made more striking through human behaviour and ideas in an animal world.

[1] *Cf.* pp. 30–32, above.

In 1962, after some nagging, he allowed a dozen of his poems to be printed in a Christmas album, *Julefest,* published by the Norwegian Red Cross Society. It was the largest collection of his published verses.

Translation into English, even carefully done, will only capture some of the meanings of the poems, not their atmosphere and nuances (like puns) in Norwegian.

The first two poems reproduced here are from the sketchbooks of his youth, probably at the age of eighteen or nineteen. The first is closely connected with the poetry of the Norwegian Sigbjørn Obstfelder,[2] and the second one both with Obstfelder and with 'free French' modern poetry of that period.

Bøn	**Prayer**
Min blaa blomst, min øientrøst lad mig se dig og bli glad, betro dig til mig med din blomsterrøst lad mig skjønne den og bli glad.	My blue flower, my eye's consolation let me look on you and be glad, entrust yourself to me with your flower-voice let me understand it and be glad.

Kunstnerdrøm	**An Artist's Dream**
– Og i drømmenes sølvtåke stiger jeg stille, med løftet pande og lukkede øine mot høieste tind – Og i morgenens disige gry lar lysets gud den store sol, verdenståkernes hjem skinne frem i farver.	– And in the silver mist of dreams I climb silently with uplifted brow and closed eyes towards the highest peak – And in the morning's misty dawn the god of light lets the great sun, home of the earthly mists, shine forth in colour.

Among the drafts of verse from his school years the most common poetic theme of the young is, of course, also to be found – although here the elegiac tone often encountered in his poetry is swiftly dispelled by an ironic coda.

Til dig	**To You**
– og naar en drøm fanger mit sind – da er den om dig. Naar toner glider brusende ind og lokker min tanke saa fjern en vei	– and when a dream captures my mind – then it is of you. When music glides echoing in and entices my thoughts onto so distant a path

[2] *Cf.* p. 54, above.

– da gaar den til dig.	– then it leads to you.
Og som en blind paa en øde hei	And like a blind man on a deserted moor
leter jeg efter dig.	I look for you.

An elegiac mood is often encountered, but he wonders at times how long one can manage to retain a serious air and profound thoughts:

Og nu har jeg læst saa mangen bog	And now I have read so many books
men føler mig træt og led og gnaven	but feel tired and sick and cross
– længes kun ut – som mot tauseste skog,	– only yearning – as for the most silent forest,
og sukker tungt som mot natten og graven.	and sighing deeply as for night and the grave.
Hvor kommer de fra, savnenes tog?	Where does it come from, this feeling of spleen?
– Da sagde en venlig fysiolog:	– Then a kind physiologist said:
Slikt kommer kun ifra maven!	Such things only come from the stomach!

A number of poems from the early 1920s say something about his vision of life and art. The first of them, 'Skjønnhetens gåde' ('The Mystery of Beauty), was first published in the magazine *Musik* in December 1925 (p. 281) and, 27 years later, re-appeared in the Christmas 1962 edition of *Julefest.*

Skjønnhetens gåde	**The Mystery of Beauty**
'O, kvidrende fugl, din ottesang	'Oh, twittering bird, your matins
synker som lys om vor pilgrimsgang.	sprinkle its light on our pilgrim path.
Hvad jubler du over? Hav nåde	Why are you rejoicing? Have mercy
og løs oss skjønnhetens gåde.'	and solve for us the mystery of beauty.'
'Jeg kveder et dråpa over en mark	'I am singing a song over a worm
jeg nylig knep i den tørre bark.'	I recently pinched in the dry bark.'

The following, also published in *Julefest* at Christmas 1962, may have been written after 'Skjønnhetens gåde':

Nøkken	**The Water Sprite**
Bortom blåne, bakom fjerne,	Beyond the blue, distant ridges,
inngjennom tåkens alvespinn,	in between the mist's fairy web,
nedgjennom vasne søkk –	down through watery hollows –
der ser du svarteste huldretjernet;	there you see the darkest enchanted tarn;
sokner du syv mil, fanger du inn	if you drag it seven leagues deep, you will capture
den døde, sleipe nøkk.	the dead, slimy water sprite.

'I regn og blest' is a poem Irgens-Jensen used in his song with the same title; this poem, too, was published in the Christmas 1962 *Julefest*:

I regn og blest	**In Rain and Wind**
Oppunder furuens hullete hatt *hadde en pjusket kråke hus.* *Innunder furuleggen satt* *En slunken forfrossen mus.*	Up under the pine's leaky hat a dishevelled crow had her house. In under the pine trunk sat a meager, frozen mouse.
Da svartnet skyene, huttetu! *Og stormene rev og slet:* *'Godt jeg ikke er kråke nu!'* *sa musen og grov sig ned.*	Then the clouds darkened, brr! And the storms ranted and raved: 'I'm glad I'm not a crow now!' said the mouse and dug itself in.
Regn og flom, et eneste kav; *Nu gisper musen innunder mulde.* *'Musen har gravet sin egen grav!'* *lo kråken, hun rystet av kulde.*	Rain and flood, terrential storm; Now the mouse is panting under the soil. 'The mouse has dug his own grave!' laughed the crow, shivering with cold.

'Den bakvendte verden' and 'Anekdote' were found in Irgens-Jensen's notebooks after his death. The themes might have some relevance to the situation in the beginning of the Second World War:

Den bakvendte verden	**The Backward World**
En torsk blev jaget fra hav til hav *og alltid var det det samme kav* *for å skaffe sin buk litt føde.*	A cod was hunted from sea to sea and always it was the same bustle to procure its stomach a little food.
Da mistet den torsk sin vesle forstand; *den gjorde et byks, spratt opp på land* *og gispet sig salig til døde.*	Then the cod lost its small mind; it took a bound, leapt up on land and gasped itself blissfully to death.

Anekdote	**Anecdote**
En foretagsom mann *drog om i fjerne land* *og lette etter skatte.* *Da hendte det en gang* *at skjorten kjentes trang* *Han la den efter sig i krattet.*	An enterprising man travelled in distant lands seeking for treasure. It happened one time that his shirt felt tight. He left it behind in the bushes.

Så kom vår ferdemann	Then our traveller came
til dvergefolkets land,	to the land of the dwarfs,
– ja, det var lenge efter.	– oh, that was much later.
Her fikk han være gjest	Here he became a guest
ved deres tempelfest	at their temple-feast
for slektens dype, skjulte krefter.	for the deep, hidden strengths of the race.
Nu bar de frem sin gud.	Now they carried forth their god.
Ja, mystisk så den ut	Oh, it looked mystical
mot templets mørke porte.	against the temple's dark portal.
De dverge skrek av fryd!	The dwarves shouted for joy!
Men gudens beste pryd,	But the god's best adornment,
det var såmen den gamle skjorte.	sure enough, it was the old shirt.

'Tre rømlinger', written in 1930s in the form of folk poetry with its characteristic repetitions, was later used in a choral song for male voices:

Tre rømlinger	**Three Fugitives**
Tre rømlinger, farlige fanter på flukt	Three fugitives, dangerous rascals on the run
i ruskeregn	in drizzling rain
og skoddehegn -	and a wall of mist –
mellom klipper og kløfter i djevelens slukt.	between cliffs and crevices in the devil's gorge.
Nei, sandelig drattet den første ned.	Then suddenly the first flopped down.
I ormekratt	Among the ferns
en uværsnatt	one stormy night
fant han så trygt et skjulested.	he found such a safe hiding place.
Nu takket de andre for lykke og hell	Now the others gave thanks for fortune and success
i ruskeregn	in drizzling rain
og skoddehegn –	and a wall of mist –
Nummer to vendte om. Et blaff, et smell…	Number Two turned round. A flash, a kick…
Nei, sannelig skjøt de ham ned som en hund	Really, they shot him down like a dog!
i ormekratt	Among the ferns
et uværsnatt	one stormy night
fant han så søt en hvilestund..	he found such a sweet lasting rest.

Da takket den tredje sin skjebne på ny
i ruskeregn
og skoddehegn –
og han drømte forskrekket om frelse og gry.
Han satt der så stille og kold på en sten
i ormekratt
en uværsnatt.
Hundre år efter fant de hans ben.

Then the third gave thanks for his fate
once again in drizzling rain
and a wall of mist-
And he dreamt in his fear of salvation and dawn.
He sat there so still and cold on a stone
among the ferns
one stormy night.
A hundred years later they found his bones.

Animals occur in Irgens-Jensen's verses and songs with some frequency. He portrayed the cat in two different ways, the fierce, murderous hunter and the quiet, purring, playful animal:

Katten og musen

Småmusen lå og tenkte så:
'Gid det var natt!
Da vil jeg gå,
da vil jeg gå på stabburet med mine små.'

Derinne satt en liten katt
og tenkte så:
'Gid det var natt!
Da skal jeg ta småmusen fatt,
Da skal jeg ta småmusen fatt!'

The Cat and the Mouse

The little mouse lay thinking:
'I wish it were night!
Then I would go,
then I would go to the storehouse with my little ones.'

Indoors sat a little cat
thinking:
'I wish it were night!
Then I will catch the little mouse,
then I will catch the little mouse.

Småpus

'Å, hadde jeg vinger, å, kunne jeg fly'
sukket småpus og myste mot sky.
Det kvidrer og glitrer i sol, i vind,
nu leker småfuglen min.

Jeg vilde så gjerne få leke med den,
varlig og lett og være god-venn
og streife den,

la fly igjen
og fange den inn!
Det er leken min.

The Kitten

'Oh, if only I had wings, oh, if only I could fly'
sighed the kitten, peering at the sky.
It twitters and glitters in sun, in wind,
now my little bird is playing.

I would so much like to play with it,
carefully and gently, and be its friend
and pat it,

let it fly again
and catch it!
That is my game.

But even animals of the same species can have individual traits in the fables, as in the third song in the cycle *Fabler og barnerim*:

Storebjørn og veslebjørn

Storebjørn og veslebjørn
labbet i skogene sammen.
De slo en sau i ny og ne –
så ble det vel rast og gammen!

Og venner var de i onde dage –
Hva annet kunde vel nytte?
Men ikke var det nu alltid så vel
når de skulle dele byttet.

'Jeg trenger vel mest som er så svær,'
sa digerbamse og murret –
'Jeg får få til å vokse, som liten er,'
sa veslebjørn og knurret.

Så røk de i hop da, må vite,
og brukte tenner og klør.
Men veslebjørn rispet godt ifra seg
og blev bare klemt litt mør.

'Stakkars kryp,' tenkte digerbamse –
men veslebjørn sa til seg selv:
'Jeg er ikke stor, det får så være,
men jeg er da bjørn likevel.'

Big Bear and Little Bear

Big Bear and Little Bear
padded in the forest together.
They killed a sheep once in a while –
then there was rest and delight!

And they were friends in the bad days –
What else could be of use?
But now it was not always so well
when they should divide the spoil.

'I need the most, I who am so large.'
said Big Bruin, grumbling –
'I need to grow, I who am so small,'
said Little Bear, growling.

Then they jumped up, you know,
and used their teeth and claws.
But Little Bear defended himself well,
scratching away
and just got some rough hugs.

'Poor thing,' thought Big Bruin –
but Little Bear said to himself:
'I am not big, that may well be,
but I am still a bear.'

He also used animals as metaphors to illustrate the values of life in another poem that was printed in *Julefest* at Christmas 1962:

Grevlingen og lerken

En grevling gravet sin fremtids bol
og vendte baken til morgenens sol;
da hørte den lerken kvede.

'Du flyr og fløyter, sorgløs og blind,
gad visst hvad du søker i sky og vind!
Kom ned og pass ditt rede!'

The Badger and the Lark

A badger was digging his future den
and turned his back to the morning sun;
then he heard the lark singing.

'You fly and whistle, carefree and blind,
I wonder what you are seeking in cloud and wind!
Come down and guard your nest!'

'Jeg sanker de toner av himlens blå
og drysser dem ned over store og små,
det er min sorg og min glede.'

'I pick the notes from the blue of the sky
and sprinkle them down over
great and small,
that is my sorrow and my joy.'

His best-known fable was first performed as a song in 1923, as the second of the *Fabler og barnerim*:

Bånlåt

Bjørnen han tasser blant skogens trær,
vasser i myr og strie strømmer.
Så finner han seg et multebær
og legger seg i mosen og drømmer.
'Jeg er så gla i lam –
jeg er så gla i lam', tenker bjørnen.

Lullaby

The bear he pads amongst the forest
trees,
wades in marsh and violent streams.
Then he finds himself a cloudberry
and lies down in the moss and dreams.
'I am very fond of lamb,
I am very fond of lamb,' thinks the bear.

Irgens-Jensen wrote a number of ironic verses about the stupidity of the Nazis and the terrors they brought. They are worth reproducing in full:

Sultanfest

Hør det er sultanfest idag
og trommehvirvler, bekkenslag
og jubel, skrik og trengsel.

Herolder roper ut hans ry:
'Vår ære reiste han pàny' –
Det metter folkets lengsel.

Hvor finnes slik en marmorplass,
slik gyldent, funklende palass -
stort som vårt største fengsel?'

\- - -

Men i den lumre, tunge natt
lød fuglestemmers hese skratt
fra stadens rettersteder:

'O sultan over lyst og nød,
o sultan over blod og død!
Her deles dine gleder.

Sultan's Feast

Listen, it is the sultan's feast today
and drum-rolls, cymbal clash
and jubilation, shouts and crowds.

Heralds call his fame:
'Our honour he raises anew.
That satisfies the people's longing.

Where is such a marbled square to be
found,
such a gilded, glittering palace –
as large as our largest prison?' –

\- - -

But in the warm, heavy night
the husky screech of the birds sounded
from the city's places of execution:

'Oh, sultan over desire and need,
Oh, sultan over blood and death!
Here your joys are shared.

Langt flyr ditt ry, tung er din prakt – *vi er din sande æresvakt!* *Hør! Dine gribber kveder.'*	Far flies your fame, great is your splendour – we are your true guard of honour! Listen! Your vultures are chanting.'
Anekdote (om tygget mat)	**Anecdote (about chewed food)**
De er så flinke, de vet så meget, *apene ved Utopandre.* *Er det no rart om de gjerne vil* *lyksaliggjøre andre?*	They are so clever, they know so much, the apes at Utopandre. Is it no wonder they want to make others happy
En dag fikk de fanget en løveunge *som tok seg en middagslur.* *Nå skulde denne råe sjeiken* *komme under kultur.*	One day they captured a lion cub who was taking an afternoon nap. Now this coarse sheikh would become cultivated.
Men først måtte bestet fôres grundig *og efter siste metode* *med prøvede retter som alle aper* *fant var sunde og gode.*	But first the beast must be fed properly and according to the latest method with proven dishes which all the apes found were healthy and good.
Og røtter og nøtter ble tygget og knast *med skarpe apetenner,* *all markens grøde eltet, knadd* *av gramsende apehender.*	And roots and nuts were chewed and crunched by sharp ape-teeth, all the produce of the field rubbed, kneaded by grasping ape hands.
Det ble en tip-top-total-ragout. *'Så mesk deg nå, din røver.'* *Men løven snudde sitt hode vekk.*	It became a tip-top-total ragoût. 'So stuff yourself, you robber.' But the lion turned his head away.
- - -	- - -
De er visst dumme, løver?	They seem to be stupid, the lions?

The next poem, 'Løvetanden synger i vinden' ('The Dandelion Sings in the Wind'), from 1938, has its basis in Irgens-Jensen's problems in getting rid of the dandelions in his lawn. Although he loved flowers, as his son recollected in conversation with the author, he was no gardener and his occasional attempts to weed out the masses of dandelions were to little avail:

Løvetanden synger i vinden

Flyv, flyv mine fnokker…
Nu snur gartneren ryggen til,
nu tilverks med listig spil!
Opp til flukt, mine aeroplaner,
følg uhørlige luftningers baner,
vugg og bølg i vårlig bris,
vernet av sitrende varmedis.
Synk så i muldens fang og vent
– lat som ingenting har hendt.

Flyv, flyv mine fnokker…
Tidlig på våren tar dere fatt
med å bore og sprenge i rot-trevle-kratt.
Men husk: Ubønnhørlig må dere være,
holde herskerkaldet i ære:
Treng dem undav, de bleke liljer,
de bør ikke stå seg mot hårde viljer.
Kvel de blyge, blå fioler,
hva er de mot våre flammesoler?
De sjeldne og rare får også falde,
herbariet har nok plass til dem alle.

Flyv, flyv mine fnokker…
Her går du gartner og stuller og steller,
graver, vander til dagen helder.
Jo uslere, sykere vekstene er,
jo inderligere har du dem kjær.
Hellige enfold! Møien er spildt.
For liv som vil leve, er stridt og vildt,
og ingen idyll – slik du har drømt.
Du dømmer jo livet – din sak er dømt.

The Dandelion Sings in the Wind

Fly, fly my downy seeds…
Now the gardener turns his back,
now to work with a crafty game!
Up and away, my aeroplanes,
follow the light winds' silent courses,
rock and wave in the spring-like breeze,
protected by quivering heat haze.
Then sink into the bosom of the earth and wait
– pretending that nothing has happened

Fly, fly my downy seeds…
Early in spring you set to work
with boring and bursting in root-fibre thicket.
But remember: you must be unrelenting,
honour the ruler's vocation:
Push them away, those pale lilies,
they ought not to resist our strong wills.
Strangle the shy, blue violets,
what are they against our flaming suns?
The rare and strange will also fall,
the herbarium has room enough for them all.

Fly, fly my downy seeds…
Here you walk, gardener, puttering, caring,
digging, watering till the day ends.
The more wretched, sick the plants are,
the more intensely you love them.
Blessed innocence! The toil is wasted.
For life that wants to live, is hard and wild,
and no idyll – as *you* have dreamt.
You try to judge life – your case is lost.

Flyv, flyv mine fnokker…
Du meier, luker, holder oss nede,
ja dreper oss grundig, det er din glede.
Vi spirer møisommelig frem påny
med hatets seid som vår dyre arv
sprengende på gjennom blod og marv,
stiger mot storm og skjebnegry.
Ingen krone skal duve friere,
frø seg, spre seg, ødslere, videre!

Fly, fly my downy seeds…
You mow, weed, keep us down,
yes, kill us thoroughly, that is your pleasure.
Laboriously we grow anew
with hatred's witchcraft as our noble heritage
bursting through blood and marrow,
rising towards storm and the dawn of fate.
No crown will sway more freely,
and scatter more lavishly afar.

Flyv, flyv mine fnokker…
Til alle riker bærer vi bud,
frelserbud fra vår seiersgud.
Herlig, herlig er krigeryrket.
Vi smitter sveklingen med vår styrke,
han skal få merke urgammel kraft,
lære å hylde vår mystiske saft.
Nei aldri skal han falde til ro
i sin slappe tro.

Fly, fly my downy seeds…
To all realms we carry a message,
a message of salvation from our victorious god.
Glorious, glorious is the profession of war.
We inspire the weakling with our
strength,
he'll be made to feel the ancient power,
learn to acclaim our mystic vitality.
No, he will never get peace
in his lax beliefs.

Flyv, flyv mine fnokker…
Flyv, millioner av aeroplaner,
vidt om i verden på dødsorkaner.
Engang – det tror vi, vet vi, kommer
livets mål, den store sommer,
da vi, som et bølgende hav av soler,
dekker hver plett med maktsymboler
og jubler i vinden den sunde lære:
Kraft er rett og ære.

Fly, fly my downy seeds…
Fly, millions of aeroplanes,
far round the world on death's hurricanes.
One day – we believe, we know, will come
life's goal, that great summer,
when we, like a billowing ocean of suns,
will cover every space with symbols of power
and shout into the wind the sound teaching:
Might is right and honour.

Late in life Irgens-Jensen contemplated the advent of old age, and some of these thoughts found their expression on some scrap of papers found in his home. After some pressure he allowed this meditation to be printed in the *Julefest* Christmas album in 1962:

Ved stranden

En balje med vann og en kasse med sand
står bak gjerdet i haven.
Der seiler og bygger en guttemann
og kryper rundt på maven.

Snart skal han lage et digert slott,
men ingen fillehytter,
og der skal han rydde og luke godt
og gjøre en masse nytter!

En dag står havegrinden på klem,
da smetter han ut, den Nysgjerrig-Per!
Verden bak gjerdet, mor og hjem -
er ikke verden mer.

For her kan han springe så langt han vil
på myke gulver av sand,
og sjøen den bølger og gnistrer av ild, –
og likevel er det vann.

Og skyer seiler som skip forbi
og vil vel aldri vende,
de kommer fra eventyret, de -
og skal til verdens ende.

Og gjett hva den nye skyen er.
Jo, et skinnende kongeslott!
Det finnes ikke no' gjerde der!
Han stirrer – til alt blir grått.

……

Siden gikk leken ofte i stå.
Det ble ikke flere borger av sand,
skyer seilte bort, og så –
var han en gammel mann.

By the Shore

A tub of water and a box of sand
stand behind the fence in the garden.
There a small boy is sailing and building
and crawling around on his stomach.

Soon he will make an enormous palace,
but no hovels, and there he will tidy and
weed well and make himself very useful!

One day the garden gate stands ajar,
then he slips out, the Nosy Parker!
The world behind the fence, mother
and home
is not the world any longer.

For here he can run as far as he wants
on soft floors of sand,
and the sea it billows and sparkles with
fire,
and yet it is still water.

And clouds sail by like ships
and will probably never turn,
they come from the fairy-tale, they do
and are going to the end of the world.

And guess what that new cloud is.
Yes, a glittering palace of kings!
There are no fences there!
He stares until everything becomes
grey.

……

Later the game often ground to a stop.
Finished the building of castles of sand,
the clouds sailed away, and then –
he was an old man.

Bibliography and Other Sources

The text contains a large number of quotations of reviews and short articles from newspapers and journals. Those sources are not included in this Bibliography; full references are given in the text.

1. Books and Theses

A. Irgens-Jensen, his Family and Music

ANKER, ØYVIND, *Jensen & Co. Jubileumsskrift*, Jensen & Co, Oslo, 1966

FLOCK, ESTER IRGENS, *Slekten Irgens*, private publication, Bergen, 1955

HOLMSEN, CATO, *Slekten Gløersen*, private publication, Oslo, 1929

IRGENS, HEIDI, *Ludvig Irgens-Jensen: His Life and his Songs*, MA thesis, graduate college, University of Iowa, 1994

LANGBERG, LUDV. KR., *Slekten Irgens fra Røros*, private publication, Oslo, 1927

VOLLSNES, ARVID O., 'Ludvig Irgens Jensens *Passacaglia*'. MA thesis, Oslo University, 1972

———, *Modernisme på norsk – Komponisten Ludvig Irgens-Jensen*, Garantiforlaget, Oslo, 1996

———, *Komponisten Ludvig Irgens-Jensen*, Aschehoug, Oslo, 2000

B. Norwegian Music and Culture

BEYER, EDVARD, *Hans E. Kinck – livsangst og livstro*, two vols., Aschehoug, Oslo, 1956

BRØGGER, KR. FR., *Kammermusikkens historie her hjemme*, private publication, Oslo, 1943

BRUSTAD, BJARNE, *Liv og virke i ord og tonee*, Tanum, Oslo, 1971

BUE, PÅL, *Nasjonale ideologier i norsk musikk på 1920 taler*, MA thesis, Oslo University, 1974

BULL, SVERRE HAGERUP (ed.), *Musikkens Verden*, Musikkens Verden forlag, Oslo, 1951 and 1963

BÆKKELUND, GORM, *TONO. Vern om musikkverk i 50 år: 1928–1978*, Aschehoug, Oslo, 1978

ERIKSEN, THOMAS HYLLAND, *Typisk norsk*, Cappelen, Oslo, 1993

GRINDE, NILS, *Norsk musikkhistorie*, 4th edn., Musikkhuset Forlag, Oslo, 1993; English translation: *A History of Norwegian Music,* University of Nebraska Press, Lincoln, 1991

GULLVAAG OLAV, *Heimferd* (with friezes by Henry Imsland), Noregs Boklag, Oslo, 1930

———, *Heimferd, dramatisk symfoni av Ludvig Irgens Jensen*, Noregs Boklag, Oslo, 1931
Gurvin, Olav, *Frå tonalitet til atonalitet*, Aschehoug, Oslo, 1937
———, *Fartein Valen. En banebryter i nyere norsk musikk*, Lyche, Drammen/Oslo, 1962
Herresthal, Harald, and Pistone, Danièle (eds.), *Grieg et Paris*, Presses Universitaires de Caen, Caen, 1996
Holen, Astrid, 'Olavsjubileum i en krisetid', MA dissertation, Trondheim University, 1975
Huldt-Nystrøm, Hampus, *Fra munkekor til symfoniorkester. Musikkliv i det gamle Christiania og Oslo*, Filharmonisk selskap, Oslo, 1969
Hurum, Hans Jørgen, *Musikken under okkupasjonen 1940–1945*, Aschehoug, Oslo, 1946
Johansen, David Monrad, *Edvard Grieg*, Gyldendal, Oslo, 1934 (3rd edn., 1956)
Kindem, Ingeborg, *Den norske operas historie*, Mortensen, Oslo, 1941
Kjellberg, Erik, and Ling, Jan, *Klingande Sverige*, Akademiförlagen, Göteborg, 1991
Lange, Kristian, *Norsk Komponistforening gjennom 50 år*, Norsk Komponistforening, Oslo, 1967
Libæk, Rudolf J. (ed), *Cæciliaforeningen gjennom 100 år*, Cæciliaforeningen, Oslo, 1979
Lindemann, Trygve, and Solbu, Einar, *Musik-Konservatoriet i Oslo*, Tanum, Oslo, 1973
Longum, Leif, *Drømmen om det frie menneske. Norsk kuturradikalisme og mellomkrigstidens radikale trekløver Hoel – Krog – Øverland*, Universitetsforlaget, Oslo, 1986
Lunder, Åse Lahn, *Pauline Hall og hennes innsats i norsk musikkliv*, thesis, Oslo University, 1977
Nettum, Rolf Nyboe, *Norges litteraturhistorie*, Vol. IV, Cappelen, Oslo, 1991
Newbould, Brian, *Schubert and the Symphony*, Toccata Press, London, 1992
Reidarsson, Per, *Hva er i veien med vårt musikkliv?*, private publication, Oslo, 1928
Rugstad, Gunnar, *Christian Sinding 1856–1941. En biografisk og stilistisk studie*, Cappelen, Oslo, 1979
Rønneberg, Anton, *Nationaltheatret gjennom 50 år*, Gyldendal, Norsk, Oslo, 1949
Sandvik, Ole Mørch, and Schjelderup, Gerhard, *Norges Musikhistorie*, two vols., Oppi, Kristiania, 1921
Schulerud, Mentz, *Norsk kunstnerliv*, Cappelen, Oslo, 1960
Storaas, Reidar, *Tonediktaren Geirr Tveitt*, Samlaget, Oslo, 1990
Tveit (Tveitt), Nils (Geirr), *Tonalitätstheorie des Parallellen Leittonssystems*, Gyldendal, Oslo, 1937
Vollsnes, Arvid O., (ed), *Fartein Valens brever*, Vol . I: 1904–1924, Lyche, Drammen, 1987

C. Musical, Literary and Historical Background

ANON., *Historisk statistikk*, Statistisk sentralbyrå, Oslo 1983

———, *Studentene fra 1882*, Malling, Kristiania, 1907

———, *Studentene fra 1882*, Malling, Oslo, 1932

———, *Studentene fra 1913*, Malling, Oslo, 1938

CHEN, CHUAN, *Die chinesische schöne Literatur im deutschen Schrifttum*, doctoral thesis, Kiel, Glückstadt, 1933

CHRISTIANSEN, HAAKON ODD, (ed.), *Trondheim bys historie. Supplementsbind. Trondheim i går og i dag 1914–1964*, F. Brun, Trondheim, 1973

DAHL, HANS FREDRIK, *Hallo – hallo! Kringkastingen i Norge 1920–1940*, Cappelen, Oslo, 1975

EGGE, KLAUS, *Norsk Komponistforening gjennom 25 år*, Norsk Komponistforening, Oslo, 1942

FERRIER, WINIFRED, *The Life of Kathleen Ferrier*, Hamish Hamilton, London, 1955

GAUKSTAD, ØISTEIN (ed.), *David Monrad Johansen i skrift og tale*, Tanum, Oslo, 1968

INDREBØ, GUSTAV, *Nidarosnamnet og Trondhjemsnamnet i Noreg*, Noregs Mållag, Oslo, 1930

NIELSEN, CARL, *Levende musik*, Martins Forlag, Copenhagen, 1925; Norwegian edition *Levende musikk*, Gyldendal, Oslo, 1948

SEIP, DIDRIK ARUP, *Trondhjems bynavn, Resymé og tillegg*, Brun, Oslo, 1931

SLAPGARD, BJARNE, *Omkring namnestriden Trondhjem – Nidaros – Trondheim*, Rune, Trondheim, 1977

STENSETH, BODIL, *En norsk elite. Nasjonsbyggerne på Lysaker 1890–1940*, Aschehoug, Oslo, 1993

VINCENT, JOHN, *The Diatonic Modes in Modern Music*, Mills Music, NewYork/San Francisco, 1951

WALLNER, BO, *Vår tids musik i Norden*, Nordiska Musikförlaget, Stockholm, 1968

WIETH-KNUDSEN, K. A, *Den europæiske musiks skæbnetime*, private publication, Copenhagen, 1928

2. Articles

A. Irgens-Jensen and his Music

ANON., 'Yngre norske komponister', *Musik*, Nos. 5–6, May 1925, pp. 117–20

ARBO, JENS, 'Ludvig Irgens Jensen', in *Norsk biografisk leksikon*, Aschehoug, Oslo, 1936, Vol. 7, pp. 3–6

———, 'Filologen som overrasket verden med musikk', *Norsk Musikkliv*, No. 1, 1943, pp. 6–9

BADEN, CONRAD, 'Ludvig Irgens Jensen in memoriam', *Norsk Musikktidsskrift*, 1969, vol. 2, pp. 45–46

BERGGRAV, EIVIND, 'Olavs-Kantaten', *Kirke og Kultur*, Vol. 38, Oslo, 1931, pp. 120–24

HOLST BANG, ELLING, 'Baadnlaat – Siciliano av Ludvig Irgens Jensen', *Musik*, December 1924, p. 7
———, 'Ludvig Irgens Jensen', *Musik*, 1925, Nos. 5/6, pp. 7–10
EGGE, KLAUS, 'Ludvig Irgens Jensens Der Gott und die Bajadere', *Tonekunst*, 1935, No. 1, pp. 17–18, and No. 2, p. 31
FINDAHL, THEO, 'Ludvig Irgens Jensen om aktuelle musikspørsmaal' in *Tonekunst*, 1931, No. 5: reprint of article from *Adresseavisen*, Trondheim, 24 January 1931, and *Norsk Tidende*, Brooklyn, New York, 12 February 1931
KORTSEN, BJARNE, 'Noen modale særtrekk i Ludvig Irgens Jensens musikk', *Norsk Musikktidsskrift*, Oslo, 1962, Vol. 2, pp. 62–65
———, 'Ludvig Irgens Jensen: Passacaglia for Orchestra' in Bjarne Kortsen, *Contemporary Norwegian Orchestral Music*, Kortsen, Bergen, 1969
LIND, SVERRE, 'Ludvig Irgens Jensen som komponist. En skisse på grunnlag av tre orkesterverker', *Nordisk musikkultur*, Copenhagen, Vol. 3, 1953–54, pp. 111–14
WISSUM, KNUD, 'Ludvig Irgens Jensen', *Levende musik*, Copenhagen, 1946

B. Norwegian Music, Culture and History

AAS, LARS, *Trøndere i moderne norsk diktning*, Brun, Trondhjem, 1942
BENESTAD, FINN, 'Claude Debussy i norsk musikkliv frem til 1925', *Studia Musicologica Norvegica*, No. 2, Universitetsforlaget, Oslo, 1976
BUKDAHL, JØRGEN, *Det skjulte Norge*, Aschehoug, Copenhagen, 1926
EGGE, KLAUS, 'Folketonen, hardingfele og norsk komposisjon', *Tonekunst*, No. 8, 1935 pp. 94–95, and Nos. 11–12, 1935, pp. 131–33
———, 'Overflatisk musikkbedømmelse', *Tonekunst*, No. 3, 15 February 1937, pp. 31–32
———, Editorial, *Tonekunst*, 1937, No. 7, p. 151
GURVIN, OLAV (O.G.), 'Vårt musikkliv under krigen. II Den skapende kunsten', *Norsk Musikkliv*, 1945, No. 7, p. 4
———, 'Ny musikk i Norge', *Ny musikk i Norden*, Foreningen Norden, Stockholm, 1953, pp. 69–90
———, 'Ny norsk musikk', *Musikrevy*, No. 2, 1959
HALL, PAULINE, 'Musikk', in Haakon Shetelig, Fritiof Brandt and Alf Nyman (eds.), *Vår tids kunst og diktning i Skandinavia I*, J. G. Tanum, Oslo, 1948, pp. 191–221.
JOHANSEN, DAVID MONRAD, 'Nationale verdier i vor musik': lecture for the Music Teachers' Society, printed as feature over several days in *Aftenposten*, June 1924; also published in an altered version in *Deutsch-Nordisches Jahrbuch 1925*, Jena, 1925, pp. 72–83
———, 'Den norske linjen i musikken' in Gunnar Larsen (ed.), *Det norske syn*, Fabritius, Oslo, 1927, pp. 42-49
KOLSRUD, OLUF, *Olavsfest 1930. Minneskrift*, *Norvegia Sacra*, Vol. X, Oslo, 1937, pp. 349–50
LIEDMAN, SVEN ERIK, 'Det nationella som idé' in Henrik Karlsson (ed.), *'Hemländsk hundraårig sång' 1800-talets musik och det nationella*, Kungl. Musikaliska Akademien, Stockholm, 1994, pp. 46–50

LING, JAN, 'Gibt es ein Nordischer Ton?', in Peter Andraschke and Edelgard Spaude (eds.), *Welttheater. Die Künste im 19. Jahrhundert*, Rombach, Freiburg, 1992, pp. 49–57

MØRK, ULRIK, 'Hva er der i veien med vort musikkliv?', *Aftenposten*, 22 October 1928

REIDARSSON, PER, 'Fremmed og hjemlig musikk i radioen', *Hallo-hallo*, No. 19, 1933, p. 7

———, 'Melodifølelse og rase', *Hallo-hallo*, No. 29, 16–22 July 1933, pp. 5 and 31

SKYLLSTAD, KJELL, 'Norsk musikk 1920–40', lecture at Nordic Music Researchers' Congress, Helsinki, 1971

STENSETH, BODIL, 'Krig og glemsel. Norsk musikkliv i årene 1940–45', *Musikkmagasinet Ballade*, No. 1, 1995, pp. 23–28

SØRENSEN, ØYSTEIN, 'The Development of a Norwegian Identity during the Nineteenth Century', in Øystein Sørensen (ed.), *Nordic Paths to National Identity in the Niineteenth Century*, 'KULTs skriftserie' Vol. 22, Research Council of Norway, Oslo, 1994, pp. 17–35

VOLLSNES, ARVID O., 'Olavsjubileet 1930 og Heimferd', *Konsertnytt*, 1975, No. 4, pp. 4–8

———, 'Mellomkrigstidens strid mot "modernisme" – "nasjonal musikk", en forutsetning for dannelsen av "Ny Musikk"?', *Ballade*, Nos. 2–3, 1988, pp. 10–27

———, 'Heimferd – musikken som vant og forsvant, og kom tilbake', *Adresseavisen*, 6 August 1990

———, 'L'influence de la musique française sur la musique norvégienne au début du XXe siècle', in Harald Herresthal and Danièle Pistone (eds.), *Grieg et Paris*, Presses Universitaires de Caen, Caen, 1996, pp. 199–210

ØSTVEDT, ARNE ('Papageno'), 'Intervju med Klaus Egge', *Norsk musikkliv*, No. 8, 1945, pp. 8–10

ØVERLAND, ARNULF, 'Einar Solstad', in Arnulf Øverland, *I beundring og forargelse*, Aschehoug, Oslo, 1954, pp. 135–41

ØVERÅS, ASBJØRN, 'Olav Gullvåg', *Syn og Segn*, 1942, No. 1, pp. 2–16, and No. 2, pp. 76–92

C. Musical, Literary and Historical Background

PEYSER, HERBERT F., 'The Epic of the Unfinished', *Musical Quarterly*, Vol. 14, No. 4, October 1928, pp. 639–60

PISTONE, DANIÈLE: 'Musique et société dans les années vingt' in Stanislav Tucsar (ed.), *Music, Ideas and Society. Essays in Honour of Ivan Supicic*, Hrvatsko Muzikološko Društvoihre, Zagreb, 1993, pp. 237–47

STEIN, LEON, 'The Passacaglia in the Twentieth Century', *Music and Letters*, Vol. XL, 1959, pp. 150–53

VINCENT, JOHN, *The Diatonic Modes in Modern Music*, Mills Music, NewYork/San Francisco, 1951

3. Other Sources

Two recordings with Odd Grüner-Hegge, made in 1972 by Øystein Gaukstad, preserved in the National Library as UBO/NMS Lyd b/287–289; the author's transcription of parts of the tapes is with the tapes themselves in a box (page numbers in the footnotes refer to this transcription)

Interview with Ludvig Irgens-Jensen made by Torstein Gunnarson in 1969, preserved in the National Library as UBO/NMS lyd/b194–195; the author's transcription of the tapes is in the boxes (page numbers in the foototes refer to this transcription)

IRGENS JENSEN, DAGNY, 'Erindringer om min bror', manuscript in the possession of Olav Irgens-Jensen, *c.* 1984

HAUGEN, EINAR, 'De brendte våre gårder': manuscript of a radio programme for NRK in 1946 about Inger Hagerup's poem and Irgens-Jensen's music, in the possession of Olav Irgens-Jensen

Discography

Recordings listed are on CD unless otherwise indicated.

1. Orchestral Music

Air

Bournemouth Symphony Orchestra cond. Bjarte Engeset: Naxos 8.572313, recorded 2009, released 2011

Trondheim Symphony Orchestra, cond. Eivind Aadland: CPO 777 347-2, recorded 2009, released 2012

Bols vise ('Bol's Song')

Stavanger Symphony Orchestra, cond. Eivind Aadland: BIS-CD 1367, recorded 2001?, released 2002

Icelandic Symphony Orchestra, cond. Bjarte Engeset: Naxos 8.557017-18N (Norway) and 8.557018 (international), recorded 2002, released 2002

Canto d'omaggio

Bergen Philharmonic Orchestra, cond. Eivind Aadland: Simax PSC 1164, recorded 2001, released 2002

Kong Baldvines armring: Suite

Trondheim Symphony Orchestra, cond. Eivind Aadland: CPO 777 347-2, recorded 2009, released 2012

Partita sinfonica

Oslo Philharmonic Orchestra, cond. Odd Grüner-Hegge: recorded 1950, released 1951, on Mercury MG 90002 (LP), *Music of Modern Norway*. Vol. 4 (with works by Fliflet Bræin, Olsen, Monrad Johansen and Eggen)

Oslo Philharmonic Orchestra, cond. Ole Kristian Ruud: NIM CDN 31003/Simax PSC 3103, recorded 1986, released 1988

Trondheim Symphony Orchestra, cond. Eivind Aadland: CPO 777 347-2, recorded 2009, released 2012

Passacaglia

Oslo Philharmonic Orchestra, cond. Ole Kristian Ruud: NIM CDN 31003/Simax PSC 3103, recorded 1986, released 1988

Bergen Philharmonic Orchestra, cond. Eivind Aadland: Simax PSC 1164 (released also on PSC 1262), recorded 2001, released 2002

Bournemouth Symphony Orchestra cond. Bjarte Engeset: Naxos 8.572313, recorded 2009, released 2011

Trondheim Symphony Orchestra, cond. Eivind Aadland: CPO 777 347-2, recorded 2009, released 2012

Pastorale religioso

Bergen Philharmonic Orchestra, cond. Eivind Aadland: Simax PSC 1164, recorded 2001, released 2002

Rondo marziale

Trondheim Symphony Orchestra, cond. Eivind Aadland: CPO 777 347-2, recorded 2009, released 2012

Sinfonie i d-moll (Symfoni in re) (Symphony in D minor)

ORIGINAL VERSION

Bournemouth Symphony Orchestra cond. Bjarte Engeset: Naxos 8.572313, recorded 2009, released 2011

REVISED VERSION

Oslo Philharmonic Orchestra, cond. Øivin Fjeldstad: Simax PSC 3118, recorded 1969?, released 1993 (first released on LP in 1972 as Philips 6507 005)

Trondheim Symphony Orchestra, cond. Eivind Aadland: CPO 777 347-2, recorded 2009, released 2012

Tema con variazioni

Oslo Philharmonic Orchestra, cond. Odd Grüner-Hegge: Simax PSC 3118, recorded 1967?, released 1993 (first released on LP in 1972 on Philips 838 050 AY)

Trondheim Symphony Orchestra, cond. Eivind Aadland: CPO 777 347-2, recorded 2009, released 2012

2. Music for Voice(s) and Orchestra

Altar ('Altar')

Solveig Kringelborn (soprano), Norrköping Symphony Orchestra, cond. Lü Jia: NMA NMA 2, recorded 2003, released 2003 (released also on Norske Gram 5349632)

Bols vise ('Bol's Song')

Solveig Kringelborn (soprano), Norrköping Symphony Orchestra, cond. Lü Jia: NMA NMA 2, recorded 2003, released 2003 (also on Norske Gram 5349632)

Heimferd ('Homeward Journey') 1930

Anne Bolstad (soprano), Randi Stene (contralto), Ivar Gilhuus (tenor), Per Vollestad (baritone), Carsten Stabell (bass), members of the Nidaros Cathedral Choir, members of the Boys' Choir of Nidaros Cathedral, Trondheim Symphony Orchestra and Choir, cond. Ole Kristian Ruud: Simax PSC 3109, recorded 1993, released 1994

I blodet hans blømde ('In his blood blossomed') *from Heimferd*

Solveig Kringelborn (soprano), Norrköping Symphony Orchestra, cond. Lü Jia: NMA NMA 2, recorded 2003, released 2003

Japanischer Frühling ('Japanese Spring')

Karin Langebo (soprano), Oslo Philharmonic Orchestra, cond. Øivin Fjeldstad: Simax PSC 3118, recorded 1969?, released 1993 (first released on LP in 1972 as Philips 6507 005)

Ragnhild Heiland Sørensen (soprano), Bergen Philharmonic Orchestra, cond. Eivind Aadland: Simax PSC 1164, recorded 2001, released 2002

Solveig Kringelborn (soprano), Norrköping Symphony Orchestra, cond. Lü Jia: NMA NMA 2, recorded 2003, released 2003

Lutad mot gärdet ('Leaning on the Fence')

Solveig Kringelborn (soprano), Norrköping Symphony Orchestra, cond. Lü Jia: NMA NMA 2, recorded 2003, released 2003 (also on Norske Gram 5349632)

3. Chamber Music

Bols vise ('Bol's Song')

Tom Ottar Andreassen (flute), Roger Andreassen (organ): Bergen Digital BD7046CD, recorded 2006, released 2006

Violin Sonata in B flat major

Stig Nilsson (violin), Jens Harald Bratlie (piano): NIM CDN 31003/SIMAX PSC 3103, recorded 1987, released 1988

4. Songs with Piano

Altar

Kathleen Ferrier (contralto), Phyllis Spurr (piano): Decca LL1670, recorded 1949, released 1957 and multiply re-issued; most recent CD releases Decca 433 473-2 and 433 802-2 and Naxos Historical 8.112071 (2012)

Eva Gustavson (soprano), Amund Raknerud (piano): Cambria CD 1136, recorded before 1960, released 2003

Das Mädchen auf der Brücke ('The Maiden on the Bridge')

Solveig Kringlborn (soprano), Einar Henning Smebye (piano): NMA NMA 2, recorded 2003, released 2003

De brente våre gårder

Svein Bjørkøy (tenor), Tor Espen Aspaas (piano): Euridice EUCD 43, recorded 2008, released 2008

Digte av Øverland, Op. 5: No. 1, 'Besværgelse'

Solveig Kringelborn (soprano), Einar Henning Smebye (piano): NMA NMA 2, recorded 2003, released 2003

Fabler og barnerim

Vols. I and II – Åshild Skiri Refsdal (soprano), Gunnar Flagstad (piano): Thema TH198-2, recorded 1997–98, released 1998

Vol. 1, No. 2, 'Bånlåt'; Vol. 2, No. 2, 'Katten og musen', and No. 3, 'Debatten' – Solveig Kringelborn (soprano), Einar Henning Smebye (piano): NMA NMA 2, recorded 2003, released 2003

Fiskerens aftensang

Svein Bjørkøy (tenor), Tor Espen Aspaas (piano): Euridice EUCD 43, recorded 2008, released 2008

Japanischer Frühling ('Japanese Spring')

Isa Katharina Gericke (soprano), Sveinung Bjelland (piano): Simax PSC 1231, recorded 2002, released 2002

Rosenstaden ('The City of Roses')

No. 5, 'Lindegull's namn', and 'Önskestunden' (unnumbered) – Solveig Kringelborn (soprano), Einar Henning Smebye (piano): NMA NMA 2, recorded 2003, released 2003

Rosenstaden ('The City of Roses') – 'Så kom du'

Svein Bjørkøy (tenor), Tor Espen Aspaas (piano): Euridice EUCD 43, recorded 2008, released 2008

Slaviske Digte, Op. 6

No. 2, 'Guldskyen' – Solveig Kringelborn (soprano), Einar Henning Smebye (piano): NMA NMA 2, recorded 2003, released 2003

6. Male Choir

Dagvise

Quattro Stagioni: Quattro QCD 9303, released 1994

De brendte våre gårder

Dale Male Choir, cond. Lars Ragnvaldsen.: Vest-Norsk VPN-0095-0033, released 1995

På jorden et sted

Quattro Stagioni: Norsk Musikkproduksjon ARCD 1914, released 1988

Index of Irgens-Jensen's Music

General Index

Norwegian has three vowels – å, æ and ø – which are not found in the English alphabet. In Norwegian indexes they are always listed separately. For an English-speaking readership the Society of Indexers advises interfiling them with a, ae and o, just as é, è, ö, etc., are customarily interfiled with the letters they most closely resemble.

Numbers in italics indicate an illustration.

Contents of the CD

This representative cross-section of Irgens-Jensen's music contains a few historical items but most of the recordings here are commercially available (further details will be found in the Discography, pp. 343–46). Our thanks to the artists and companies who have made this compilation possible, especially Grappa/Simax (who also produced and mastered it), Thema, NMA, Naxos and the Oslo University Students' Choral Society. Further thanks go to the Department of Musicology of the University of Oslo for its contribution towards the cost of the disc.

1 *Passacaglia*: opening and first passacaglia
Bergen Philharmonic Orchestra, conducted by Eivind Aadland
Source: Simax PSC 1164
5:53
For commentary, *cf.* p. 121.

2 *Passacaglia*: conclusion
Bergen Philharmonic Orchestra, conducted by Eivind Aadland
Source: Simax PSC 1164
6:08
For commentary, *cf.* pp. 124–25.

3 *Digte av Øverland*, Op. 5: No. 1, 'Besværgelse' ('Conjuration')
Solveig Kringleborn (soprano), Einar Henning Smebye (piano)
Source: NMA NMA 2
2:37
For text, translation and commentary, *cf.* pp. 55–57.

4 Sonata for Violin and Piano in B flat major: first movement, *Allegretto* (opening)
Stig Nilsson, violin; Jens Harald Bratlie, piano
Source: NIM (Norway in Music) CDN 31003
4:03
For commentary, *cf.* pp. 82–83.

5 *Fabler og barnerim* ('Fables and Nursery Rhymes'), Vol. 1: No. 2, 'Bånlåt' ('Lullaby')
Åshild Skiri Refsdal, soprano, Gunnar Flagstad, piano
Source: Thema TH 198-2

1:21
For commentary, *cf.* pp. 73–76.

6 *Tema con variazioni*: beginning
Oslo Philharmonic Orchestra, conducted by Odd Grüner-Hegge
Source: Simax PSC 3118
6:12
For commentary, *cf.* pp. 88–89.

7 *Tema con variazioni*: conclusion
Oslo Philharmonic Orchestra, conducted by Odd Grüner-Hegge
Source: Simax PSC 3118
4:26
For commentary, *cf.* pp. 89–92.

8 *Heimferd* ('Homeward Journey'): Stiklestad – Matins, Old Lay of Bjarki
Ivar Gilhuus, tenor; Harald Bjørkøy, tenor; Per Vollestad, baryton; Carsten Stabell, bass; Trondheim Symphony Orchestra, conducted by Ole Kristian Ruud
Source: Simax PSC 3109
4:35
For commentary, *cf.* p. 153.

9 *Heimferd*: final battle (fugue)
Trondheim Symphony Orchestra, conducted by Ole Kristian Ruud
Source: Simax PSC 3109
3:47
For commentary, *cf.* p. 153.

10 *Heimferd*: closing chorale
Anne Bolstad, soprano; Trondheim Symphony Orchestra and Chorus, conducted by Ole Kristian Ruud
Source: Simax PSC 3109
5:31
For commentary, *cf.* p. 155.

11 *Partita sinfonica*: 'Bols vise' ('Bol's Song')
Oslo Philharmonic Orchestra, conducted by Ole Kristian Ruud
Source: NIM (Norway in Music) CDN 31003
3:02
For commentary, *cf.* p. 190.

12 *Altar*
Solveig Kringelborn (soprano), Norrköping Symphony Orchestra, conducted by Lü Jia
Source: NMA NMA 2
2:53
For commentary, *cf.* pp. 198–200 and 201.

13 *Lutad mot gärdet* ('Leaning on the fence')
Solveig Kringelborn (soprano); Norrköping Symphony Orchestra, conducted by Lü Jia
Source: NMA NMA 2
1:55
For commentary, *cf.* p. 198.

14 Symphony in D minor: I. *Allegro* (beginning)
Bournemouth Symphony Orchestra, conductor Bjarte Engeset.
Source: Naxos 8.572313
8:46
For commentary, *cf.* pp. 220–21.

15 *Malmfuru* ('A Pine-Mast')
Oslo University Students' Choral Society, conducted by Sverre Bruland (1968)
Source: Archive of the Oslo University Students' Choral Society
1:51
For commentary, *cf.* pp. 212–13.

16 *På jorden et sted* ('Somewhere on Earth')
Oslo University Students' Choral Society, conducted by Sverre Bruland (1968)
Source: Archive of the Oslo University Students' Choral Society
1:51
For commentary, *cf.* p. 244.

17 *Japanischer Frühling*: No. 6, 'Betrachtung' ('Contemplation')
Ragnhild Heiland Sørensen (soprano), Bergen Philharmonic Orchestra, conducted by Eivind Aadland
Source: PSC 1164
3:34
For commentary, *cf.* p. 251.

18 *Japanischer Frühling*: No. 7, 'Nichts leichter' ('Nothing easier')
Ragnhild Heiland Sørensen (soprano), Bergen Philharmonic Orchestra, conducted by Eivind Aadland
Source: PSC 1164
2:15
For commentary, *cf.* p. 251.

19 Ludvig Irgens-Jensen speaking
Source: private tape
1:52

This excerpt comes from the 1969 NRK radio interview Irgens-Jensen gave to the producer Torstein Gunnarson a few days before his 75th birthday; it was intended for a celebratory programme which, with Irgens-Jensen's death, became a memorial broadcast. Gunnarson told this author that the shy Irgens-Jensen would have preferred to leave the studio immediately – he almost had to pull the composer back into the chair. Gunnarson nonetheless succeeded in creating a conversation, and Irgens-Jensen's answer to one of his questions ('Was it difficult or easy for you to avoid the trends and directions which were of current interest?') gives a sample of his voice:

> Jeg tenkte ikke så meget på det der, tror jeg. Jeg gjorde ikke det. Det var visst vanskelig den gang også for de som skulle... finne seg selv, sånn. Jeg... jeg strevet og slet med å få sammen noe og formmessig, husker jeg, i unge år, sånn. Og... så ble det etterhvert noen sanger og greier, og det... og det var... og de tilfredstilte meg. Og... Jeg var jo... skal vi se, jeg var jo... Jeg fulgte i grunnen ganske godt med i... i det jeg kunne få fatt i av noter og kjøpt, sånn. Jeg kan nevne for eksempel Schönbergs atonale ting, de kjente jeg allerede fra 1913, da jeg fikk fatt i og sånn, og spilte dem med en viss interesse. Men, det... det lå jo ikke noe for meg. Hele tiden var jeg jo veldig begeistret for Max Reger, og det var i grunnen... ja, det var i grunnen... først da jeg kom litt bort fra det at jeg begynte å skrive selv, sånn i 17–18 først, tror jeg det var....[1]

Total time: 73:51

[1] 'I did not think very much about it, I believe. I didn't. It was certainly difficult then, too, for those who wanted to... find themselves, so to speak. I... I toiled and struggled with getting something together and give it shape, I remember, in my youth, so to speak. And... then gradually there were some songs and things, and that... and that was... they satisfied me. And... I did... I did, shall we say... After all, I kept up quite well with... with what I could get hold of as notes and bought, so to speak. I can name by way of example Schoenberg's atonal things, I knew them from 1913 already when I got hold of them and, so to speak, and played them with some interest. But it... there was nothing in it for me. All that time I was very enthusiastic about Max Reger, and it was basically... yes, it was basically... not until I had moved away a little from it that I began to write myself, in 17–18 or so, I think it was....'